Willia[illegible]

H[illegible]DY L[illegible]RR

An Incredible Life

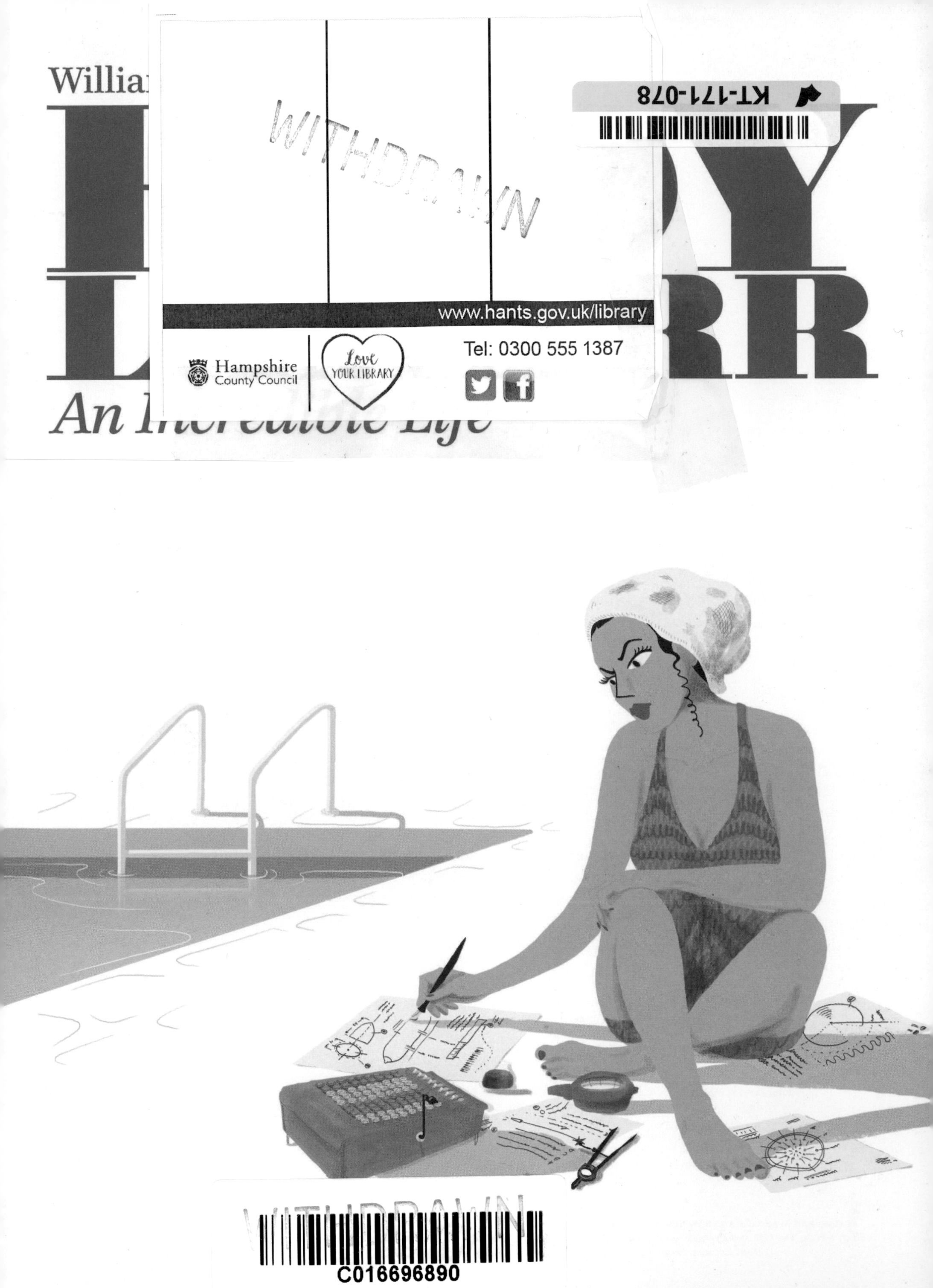

WILLIAM ROY
Story

SYLVAIN DORANGE
Art

❈

MONTANA KANE
Translation

❈

**FABRICE SAPOLSKY
& ALEX DONOGHUE**
US Edition Editors

AMANDA LUCIDO
Assistant Editor

VINCENT HENRY
Original Edition Editor

JERRY FRISSEN
Senior Art Director

FABRICE GIGER
Publisher

Rights & Licensing - licensing@humanoids.com
Press and Social Media - pr@humanoids.com

HEDY LAMARR: AN INCREDIBLE LIFE
This title is a publication of Humanoids, Inc. 8033 Sunset Blvd. #628, Los Angeles, CA 90046.
Copyright © 2018 Humanoids, Inc., Los Angeles (USA). All rights reserved. Humanoids and its logos are ® and © 2018 Humanoids, Inc.
Library of Congress Control Number: 2018944654

Life Drawn is an imprint of Humanoids, Inc.

First published in France under the title "Hedy Lamarr: La plus belle femme du monde" — Copyright © 2018 La Boîte à Bulles,
William Roy & Sylvain Dorange. All rights reserved. All characters, the distinctive likenesses thereof and all related indicia
are trademarks of La Boîte à Bulles Sarl and / or of William Roy & Sylvain Dorange.

No portion of this book may be reproduced by any means without the express
written consent of the copyright holder except for artwork used for review purposes. Printed in PRC.

Sources used for the creation of this volume include (but are not limited to):
Ecstasy and Me, My Life as a Woman by Hedy Lamarr, *Fawcett Crest Books*, **Beautiful, The Life of Hedy Lamarr** by Stephen Michael Shearer, *Thomas Dunne Books*,
Hedy's Folly, The Life and Breakthrough Inventions of Hedy Lamarr by Richard Rhodes, *Vintage*, **Calling Hedy Lamarr**, a Georg Misch documentary, *Mischief Films*,
Hedy Lamarr, Secrets of a Hollywood Star, a Donatello and Fosco Dubini documentary, *3Sat*, *Dubini FilmProduktion, MI Films*

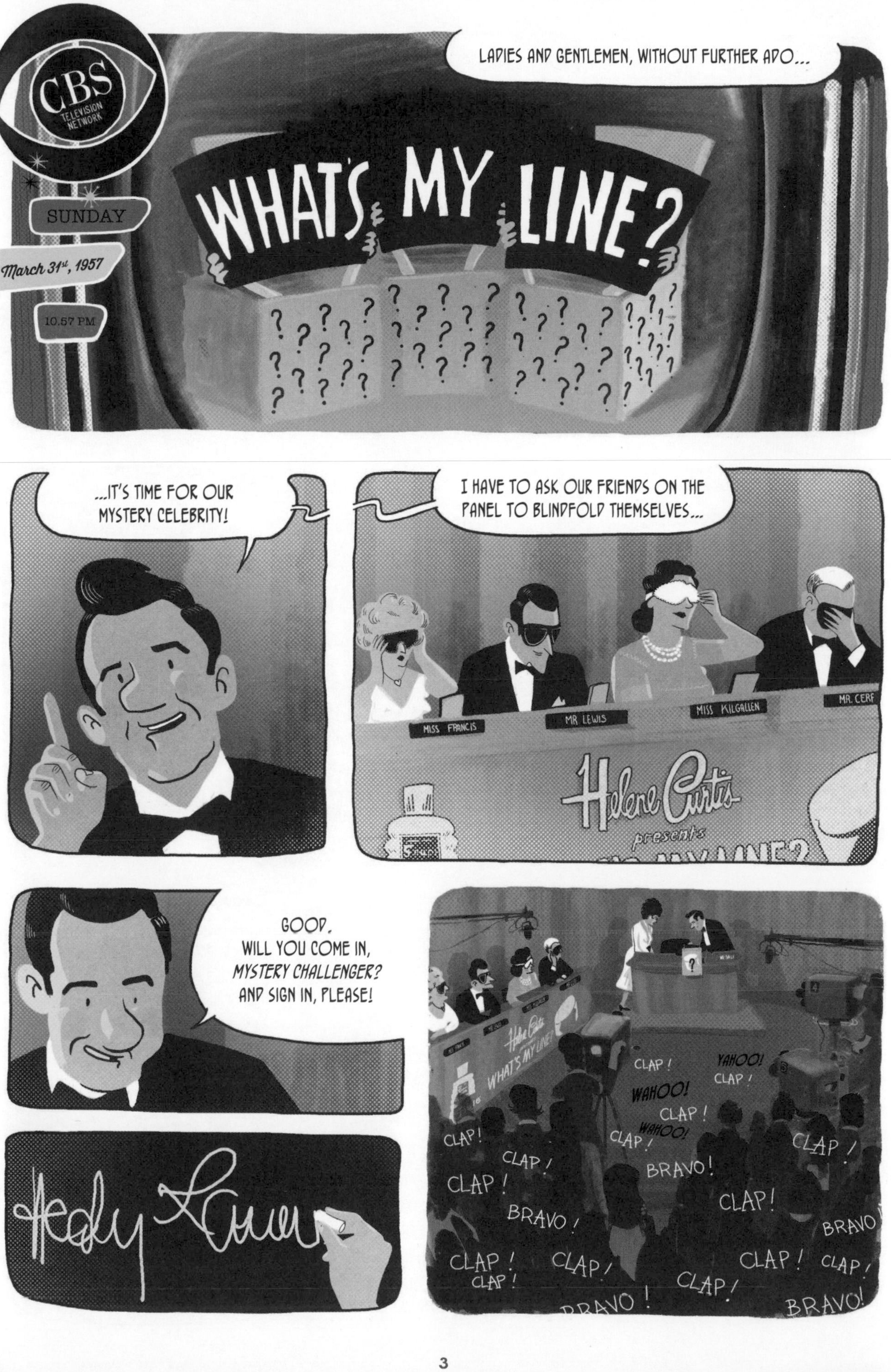
CBS
TELEVISION NETWORK
SUNDAY
March 31st, 1957
10.57 PM
WHAT'S MY LINE?
LADIES AND GENTLEMEN, WITHOUT FURTHER ADO...
...IT'S TIME FOR OUR MYSTERY CELEBRITY!
I HAVE TO ASK OUR FRIENDS ON THE PANEL TO BLINDFOLD THEMSELVES...
MISS FRANCIS
MR LEWIS
MISS KILGALLEN
MR. CERF
Helene Curtis
presents
GOOD. WILL YOU COME IN, *MYSTERY CHALLENGER?* AND SIGN IN, PLEASE!
WHAT'S MY LINE?
CLAP! YAHOO! CLAP! WAHOO! CLAP! WAHOO! CLAP!
CLAP! CLAP! CLAP! BRAVO! CLAP! CLAP! BRAVO! BRAVO!
CLAP! CLAP! CLAP! CLAP! CLAP! CLAP! BRAVO! BRAVO!

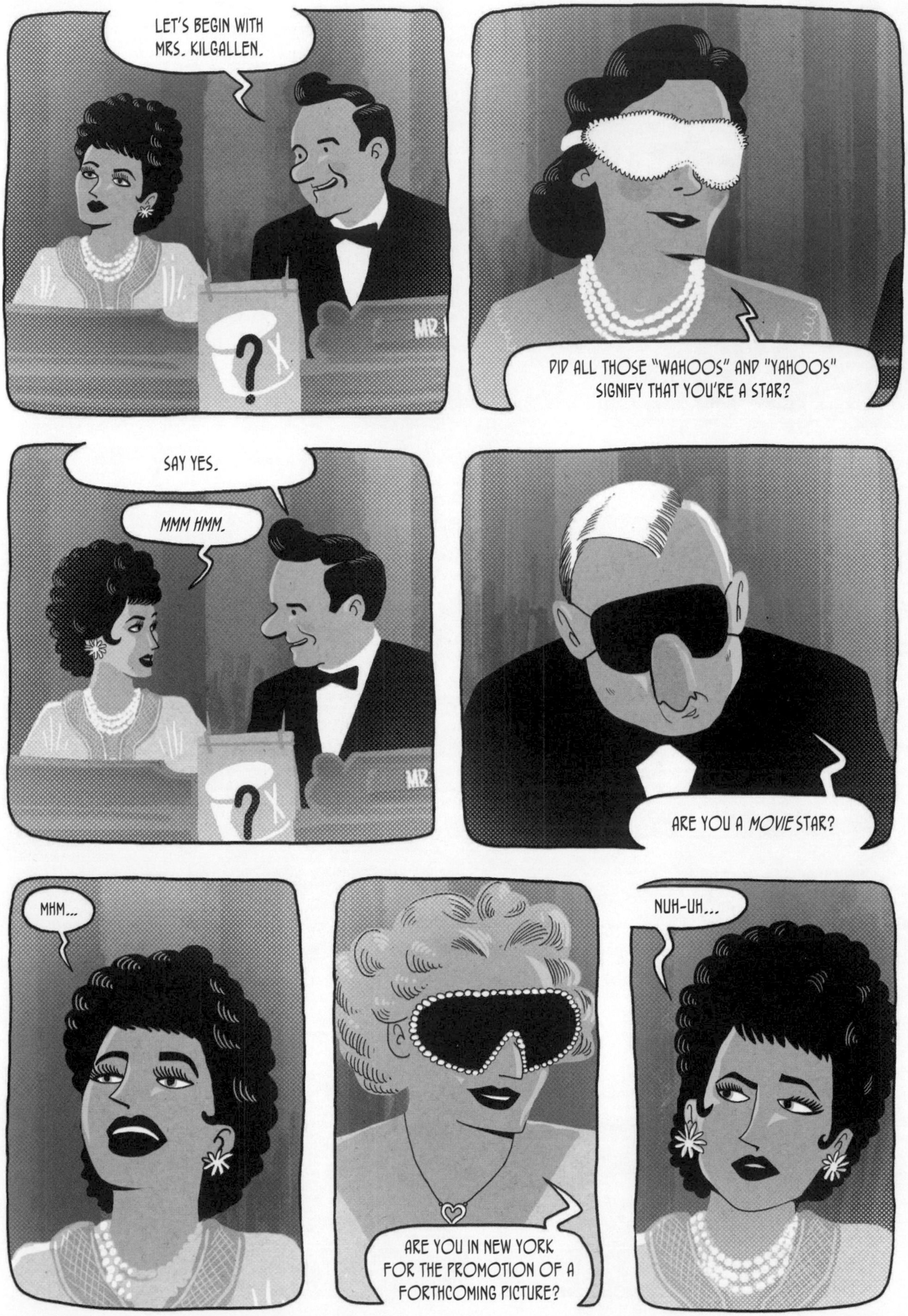
LET'S BEGIN WITH MRS. KILGALLEN.
MR.
DID ALL THOSE "WAHOOS" AND "YAHOOS" SIGNIFY THAT YOU'RE A STAR?
SAY YES.
MMM HMM.
MR.
ARE YOU A MOVIE STAR?
MHM...
ARE YOU IN NEW YORK FOR THE PROMOTION OF A FORTHCOMING PICTURE?
NUH-UH...

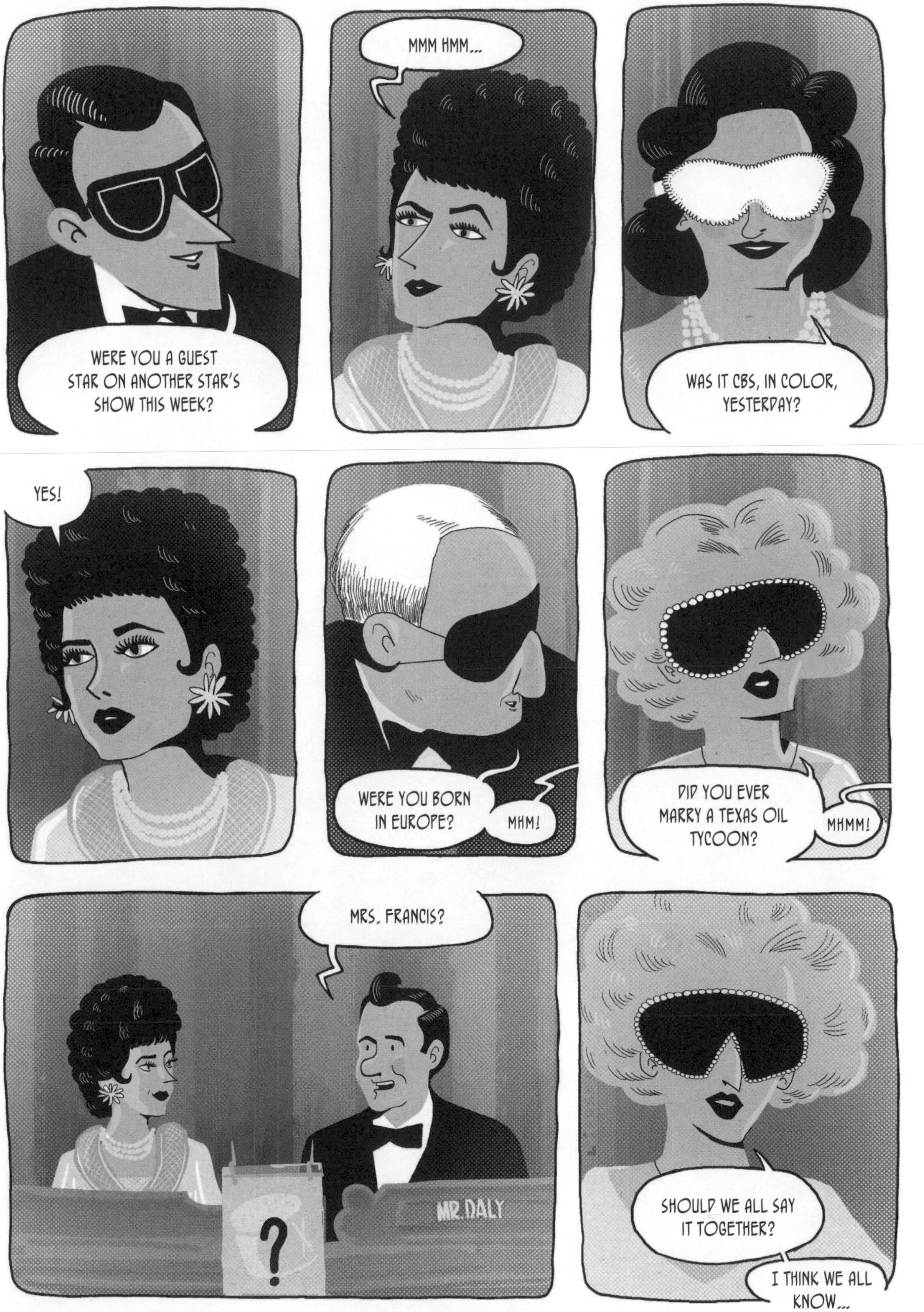
WERE YOU A GUEST STAR ON ANOTHER STAR'S SHOW THIS WEEK?
MMM HMM...
WAS IT CBS, IN COLOR, YESTERDAY?
YES!
WERE YOU BORN IN EUROPE?
MHM!
DID YOU EVER MARRY A TEXAS OIL TYCOON?
MHMM!
MRS. FRANCIS?
MR. DALY
?
SHOULD WE ALL SAY IT TOGETHER?
I THINK WE ALL KNOW...

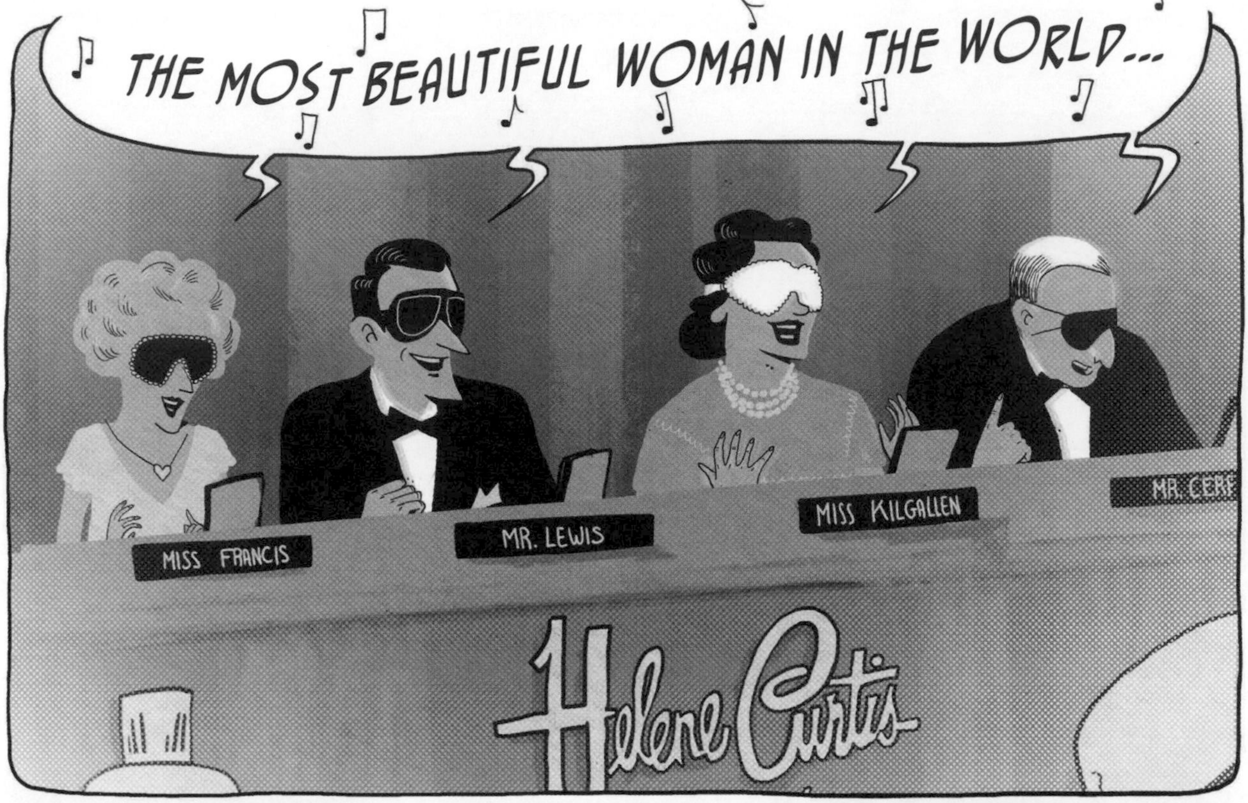
THE MOST BEAUTIFUL WOMAN IN THE WORLD...
MISS FRANCIS
MR. LEWIS
MISS KILGALLEN
MR. CERF
Helene Curtis

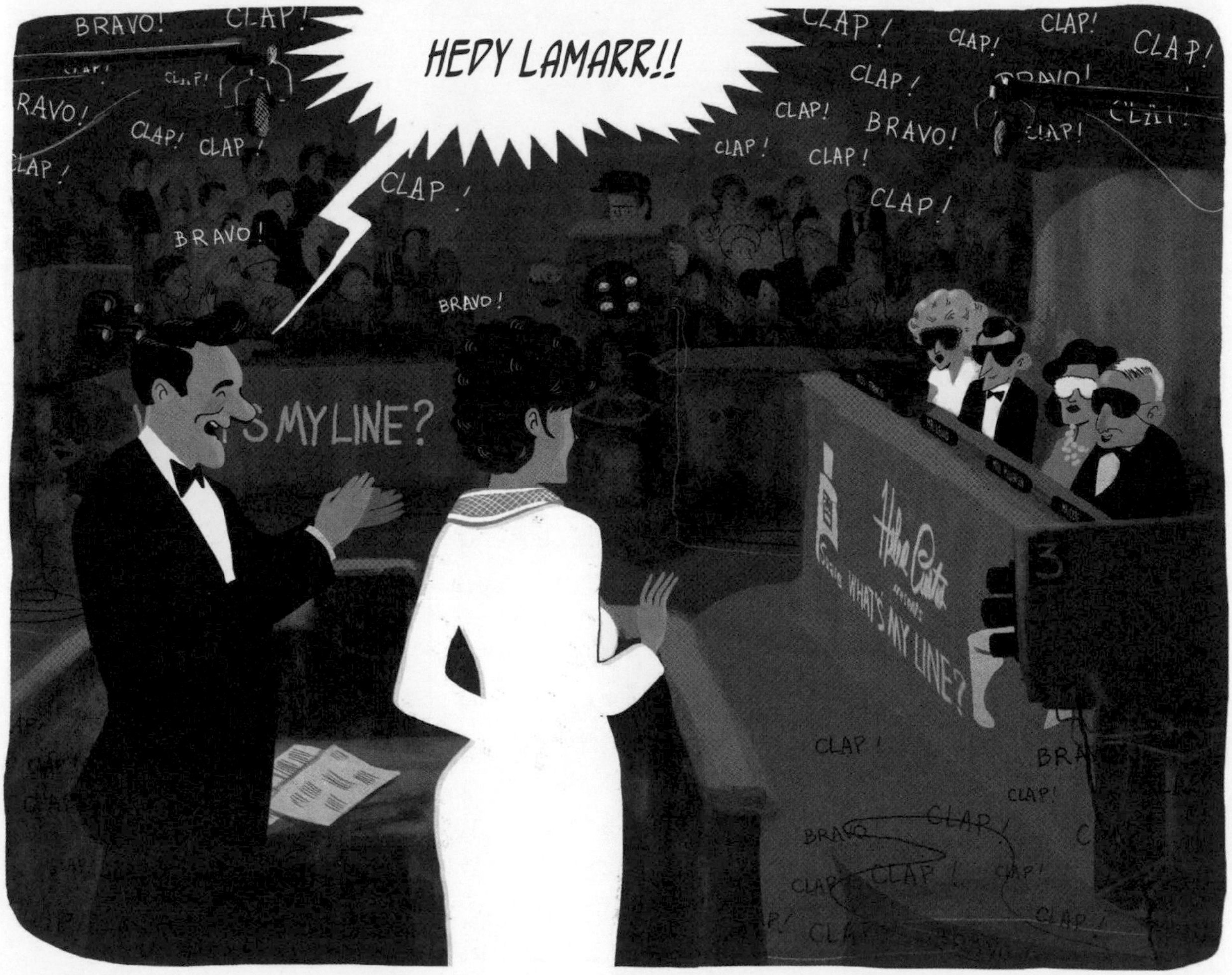
HEDY LAMARR!!
BRAVO!
CLAP!
CLAP!
CLAP!
CLAP!
CLAP!
BRAVO!
CLAP!
CLAP!
CLAP!
CLAP!
BRAVO!
CLAP!
BRAVO!
CLAP!
Helene Curtis
WHAT'S MY LINE?
CLAP!
CLAP!

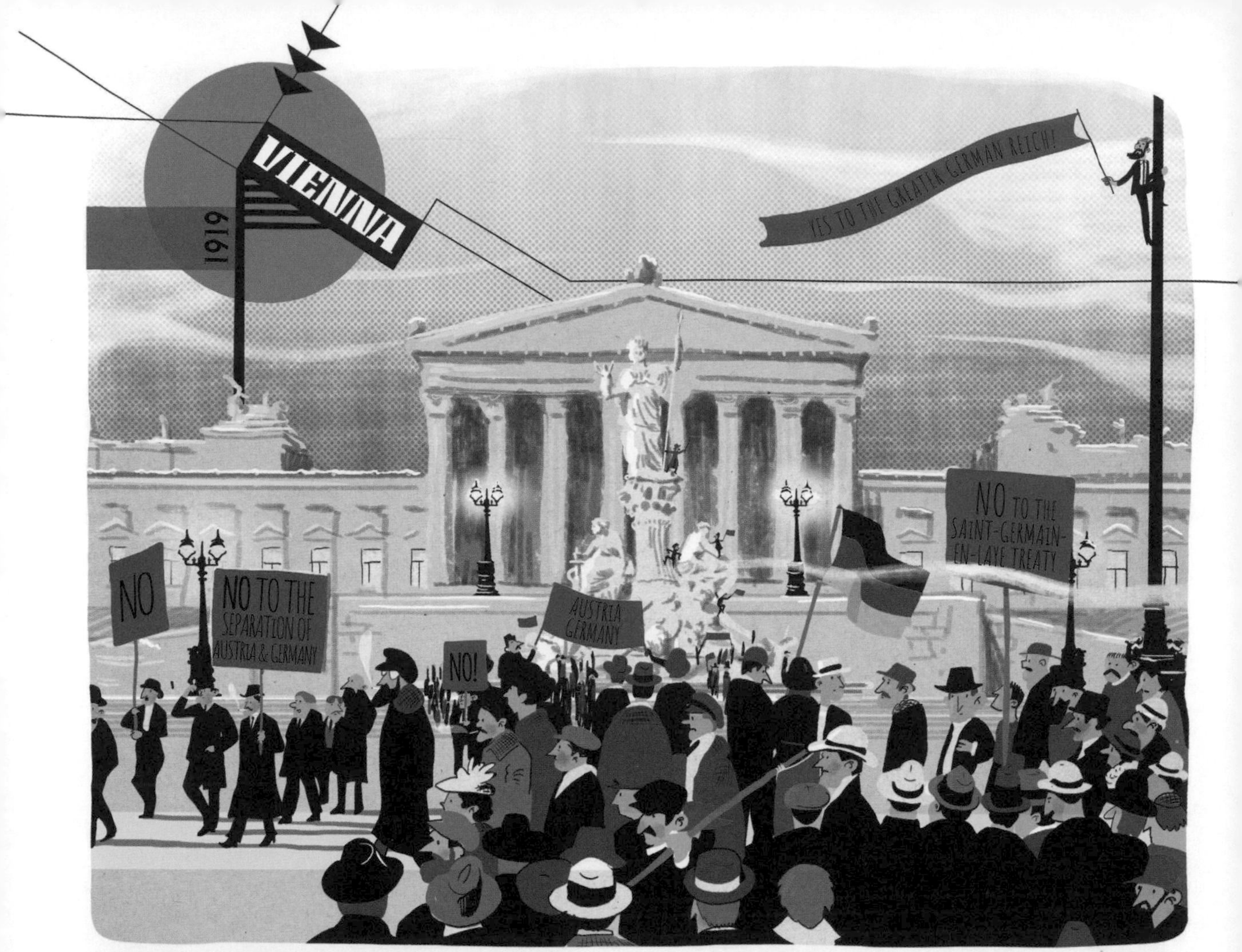
1919
VIENNA
YES TO THE GREATER GERMAN REICH!
NO
NO TO THE SEPARATION OF AUSTRIA & GERMANY
AUSTRIA GERMANY
NO!
NO TO THE SAINT-GERMAIN-EN-LAYE TREATY

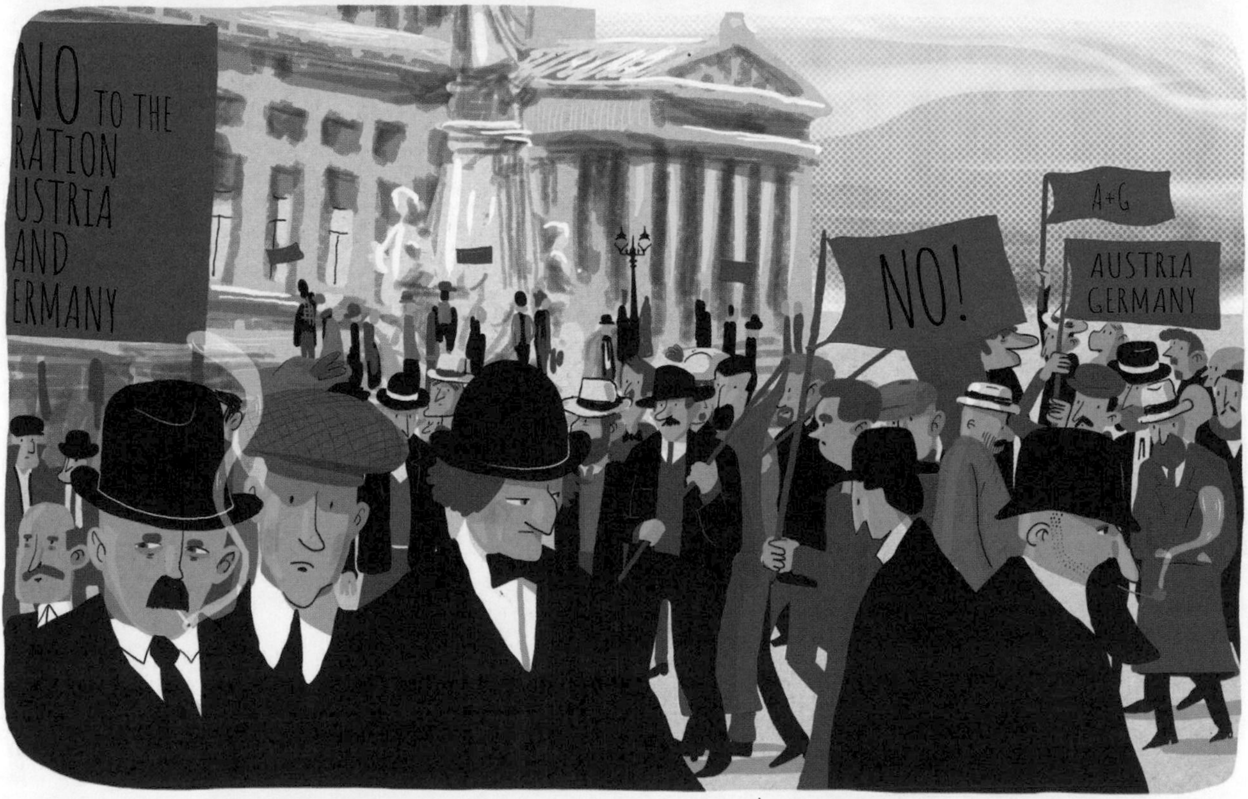
NO TO THE
RATION
USTRIA
AND
ERMANY
NO!
A+G
AUSTRIA GERMANY

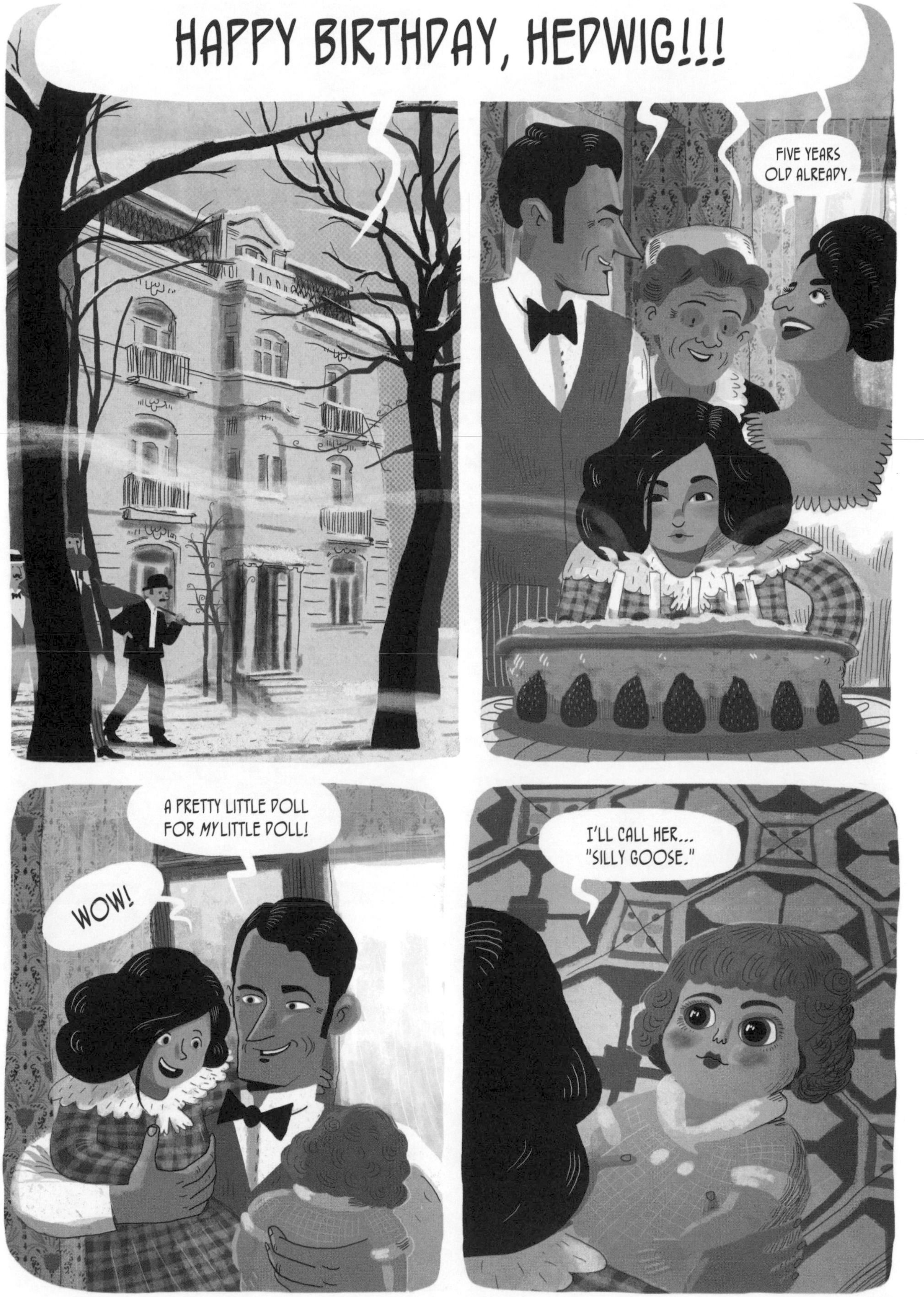
HAPPY BIRTHDAY, HEDWIG!!!
FIVE YEARS OLD ALREADY.
A PRETTY LITTLE DOLL FOR MY LITTLE DOLL!
WOW!
I'LL CALL HER... "SILLY GOOSE."

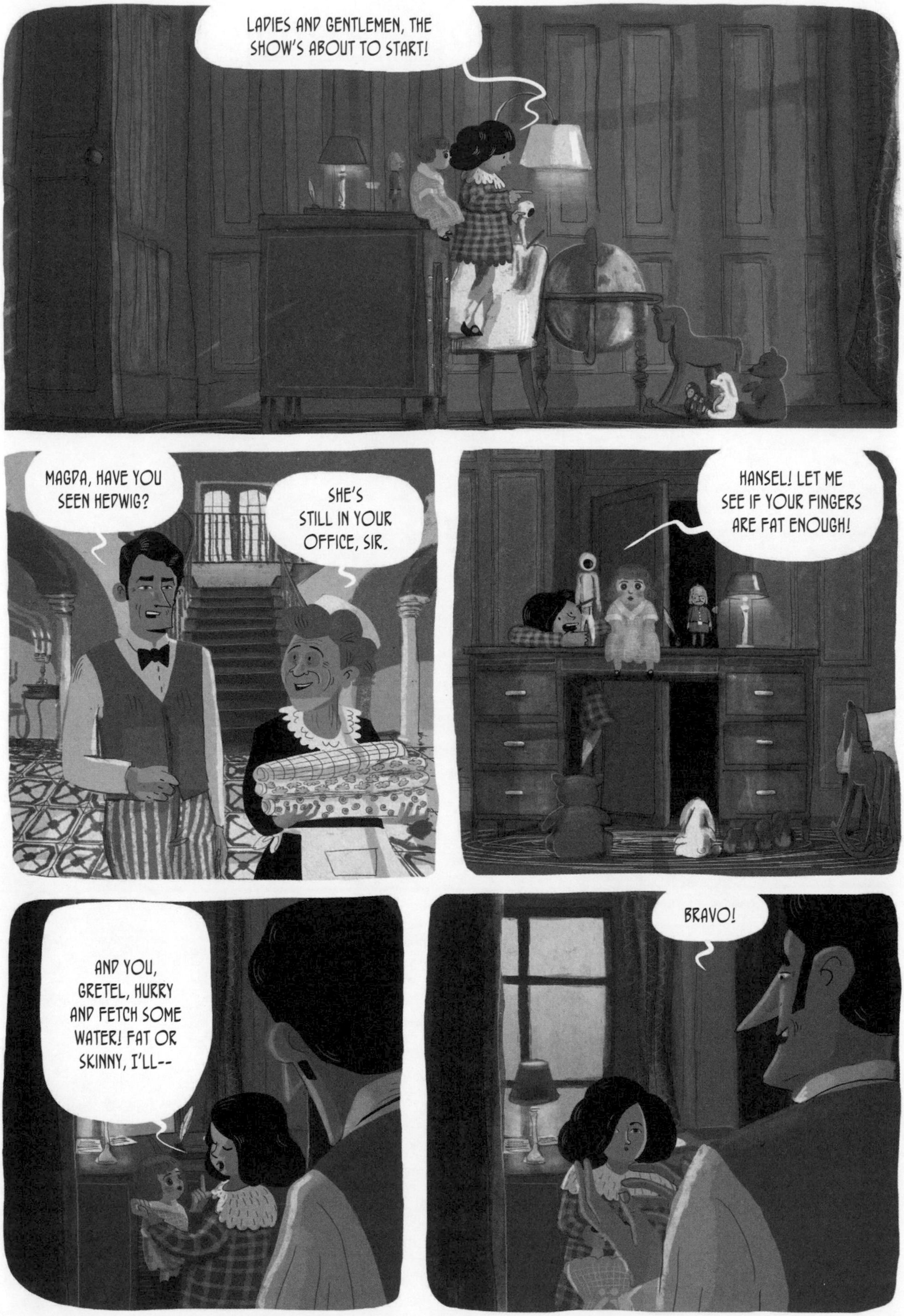
LADIES AND GENTLEMEN, THE SHOW'S ABOUT TO START!
MAGDA, HAVE YOU SEEN HEDWIG?
SHE'S STILL IN YOUR OFFICE, SIR.
HANSEL! LET ME SEE IF YOUR FINGERS ARE FAT ENOUGH!
AND YOU, GRETEL, HURRY AND FETCH SOME WATER! FAT OR SKINNY, I'LL--
BRAVO!

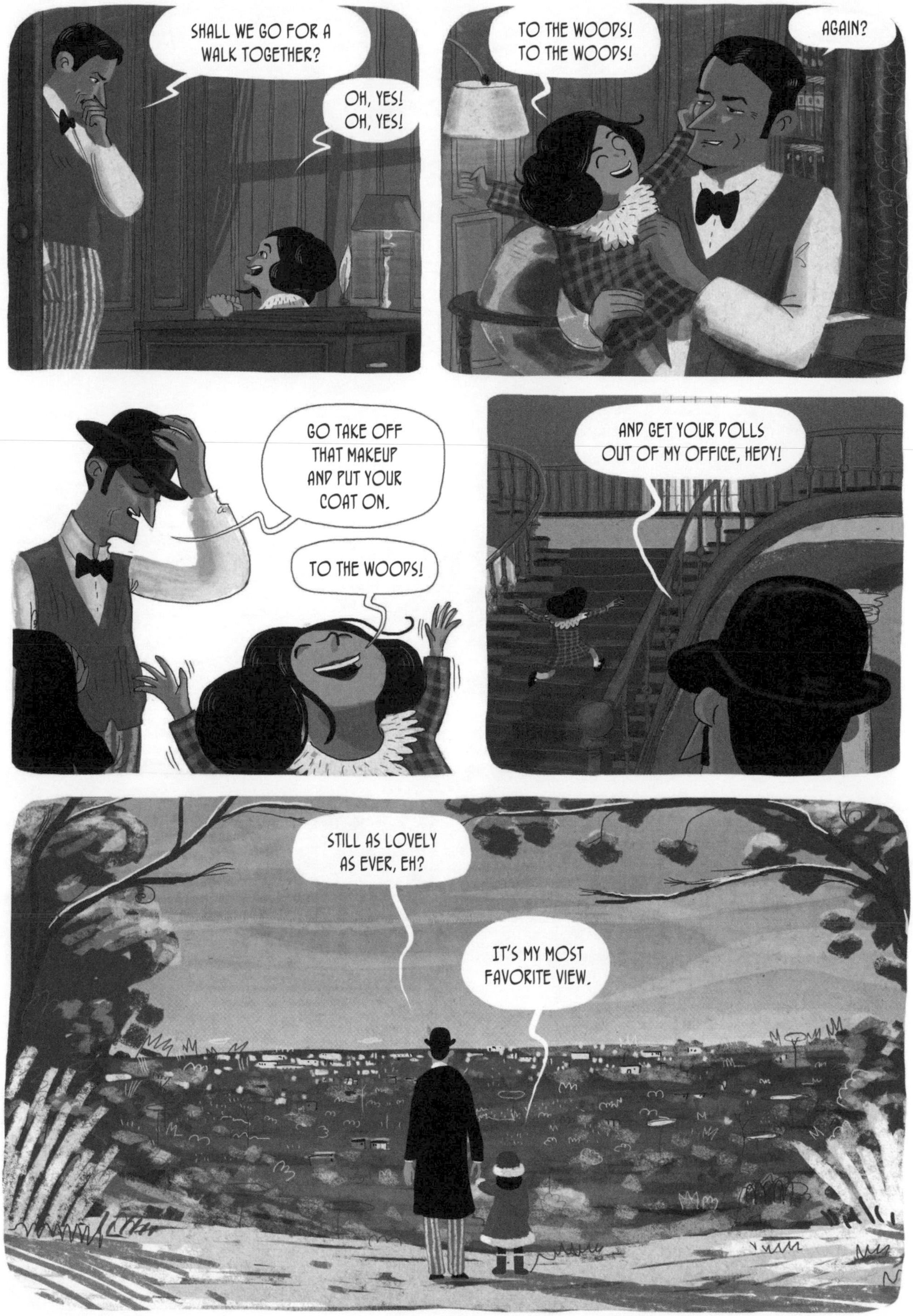
SHALL WE GO FOR A WALK TOGETHER?
OH, YES! OH, YES!
TO THE WOODS! TO THE WOODS!
AGAIN?
GO TAKE OFF THAT MAKEUP AND PUT YOUR COAT ON.
TO THE WOODS!
AND GET YOUR DOLLS OUT OF MY OFFICE, HEDY!
STILL AS LOVELY AS EVER, EH?
IT'S MY MOST FAVORITE VIEW.

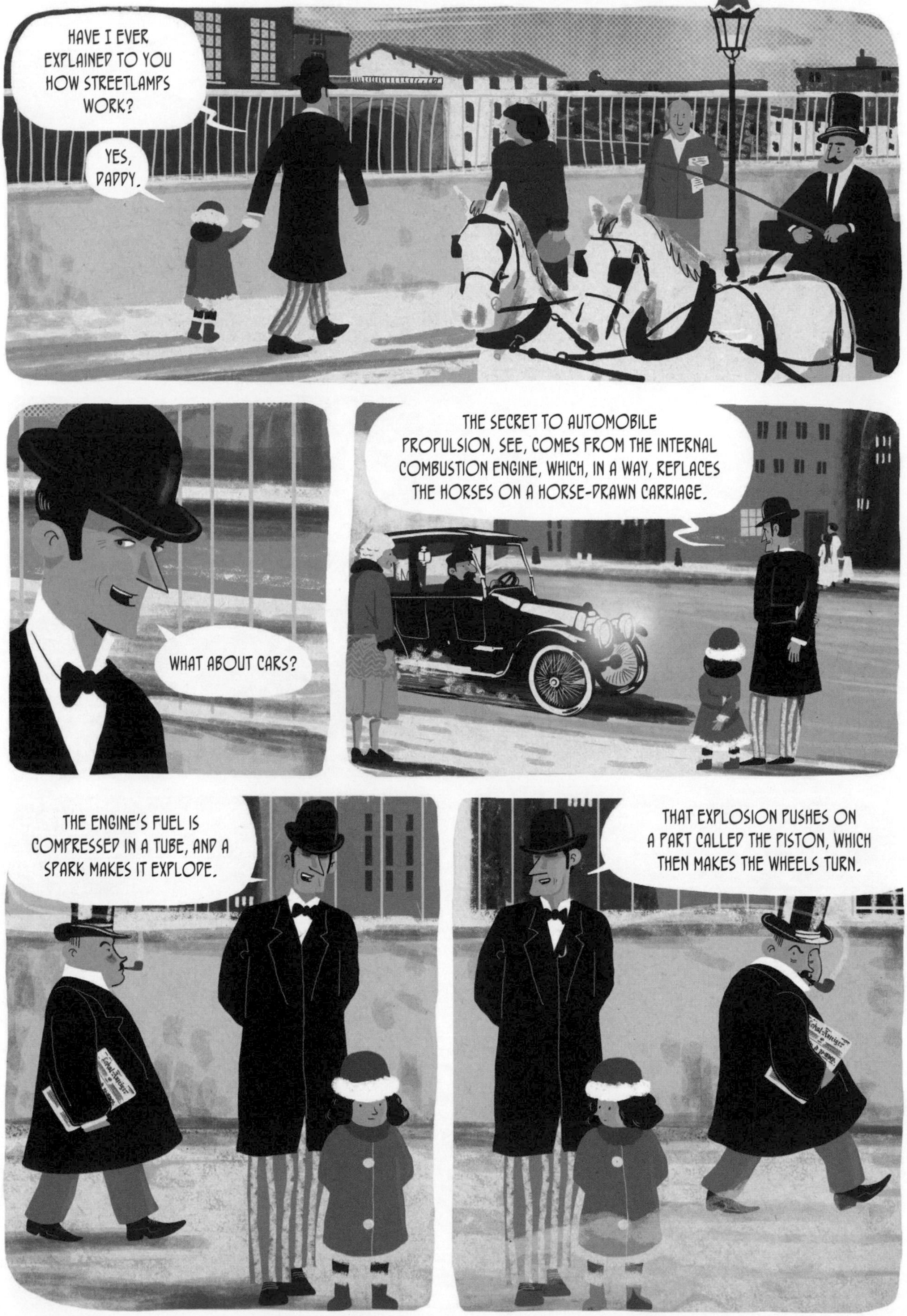
HAVE I EVER EXPLAINED TO YOU HOW STREETLAMPS WORK?
YES, DADDY.
WHAT ABOUT CARS?
THE SECRET TO AUTOMOBILE PROPULSION, SEE, COMES FROM THE INTERNAL COMBUSTION ENGINE, WHICH, IN A WAY, REPLACES THE HORSES ON A HORSE-DRAWN CARRIAGE.
THE ENGINE'S FUEL IS COMPRESSED IN A TUBE, AND A SPARK MAKES IT EXPLODE.
THAT EXPLOSION PUSHES ON A PART CALLED THE PISTON, WHICH THEN MAKES THE WHEELS TURN.

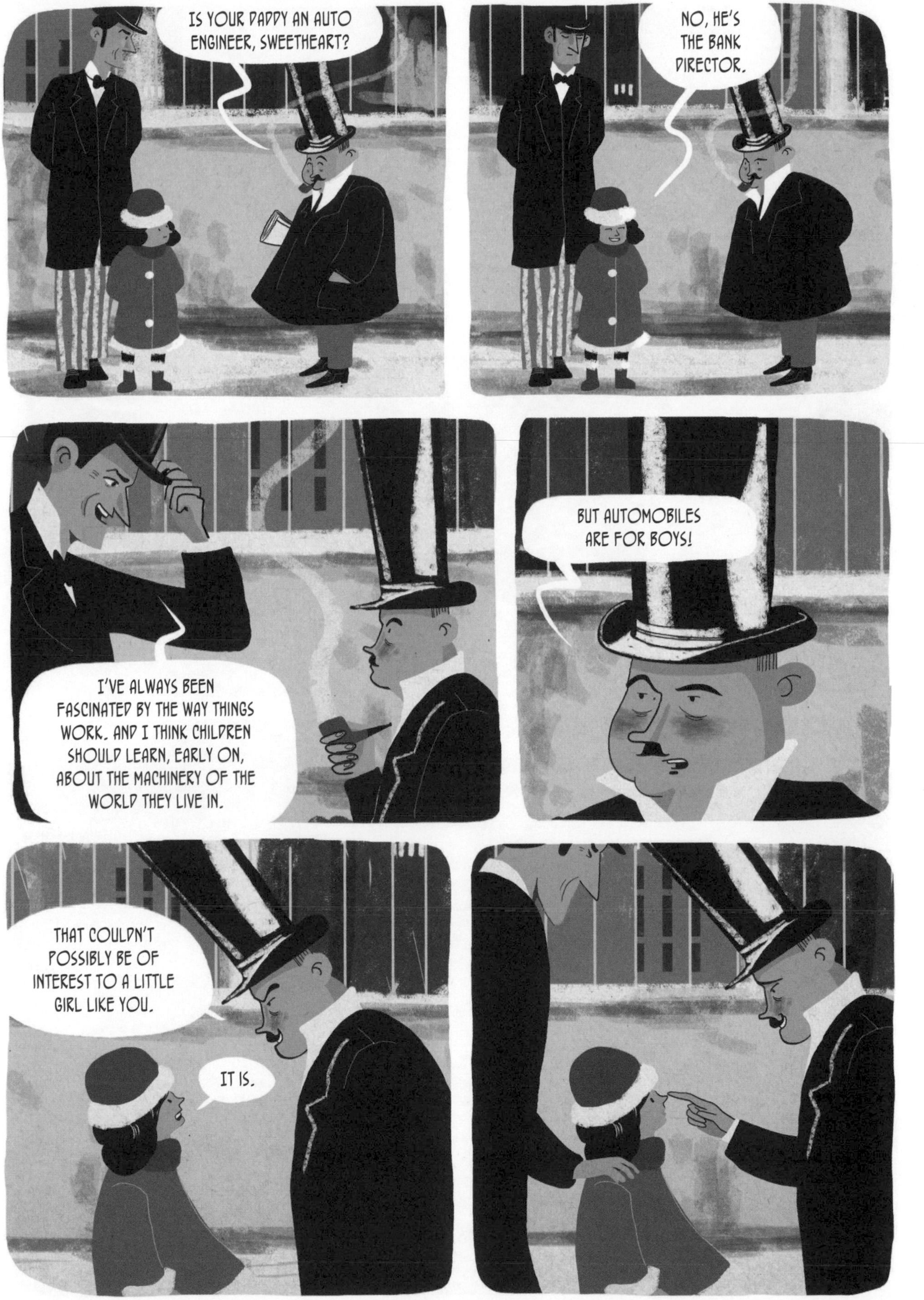
IS YOUR DADDY AN AUTO ENGINEER, SWEETHEART?
NO, HE'S THE BANK DIRECTOR.
I'VE ALWAYS BEEN FASCINATED BY THE WAY THINGS WORK. AND I THINK CHILDREN SHOULD LEARN, EARLY ON, ABOUT THE MACHINERY OF THE WORLD THEY LIVE IN.
BUT AUTOMOBILES ARE FOR BOYS!
THAT COULDN'T POSSIBLY BE OF INTEREST TO A LITTLE GIRL LIKE YOU.
IT IS.

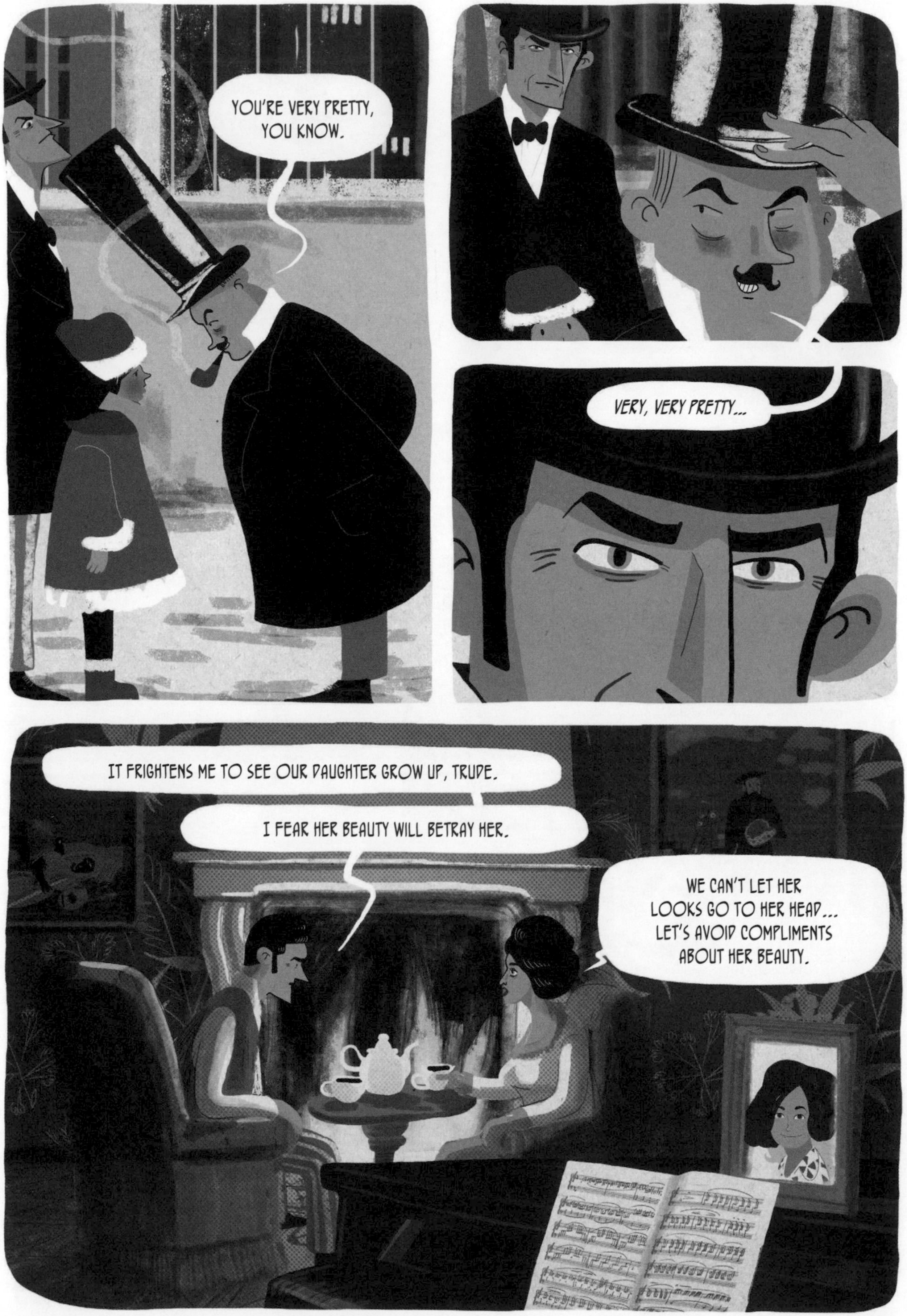
YOU'RE VERY PRETTY, YOU KNOW.
VERY, VERY PRETTY...
IT FRIGHTENS ME TO SEE OUR DAUGHTER GROW UP, TRUDE.
I FEAR HER BEAUTY WILL BETRAY HER.
WE CAN'T LET HER LOOKS GO TO HER HEAD... LET'S AVOID COMPLIMENTS ABOUT HER BEAUTY.

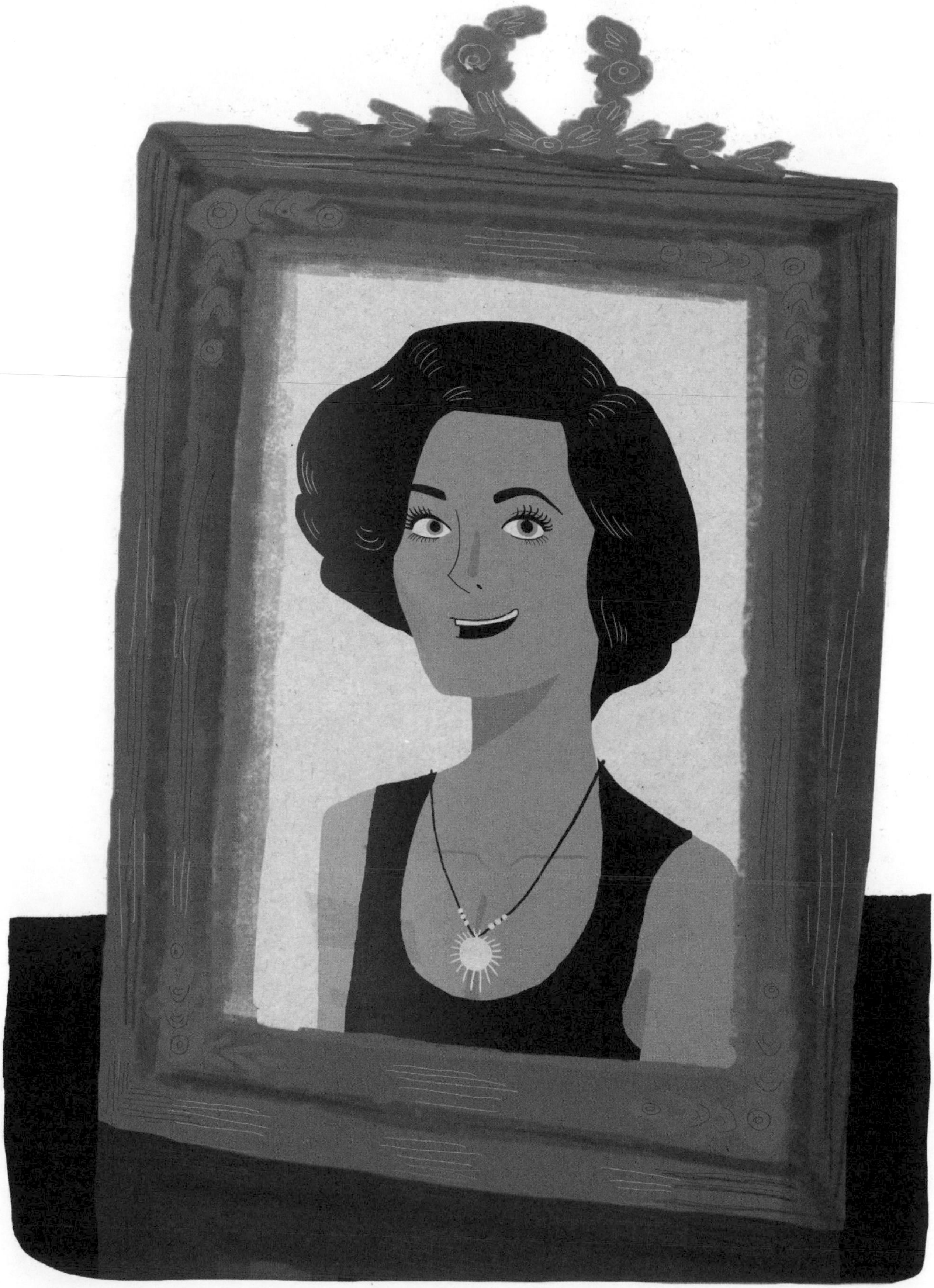

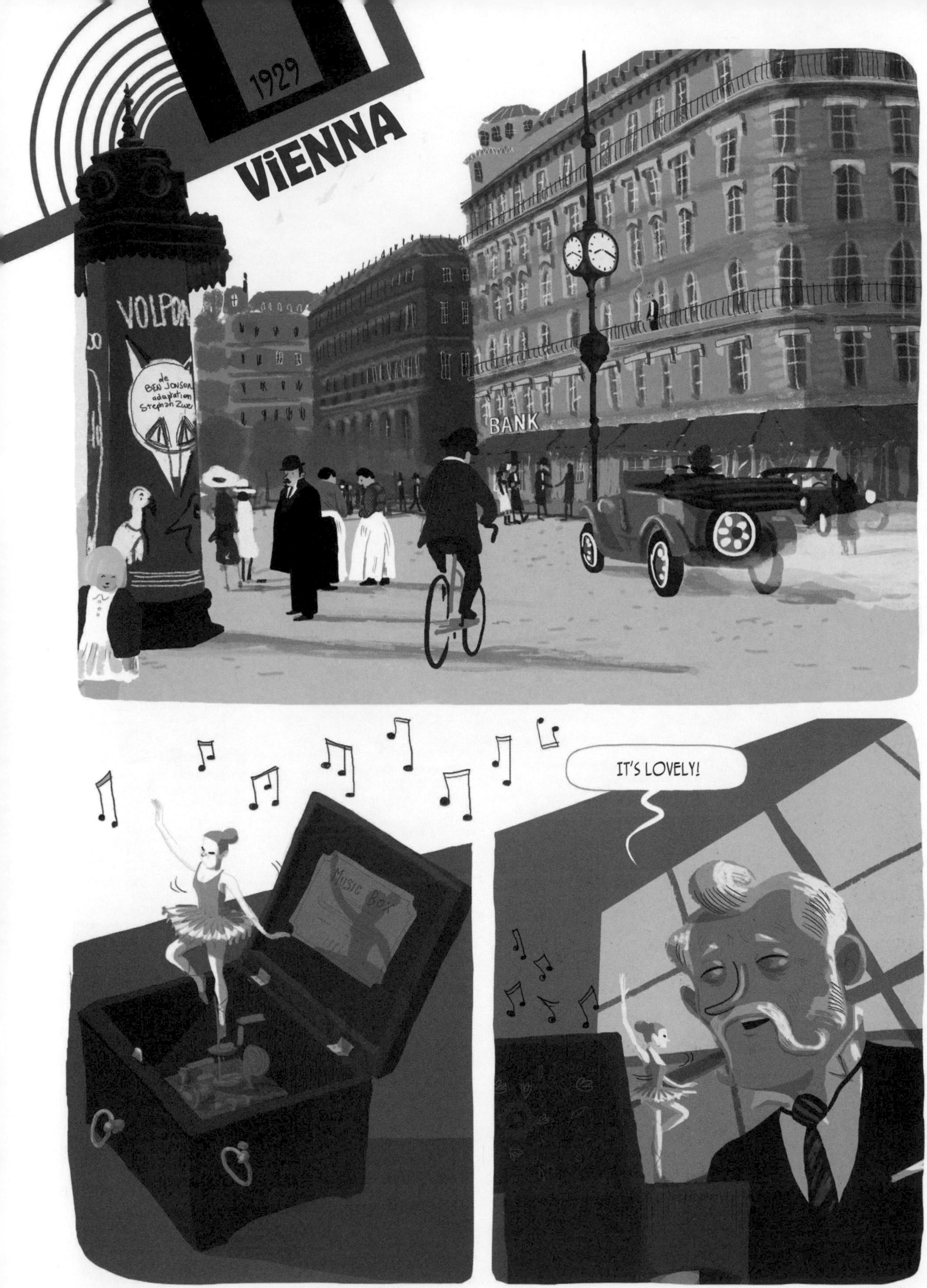
1929
VIENNA
VOLPON
de BEN JONSON adaptation Stephan Zwe
BANK
Music Box
IT'S LOVELY!

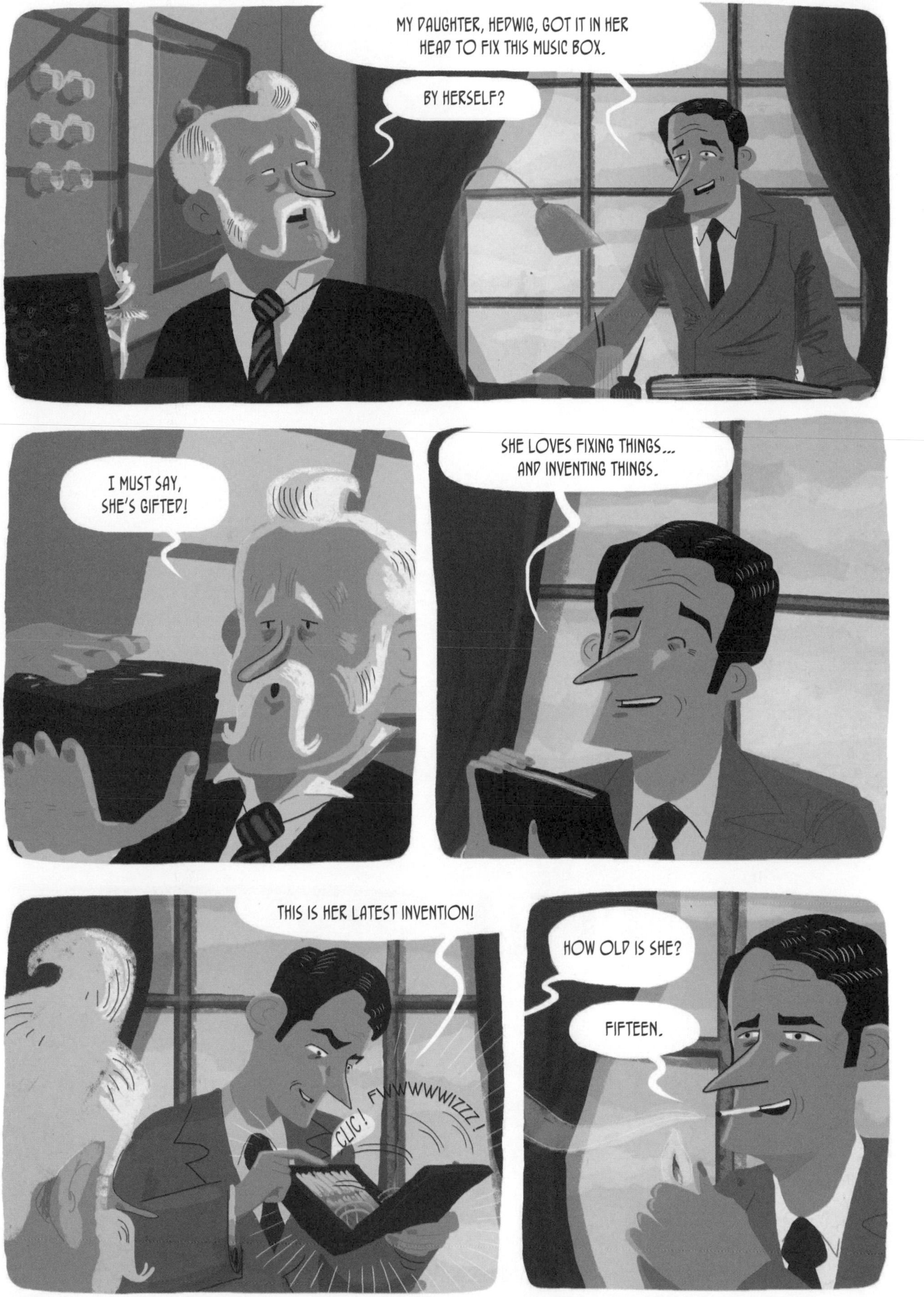
MY DAUGHTER, HEDWIG, GOT IT IN HER HEAD TO FIX THIS MUSIC BOX.
BY HERSELF?
I MUST SAY, SHE'S GIFTED!
SHE LOVES FIXING THINGS... AND INVENTING THINGS.
THIS IS HER LATEST INVENTION!
CLIC!
FWWWWWIZZZ!
HOW OLD IS SHE?
FIFTEEN.

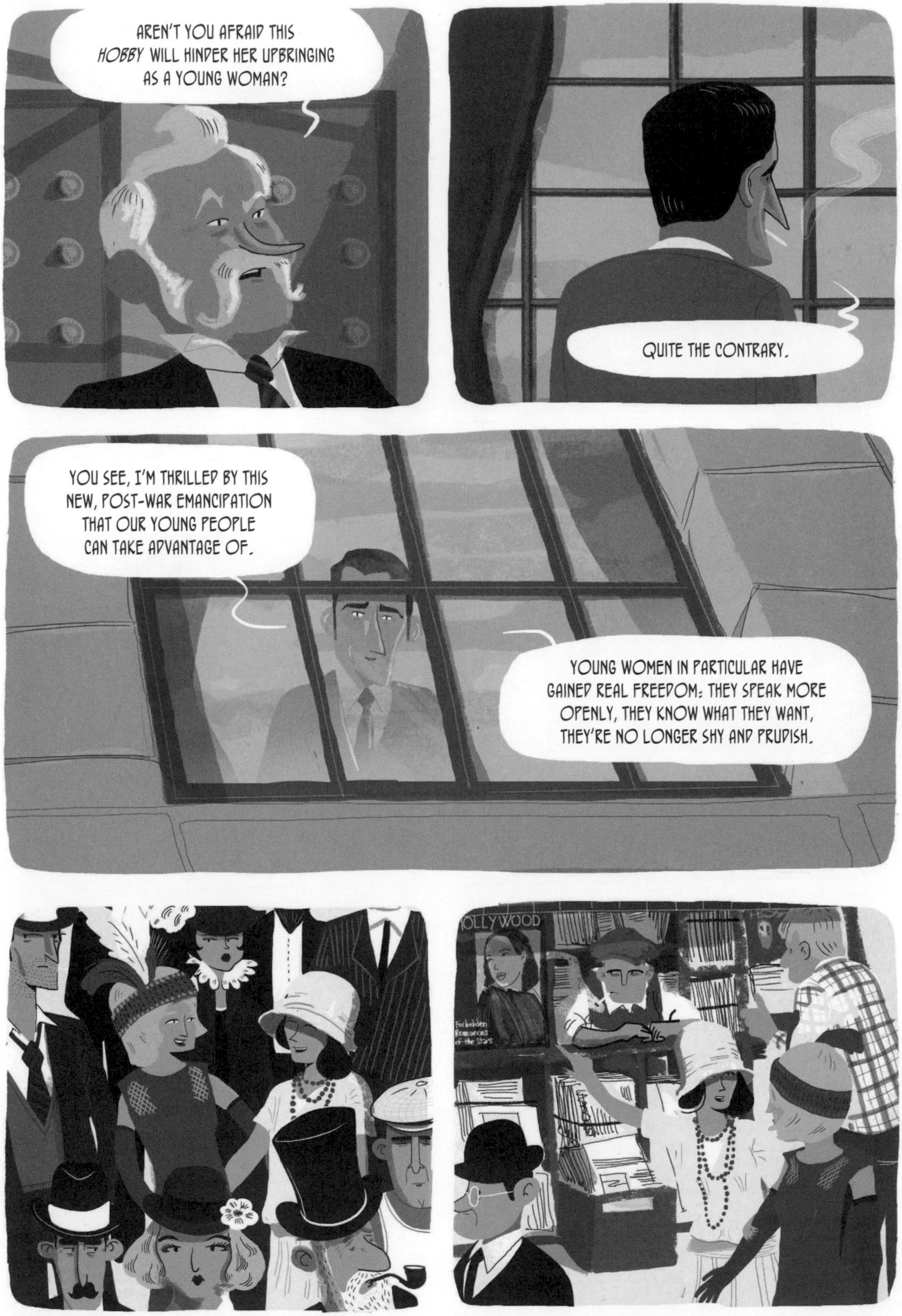
AREN'T YOU AFRAID THIS *HOBBY* WILL HINDER HER UPBRINGING AS A YOUNG WOMAN?
QUITE THE CONTRARY.
YOU SEE, I'M THRILLED BY THIS NEW, POST-WAR EMANCIPATION THAT OUR YOUNG PEOPLE CAN TAKE ADVANTAGE OF.
YOUNG WOMEN IN PARTICULAR HAVE GAINED REAL FREEDOM: THEY SPEAK MORE OPENLY, THEY KNOW WHAT THEY WANT, THEY'RE NO LONGER SHY AND PRUDISH.
OLLYWOOD
Forbidden Romances of the Stars

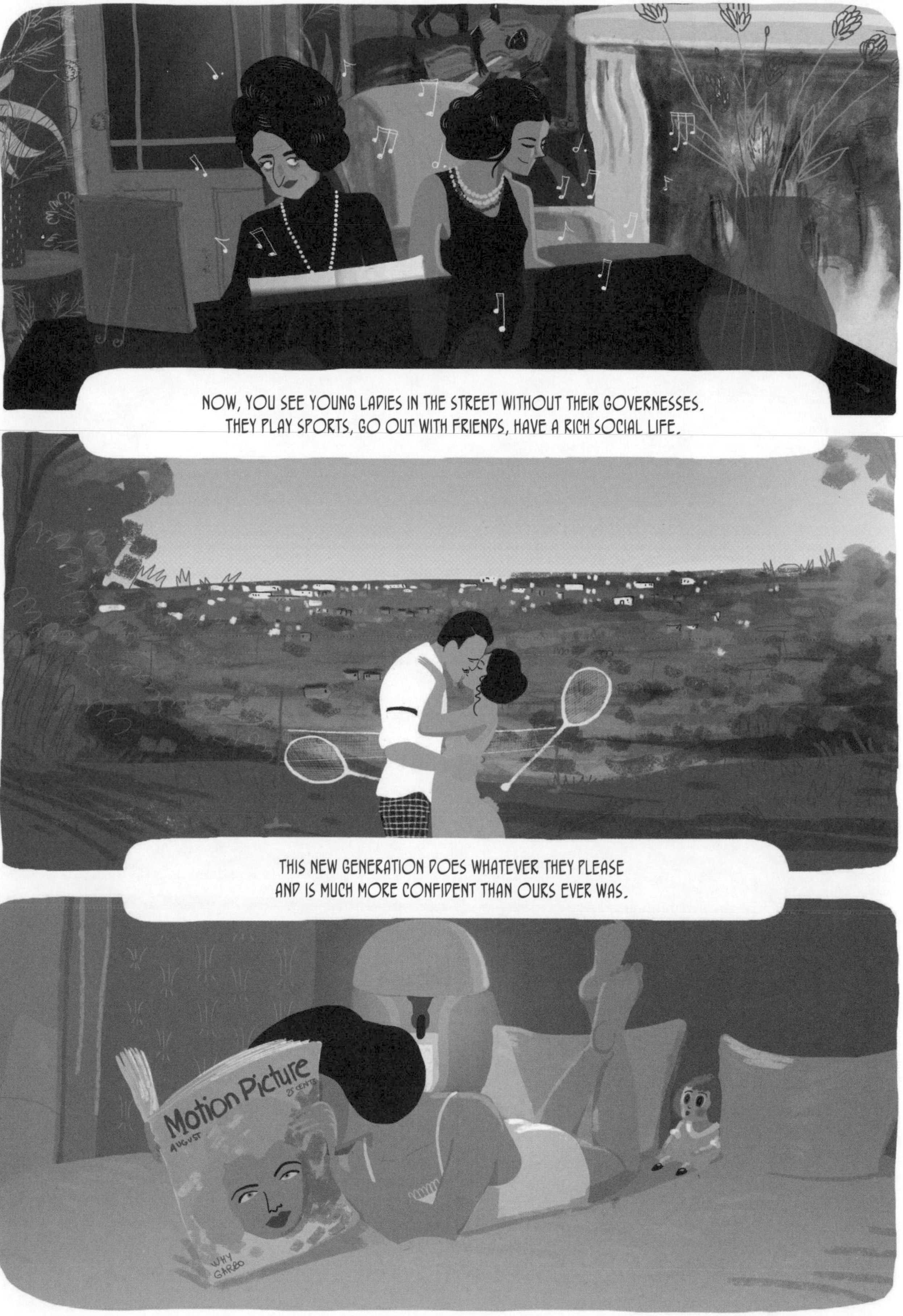
NOW, YOU SEE YOUNG LADIES IN THE STREET WITHOUT THEIR GOVERNESSES.
THEY PLAY SPORTS, GO OUT WITH FRIENDS, HAVE A RICH SOCIAL LIFE.
THIS NEW GENERATION DOES WHATEVER THEY PLEASE
AND IS MUCH MORE CONFIDENT THAN OURS EVER WAS.
Motion Picture
25 CENTS
AUGUST
WHY GARBO

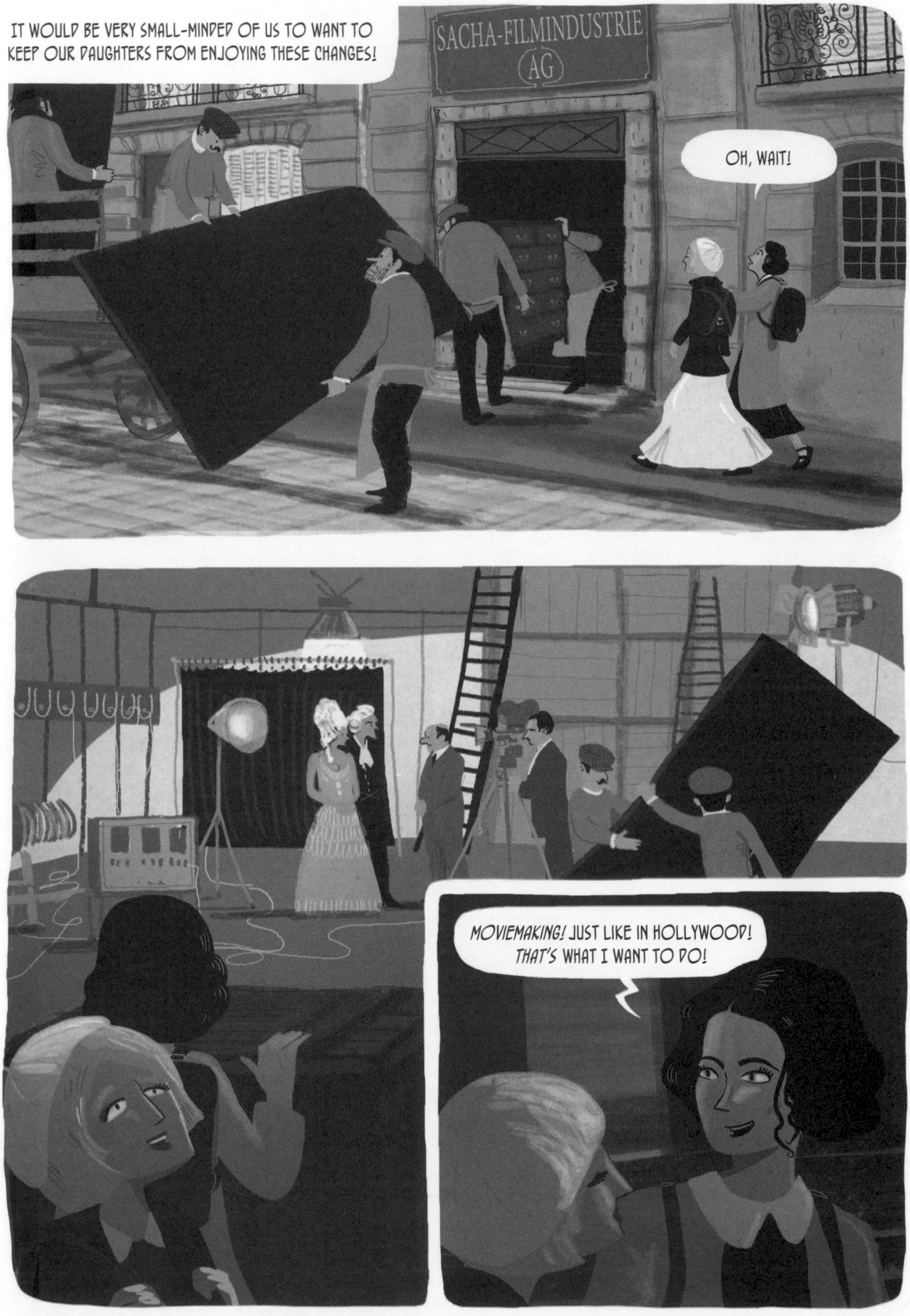
IT WOULD BE VERY SMALL-MINDED OF US TO WANT TO KEEP OUR DAUGHTERS FROM ENJOYING THESE CHANGES!
SACHA-FILMINDUSTRIE AG
OH, WAIT!
MOVIEMAKING! JUST LIKE IN HOLLYWOOD! THAT'S WHAT I WANT TO DO!

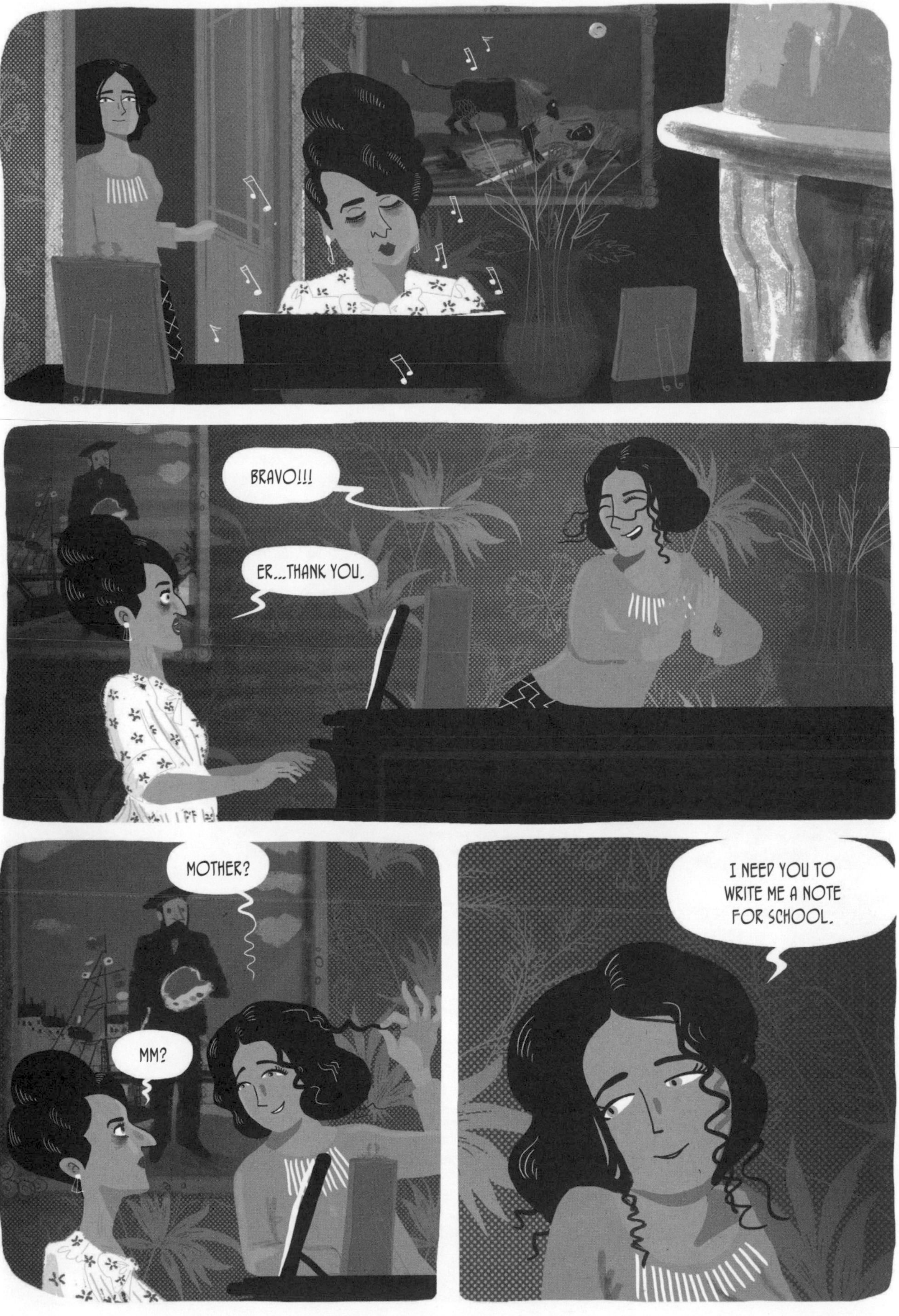
BRAVO!!!
ER...THANK YOU.
MOTHER?
MM?
I NEED YOU TO WRITE ME A NOTE FOR SCHOOL.

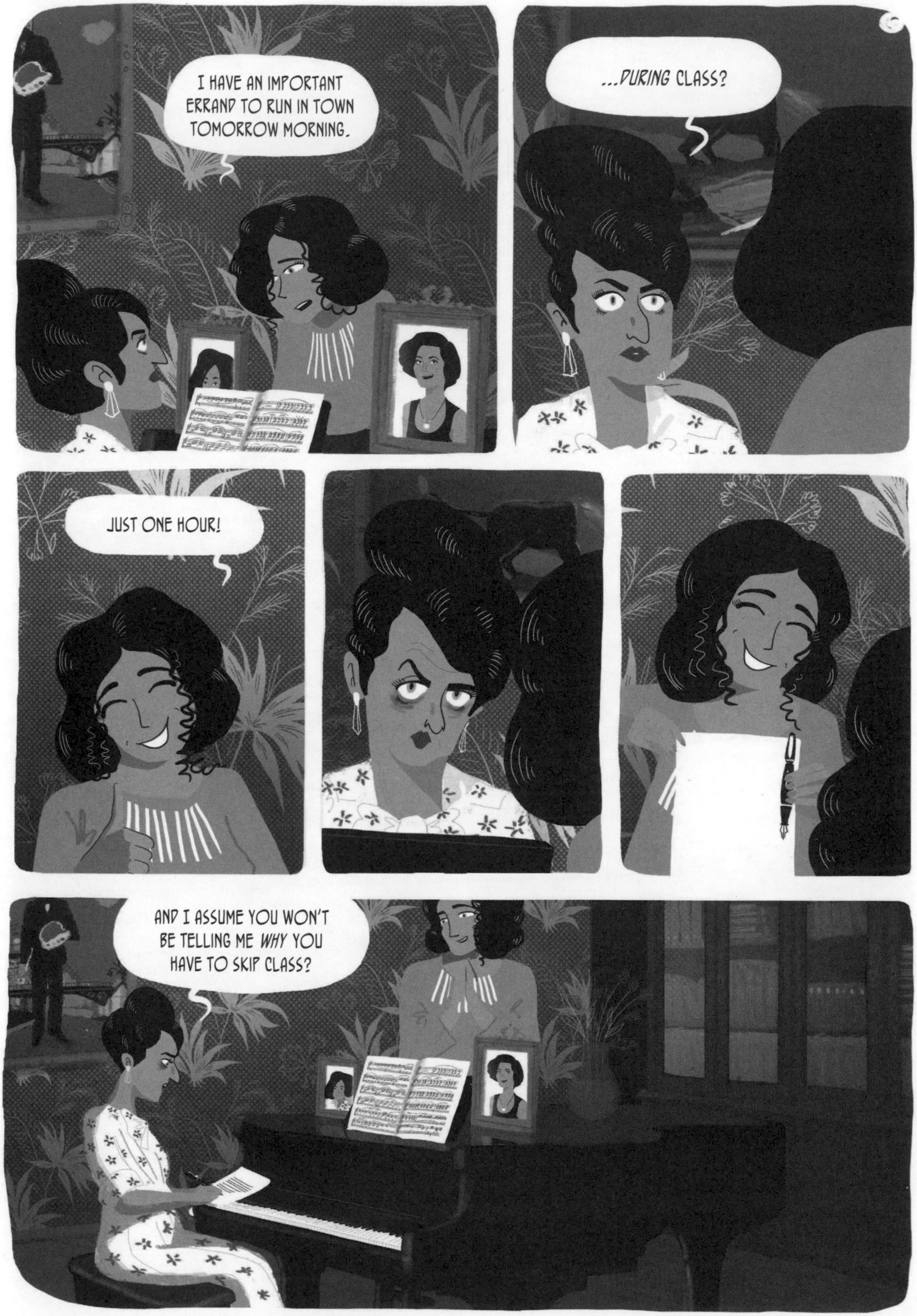
I HAVE AN IMPORTANT ERRAND TO RUN IN TOWN TOMORROW MORNING.
...DURING CLASS?
JUST ONE HOUR!
AND I ASSUME YOU WON'T BE TELLING ME WHY YOU HAVE TO SKIP CLASS?

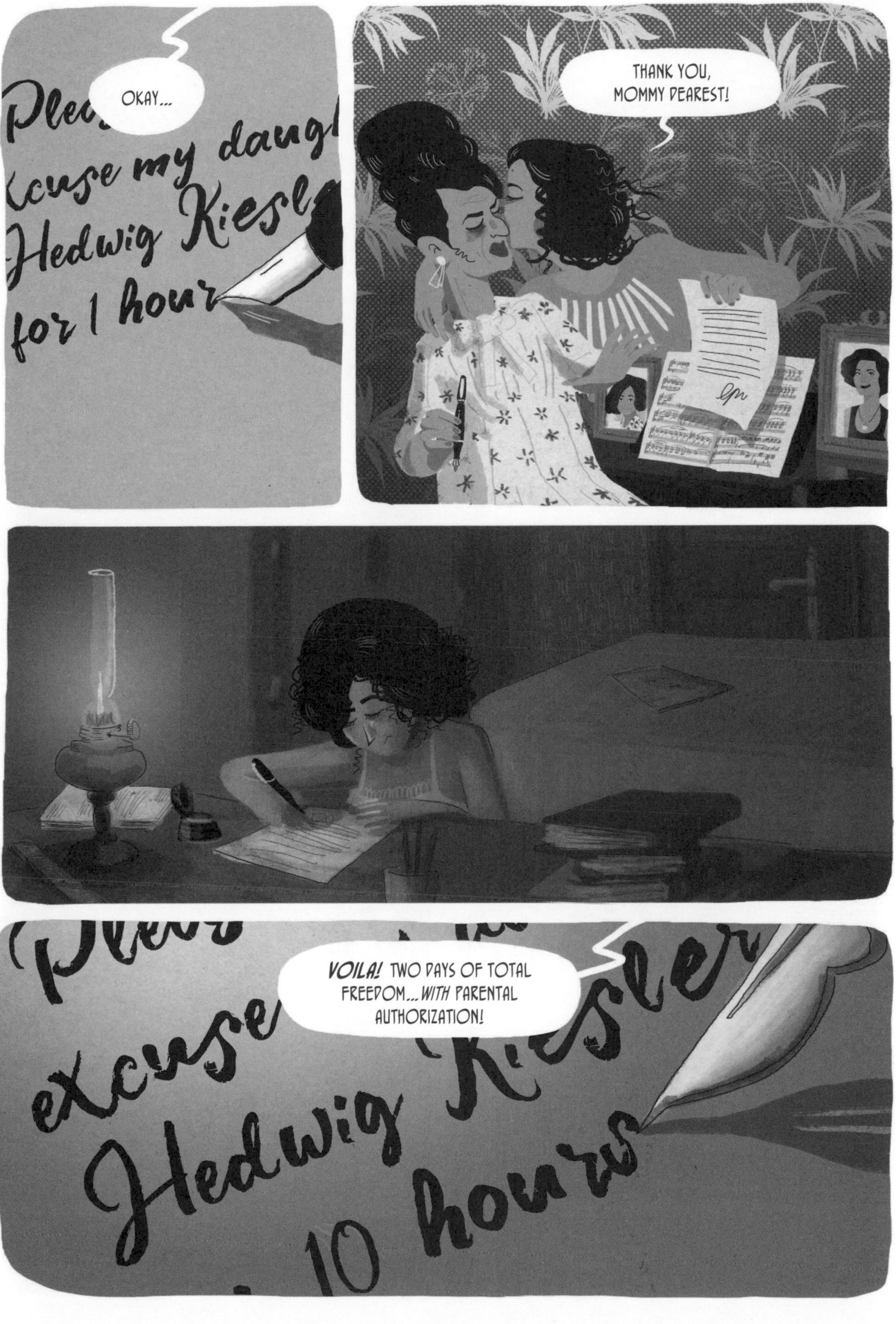
OKAY...
THANK YOU, MOMMY DEAREST!
VOILA! TWO DAYS OF TOTAL FREEDOM...*WITH* PARENTAL AUTHORIZATION!

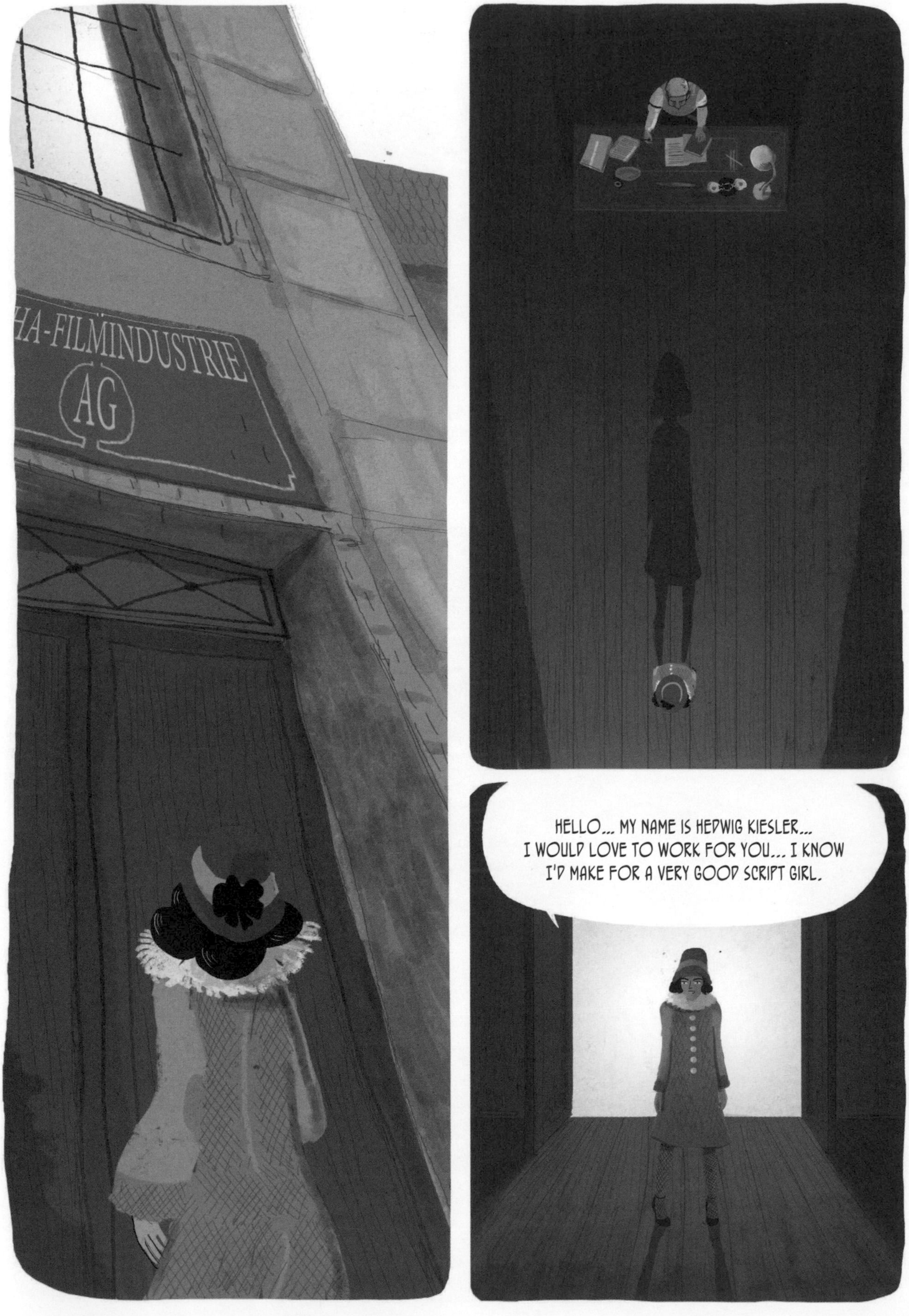
HA-FILMINDUSTRIE
AG
HELLO... MY NAME IS HEDWIG KIESLER... I WOULD LOVE TO WORK FOR YOU... I KNOW I'D MAKE FOR A VERY GOOD SCRIPT GIRL.

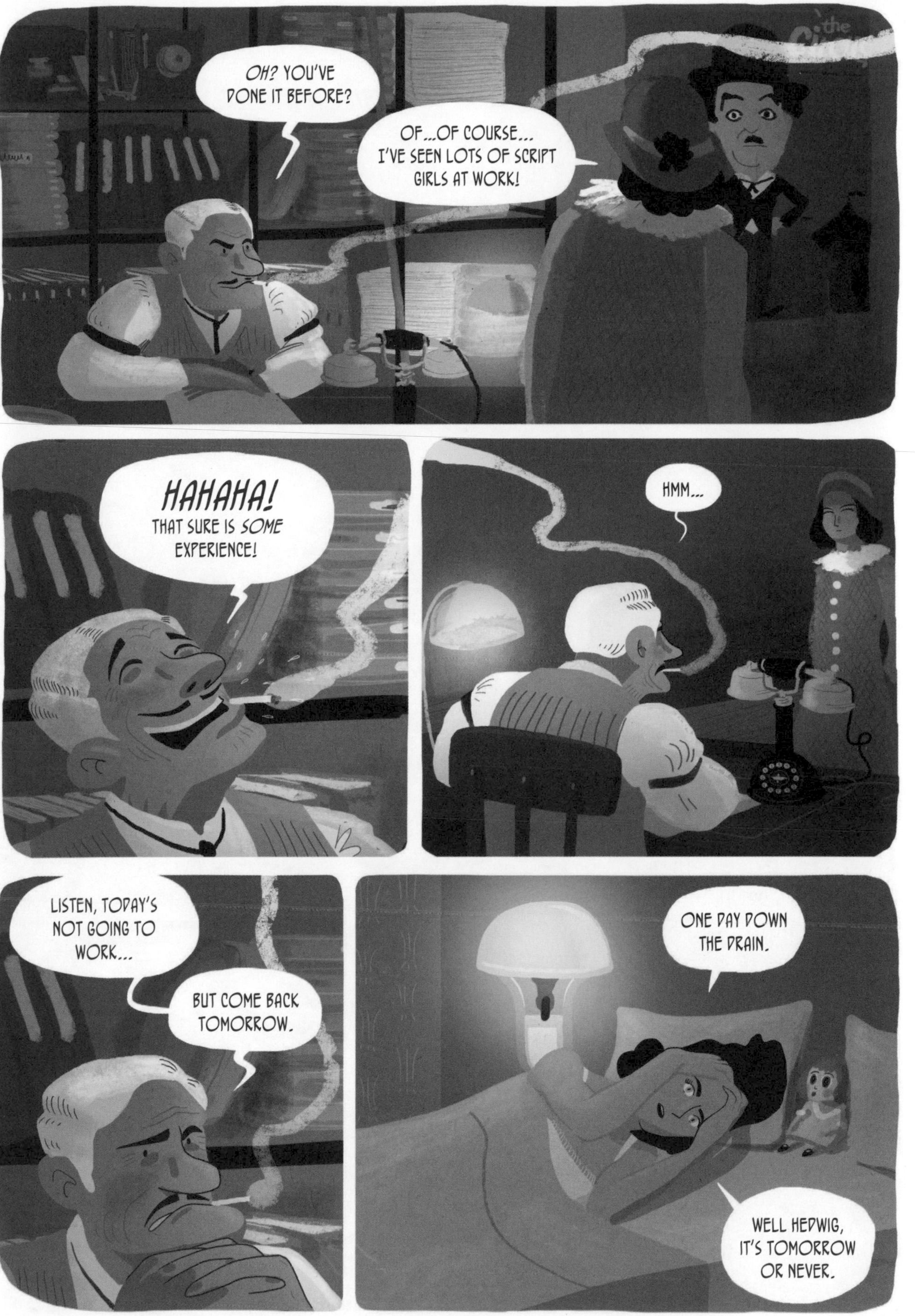
OH? YOU'VE DONE IT BEFORE?
OF...OF COURSE... I'VE SEEN LOTS OF SCRIPT GIRLS AT WORK!
HAHAHA! THAT SURE IS SOME EXPERIENCE!
HMM...
LISTEN, TODAY'S NOT GOING TO WORK...
BUT COME BACK TOMORROW.
ONE DAY DOWN THE DRAIN.
WELL HEDWIG, IT'S TOMORROW OR NEVER.

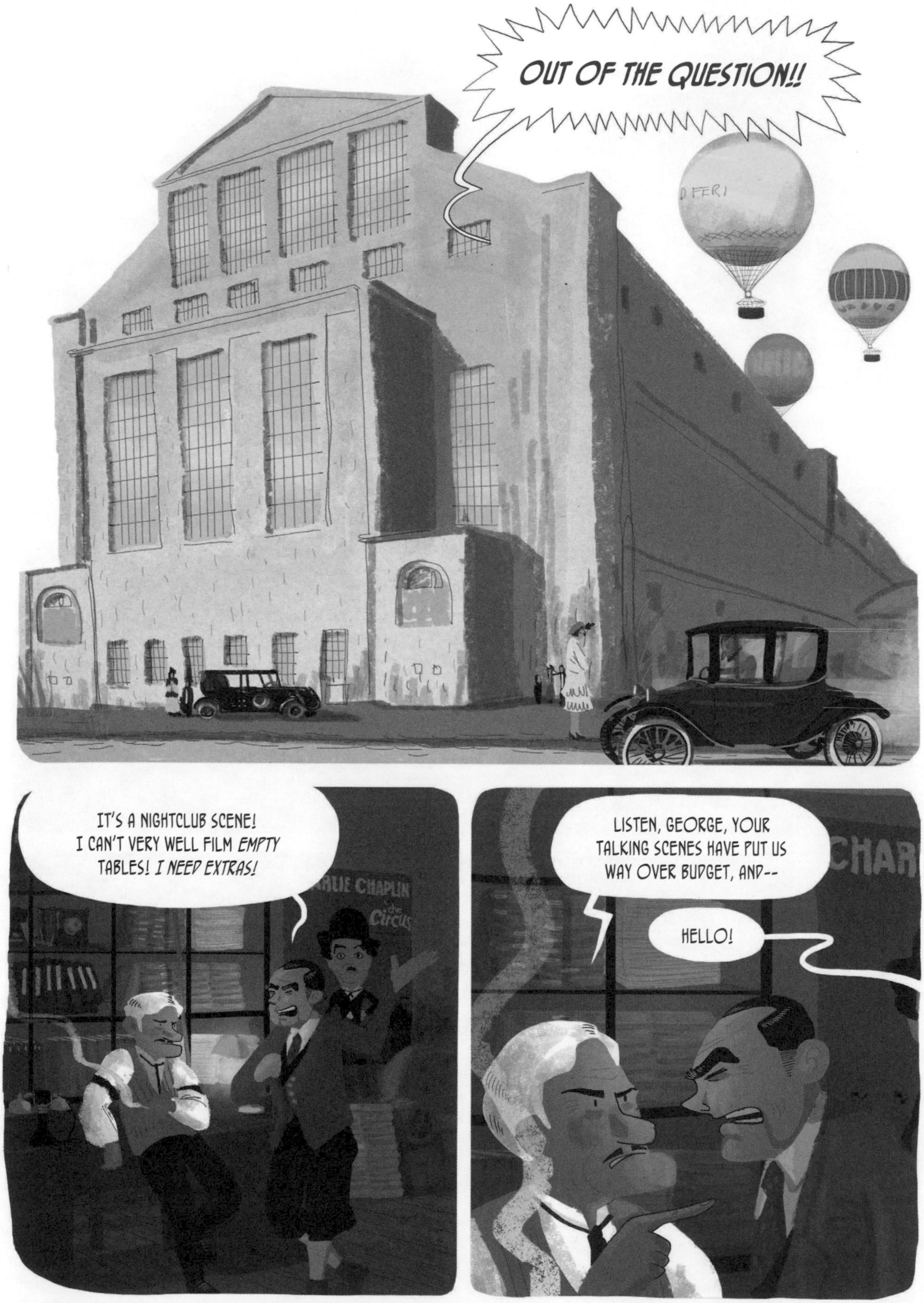
OUT OF THE QUESTION!!
IT'S A NIGHTCLUB SCENE! I CAN'T VERY WELL FILM *EMPTY* TABLES! *I NEED EXTRAS!*
LISTEN, GEORGE, YOUR TALKING SCENES HAVE PUT US WAY OVER BUDGET, AND--
HELLO!

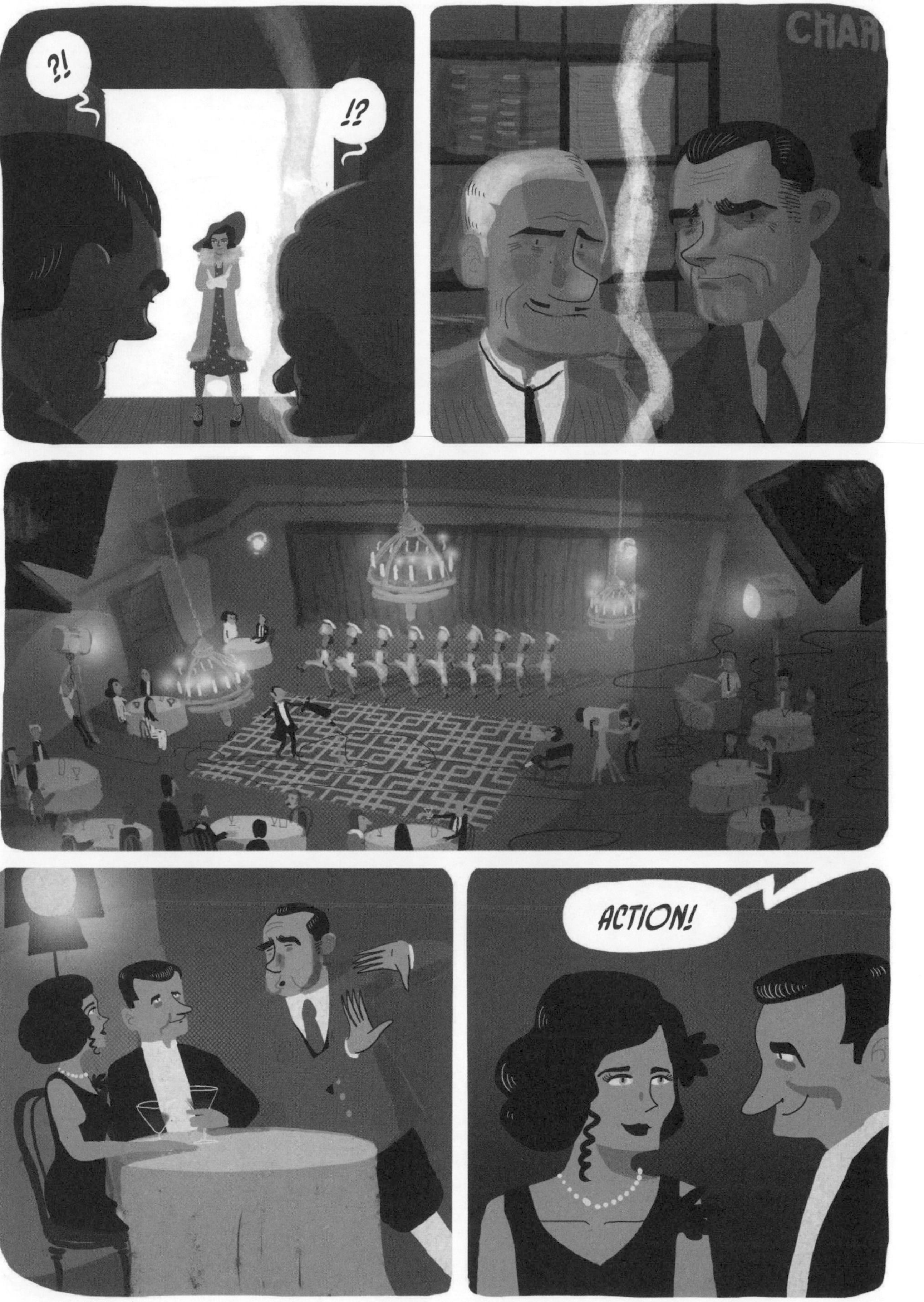
?!
!?
ACTION!

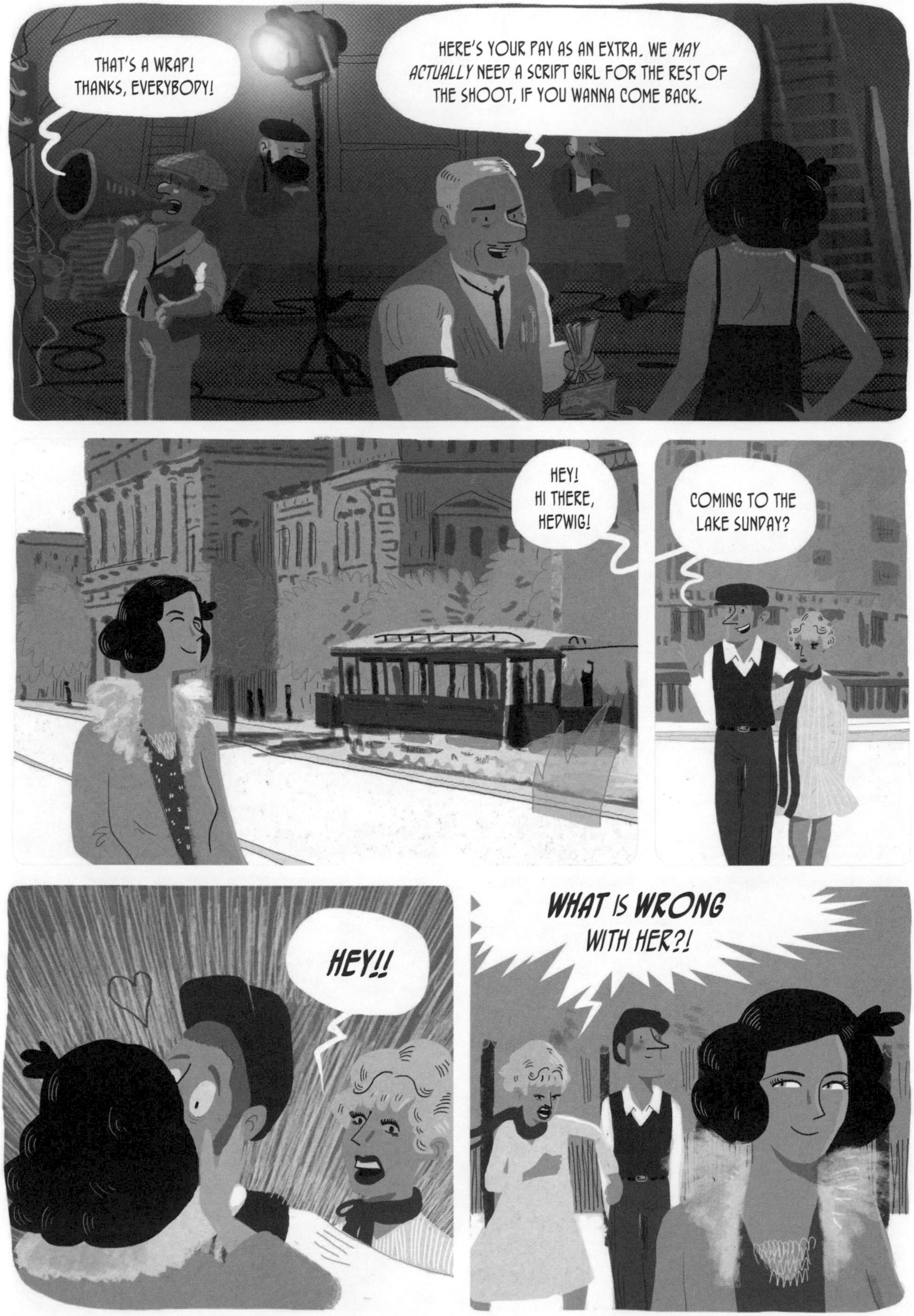
THAT'S A WRAP! THANKS, EVERYBODY!
HERE'S YOUR PAY AS AN EXTRA. WE *MAY* *ACTUALLY* NEED A SCRIPT GIRL FOR THE REST OF THE SHOOT, IF YOU WANNA COME BACK.
HEY! HI THERE, HEDWIG!
COMING TO THE LAKE SUNDAY?
HEY!!
WHAT IS WRONG WITH HER?!

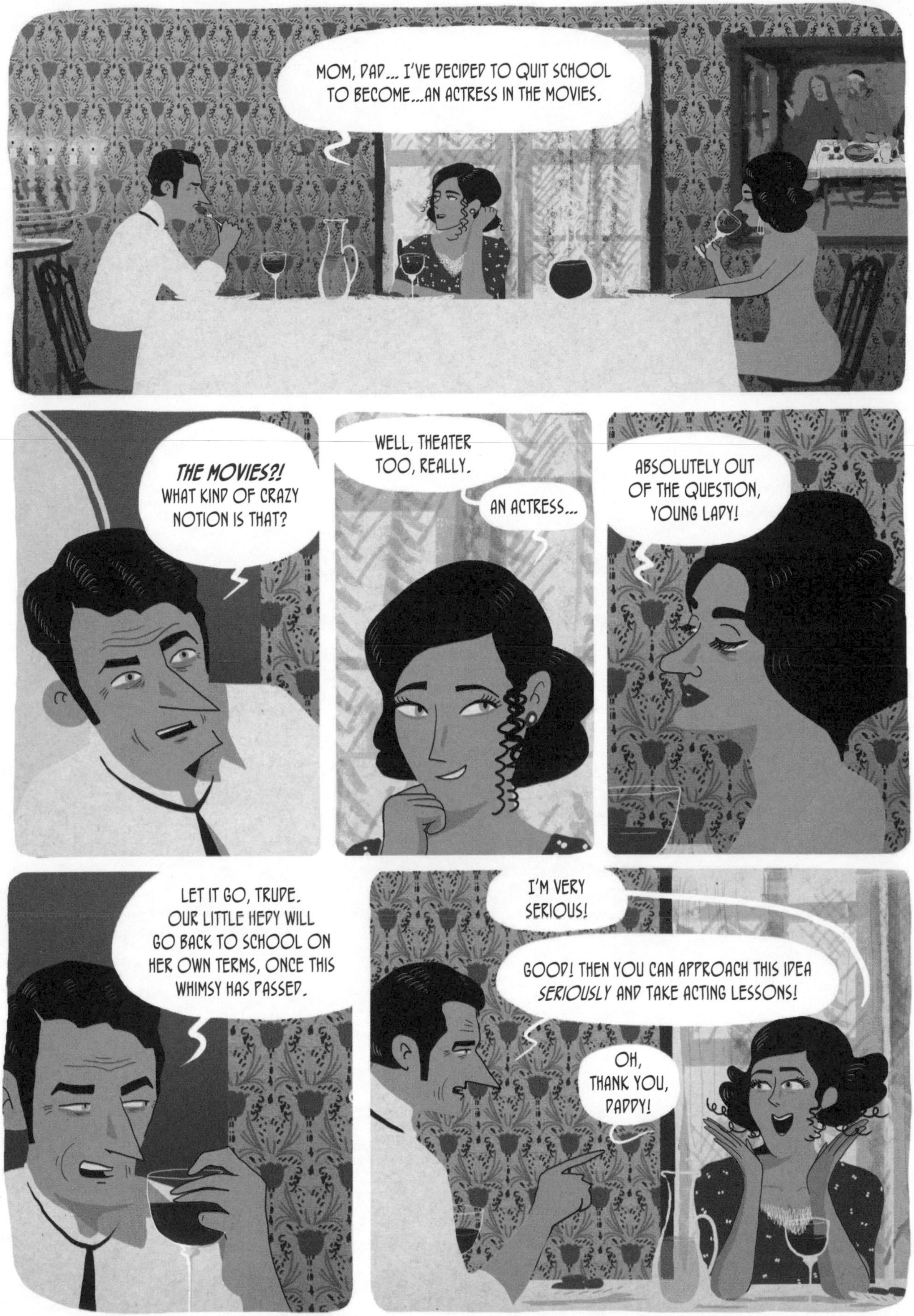
MOM, DAD... I'VE DECIDED TO QUIT SCHOOL TO BECOME...AN ACTRESS IN THE MOVIES.
THE MOVIES?! WHAT KIND OF CRAZY NOTION IS THAT?
WELL, THEATER TOO, REALLY.
AN ACTRESS...
ABSOLUTELY OUT OF THE QUESTION, YOUNG LADY!
LET IT GO, TRUDE. OUR LITTLE HEDY WILL GO BACK TO SCHOOL ON HER OWN TERMS, ONCE THIS WHIMSY HAS PASSED.
I'M VERY SERIOUS!
GOOD! THEN YOU CAN APPROACH THIS IDEA *SERIOUSLY* AND TAKE ACTING LESSONS!
OH, THANK YOU, DADDY!

EXTAƒE
(1933)
Dir: Gustav Machaty

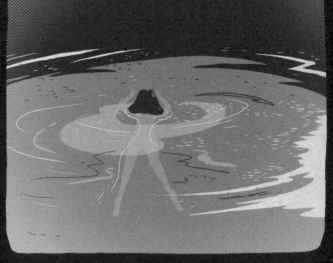

NONI!

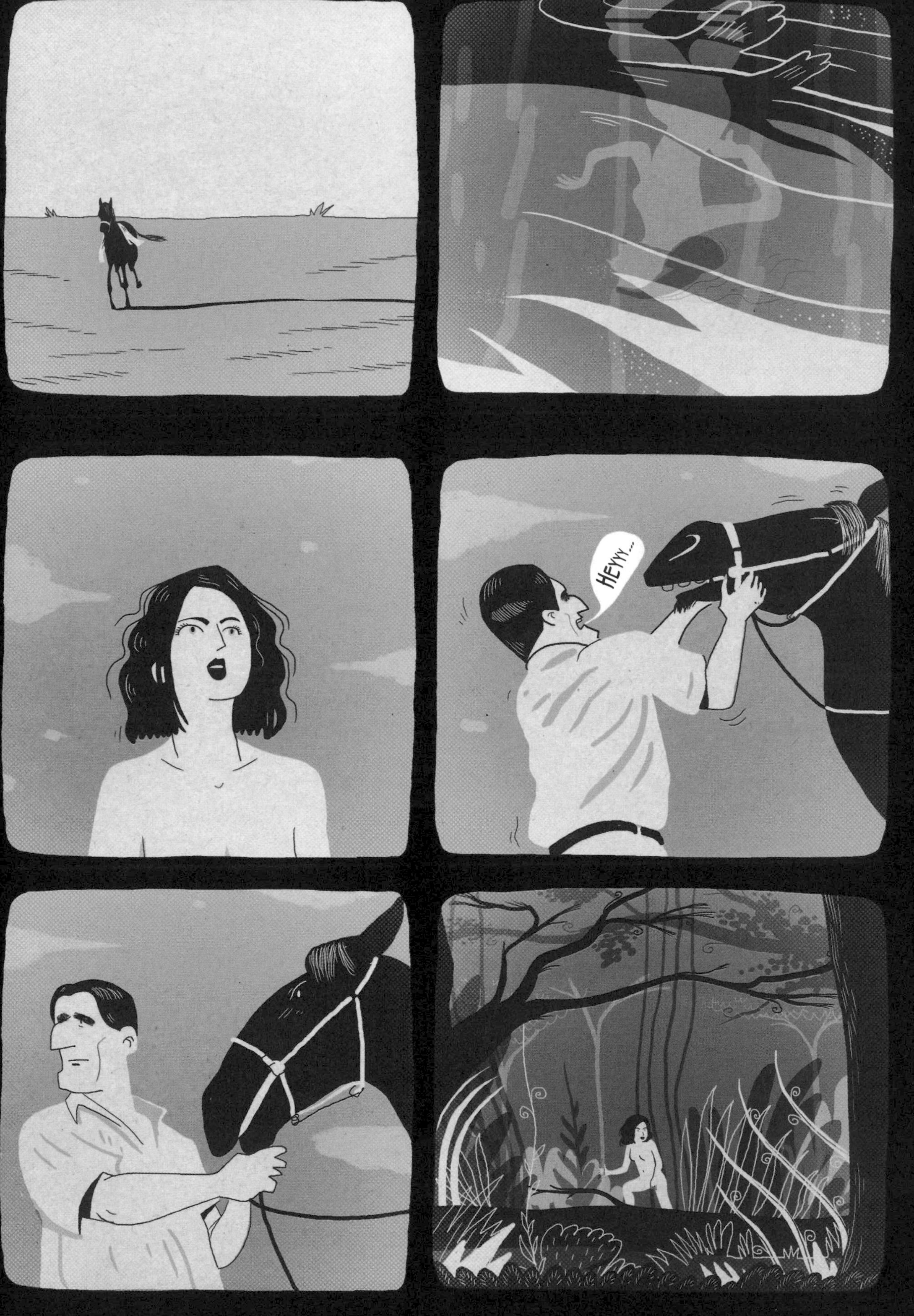
HEYYY...

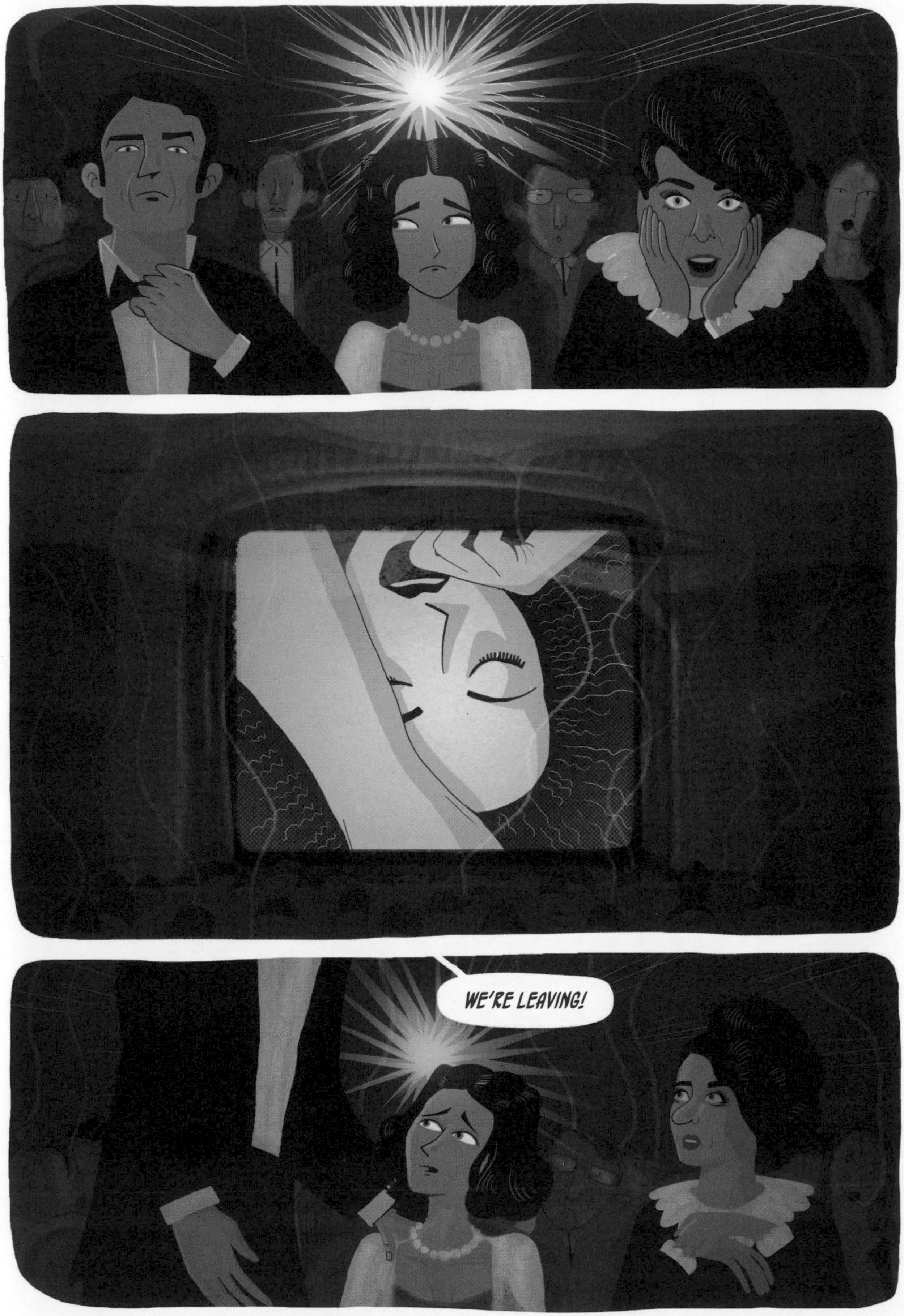
WE'RE LEAVING!

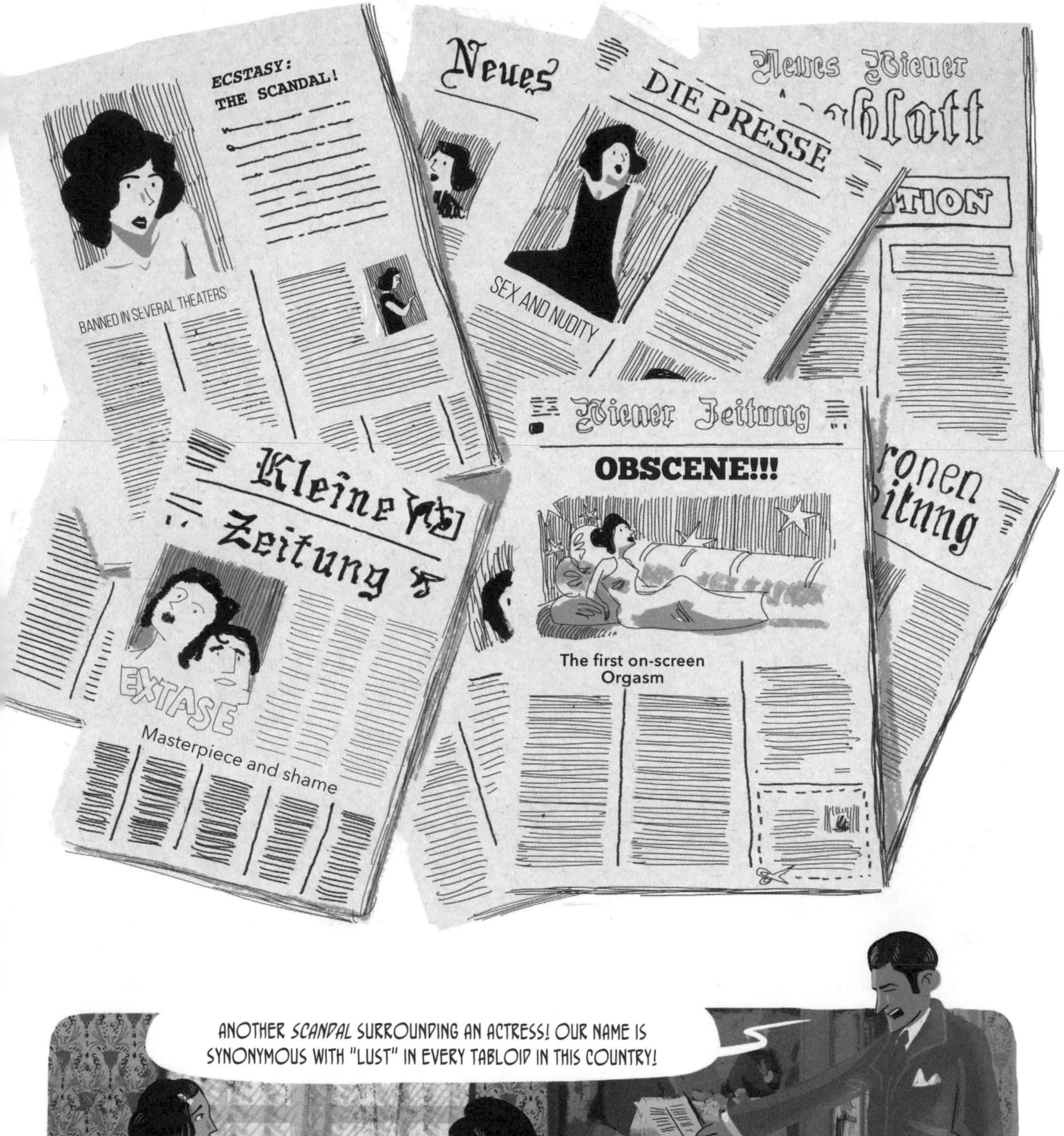
ECSTASY: THE SCANDAL!
BANNED IN SEVERAL THEATERS
Neues
DIE PRESSE
SEX AND NUDITY
Neues Wiener
Kleine
Zeitung
EXTASE
Masterpiece and shame
Wiener Zeitung
OBSCENE!!!
The first on-screen Orgasm

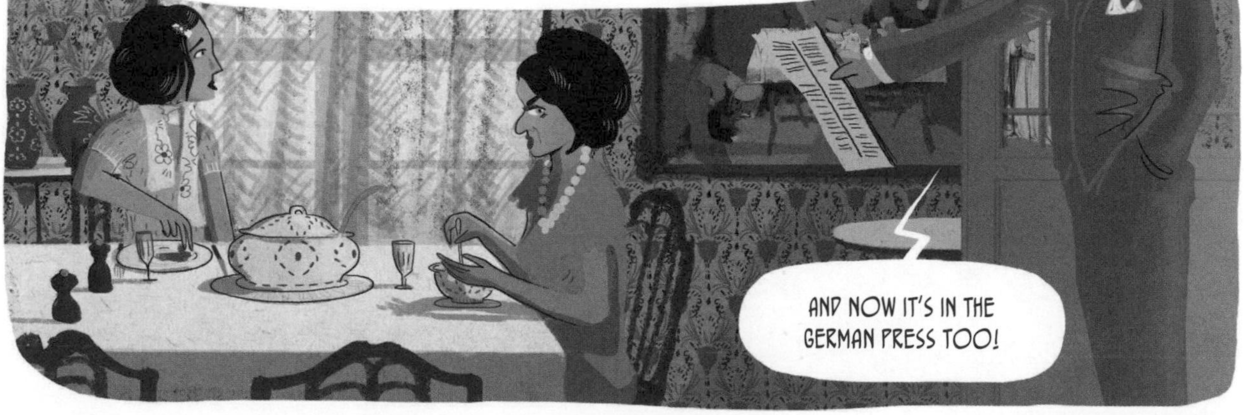
ANOTHER *SCANDAL* SURROUNDING AN ACTRESS! OUR NAME IS SYNONYMOUS WITH "LUST" IN EVERY TABLOID IN THIS COUNTRY!
AND NOW IT'S IN THE GERMAN PRESS TOO!

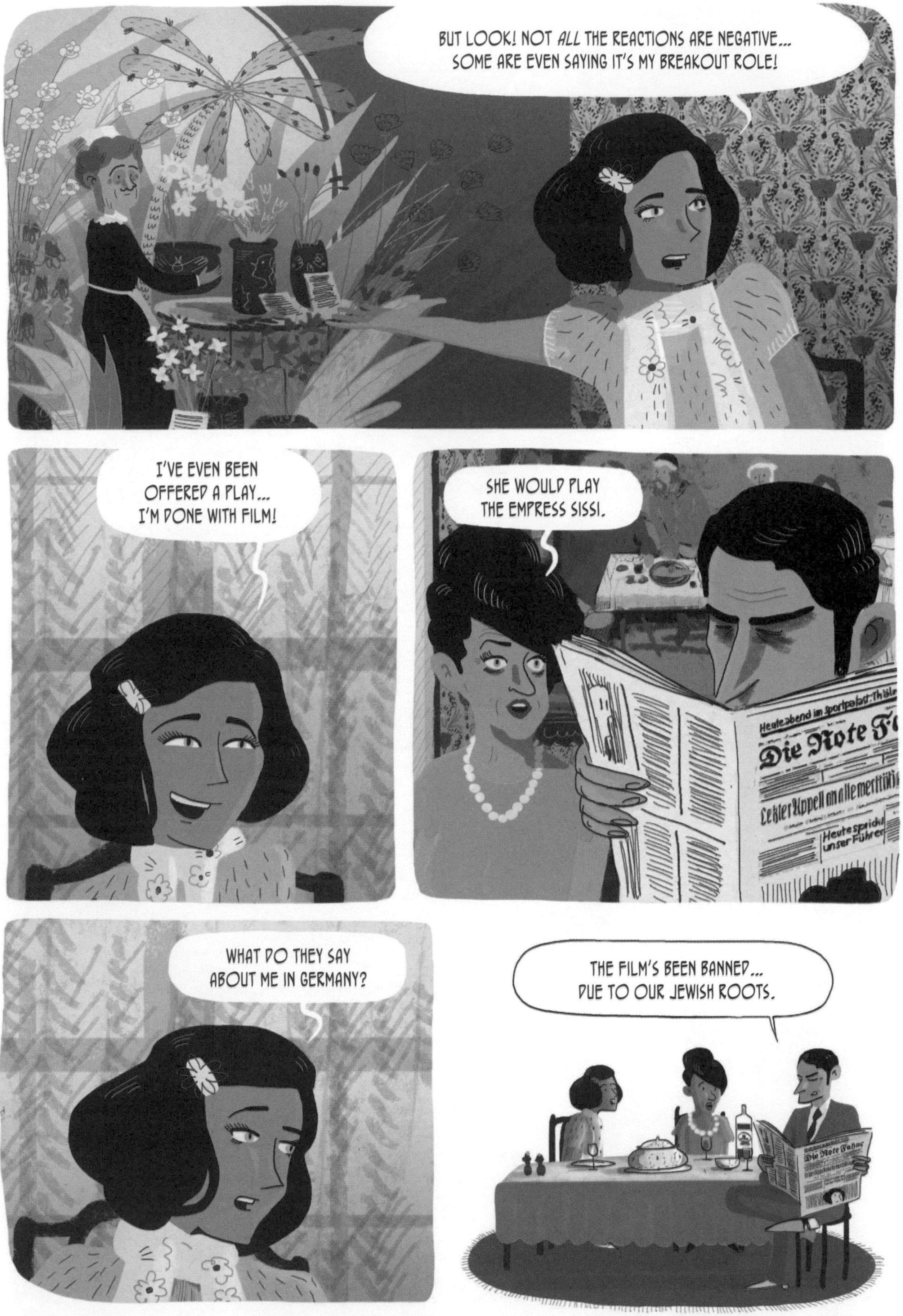
BUT LOOK! NOT *ALL* THE REACTIONS ARE NEGATIVE... SOME ARE EVEN SAYING IT'S MY BREAKOUT ROLE!
I'VE EVEN BEEN OFFERED A PLAY... I'M DONE WITH FILM!
SHE WOULD PLAY THE EMPRESS SISSI.
WHAT DO THEY SAY ABOUT ME IN GERMANY?
THE FILM'S BEEN BANNED... DUE TO OUR JEWISH ROOTS.

Pisustag, 31. Zan 1933
Rr. 25 — 71. Jabegang

Breis Gr. 30 für Piell und Brouins

Wiener
Sonn=und=Montags=Zeitnng

ADOLF HITLER: "THE TASK BEFORE US IS THE MOST DIFFICULT WHICH HAS FACED GERMAN STATESMEN IN LIVING MEMORY."

A New Chancellor for Germany

WHILE EVERYBODY THOUGHT HE'D GROWN WEAKER THESE PAST TEN YEARS, ADOLF HITLER HAS ACHIEVED A POWERFUL COMEBACK IN VERY LITTLE TIME, FASTER THAN ANYONE ELSE IN GERMAN HISTORY. THANKS TO SUPPORT FROM THE RIGHT AND THE INVOLVEMENT OF ALFRED HUGENBERG'S DNVP, HITLER, WHOM THE PUBLIC THOUGHT OF AS DEFEATED IN THE LEGISLATIVE ELECTION OF THIS PAST NOVEMBER, BECAME CHANCELLOR OF THE WEIMAR REPUBLIC ON MONDAY, JANUARY 30TH AT NOON. PLENTY OF RUMORS HAVE BEEN CIRCULATING EVER SINCE: WHAT'S THE REAL DEAL WITH HIS NEW GOVERNMENT? SHOULD HITLER BE VIEWED AS SIMPLY AN INTERIM LEADER AND THE NATIONAL SOCIALIST GERMAN WORKERS' PARTY A MERE CHAPTER IN GERMANY'S POLITICAL HISTORY? WHATEVER THE CASE, THE NEW CHANCELLOR BEGAN HIS TENURE WITH A POWERFUL AND SYMBOLIC MESSAGE: THOUSANDS OF SAS MARCHED IN A PARADE LAST NIGHT ON UNTER DEN LINDEN, AS HITLER LOOKED ON, IN AN EVENT THAT MARKED HIS TAKING OVER CONTROL OF BERLIN AND PROBABLY INDICATES THE BEGINNING OF A WITCH HUNT AGAINST THOSE WHO OPPOSED HIM. LET'S BE CAREFUL NOT TO LET GERMANY TAKE A LEAP INTO DARKNESS.

IS THE ANNEXATION OF AUSTRIA NEXT?

THAT'S A HYPOTHESIS TO TAKE SERIOUSLY. THE IDEA IS ALREADY PRESENT IN THE OPENING PARAGRAPH OF HIS MANIFESTO, MEIN KAMPF, WHICH HE STARTED WRI-TING DURING HIS NINE-MONTH-LONG INCAR-CERATION IN THE LANDSBERG PRISON, AND IN

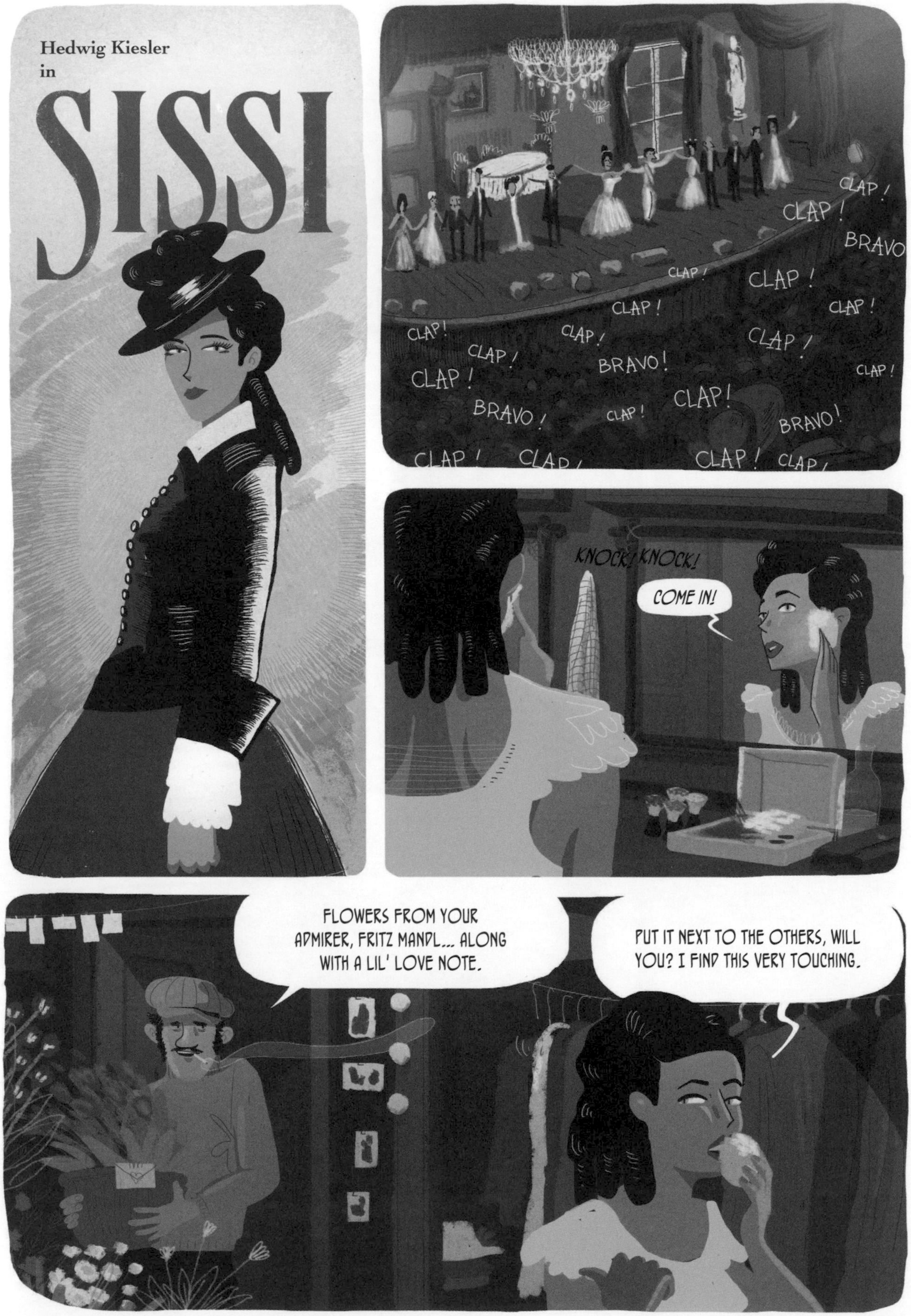
Hedwig Kiesler
in
SISSI
CLAP!
CLAP!
BRAVO
CLAP!
CLAP!
CLAP!
CLAP!
CLAP!
CLAP!
CLAP!
CLAP!
BRAVO!
CLAP!
BRAVO!
CLAP!
CLAP!
BRAVO!
KNOCK! KNOCK!
COME IN!
FLOWERS FROM YOUR ADMIRER, FRITZ MANDL... ALONG WITH A LIL' LOVE NOTE.
PUT IT NEXT TO THE OTHERS, WILL YOU? I FIND THIS VERY TOUCHING.

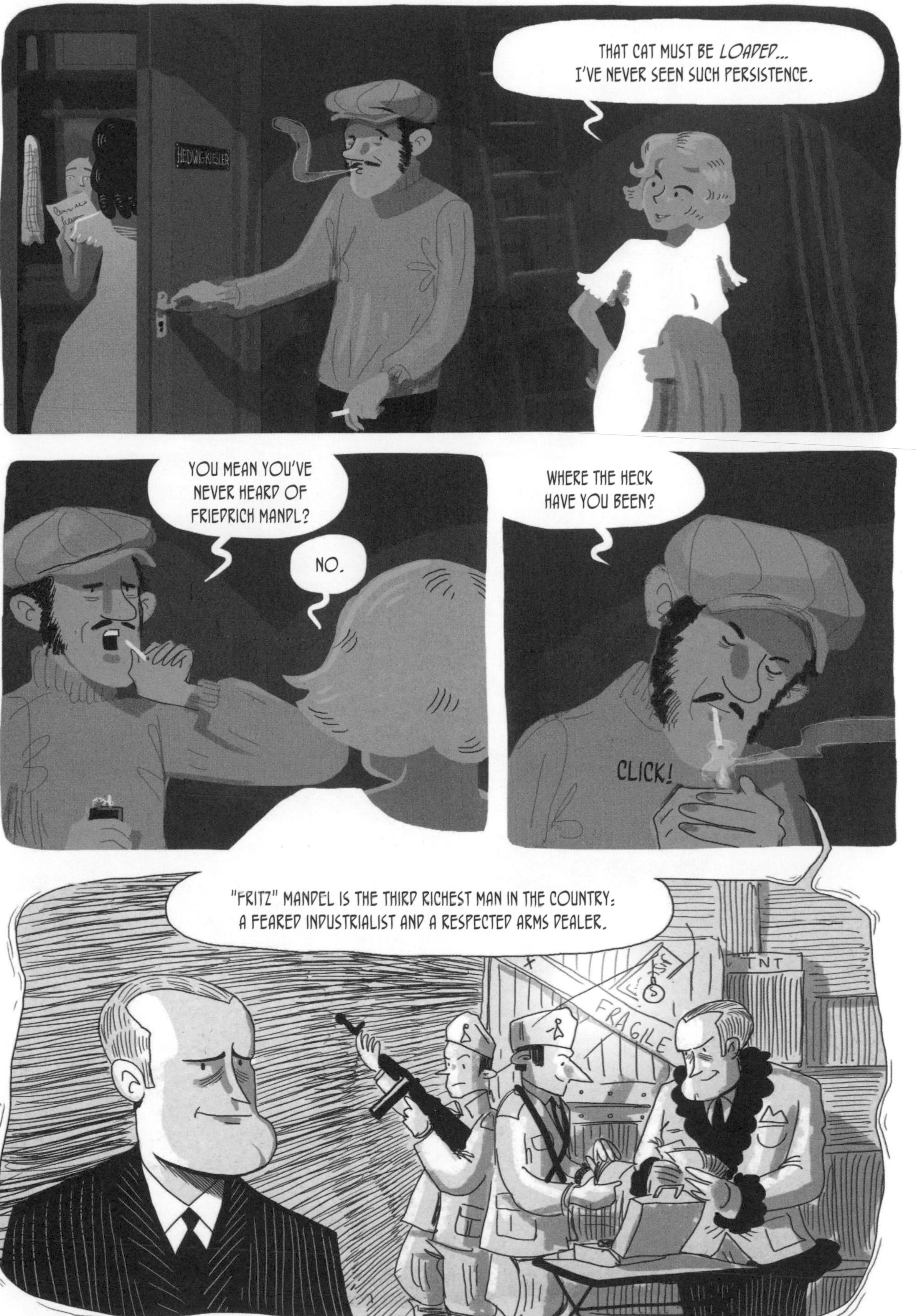
THAT CAT MUST BE *LOADED*... I'VE NEVER SEEN SUCH PERSISTENCE.
HEDWIG KIESLER
YOU MEAN YOU'VE NEVER HEARD OF FRIEDRICH MANDL?
NO.
WHERE THE HECK HAVE YOU BEEN?
CLICK!
"FRITZ" MANDEL IS THE THIRD RICHEST MAN IN THE COUNTRY: A FEARED INDUSTRIALIST AND A RESPECTED ARMS DEALER.
TNT
FRAGILE

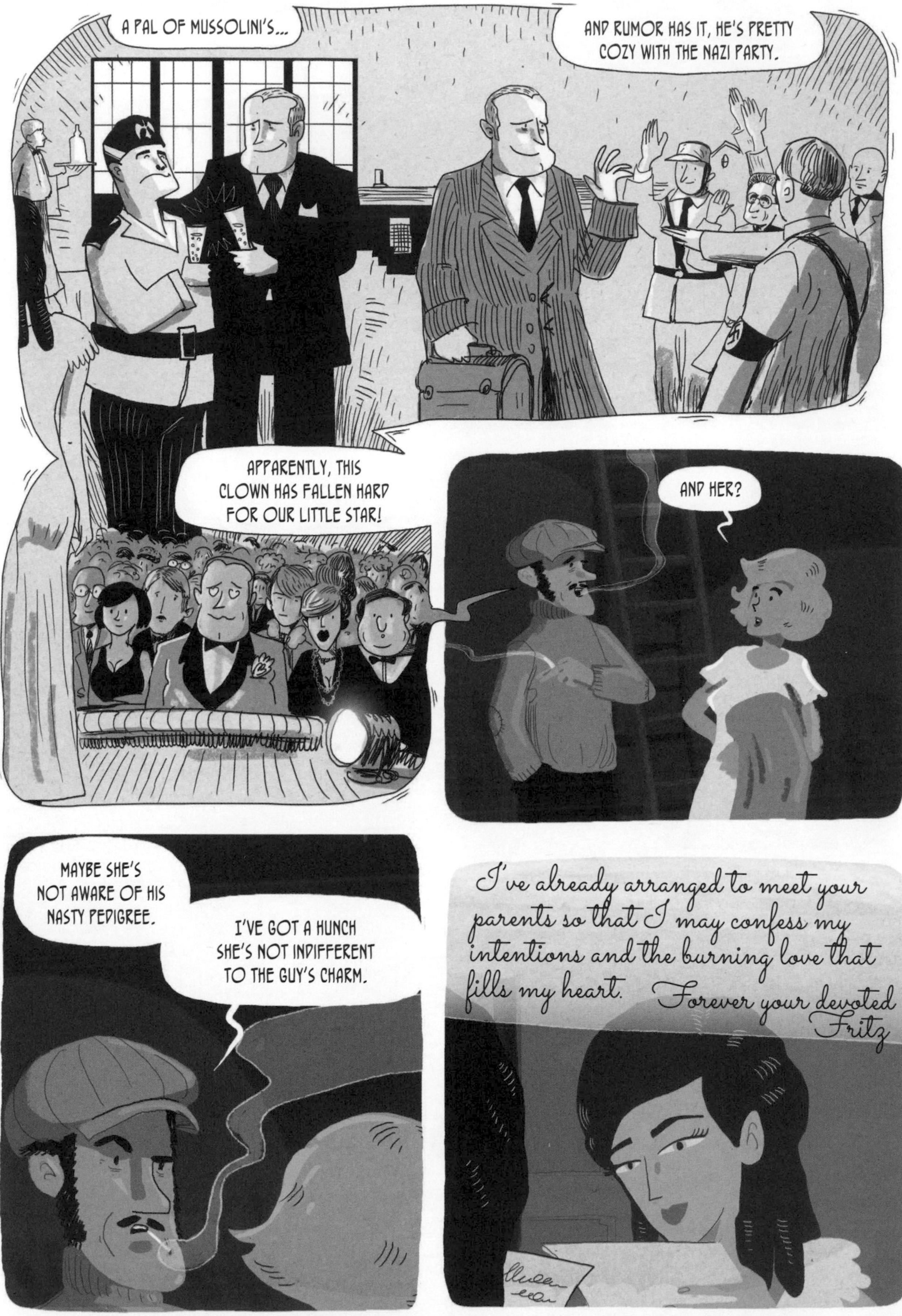
A PAL OF MUSSOLINI'S...
AND RUMOR HAS IT, HE'S PRETTY COZY WITH THE NAZI PARTY.
APPARENTLY, THIS CLOWN HAS FALLEN HARD FOR OUR LITTLE STAR!
AND HER?
MAYBE SHE'S NOT AWARE OF HIS NASTY PEDIGREE.
I'VE GOT A HUNCH SHE'S NOT INDIFFERENT TO THE GUY'S CHARM.
I've already arranged to meet your parents so that I may confess my intentions and the burning love that fills my heart. Forever your devoted Fritz

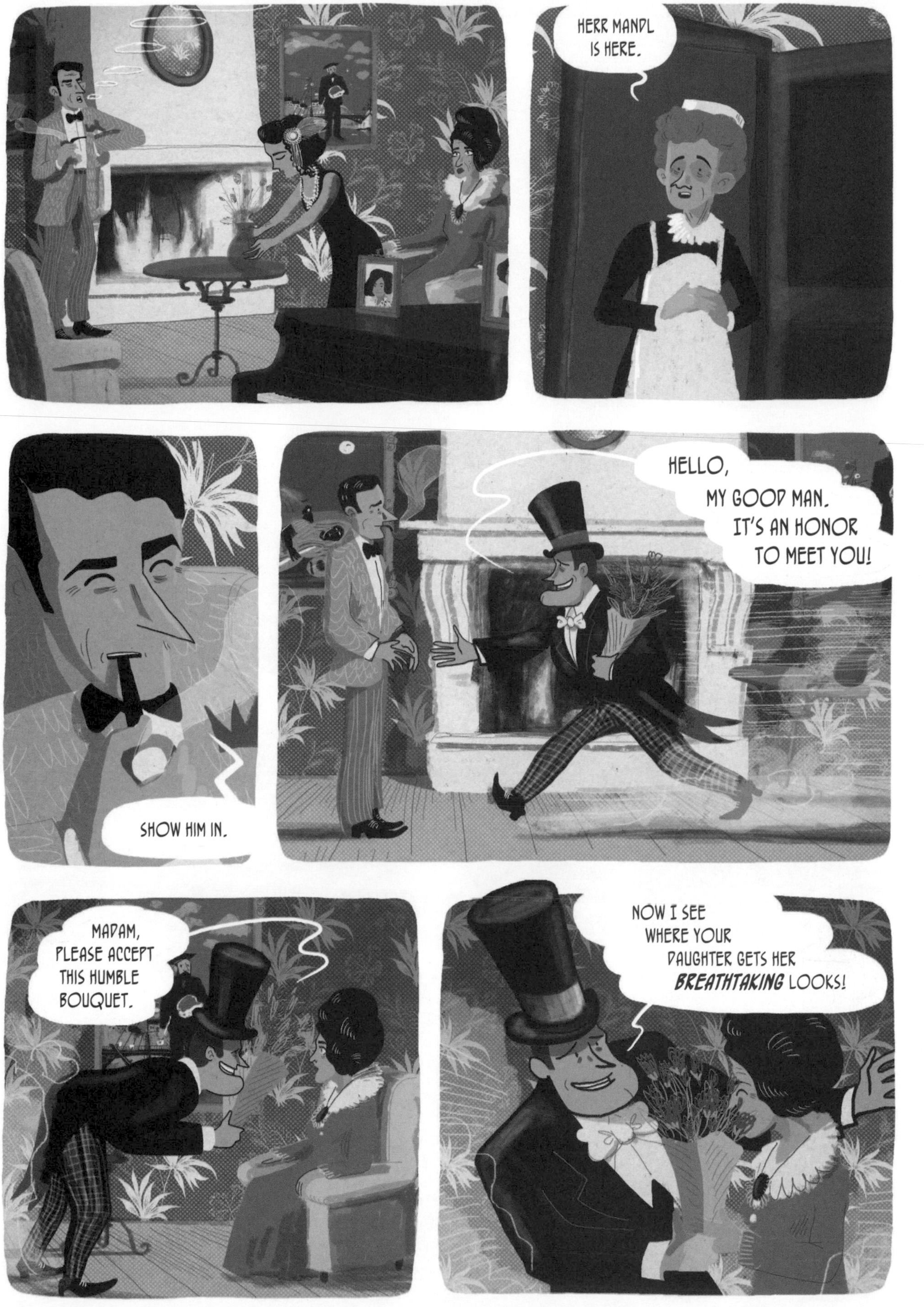
HERR MANDL IS HERE.
SHOW HIM IN.
HELLO, MY GOOD MAN. IT'S AN HONOR TO MEET YOU!
MADAM, PLEASE ACCEPT THIS HUMBLE BOUQUET.
NOW I SEE WHERE YOUR DAUGHTER GETS HER BREATHTAKING LOOKS!

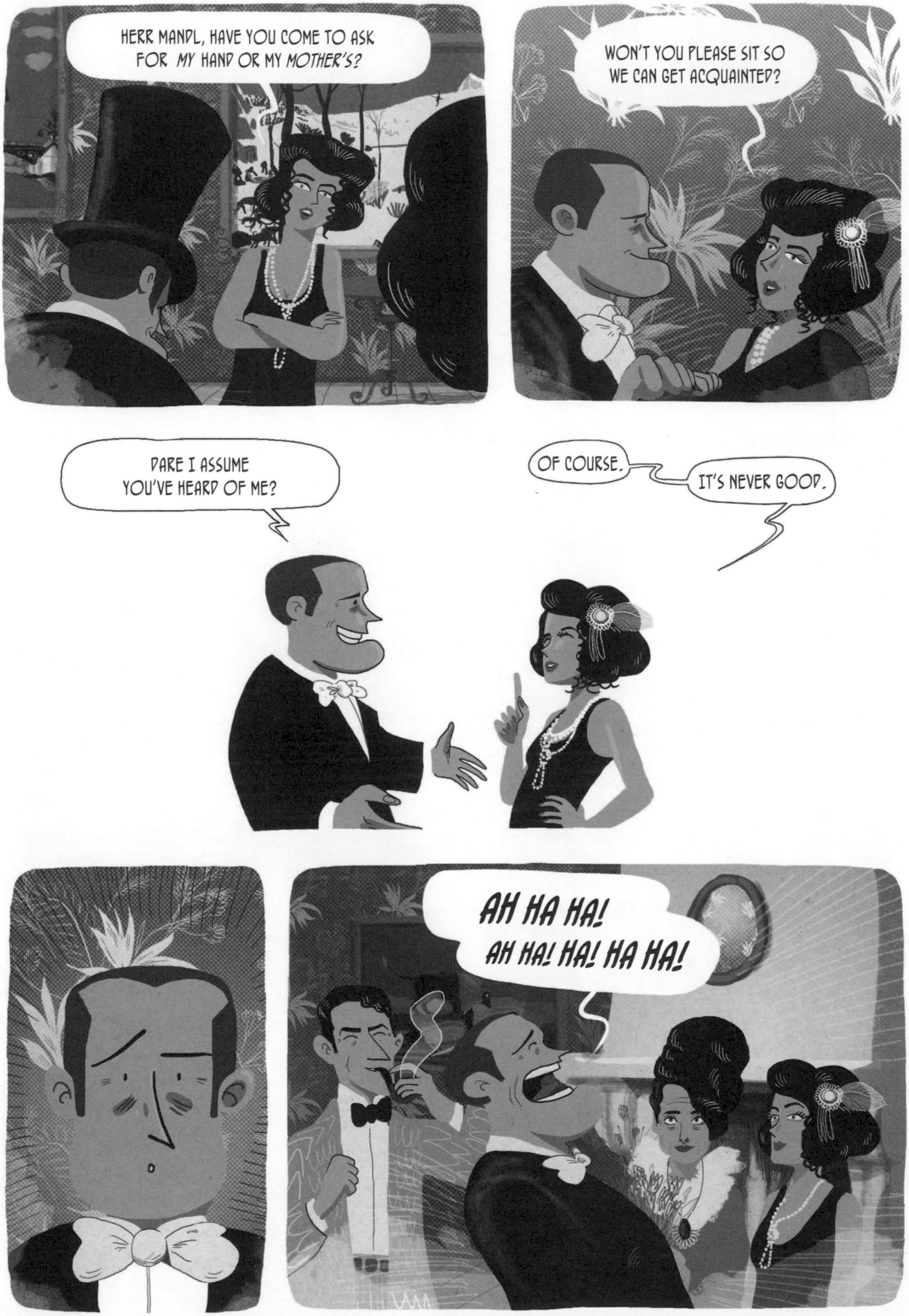
HERR MANDL, HAVE YOU COME TO ASK FOR *MY* HAND OR MY *MOTHER'S?*
WON'T YOU PLEASE SIT SO WE CAN GET ACQUAINTED?
DARE I ASSUME YOU'VE HEARD OF ME?
OF COURSE.
IT'S NEVER GOOD.
AH HA HA! AH HA! HA! HA HA!

Friedrich & Hedwig Mandl Wedding

August 10th, 1933

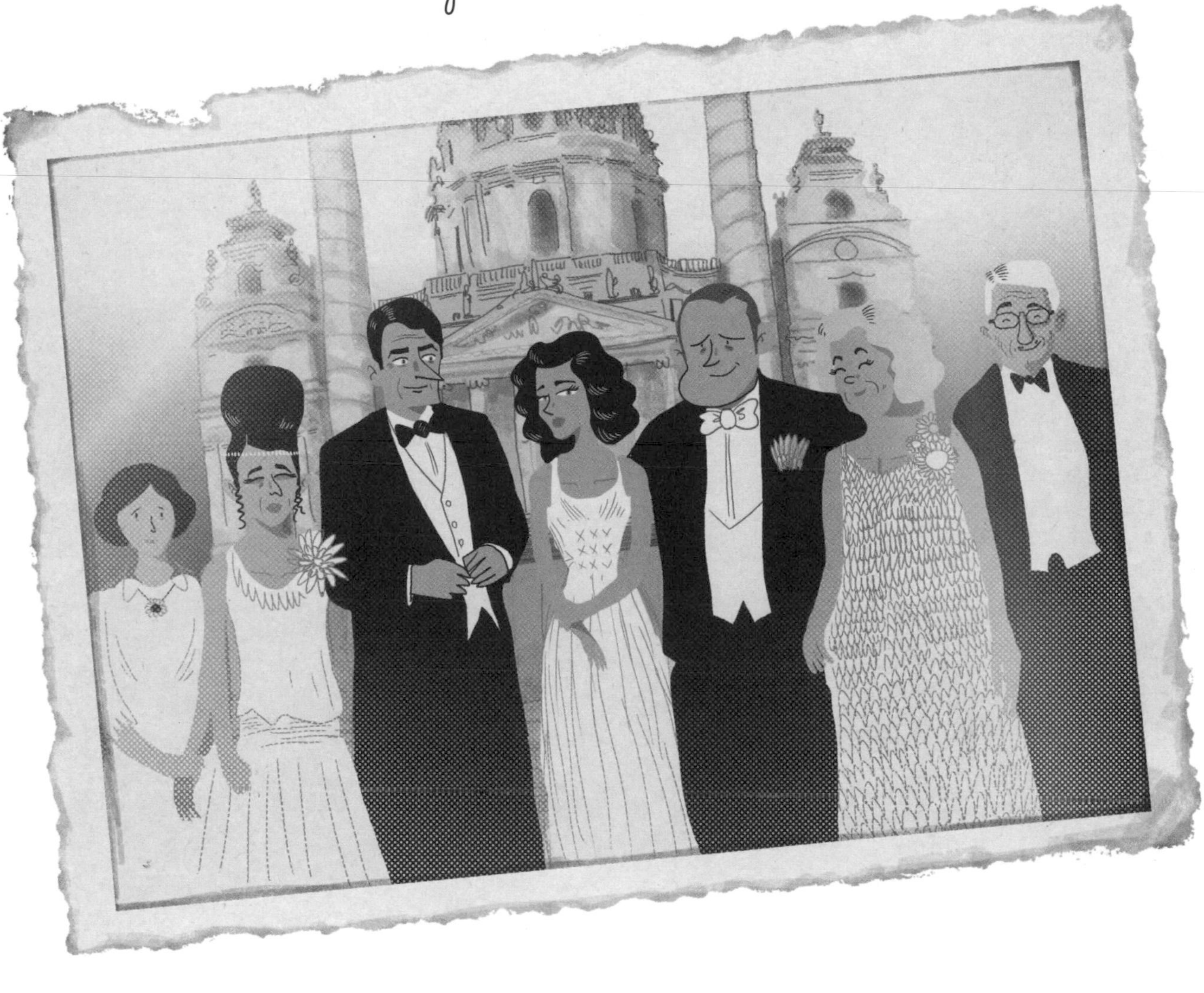

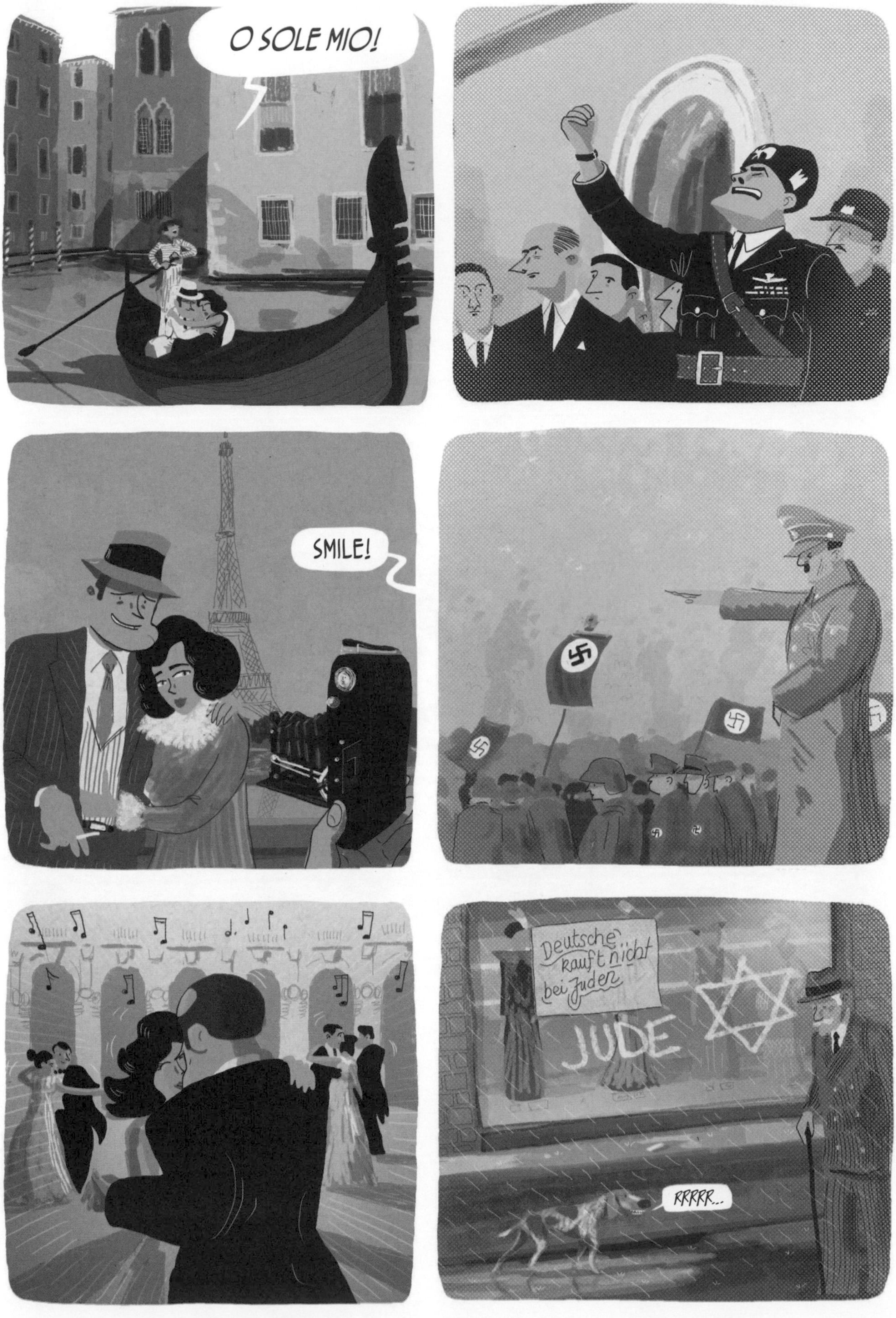
O SOLE MIO!
SMILE!
Deutsche kauft nicht bei Juden
JUDE
RRRRR...

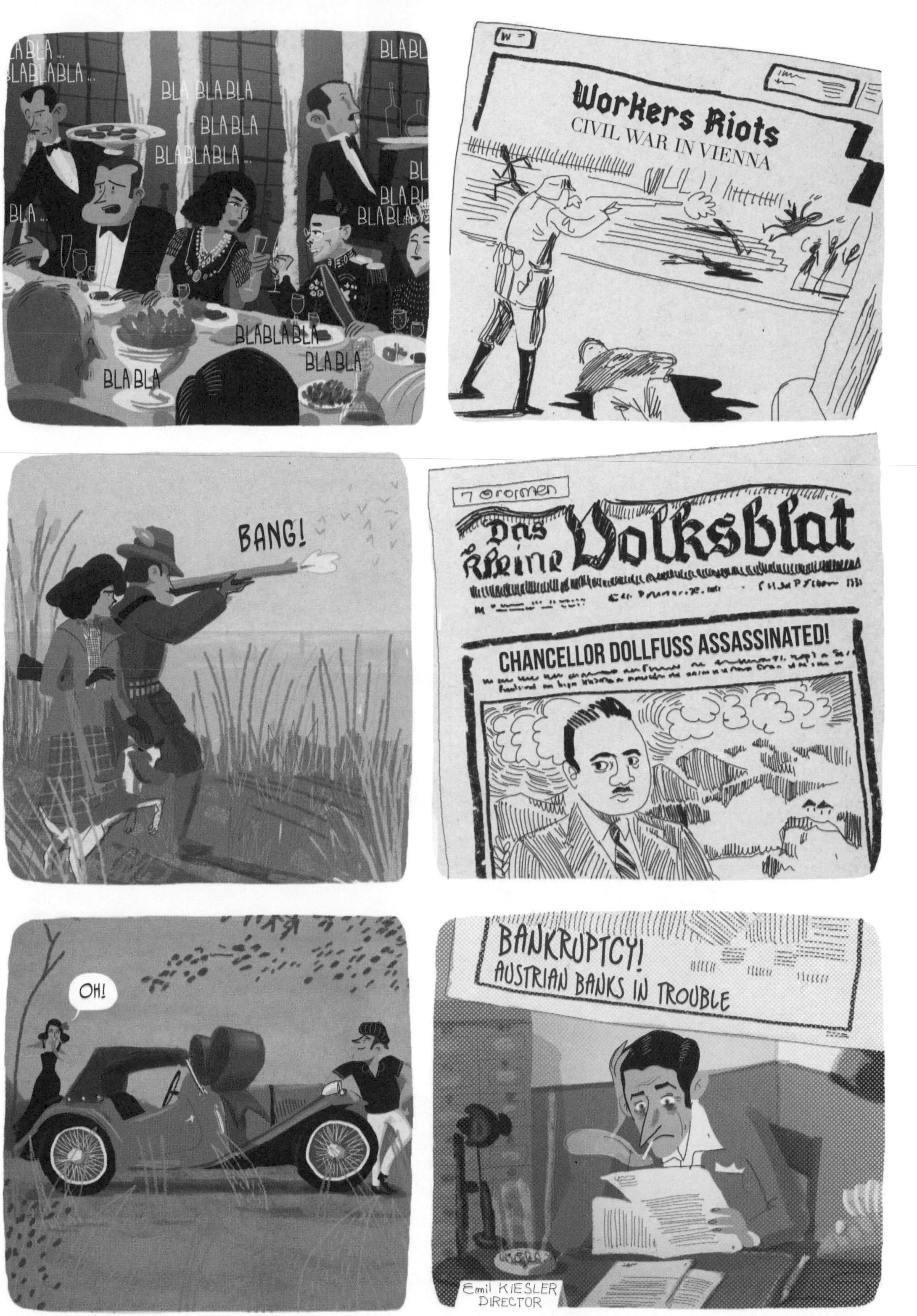

BLA...
BLABLABLA...
BLA BLA BLA
BLA BLA
BLABLABLA...
BLA...
BLABLABLA
BLA BLA
BLA BLA
BLABL
BLA BL
BLABLA
Workers Riots
CIVIL WAR IN VIENNA
BANG!
Das Kleine Volksblat
CHANCELLOR DOLLFUSS ASSASSINATED!
OH!
BANKRUPTCY!
AUSTRIAN BANKS IN TROUBLE
Emil KIESLER
DIRECTOR

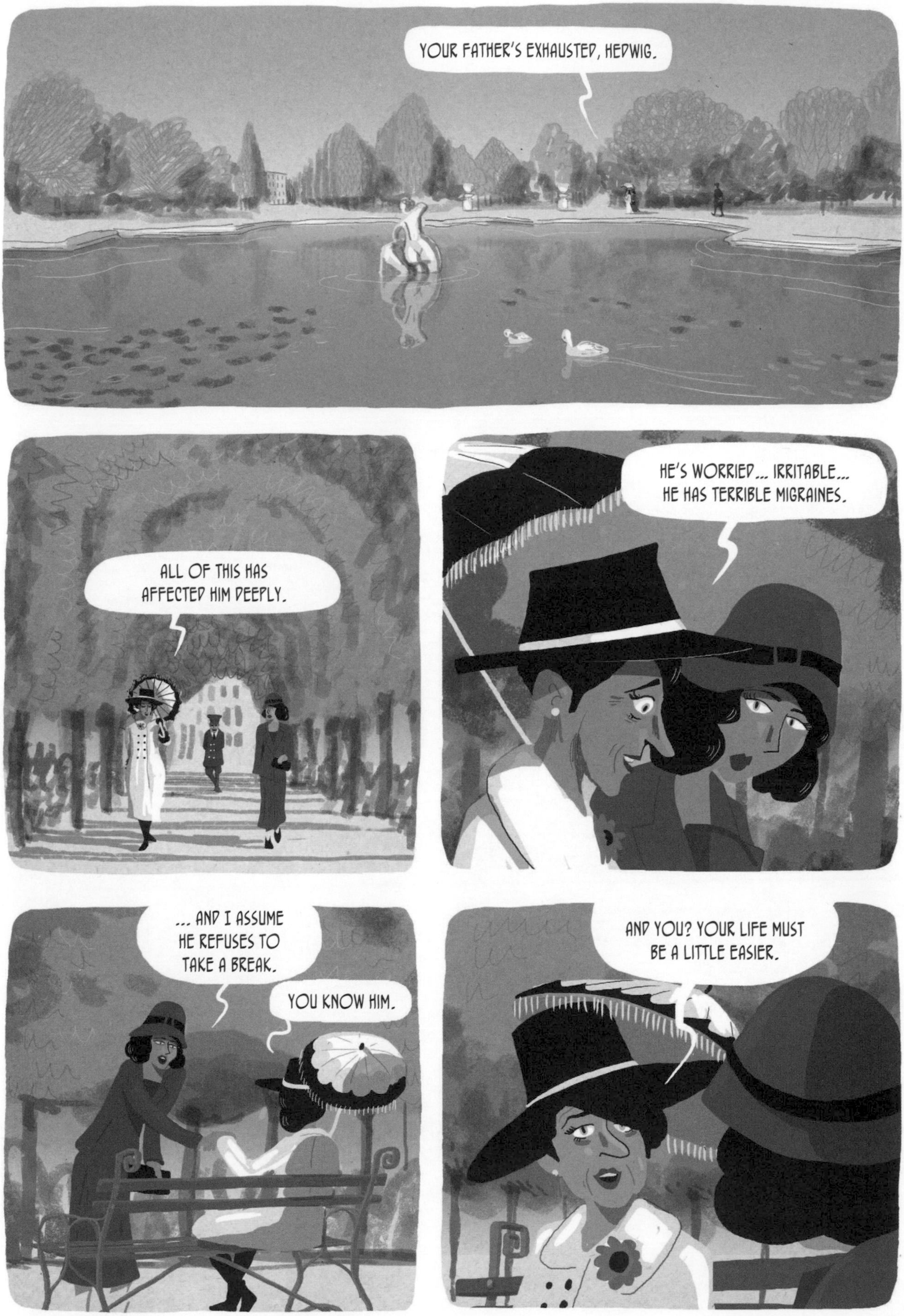
YOUR FATHER'S EXHAUSTED, HEDWIG.
ALL OF THIS HAS AFFECTED HIM DEEPLY.
HE'S WORRIED... IRRITABLE... HE HAS TERRIBLE MIGRAINES.
... AND I ASSUME HE REFUSES TO TAKE A BREAK.
YOU KNOW HIM.
AND YOU? YOUR LIFE MUST BE A LITTLE EASIER.

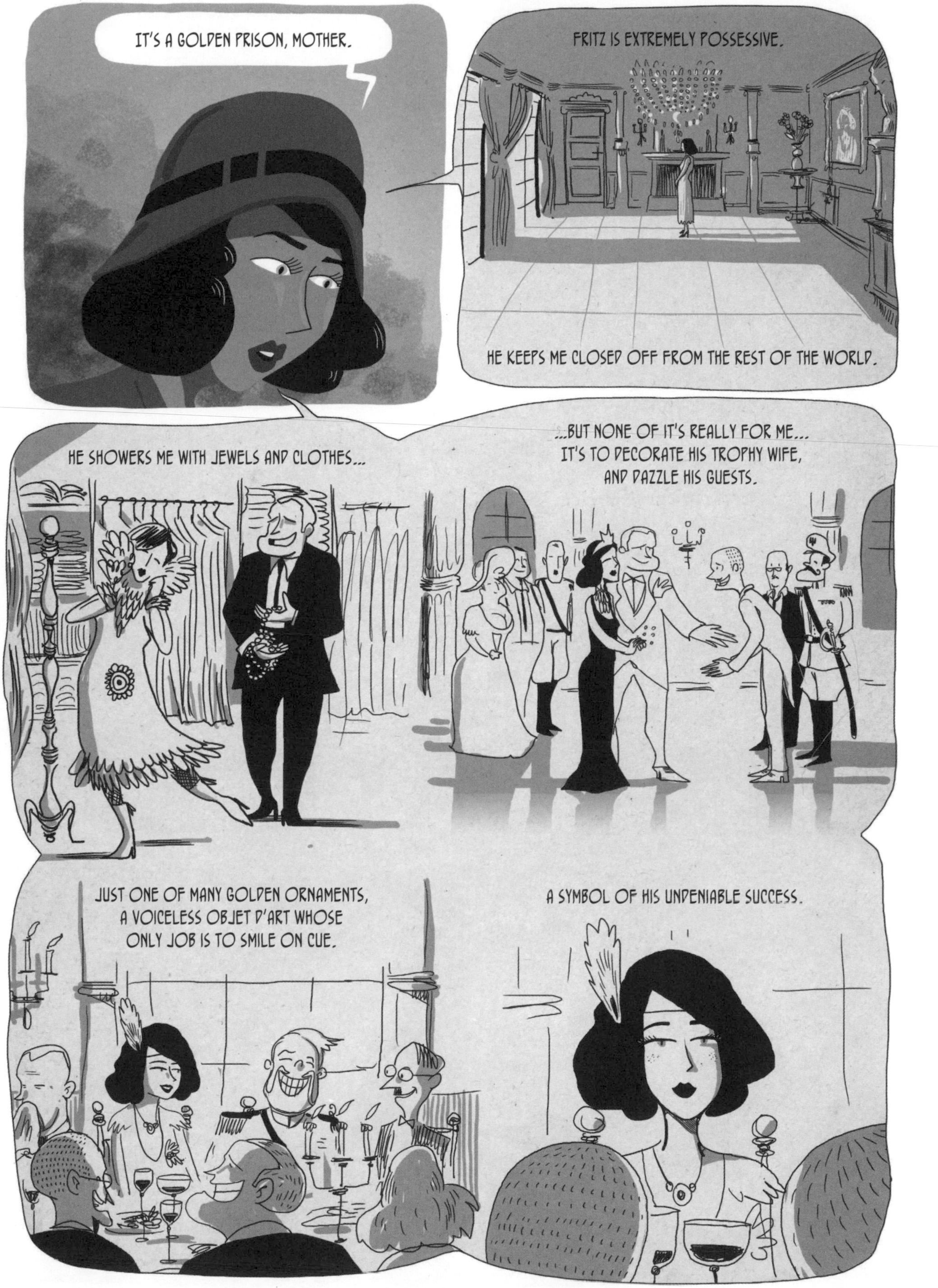
IT'S A GOLDEN PRISON, MOTHER.
FRITZ IS EXTREMELY POSSESSIVE.
HE KEEPS ME CLOSED OFF FROM THE REST OF THE WORLD.
HE SHOWERS ME WITH JEWELS AND CLOTHES...
...BUT NONE OF IT'S REALLY FOR ME... IT'S TO DECORATE HIS TROPHY WIFE, AND DAZZLE HIS GUESTS.
JUST ONE OF MANY GOLDEN ORNAMENTS, A VOICELESS OBJET D'ART WHOSE ONLY JOB IS TO SMILE ON CUE.
A SYMBOL OF HIS UNDENIABLE SUCCESS.

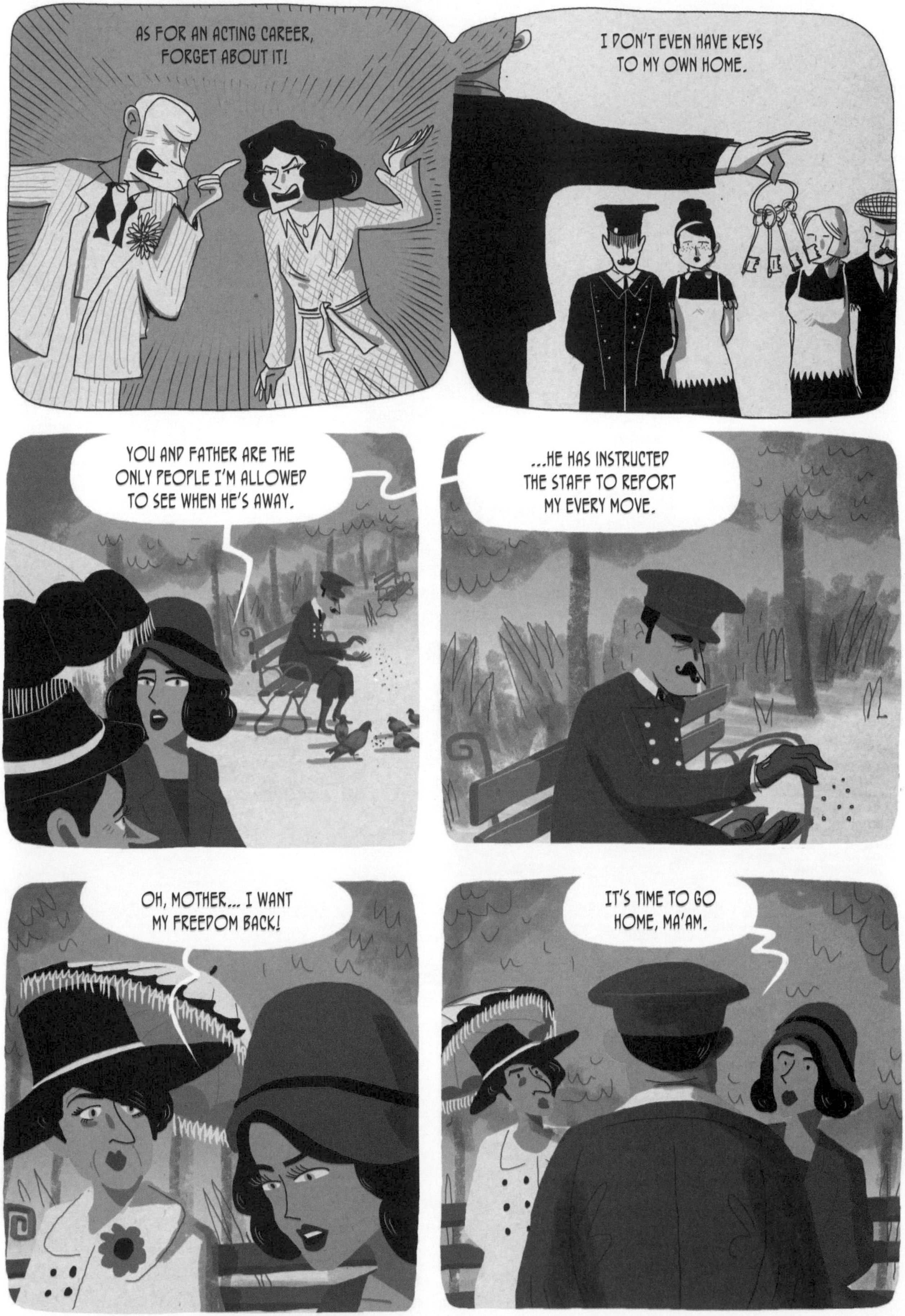
AS FOR AN ACTING CAREER, FORGET ABOUT IT!
I DON'T EVEN HAVE KEYS TO MY OWN HOME.
YOU AND FATHER ARE THE ONLY PEOPLE I'M ALLOWED TO SEE WHEN HE'S AWAY.
...HE HAS INSTRUCTED THE STAFF TO REPORT MY EVERY MOVE.
OH, MOTHER... I WANT MY FREEDOM BACK!
IT'S TIME TO GO HOME, MA'AM.

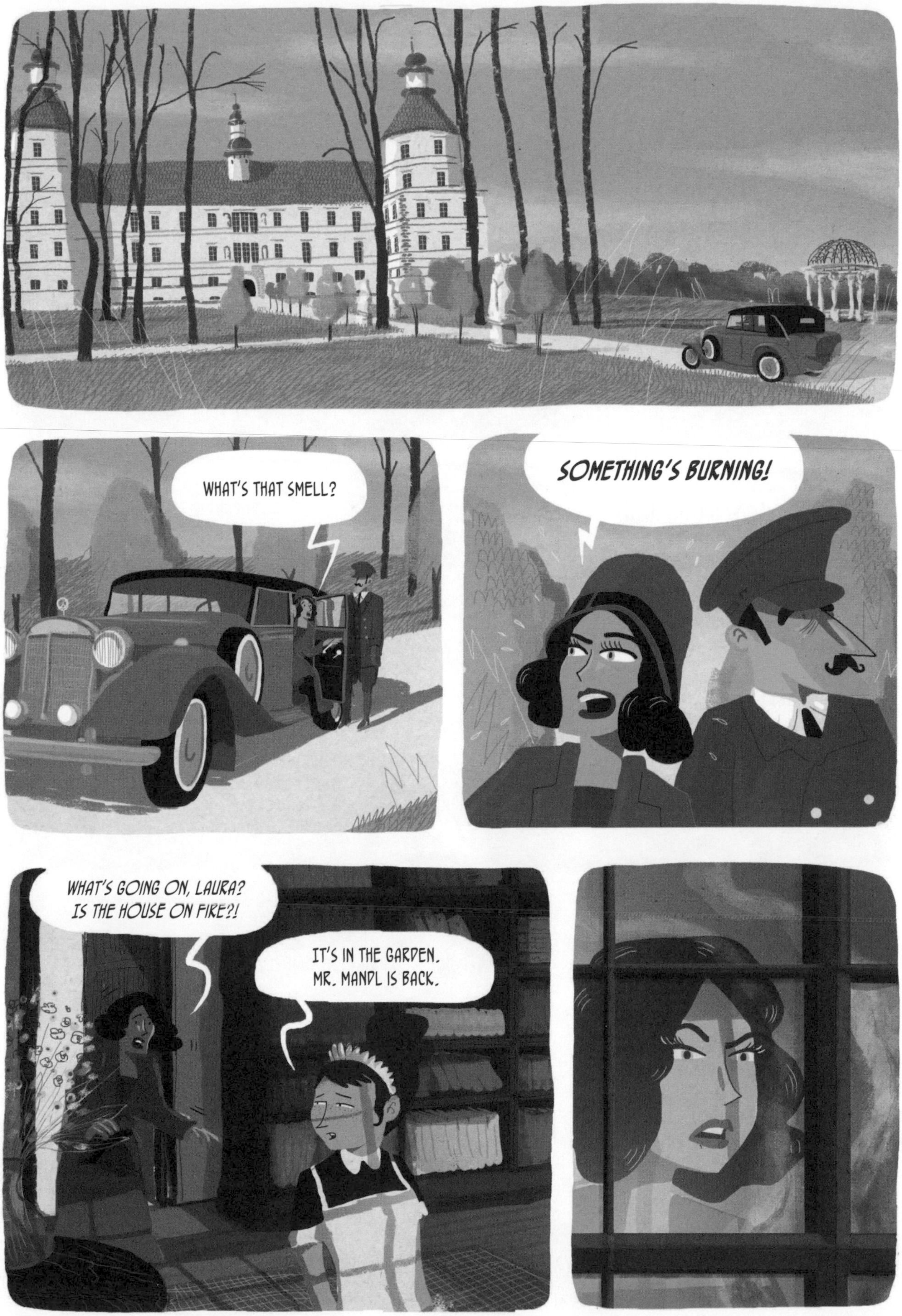
WHAT'S THAT SMELL?
SOMETHING'S BURNING!
WHAT'S GOING ON, LAURA? IS THE HOUSE ON FIRE?!
IT'S IN THE GARDEN. MR. MANDL IS BACK.

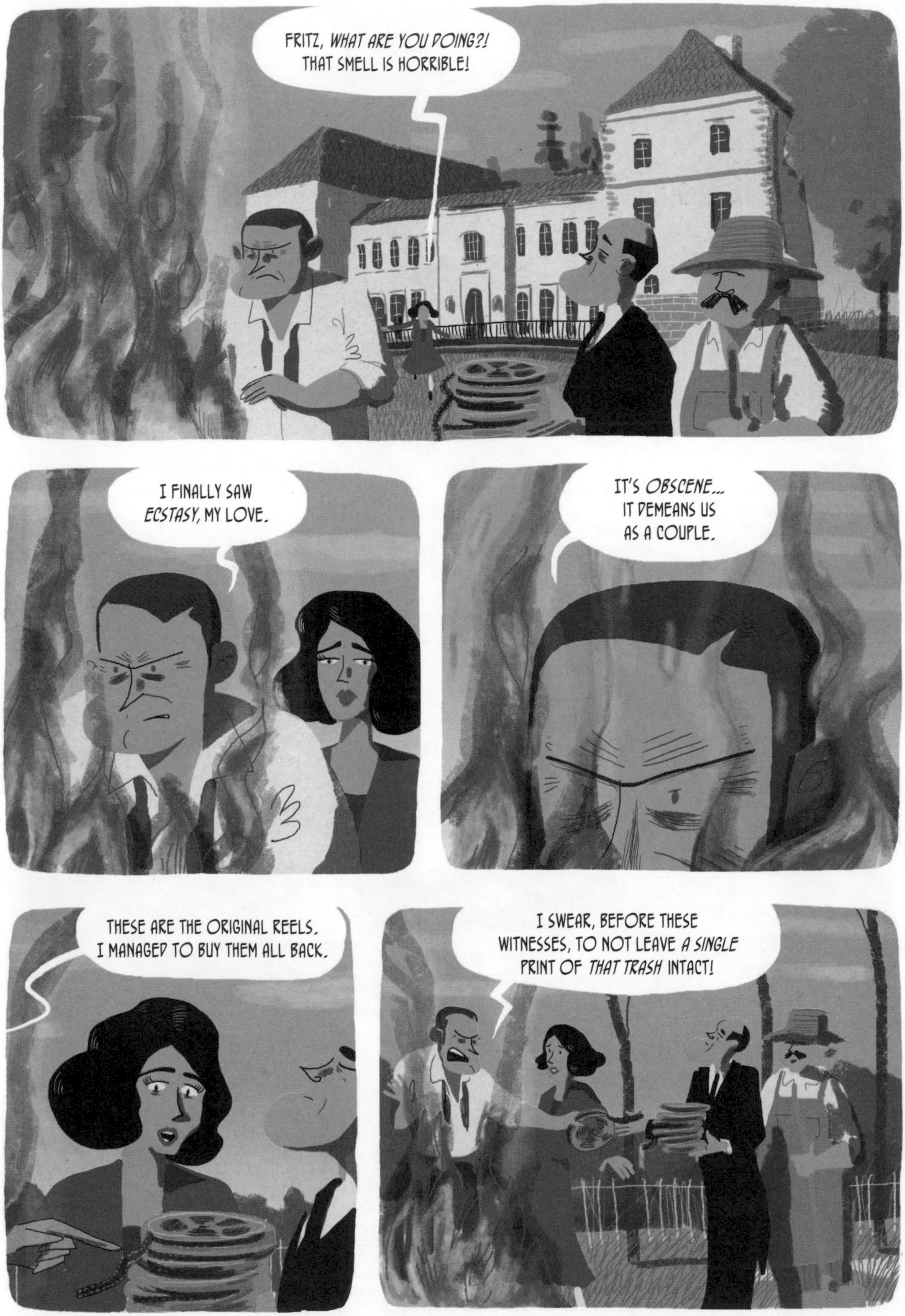
FRITZ, WHAT ARE YOU DOING?! THAT SMELL IS HORRIBLE!
I FINALLY SAW ECSTASY, MY LOVE.
IT'S OBSCENE... IT DEMEANS US AS A COUPLE.
THESE ARE THE ORIGINAL REELS. I MANAGED TO BUY THEM ALL BACK.
I SWEAR, BEFORE THESE WITNESSES, TO NOT LEAVE A SINGLE PRINT OF THAT TRASH INTACT!

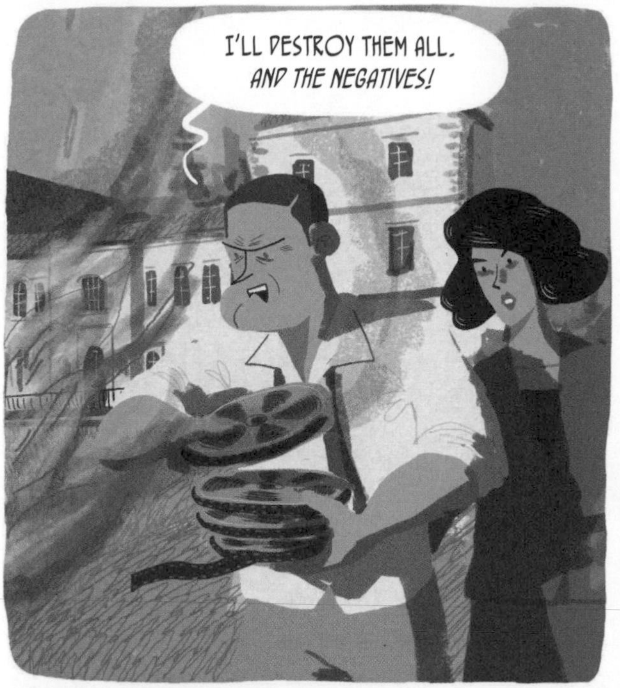
I'LL DESTROY THEM ALL.
AND THE NEGATIVES!
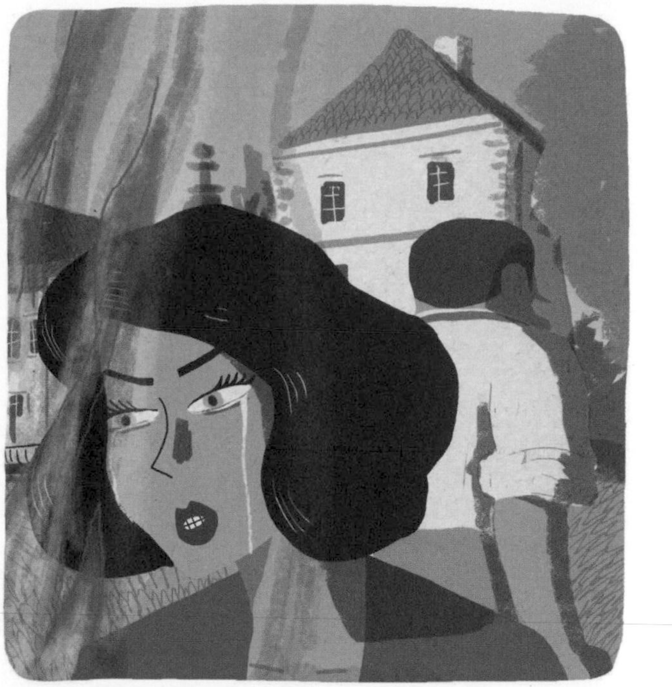
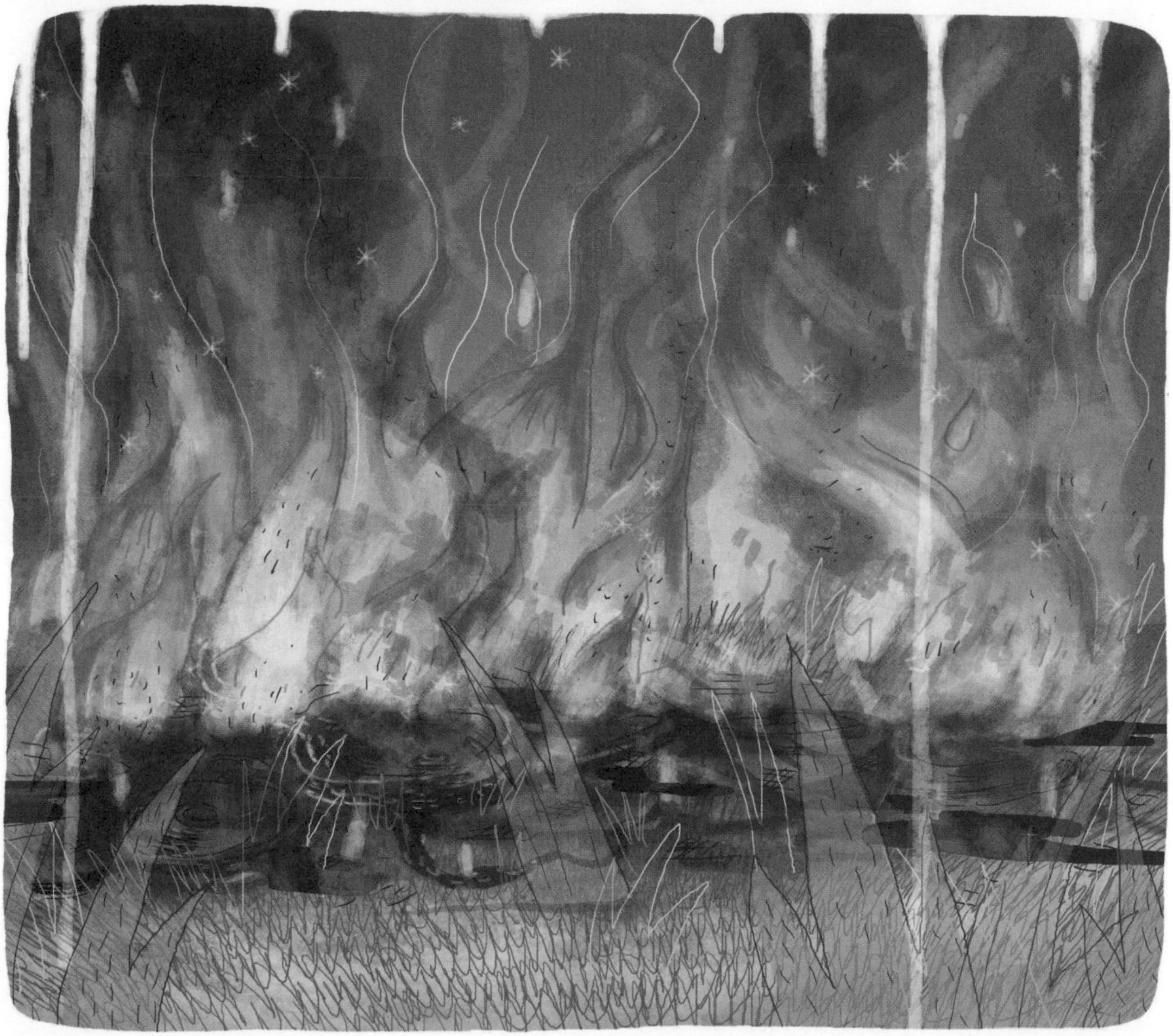

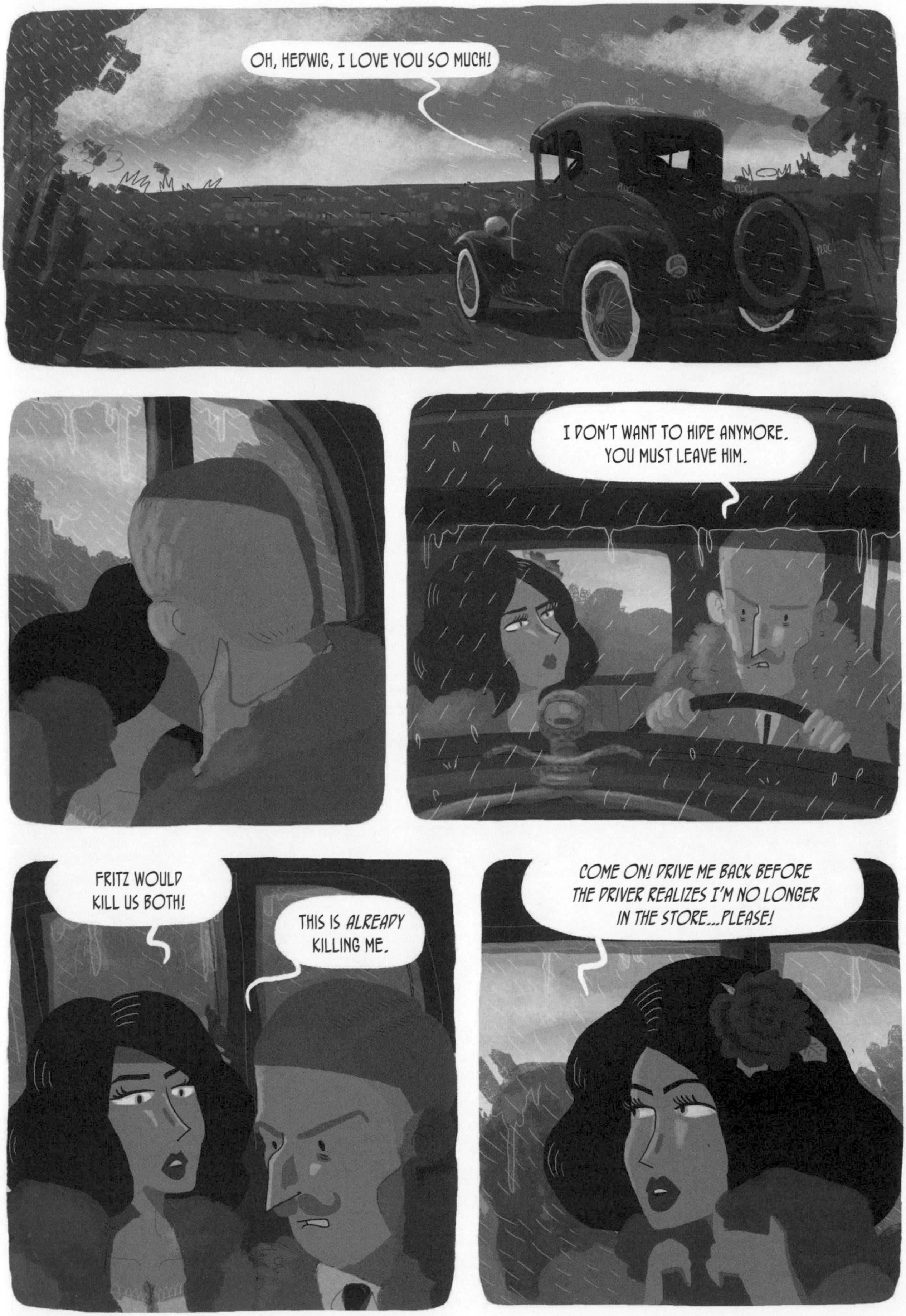
OH, HEDWIG, I LOVE YOU SO MUCH!
I DON'T WANT TO HIDE ANYMORE. YOU MUST LEAVE HIM.
FRITZ WOULD KILL US BOTH!
THIS IS *ALREADY* KILLING ME.
COME ON! DRIVE ME BACK BEFORE THE DRIVER REALIZES I'M NO LONGER IN THE STORE...PLEASE!

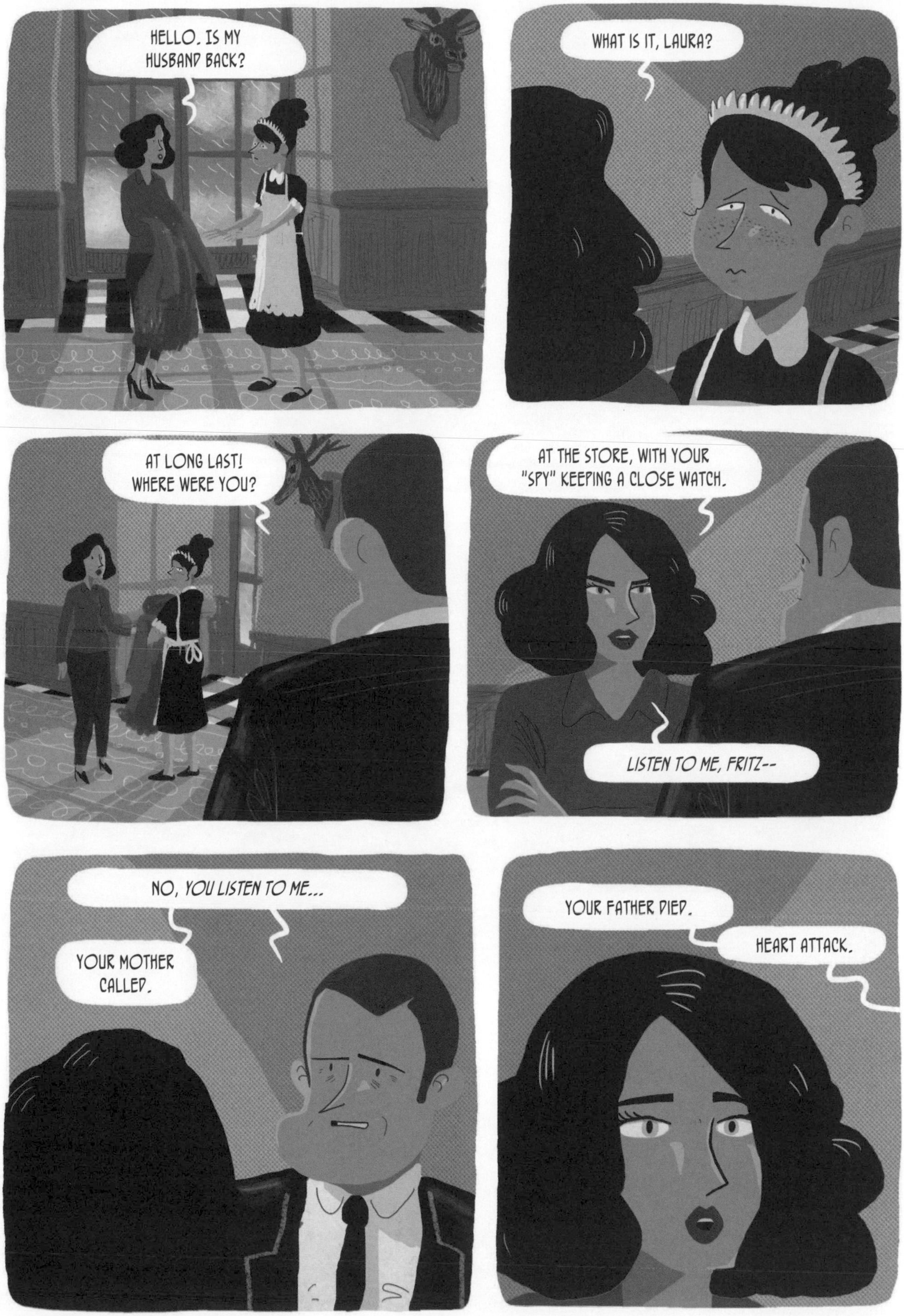
HELLO. IS MY HUSBAND BACK?
WHAT IS IT, LAURA?
AT LONG LAST! WHERE WERE YOU?
AT THE STORE, WITH YOUR "SPY" KEEPING A CLOSE WATCH.
LISTEN TO ME, FRITZ--
NO, YOU LISTEN TO ME...
YOUR MOTHER CALLED.
YOUR FATHER DIED.
HEART ATTACK.

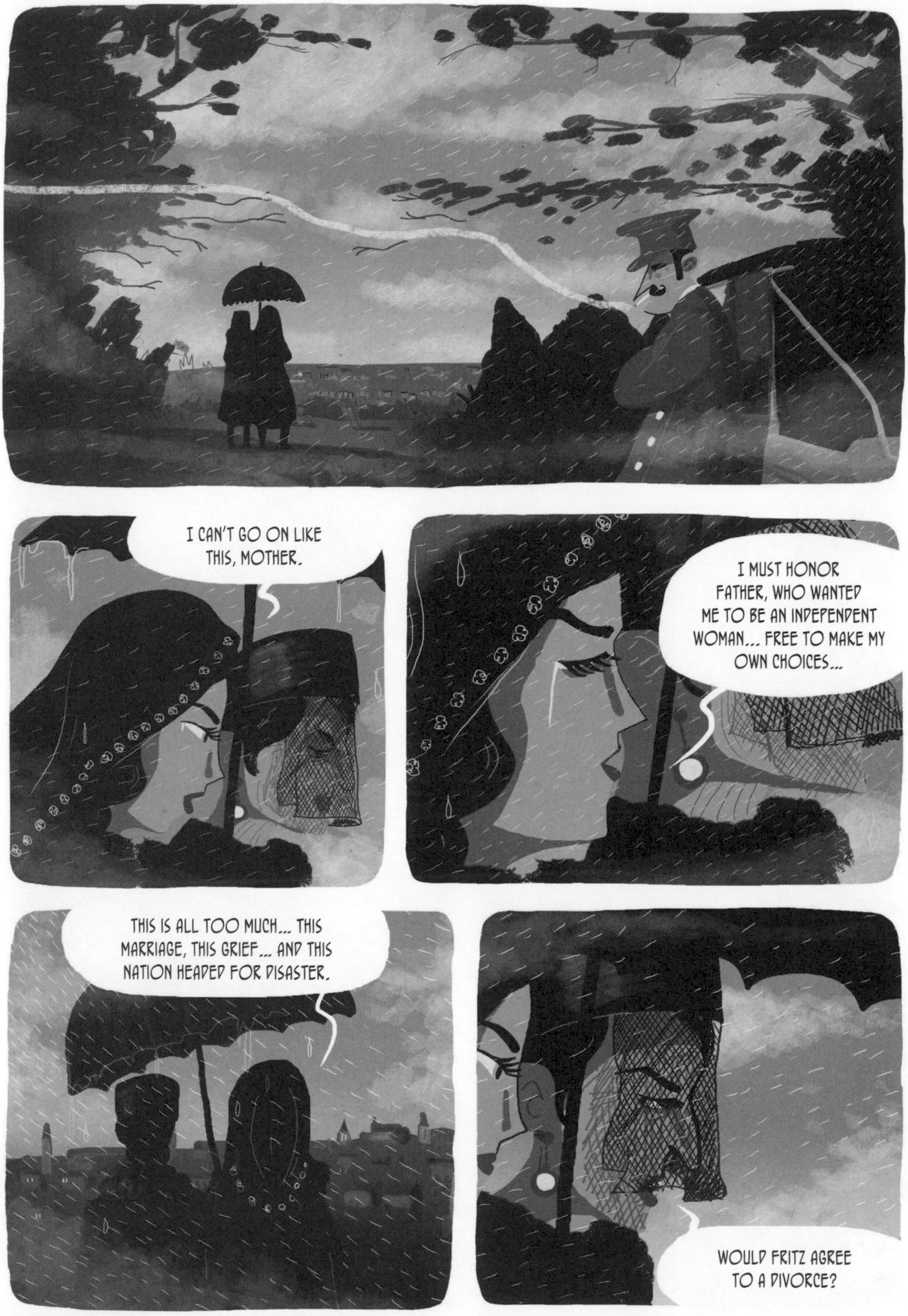
I CAN'T GO ON LIKE THIS, MOTHER.
I MUST HONOR FATHER, WHO WANTED ME TO BE AN INDEPENDENT WOMAN... FREE TO MAKE MY OWN CHOICES...
THIS IS ALL TOO MUCH... THIS MARRIAGE, THIS GRIEF... AND THIS NATION HEADED FOR DISASTER.
WOULD FRITZ AGREE TO A DIVORCE?

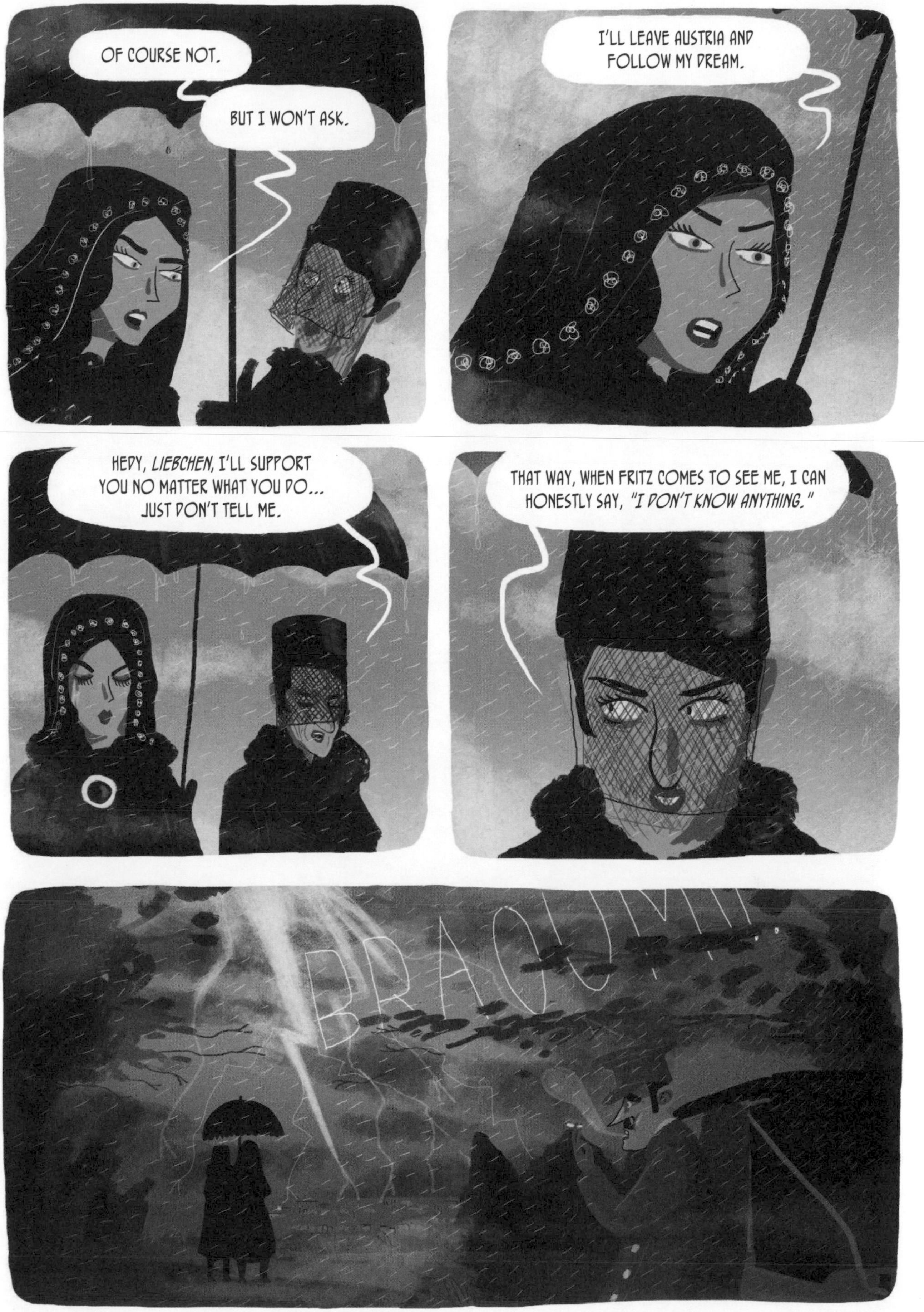
OF COURSE NOT.
BUT I WON'T ASK.
I'LL LEAVE AUSTRIA AND FOLLOW MY DREAM.
HEDY, *LIEBCHEN*, I'LL SUPPORT YOU NO MATTER WHAT YOU DO... JUST DON'T TELL ME.
THAT WAY, WHEN FRITZ COMES TO SEE ME, I CAN HONESTLY SAY, *"I DON'T KNOW ANYTHING."*

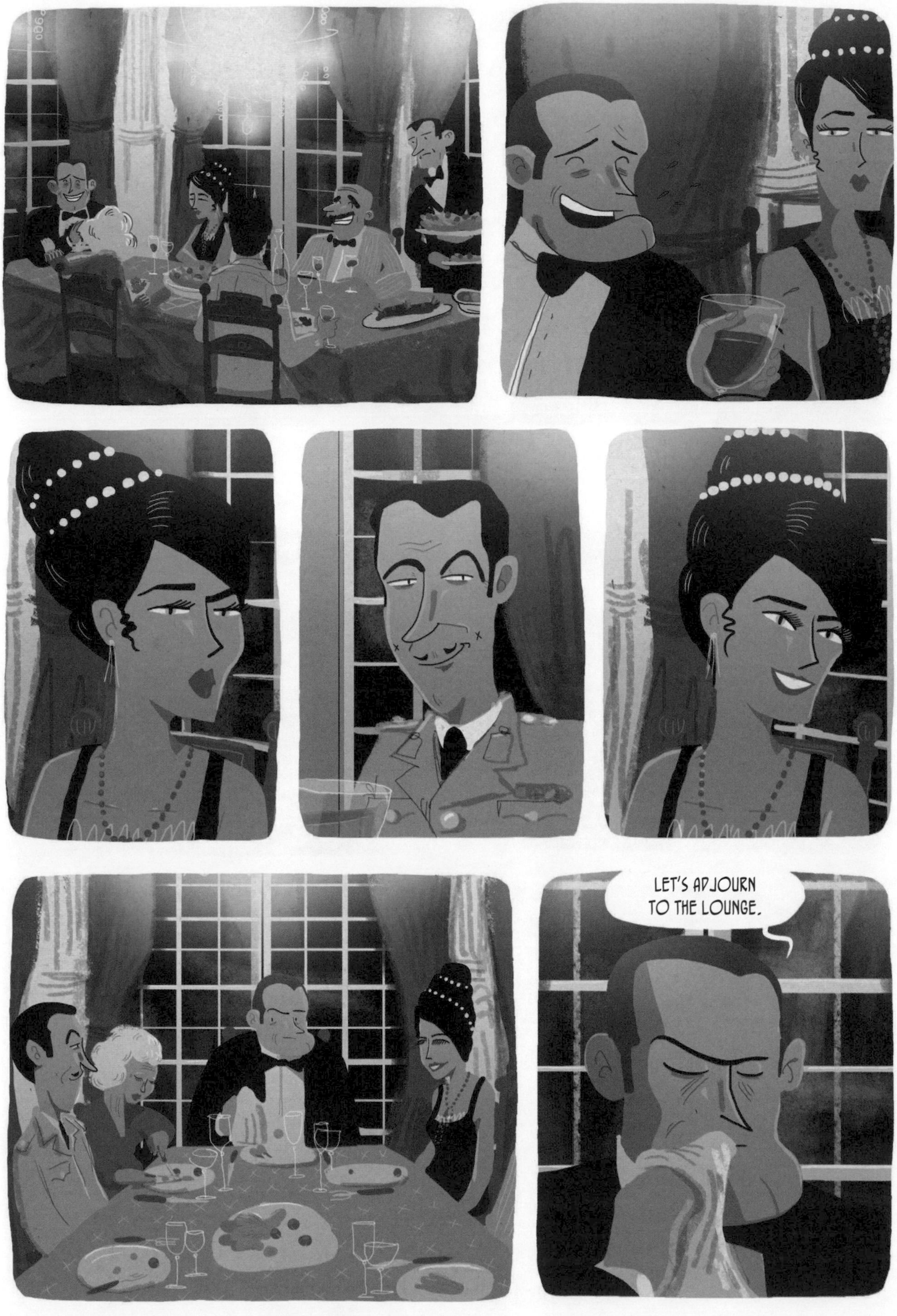
LET'S ADJOURN TO THE LOUNGE.

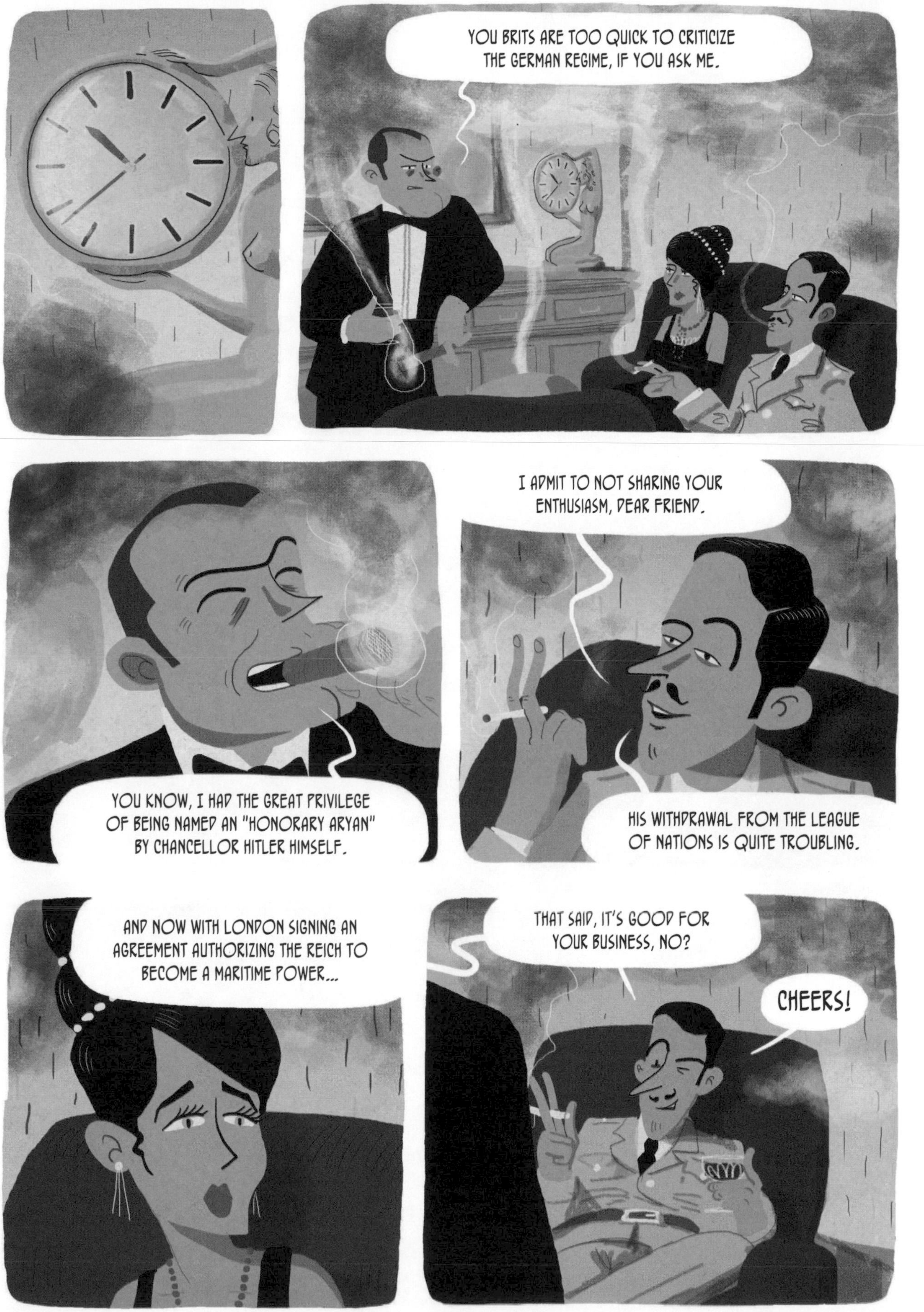
YOU BRITS ARE TOO QUICK TO CRITICIZE THE GERMAN REGIME, IF YOU ASK ME.
YOU KNOW, I HAD THE GREAT PRIVILEGE OF BEING NAMED AN "HONORARY ARYAN" BY CHANCELLOR HITLER HIMSELF.
I ADMIT TO NOT SHARING YOUR ENTHUSIASM, DEAR FRIEND.
HIS WITHDRAWAL FROM THE LEAGUE OF NATIONS IS QUITE TROUBLING.
AND NOW WITH LONDON SIGNING AN AGREEMENT AUTHORIZING THE REICH TO BECOME A MARITIME POWER...
THAT SAID, IT'S GOOD FOR YOUR BUSINESS, NO?
CHEERS!

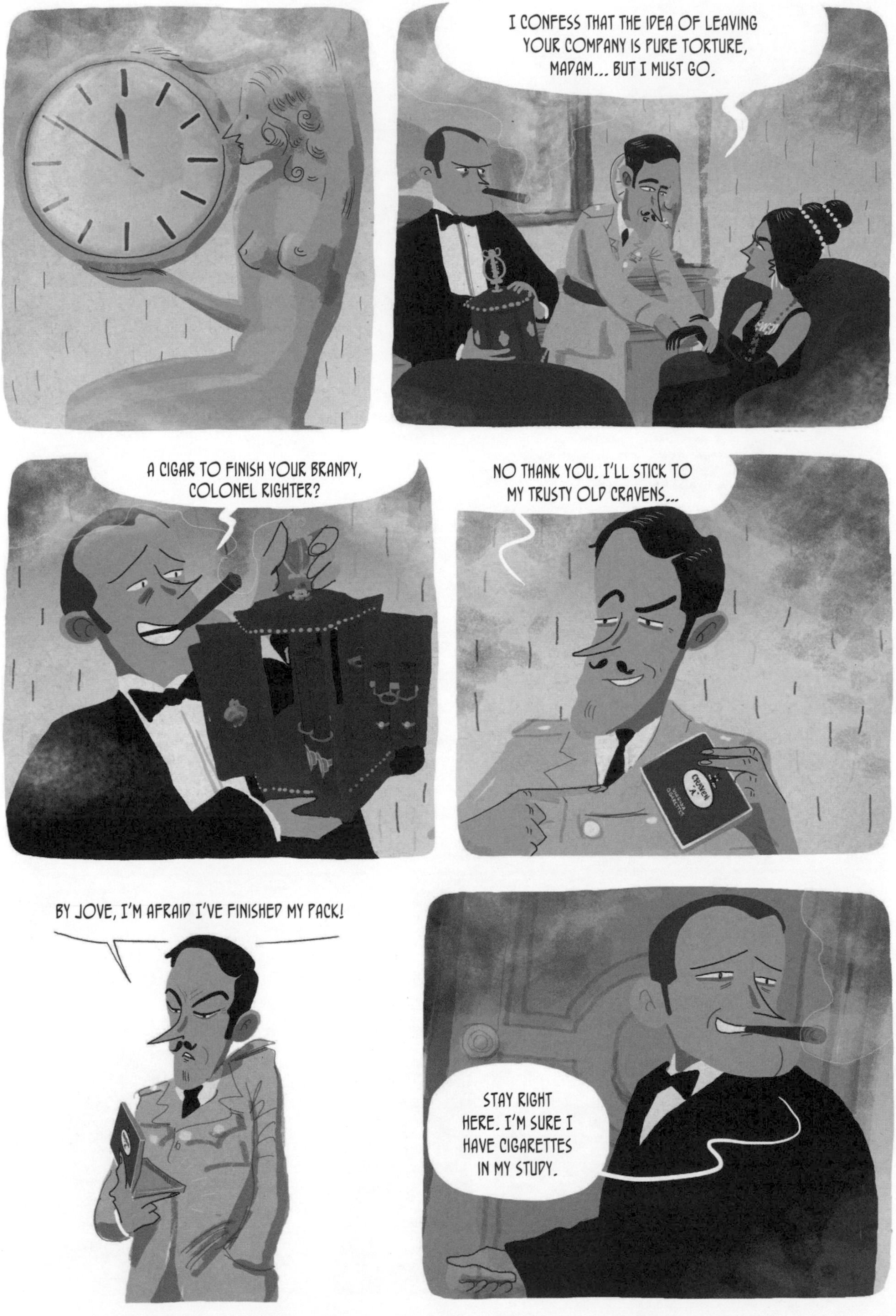
I CONFESS THAT THE IDEA OF LEAVING YOUR COMPANY IS PURE TORTURE, MADAM... BUT I MUST GO.
A CIGAR TO FINISH YOUR BRANDY, COLONEL RIGHTER?
NO THANK YOU. I'LL STICK TO MY TRUSTY OLD CRAVENS...
BY JOVE, I'M AFRAID I'VE FINISHED MY PACK!
STAY RIGHT HERE. I'M SURE I HAVE CIGARETTES IN MY STUDY.

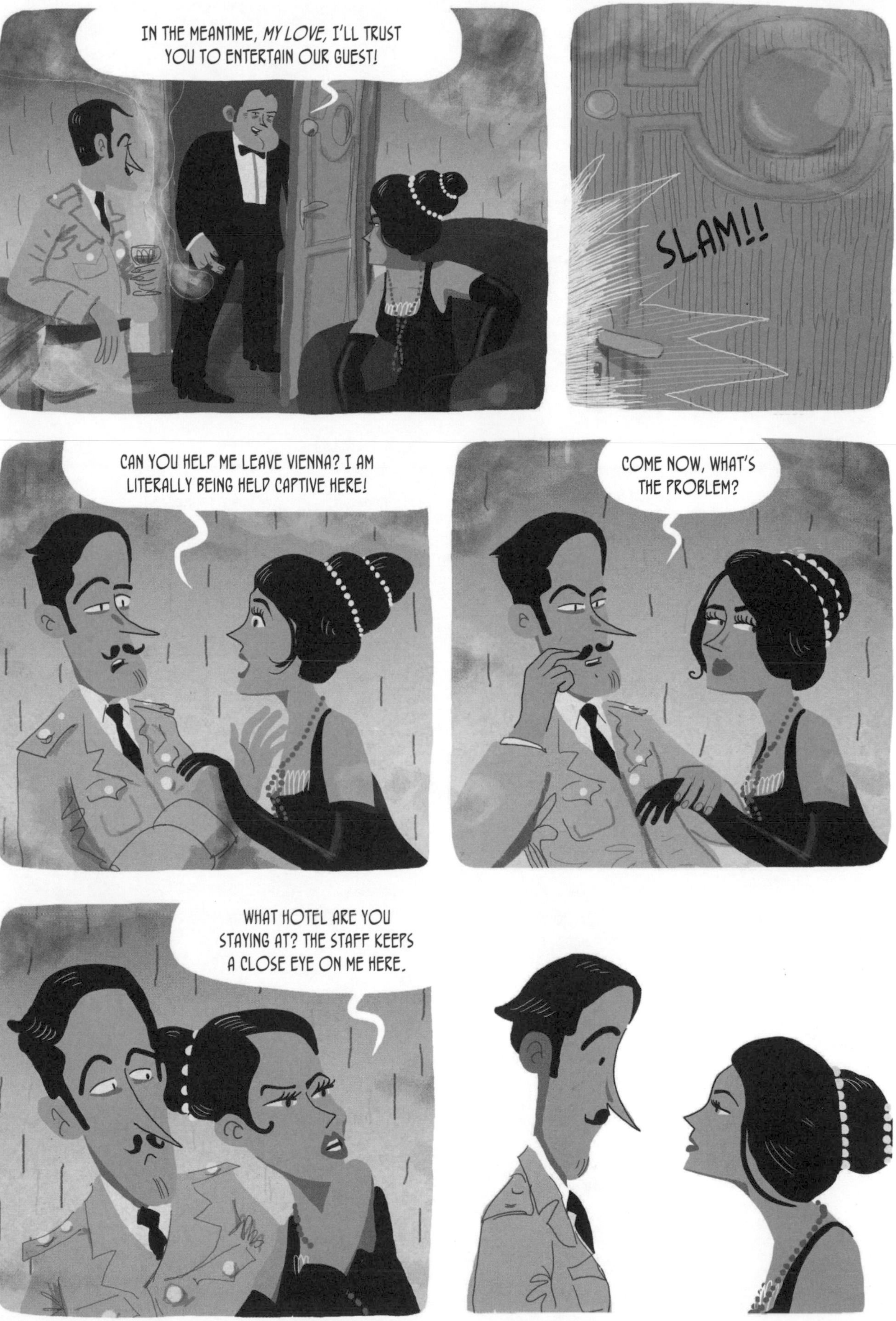
IN THE MEANTIME, MY LOVE, I'LL TRUST YOU TO ENTERTAIN OUR GUEST!
SLAM!!
CAN YOU HELP ME LEAVE VIENNA? I AM LITERALLY BEING HELD CAPTIVE HERE!
COME NOW, WHAT'S THE PROBLEM?
WHAT HOTEL ARE YOU STAYING AT? THE STAFF KEEPS A CLOSE EYE ON ME HERE.

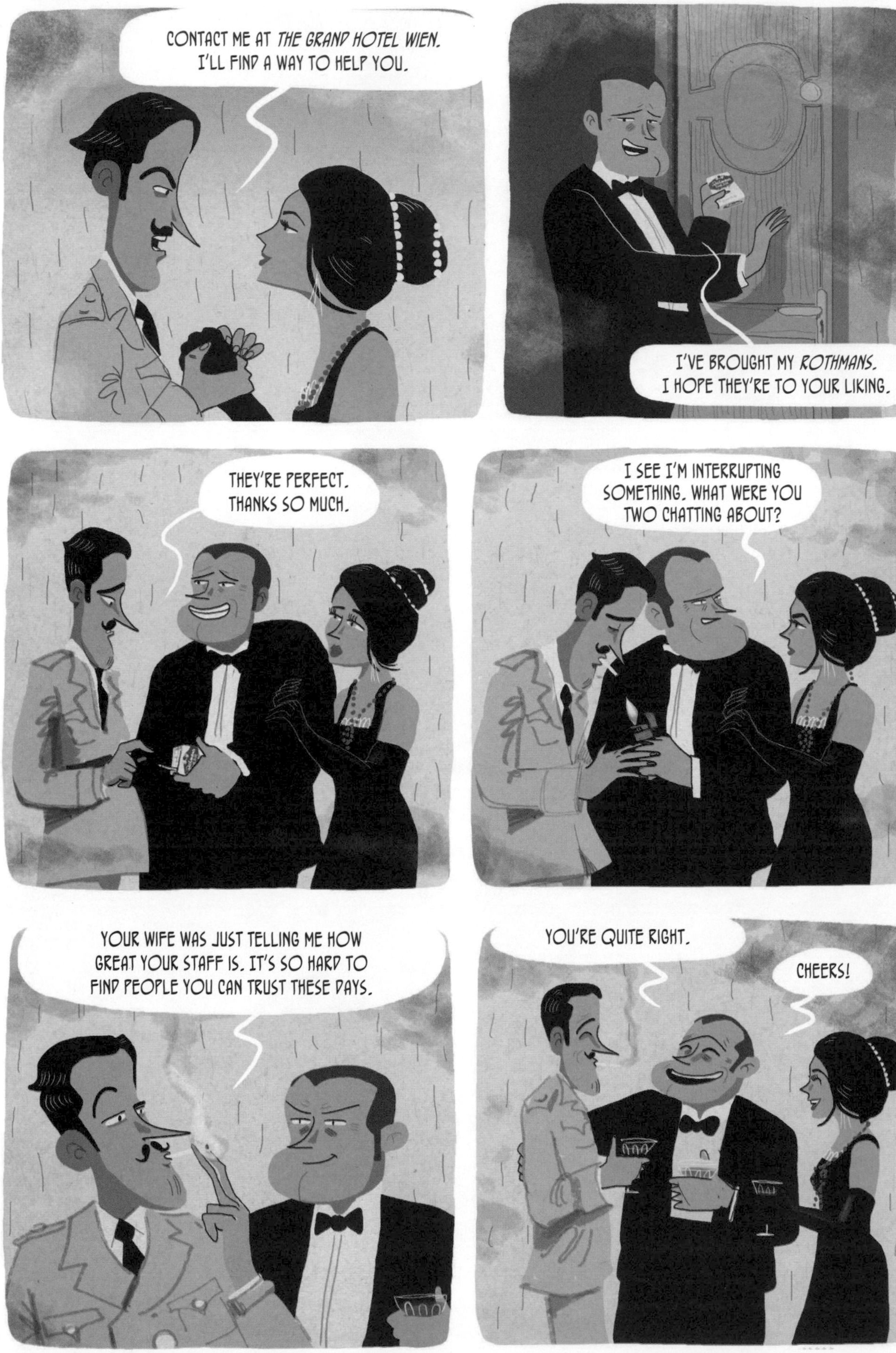
CONTACT ME AT *THE GRAND HOTEL WIEN.* I'LL FIND A WAY TO HELP YOU.
I'VE BROUGHT MY *ROTHMANS.* I HOPE THEY'RE TO YOUR LIKING.
THEY'RE PERFECT. THANKS SO MUCH.
I SEE I'M INTERRUPTING SOMETHING. WHAT WERE YOU TWO CHATTING ABOUT?
YOUR WIFE WAS JUST TELLING ME HOW GREAT YOUR STAFF IS. IT'S SO HARD TO FIND PEOPLE YOU CAN TRUST THESE DAYS.
YOU'RE QUITE RIGHT.
CHEERS!

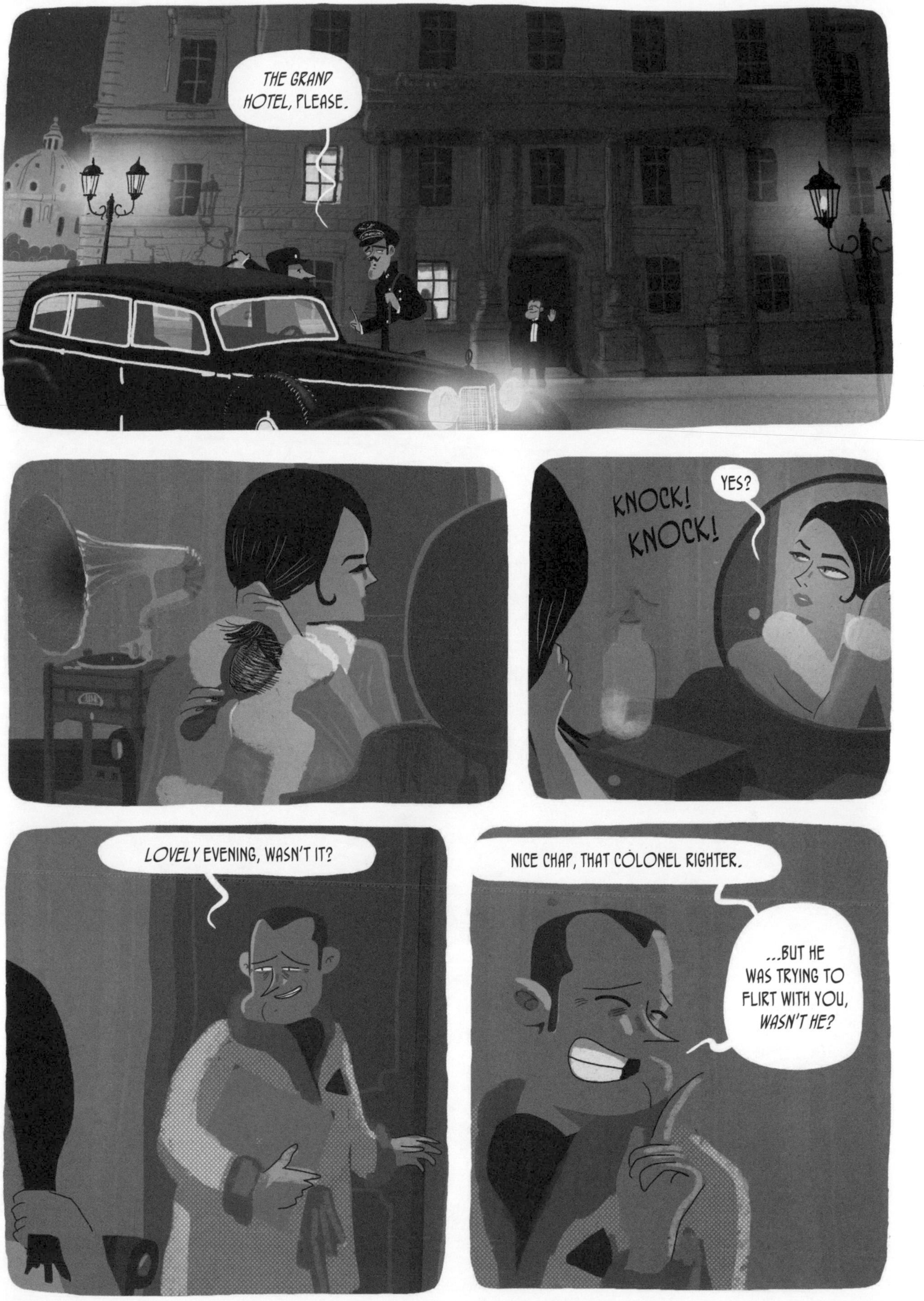
THE GRAND HOTEL, PLEASE.
KNOCK! KNOCK!
YES?
LOVELY EVENING, WASN'T IT?
NICE CHAP, THAT COLONEL RIGHTER.
...BUT HE WAS TRYING TO FLIRT WITH YOU, WASN'T HE?

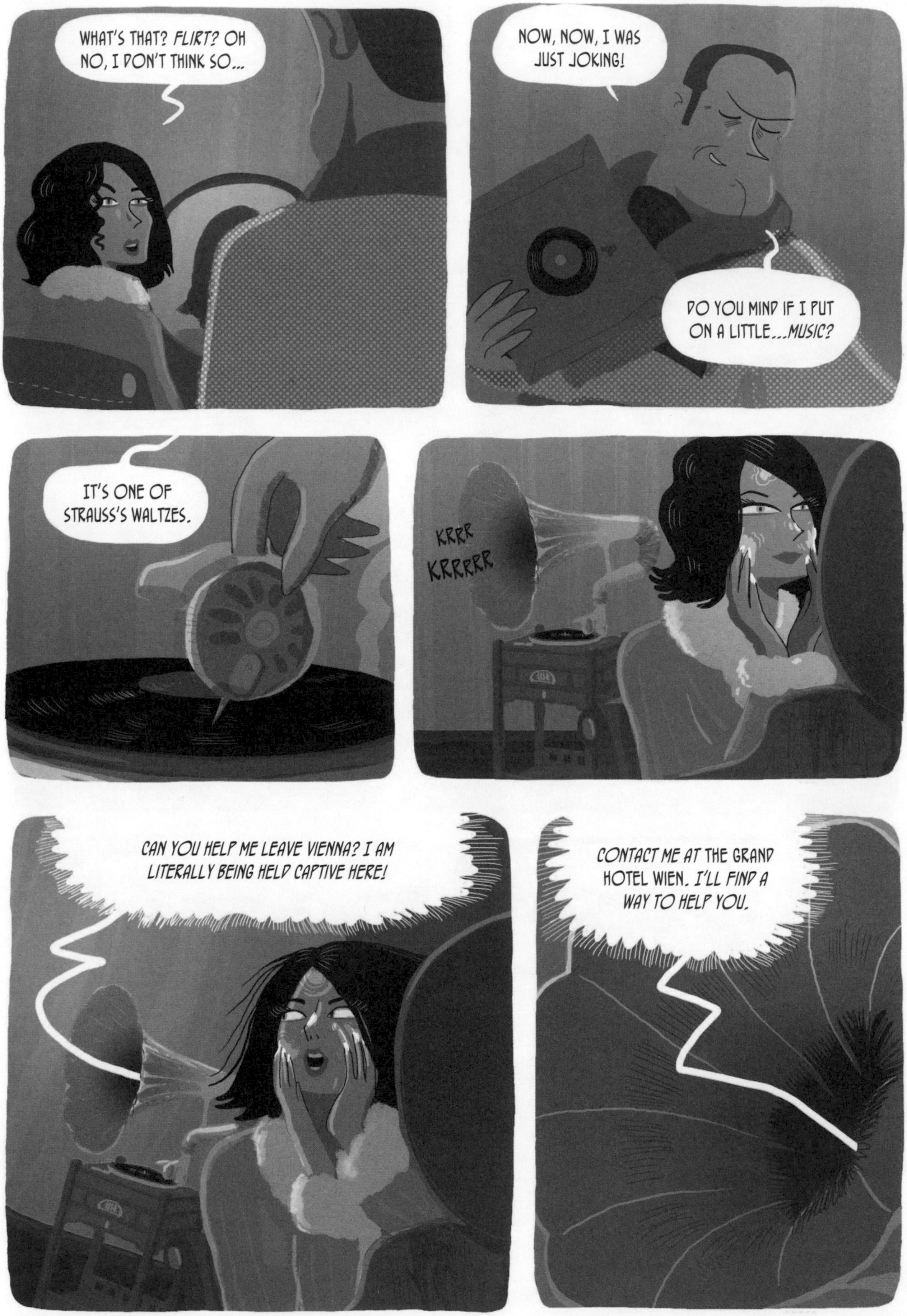
WHAT'S THAT? FLIRT? OH NO, I DON'T THINK SO...
NOW, NOW, I WAS JUST JOKING!
DO YOU MIND IF I PUT ON A LITTLE...MUSIC?
IT'S ONE OF STRAUSS'S WALTZES.
KRRR KRRRRR
CAN YOU HELP ME LEAVE VIENNA? I AM LITERALLY BEING HELD CAPTIVE HERE!
CONTACT ME AT THE GRAND HOTEL WIEN. I'LL FIND A WAY TO HELP YOU.

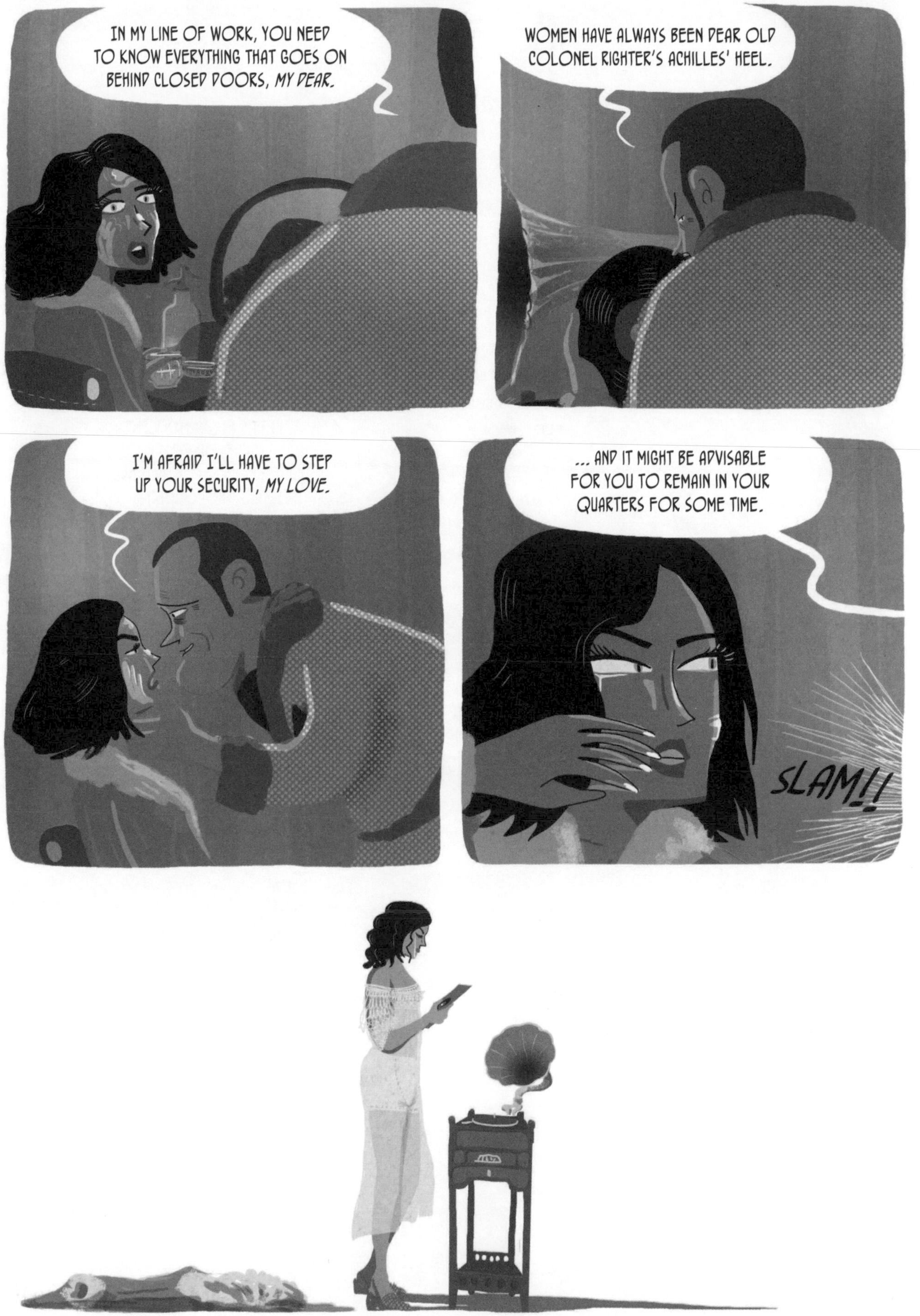
IN MY LINE OF WORK, YOU NEED TO KNOW EVERYTHING THAT GOES ON BEHIND CLOSED DOORS, *MY DEAR.*
WOMEN HAVE ALWAYS BEEN DEAR OLD COLONEL RIGHTER'S ACHILLES' HEEL.
I'M AFRAID I'LL HAVE TO STEP UP YOUR SECURITY, *MY LOVE.*
... AND IT MIGHT BE ADVISABLE FOR YOU TO REMAIN IN YOUR QUARTERS FOR SOME TIME.
SLAM!!

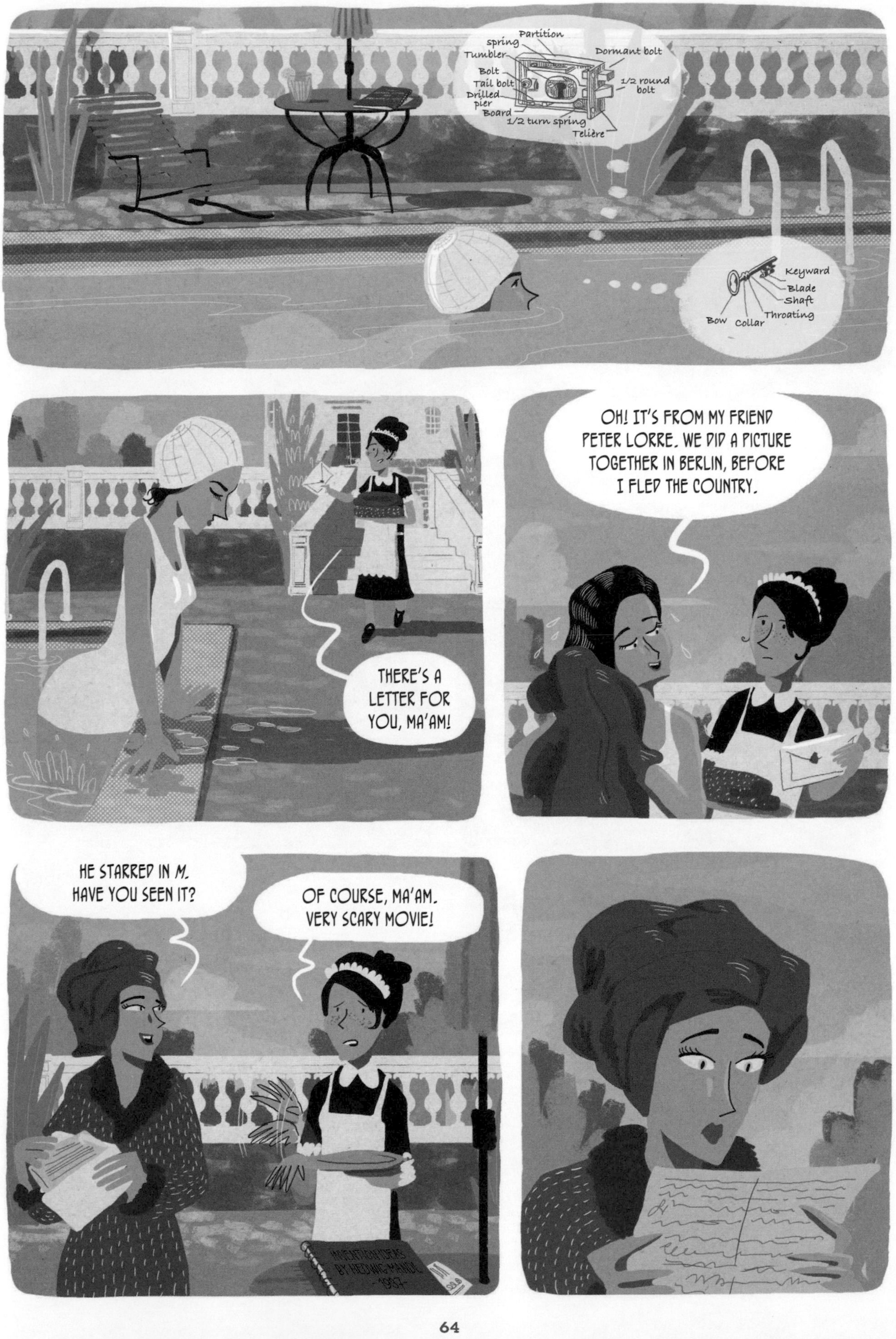
Partition
spring
Tumbler
Dormant bolt
Bolt
Tail bolt
Drilled pier
1/2 round bolt
Board
1/2 turn spring
Telière
Keyward
Blade
Shaft
Throating
Bow
Collar
THERE'S A LETTER FOR YOU, MA'AM!
OH! IT'S FROM MY FRIEND PETER LORRE. WE DID A PICTURE TOGETHER IN BERLIN, BEFORE I FLED THE COUNTRY.
HE STARRED IN *M*. HAVE YOU SEEN IT?
OF COURSE, MA'AM. VERY SCARY MOVIE!

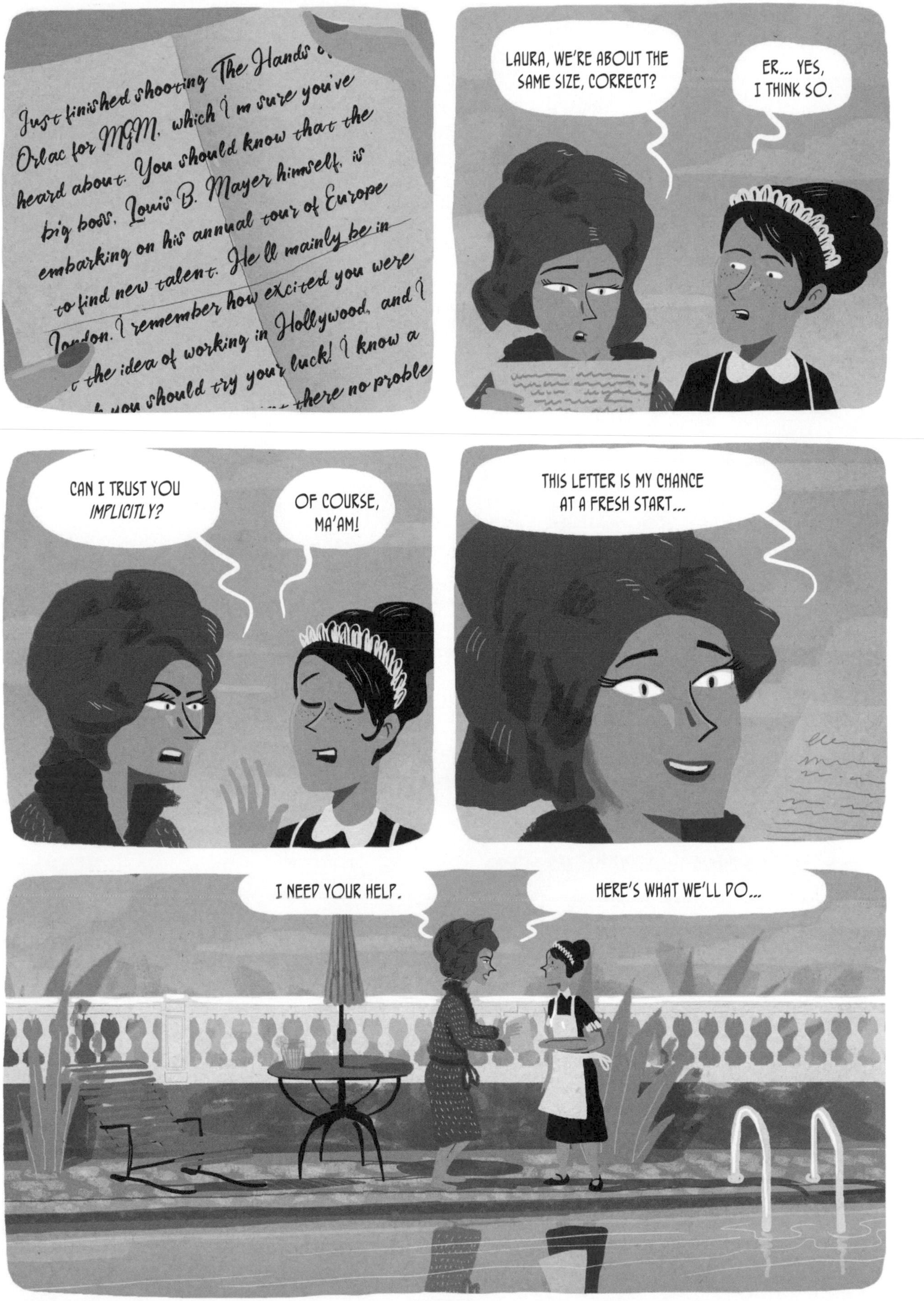
Just finished shooting The Hands
Orlac for MGM, which I'm sure you've
heard about. You should know that the
big boss, Louis B. Mayer himself, is
embarking on his annual tour of Europe
to find new talent. He'll mainly be in
London. I remember how excited you were
the idea of working in Hollywood, and I
you should try your luck! I know a
there
LAURA, WE'RE ABOUT THE SAME SIZE, CORRECT?
ER... YES, I THINK SO.
CAN I TRUST YOU *IMPLICITLY?*
OF COURSE, MA'AM!
THIS LETTER IS MY CHANCE AT A FRESH START...
I NEED YOUR HELP.
HERE'S WHAT WE'LL DO...

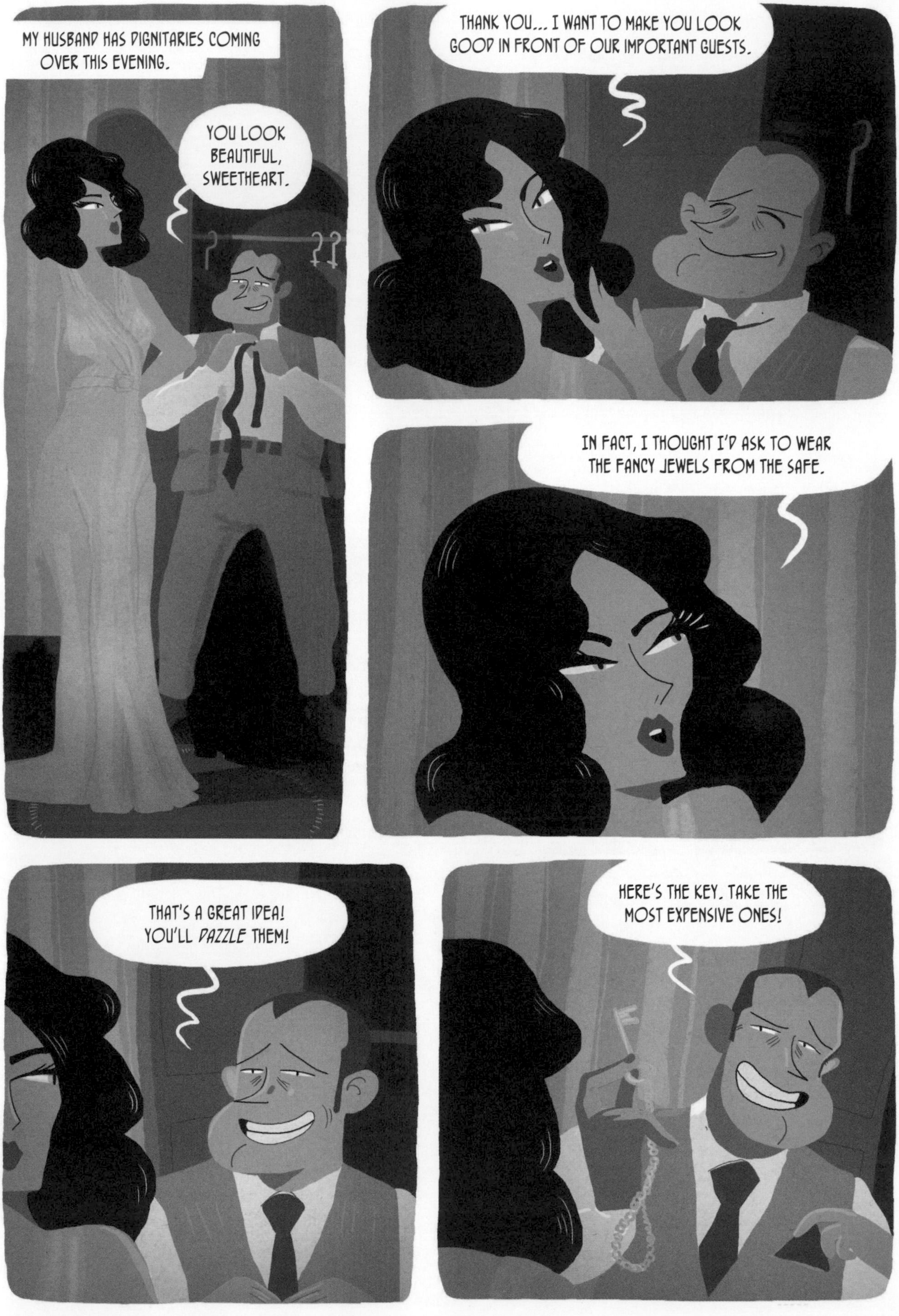

MY HUSBAND HAS DIGNITARIES COMING OVER THIS EVENING.
YOU LOOK BEAUTIFUL, SWEETHEART.
THANK YOU... I WANT TO MAKE YOU LOOK GOOD IN FRONT OF OUR IMPORTANT GUESTS.
IN FACT, I THOUGHT I'D ASK TO WEAR THE FANCY JEWELS FROM THE SAFE.
THAT'S A GREAT IDEA! YOU'LL *DAZZLE* THEM!
HERE'S THE KEY. TAKE THE MOST EXPENSIVE ONES!

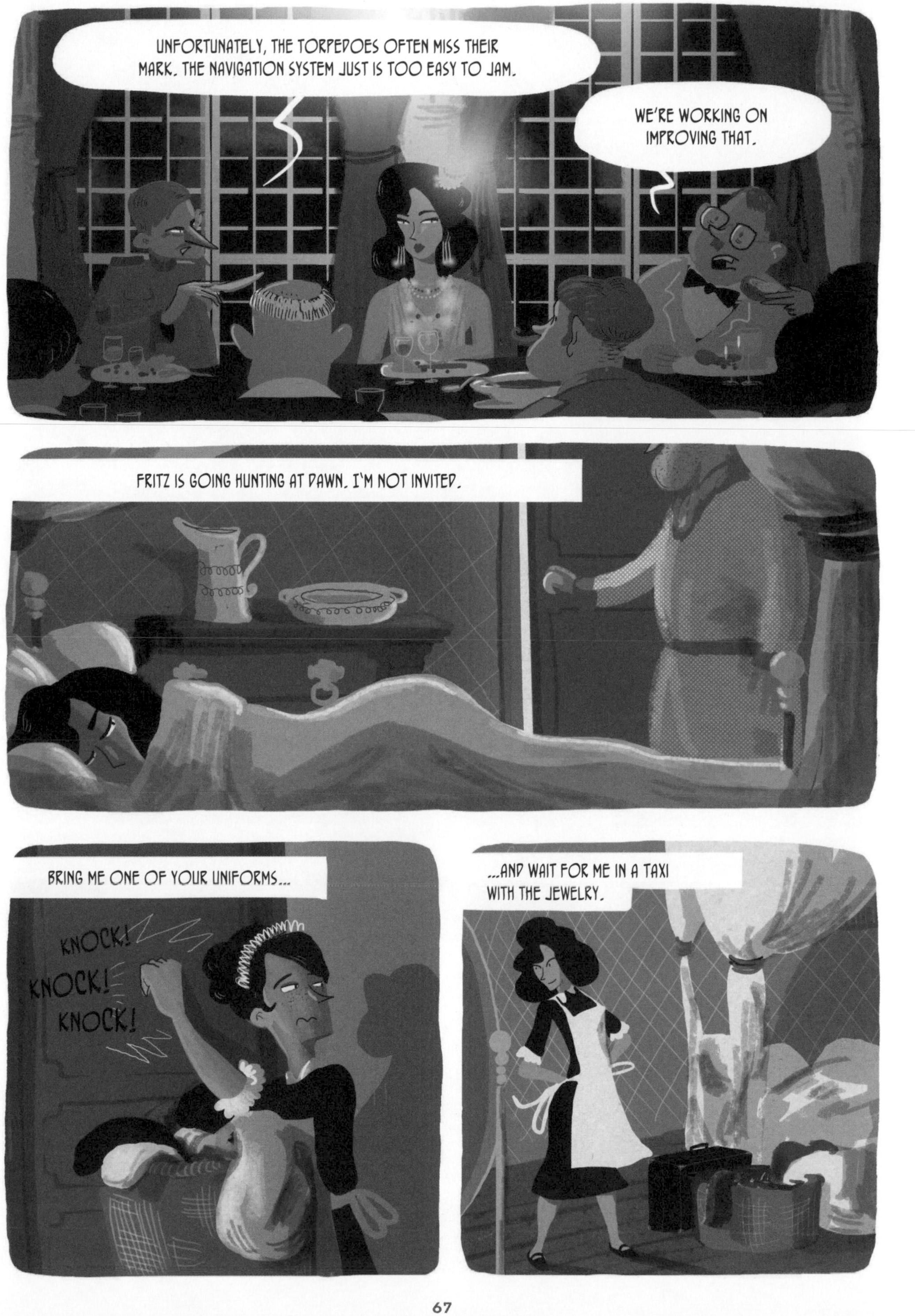
UNFORTUNATELY, THE TORPEDOES OFTEN MISS THEIR MARK. THE NAVIGATION SYSTEM JUST IS TOO EASY TO JAM.
WE'RE WORKING ON IMPROVING THAT.
FRITZ IS GOING HUNTING AT DAWN. I'M NOT INVITED.
BRING ME ONE OF YOUR UNIFORMS...
KNOCK! KNOCK! KNOCK!
...AND WAIT FOR ME IN A TAXI WITH THE JEWELRY.

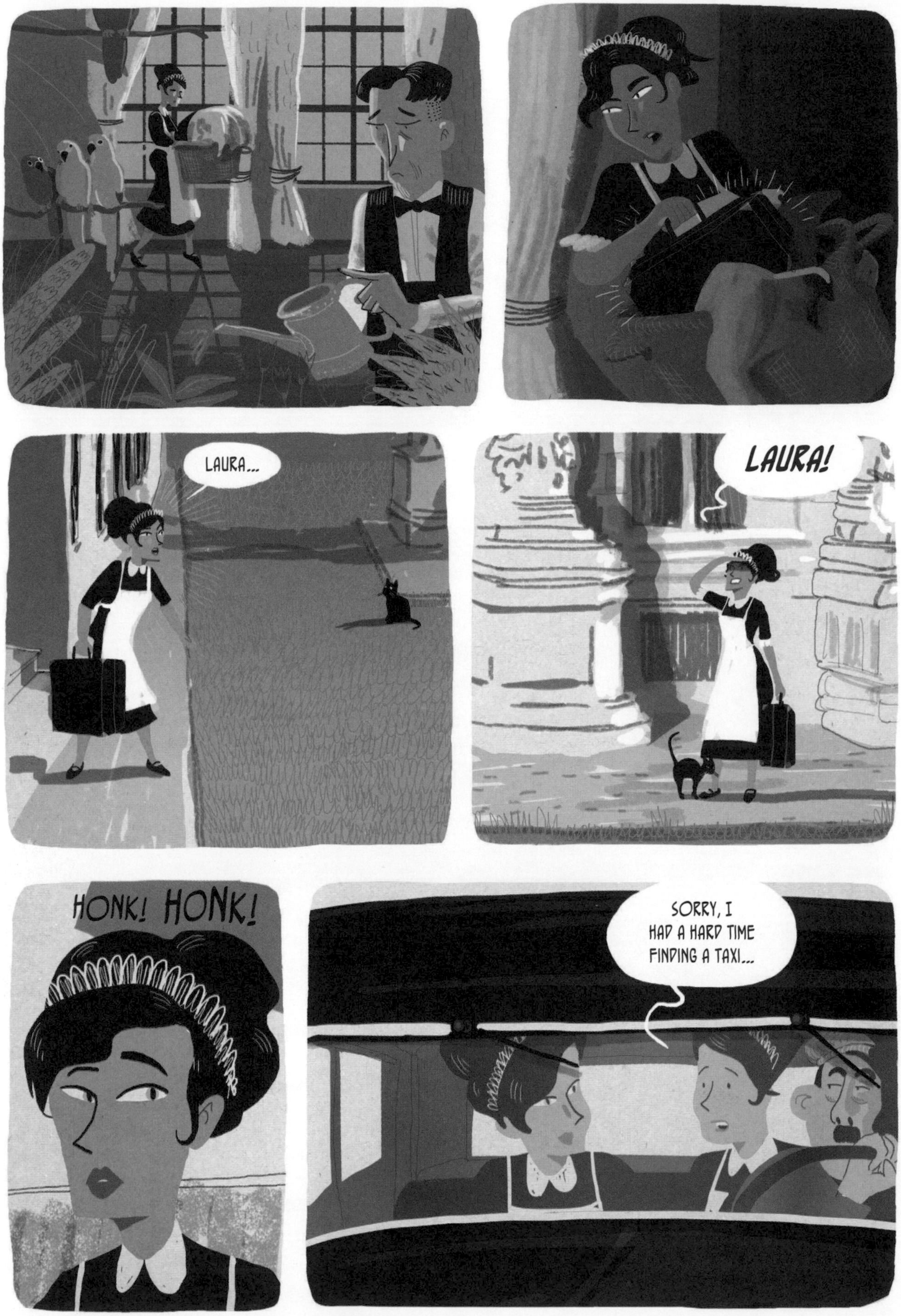
LAURA...
LAURA!
HONK! HONK!
SORRY, I HAD A HARD TIME FINDING A TAXI...

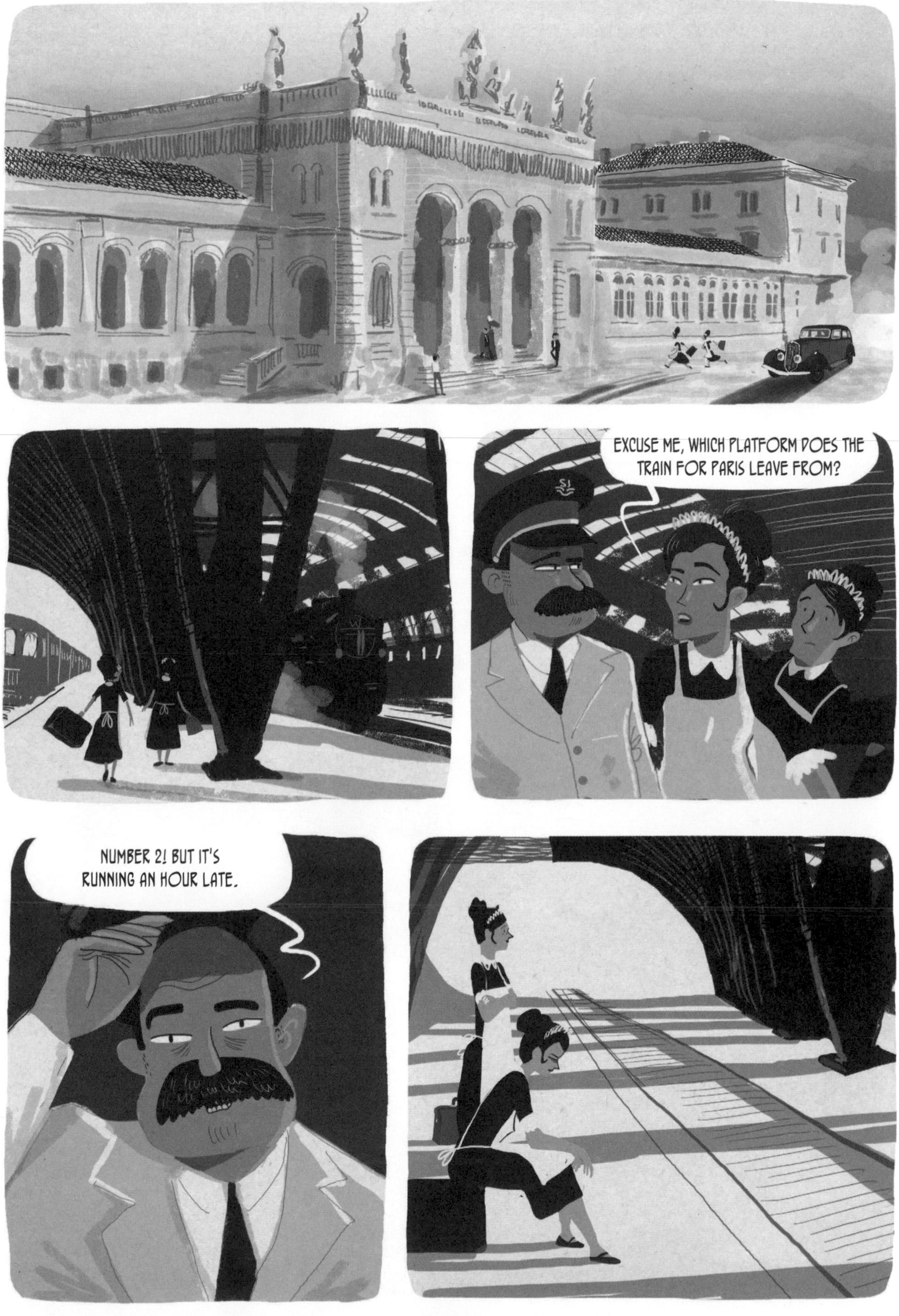
EXCUSE ME, WHICH PLATFORM DOES THE TRAIN FOR PARIS LEAVE FROM?
NUMBER 2! BUT IT'S RUNNING AN HOUR LATE.

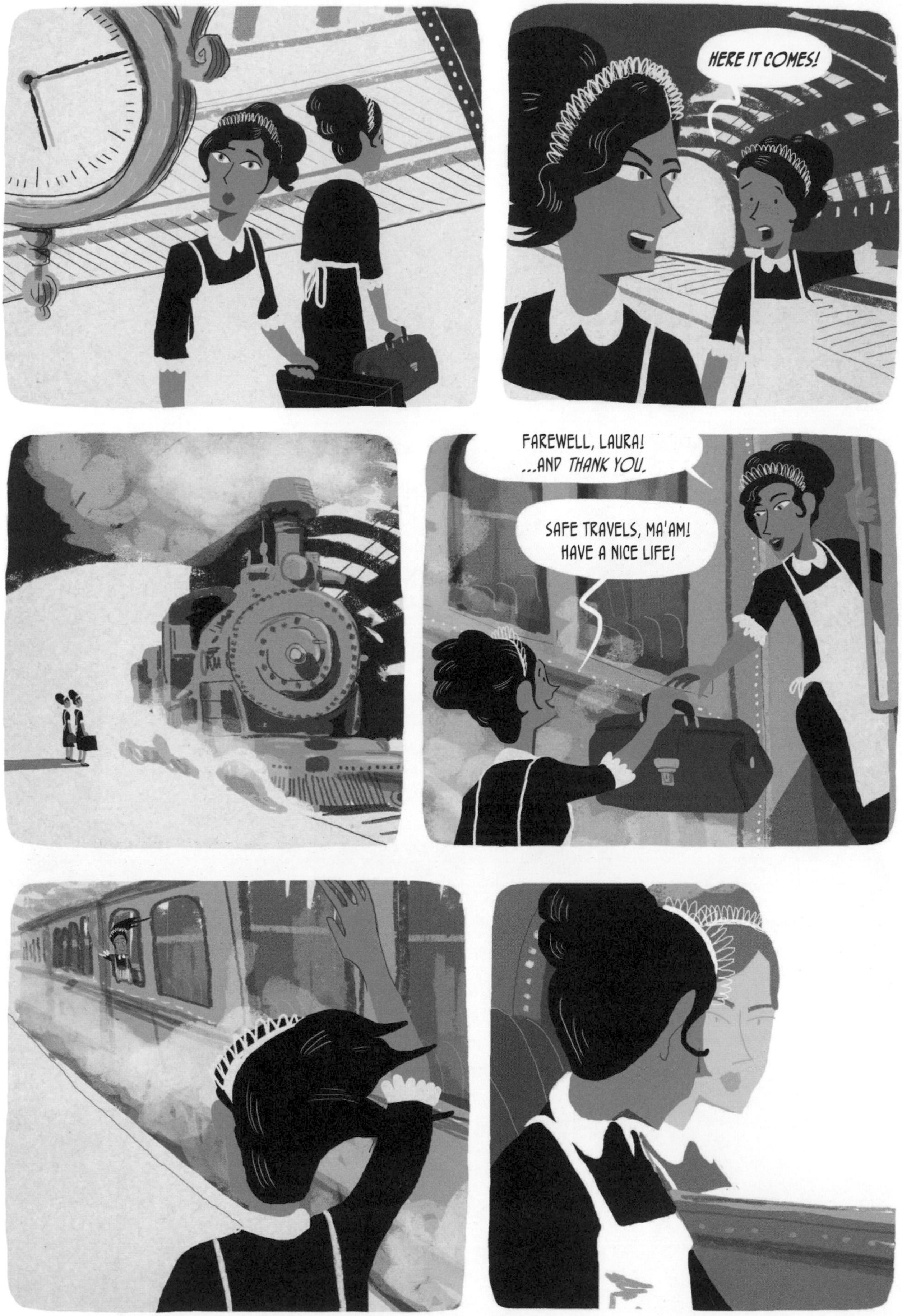
HERE IT COMES!
FAREWELL, LAURA!
...AND THANK YOU.
SAFE TRAVELS, MA'AM!
HAVE A NICE LIFE!

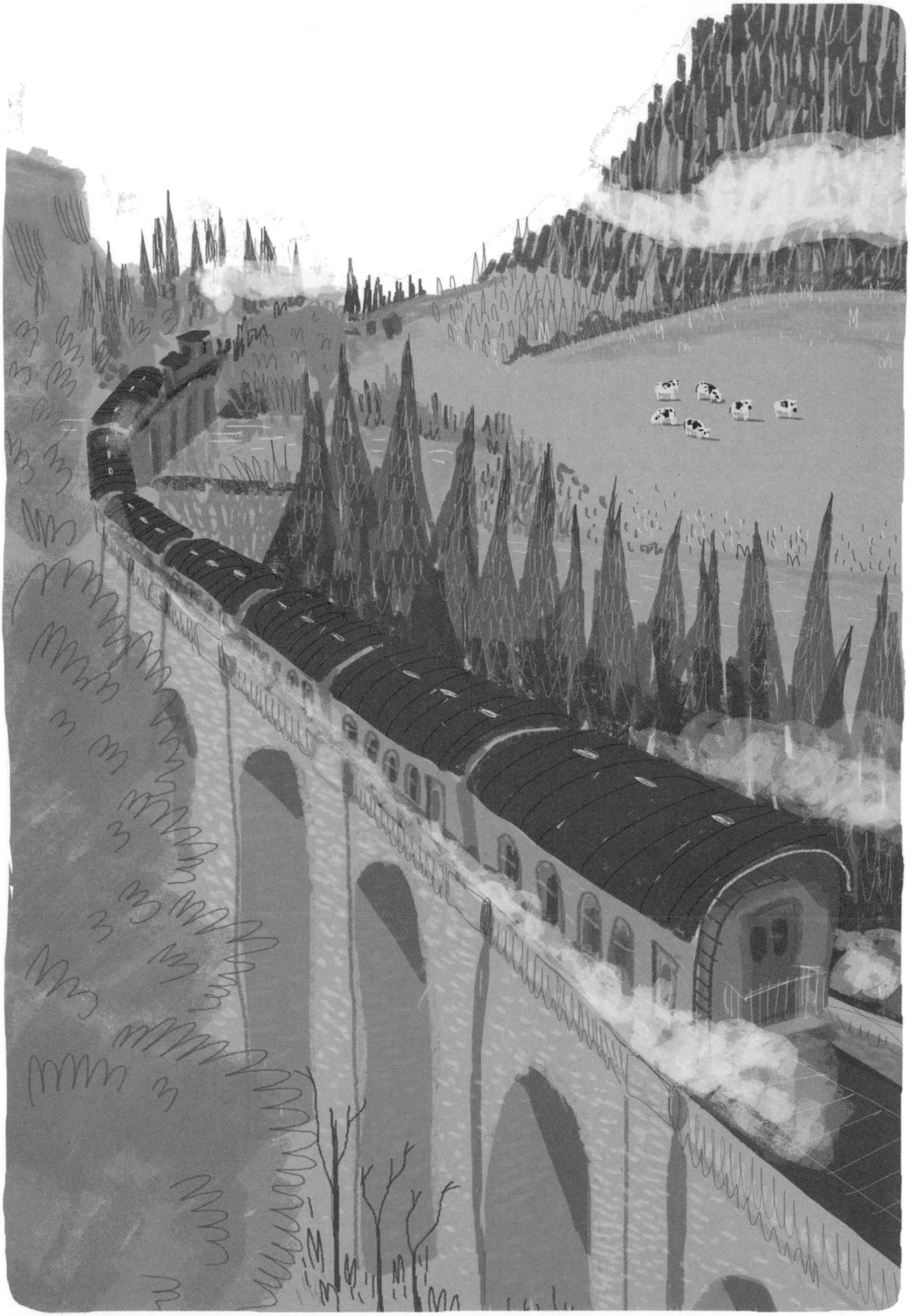

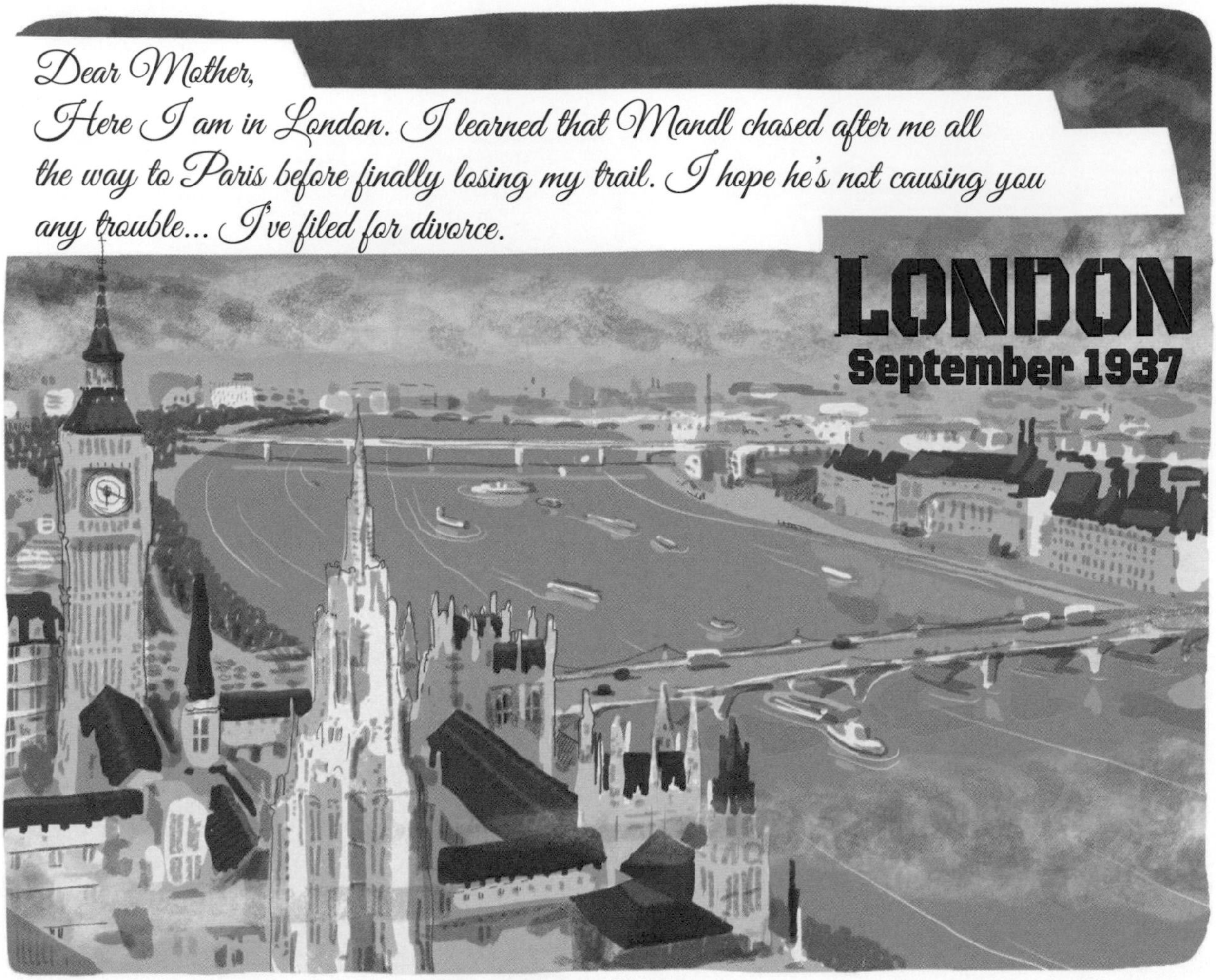
Dear Mother,
Here I am in London. I learned that Mandl chased after me all the way to Paris before finally losing my trail. I hope he's not causing you any trouble... I've filed for divorce.
LONDON
September 1937

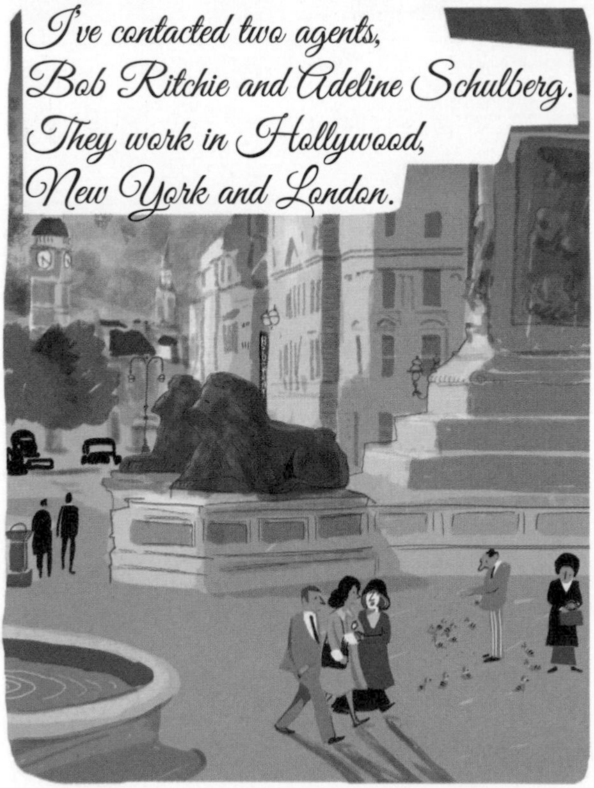
I've contacted two agents, Bob Ritchie and Adeline Schulberg. They work in Hollywood, New York and London.

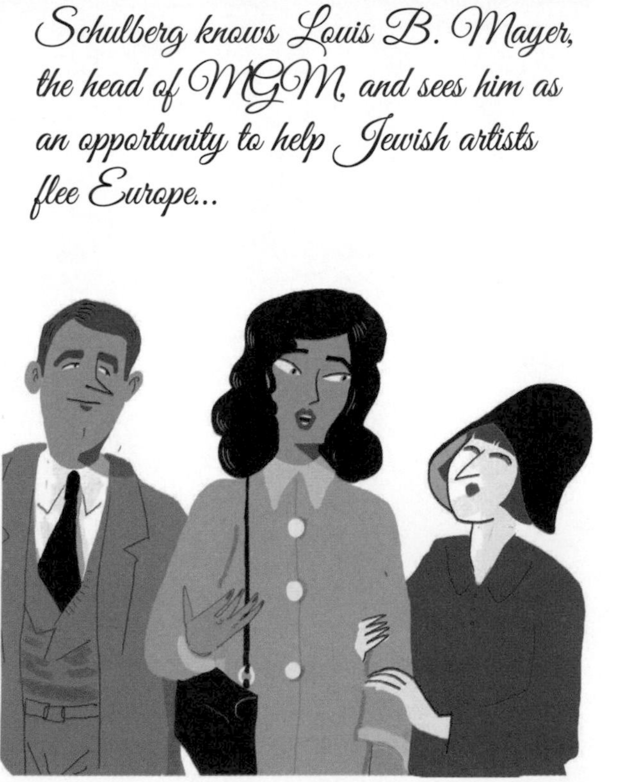
Schulberg knows Louis B. Mayer, the head of MGM, and sees him as an opportunity to help Jewish artists flee Europe...

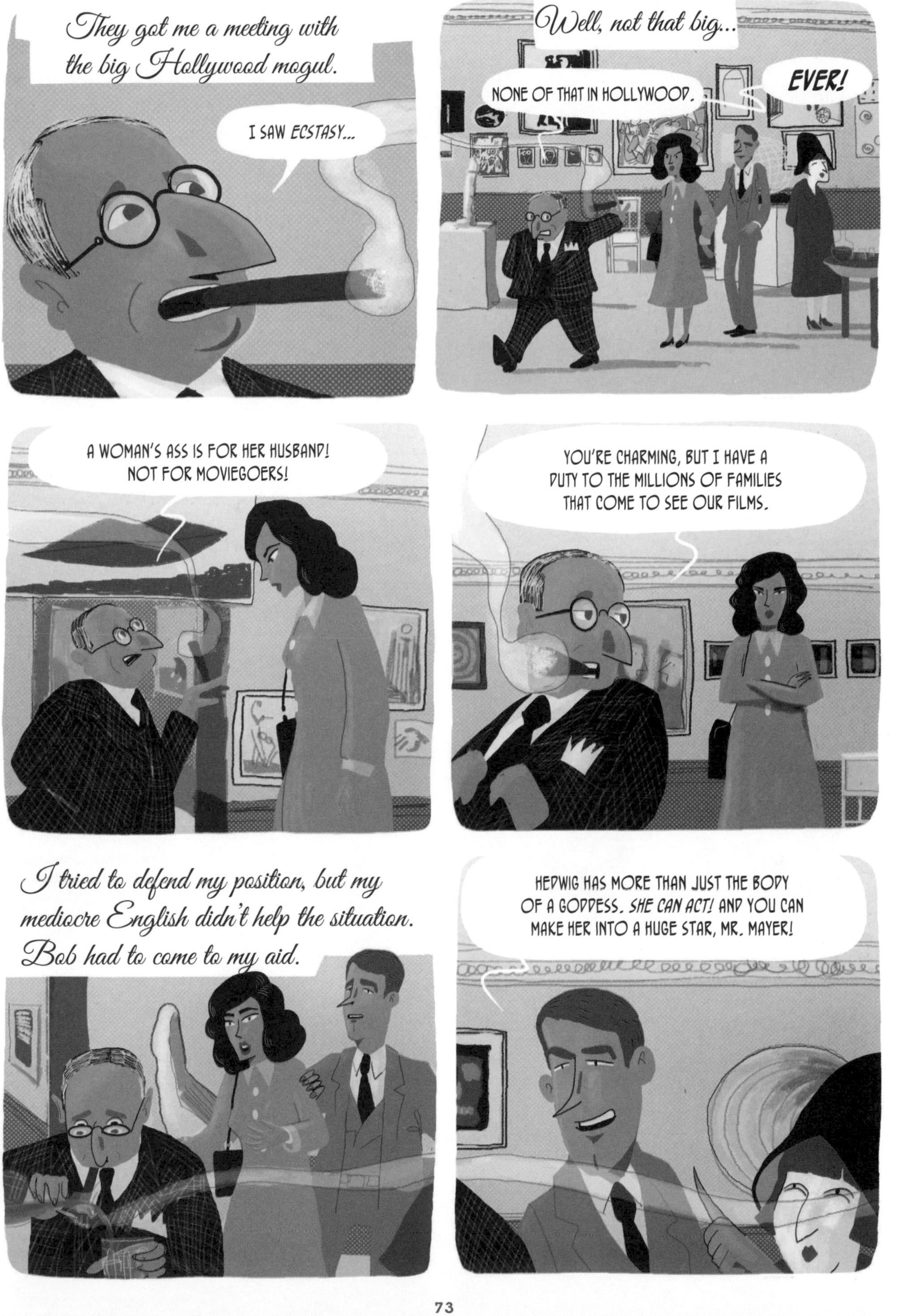
They got me a meeting with the big Hollywood mogul.
I SAW ECSTASY...
Well, not that big...
NONE OF THAT IN HOLLYWOOD.
EVER!
A WOMAN'S ASS IS FOR HER HUSBAND! NOT FOR MOVIEGOERS!
YOU'RE CHARMING, BUT I HAVE A DUTY TO THE MILLIONS OF FAMILIES THAT COME TO SEE OUR FILMS.
I tried to defend my position, but my mediocre English didn't help the situation. Bob had to come to my aid.
HEDWIG HAS MORE THAN JUST THE BODY OF A GODDESS. SHE CAN ACT! AND YOU CAN MAKE HER INTO A HUGE STAR, MR. MAYER!

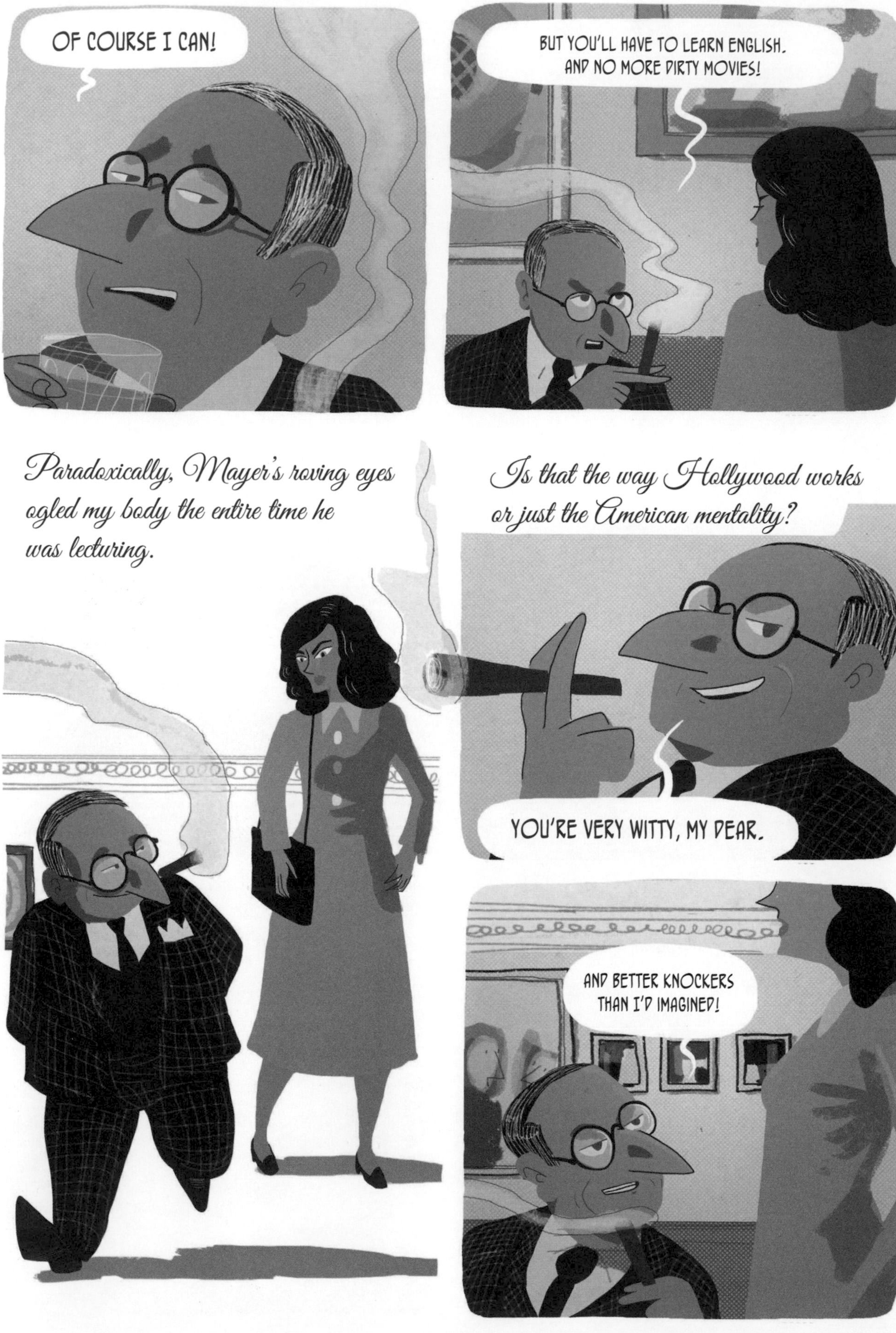
OF COURSE I CAN!
BUT YOU'LL HAVE TO LEARN ENGLISH. AND NO MORE DIRTY MOVIES!
Paradoxically, Mayer's roving eyes ogled my body the entire time he was lecturing.
Is that the way Hollywood works or just the American mentality?
YOU'RE VERY WITTY, MY DEAR.
AND BETTER KNOCKERS THAN I'D IMAGINED!

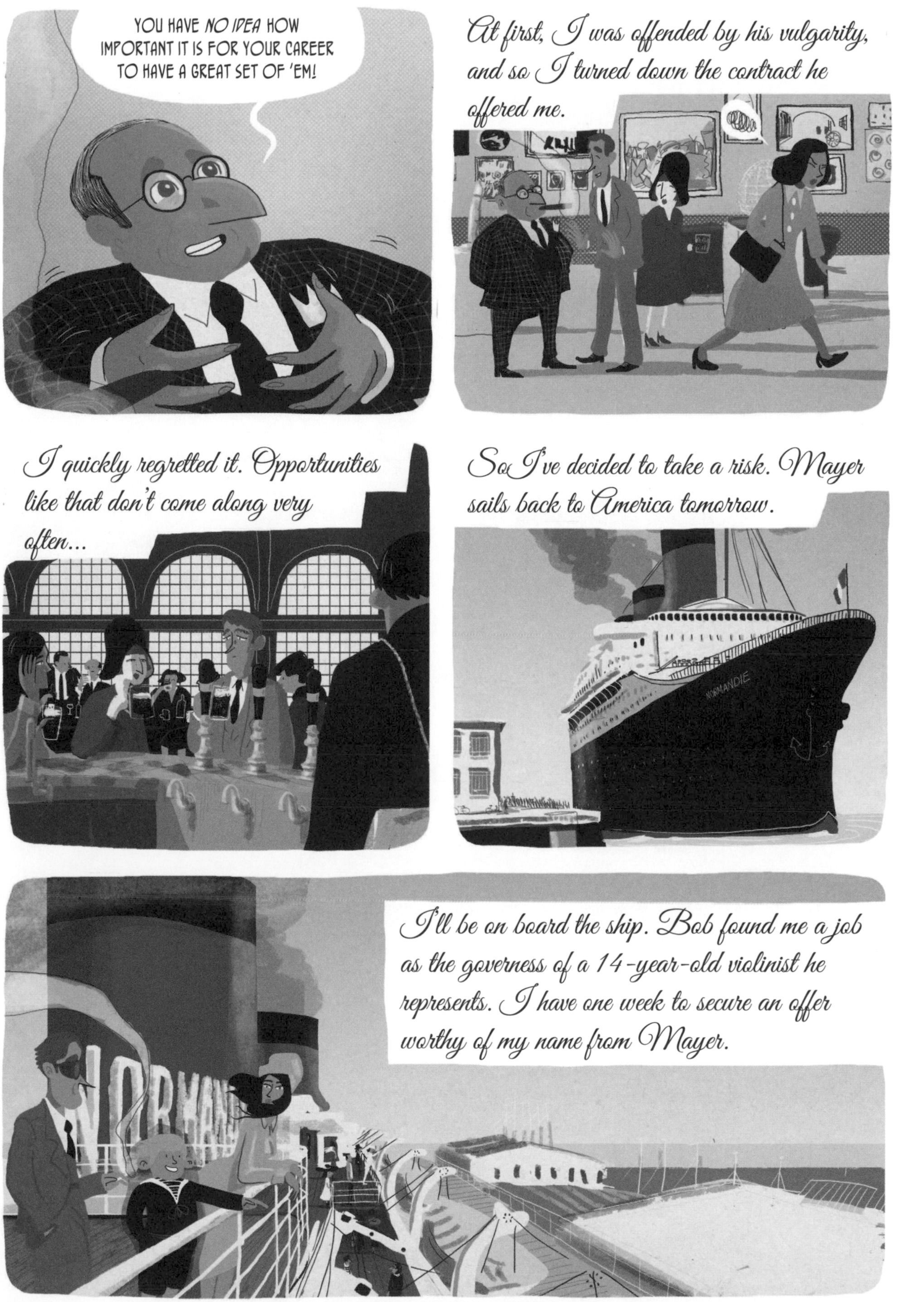
YOU HAVE NO IDEA HOW IMPORTANT IT IS FOR YOUR CAREER TO HAVE A GREAT SET OF 'EM!
At first, I was offended by his vulgarity, and so I turned down the contract he offered me.
I quickly regretted it. Opportunities like that don't come along very often...
So I've decided to take a risk. Mayer sails back to America tomorrow.
NORMANDIE
I'll be on board the ship. Bob found me a job as the governess of a 14-year-old violinist he represents. I have one week to secure an offer worthy of my name from Mayer.

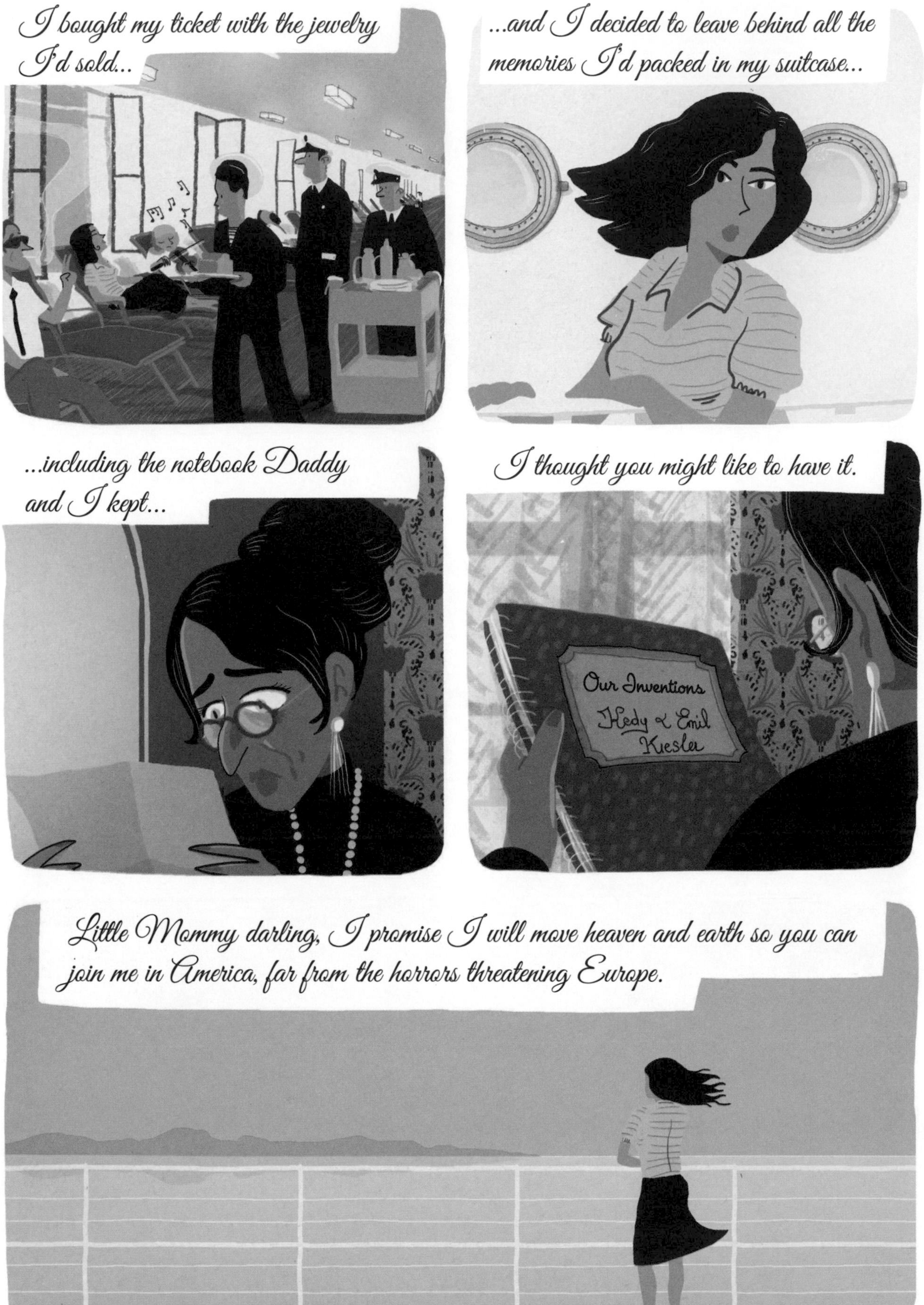
I bought my ticket with the jewelry I'd sold...
...and I decided to leave behind all the memories I'd packed in my suitcase...
...including the notebook Daddy and I kept...
I thought you might like to have it.
Our Inventions
Hedy & Emil Kiesler
Little Mommy darling, I promise I will move heaven and earth so you can join me in America, far from the horrors threatening Europe.

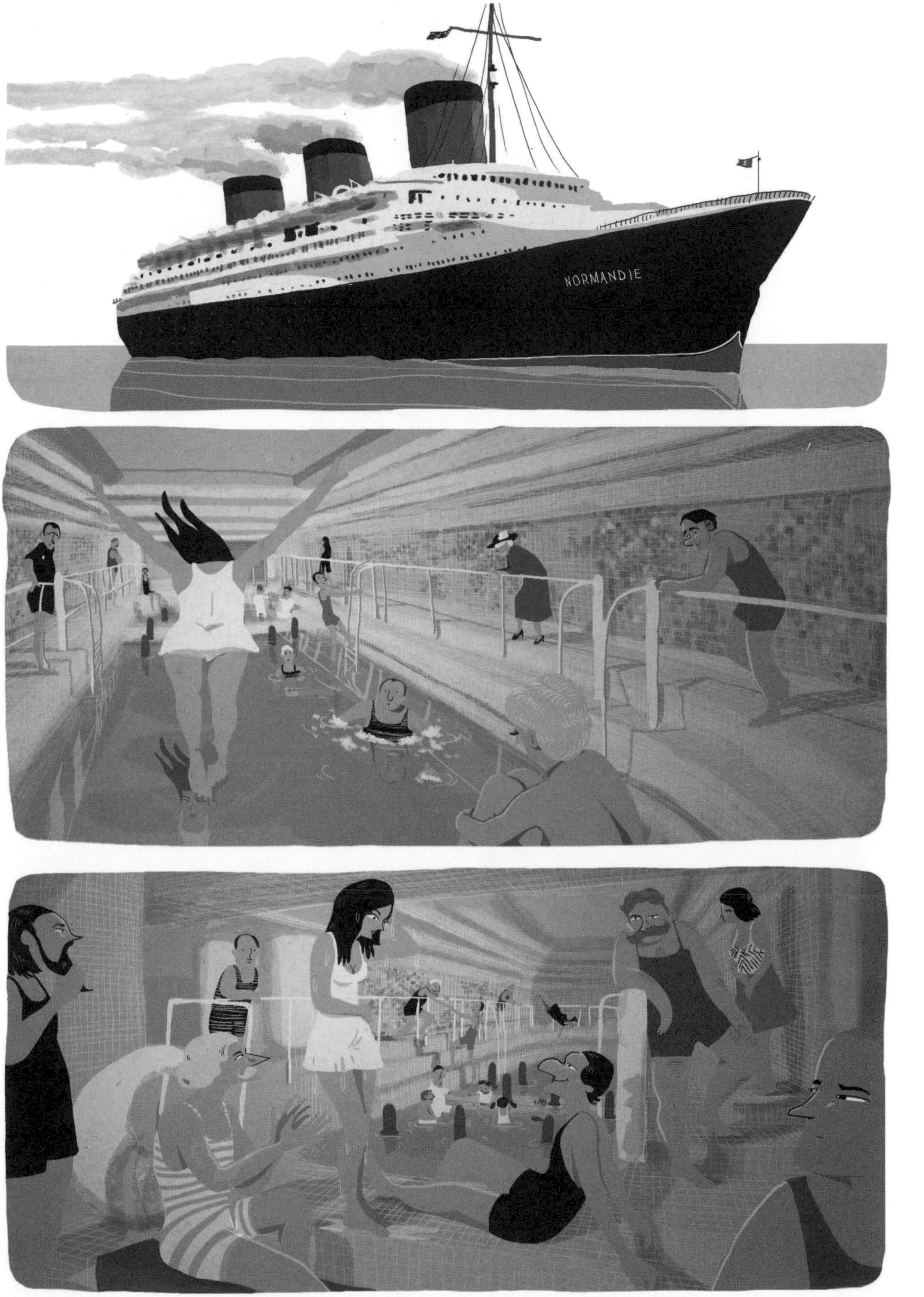
NORMANDIE

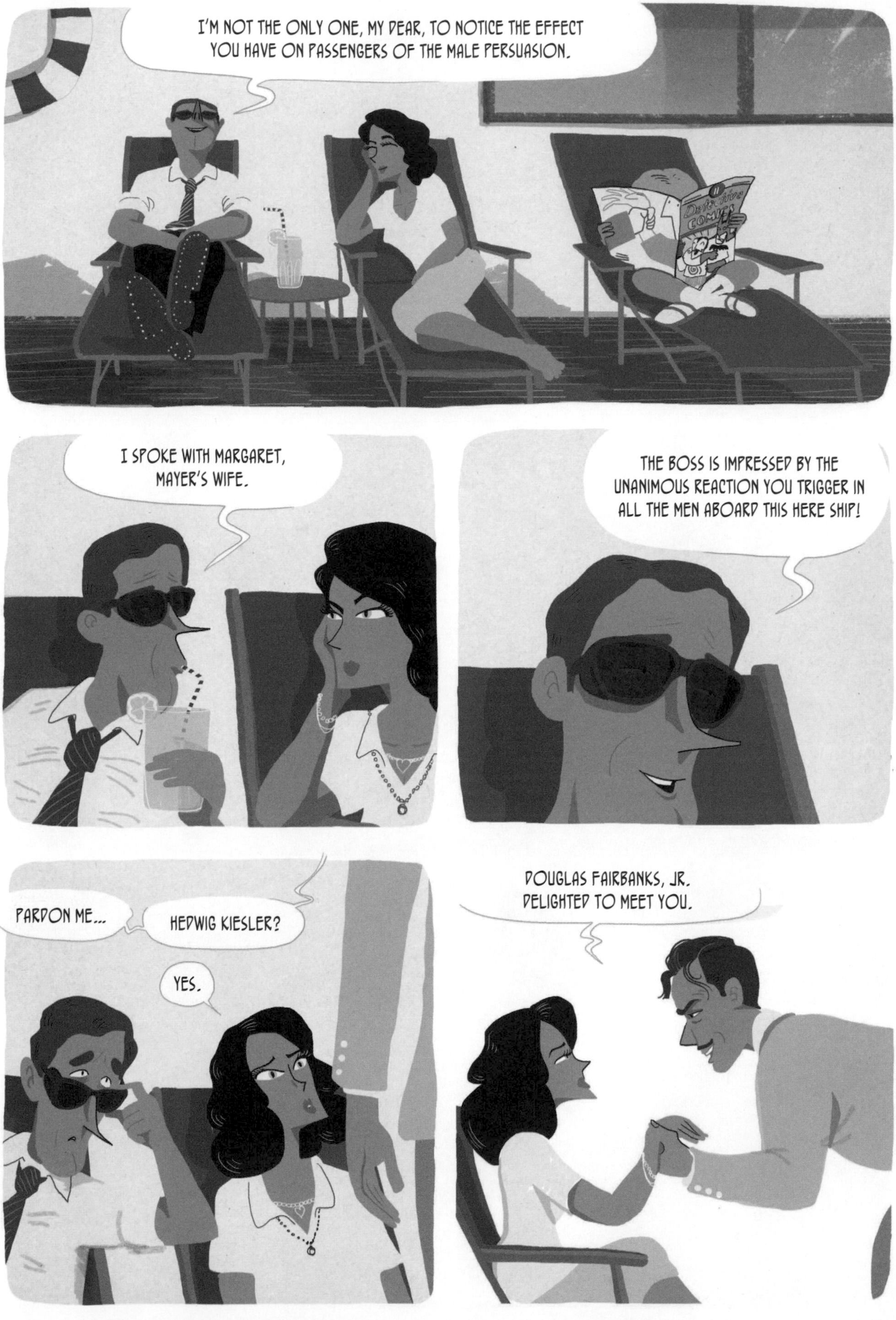
I'M NOT THE ONLY ONE, MY DEAR, TO NOTICE THE EFFECT YOU HAVE ON PASSENGERS OF THE MALE PERSUASION.
Detective COMICS
I SPOKE WITH MARGARET, MAYER'S WIFE.
THE BOSS IS IMPRESSED BY THE UNANIMOUS REACTION YOU TRIGGER IN ALL THE MEN ABOARD THIS HERE SHIP!
PARDON ME...
HEDWIG KIESLER?
YES.
DOUGLAS FAIRBANKS, JR. DELIGHTED TO MEET YOU.

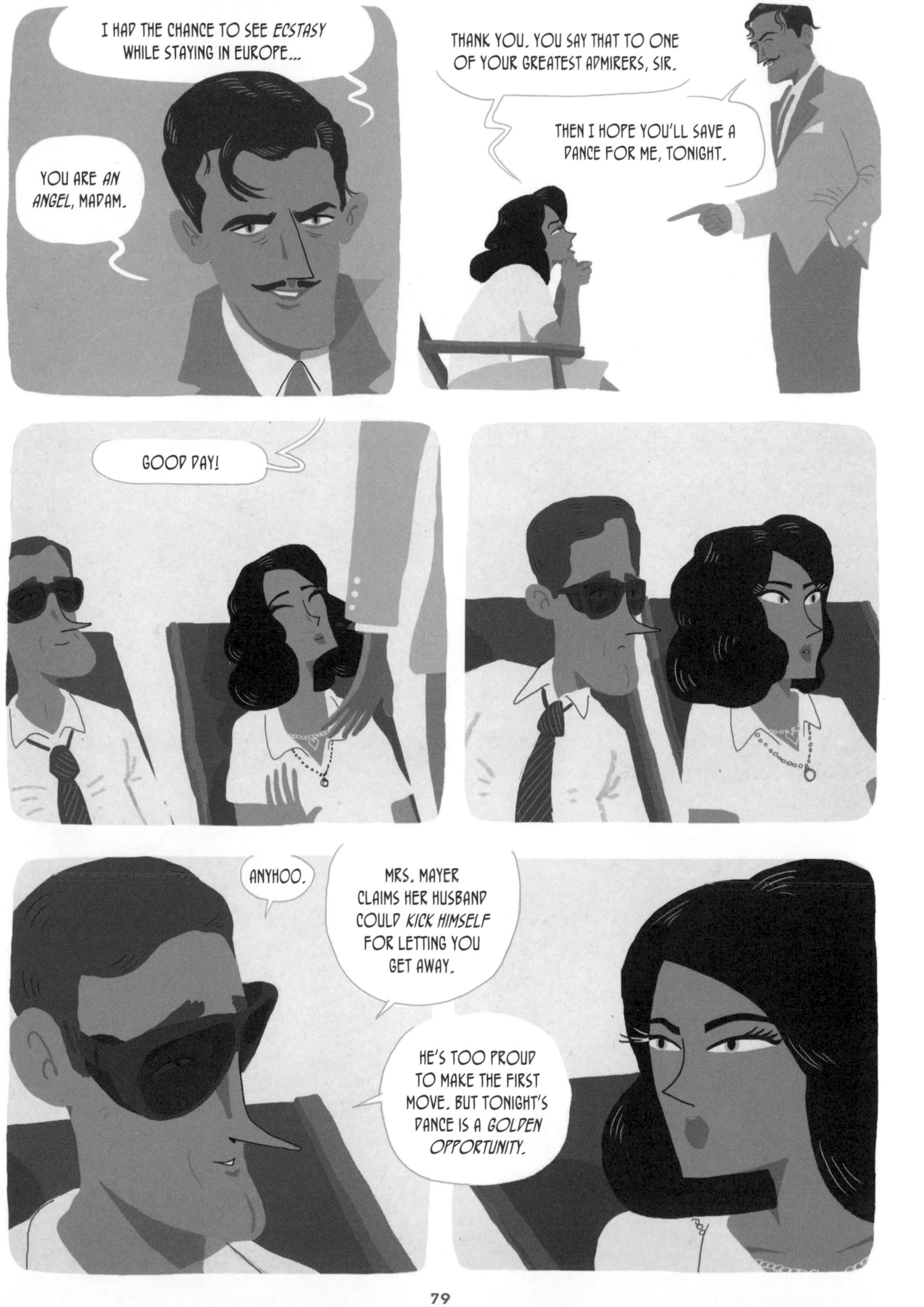
I HAD THE CHANCE TO SEE *ECSTASY* WHILE STAYING IN EUROPE...
YOU ARE *AN ANGEL*, MADAM.
THANK YOU. YOU SAY THAT TO ONE OF YOUR GREATEST ADMIRERS, SIR.
THEN I HOPE YOU'LL SAVE A DANCE FOR ME, TONIGHT.
GOOD DAY!
ANYHOO.
MRS. MAYER CLAIMS HER HUSBAND COULD *KICK HIMSELF* FOR LETTING YOU GET AWAY.
HE'S TOO PROUD TO MAKE THE FIRST MOVE. BUT TONIGHT'S DANCE IS A *GOLDEN OPPORTUNITY*.

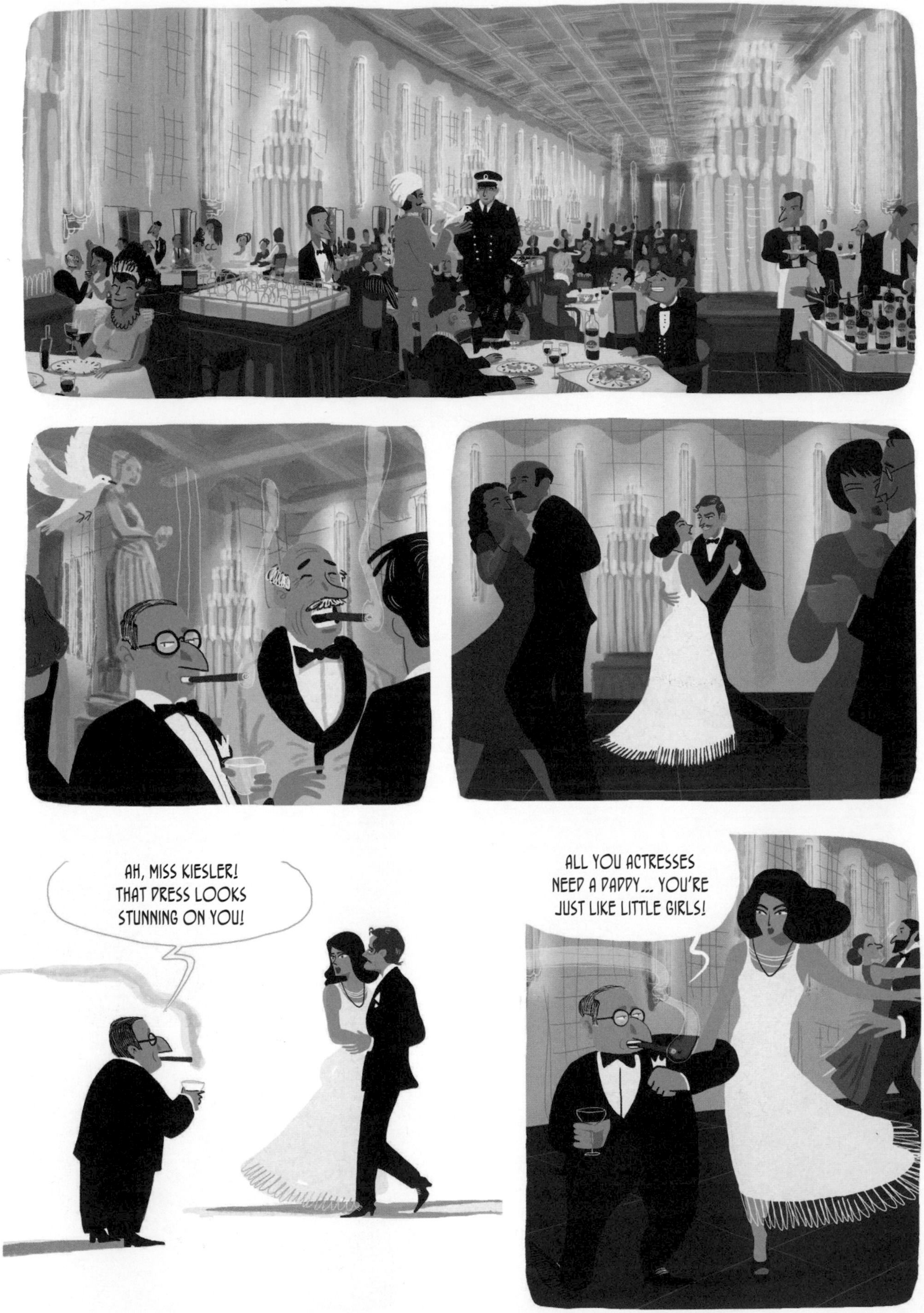
AH, MISS KIESLER! THAT DRESS LOOKS STUNNING ON YOU!
ALL YOU ACTRESSES NEED A DADDY... YOU'RE JUST LIKE LITTLE GIRLS!

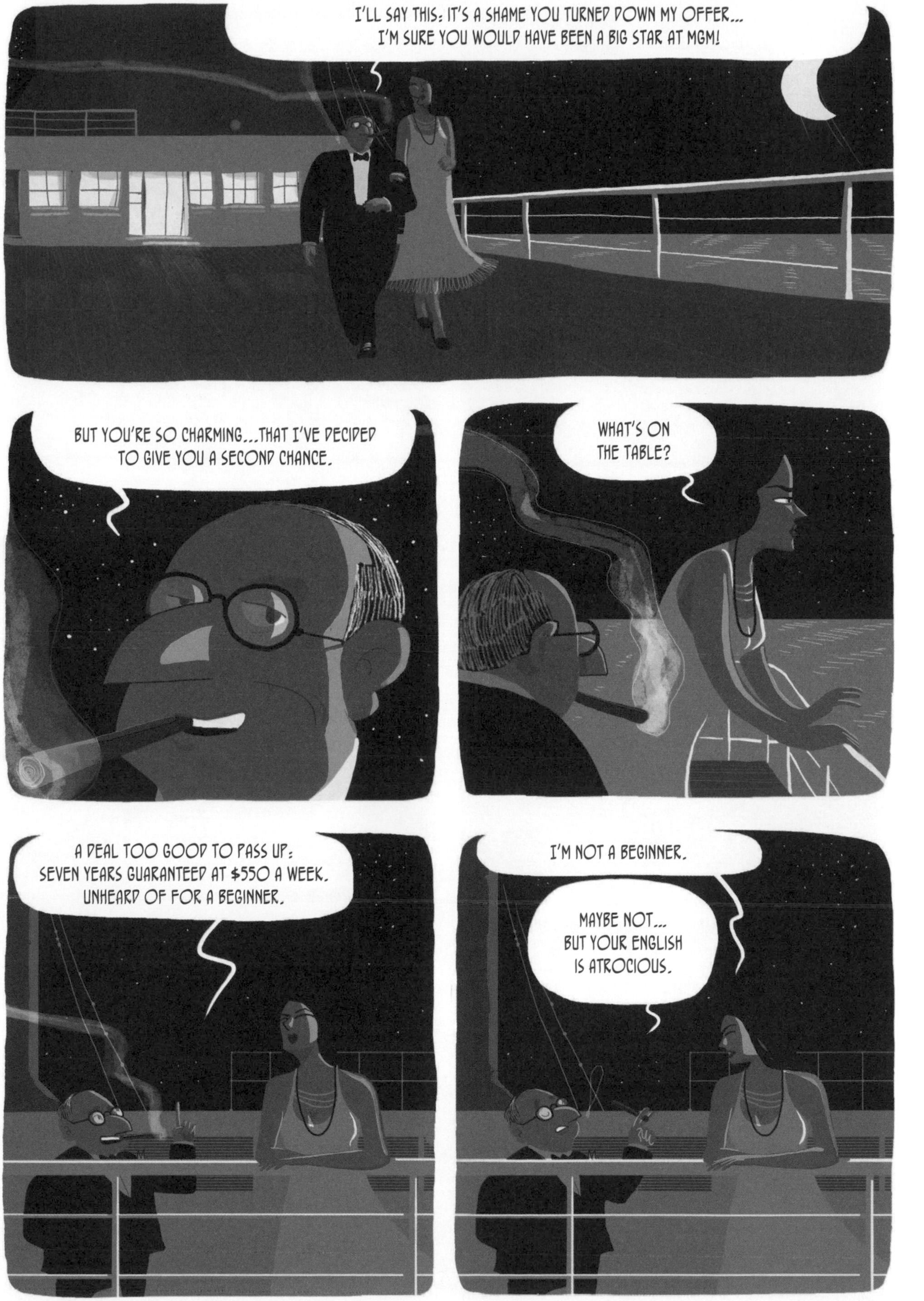
I'LL SAY THIS: IT'S A SHAME YOU TURNED DOWN MY OFFER... I'M SURE YOU WOULD HAVE BEEN A BIG STAR AT MGM!
BUT YOU'RE SO CHARMING...THAT I'VE DECIDED TO GIVE YOU A SECOND CHANCE.
WHAT'S ON THE TABLE?
A DEAL TOO GOOD TO PASS UP: SEVEN YEARS GUARANTEED AT $550 A WEEK. UNHEARD OF FOR A BEGINNER.
I'M NOT A BEGINNER.
MAYBE NOT... BUT YOUR ENGLISH IS ATROCIOUS.

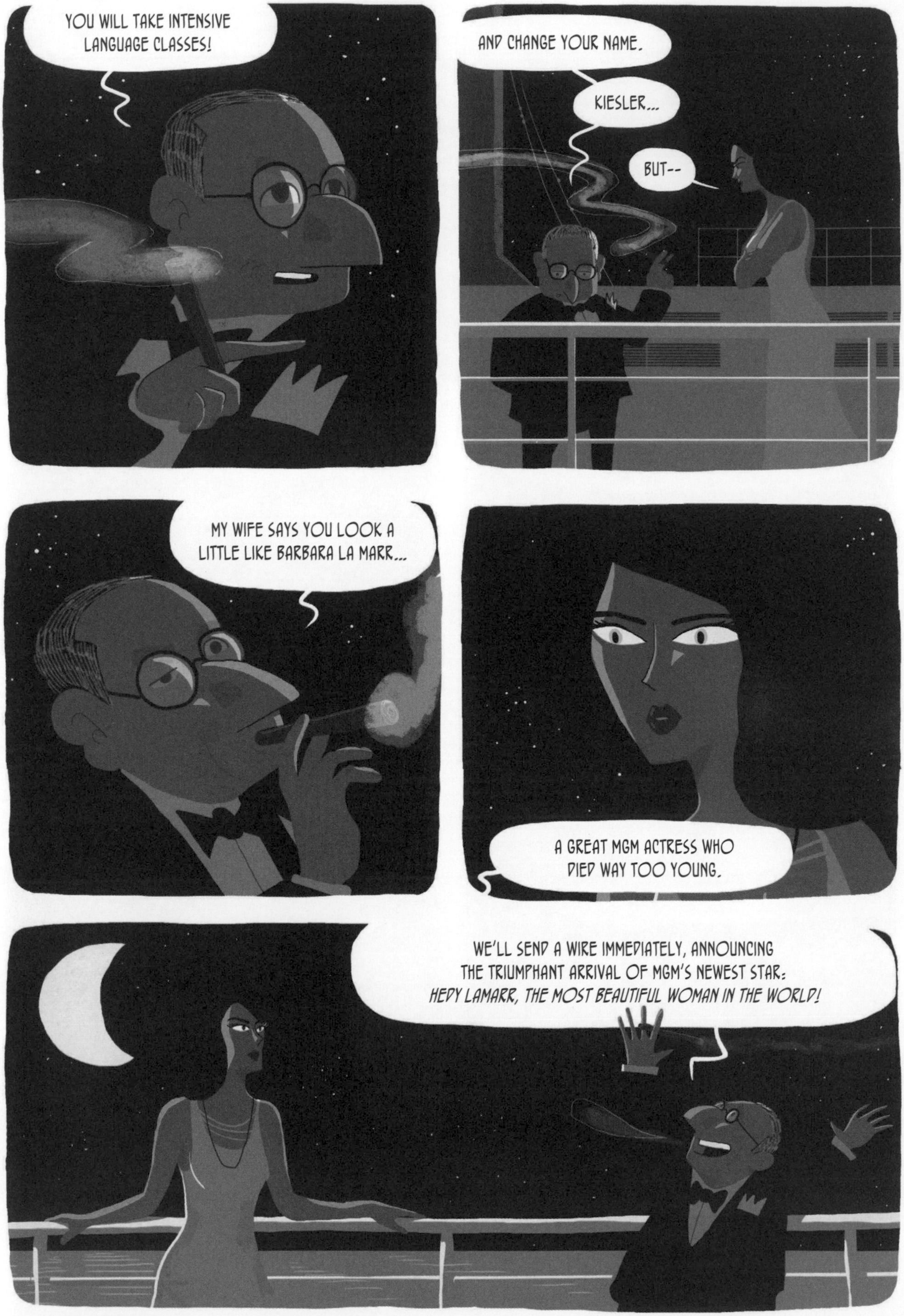
YOU WILL TAKE INTENSIVE LANGUAGE CLASSES!
AND CHANGE YOUR NAME.
KIESLER...
BUT--
MY WIFE SAYS YOU LOOK A LITTLE LIKE BARBARA LA MARR...
A GREAT MGM ACTRESS WHO DIED WAY TOO YOUNG.
WE'LL SEND A WIRE IMMEDIATELY, ANNOUNCING THE TRIUMPHANT ARRIVAL OF MGM'S NEWEST STAR: *HEDY LAMARR, THE MOST BEAUTIFUL WOMAN IN THE WORLD!*

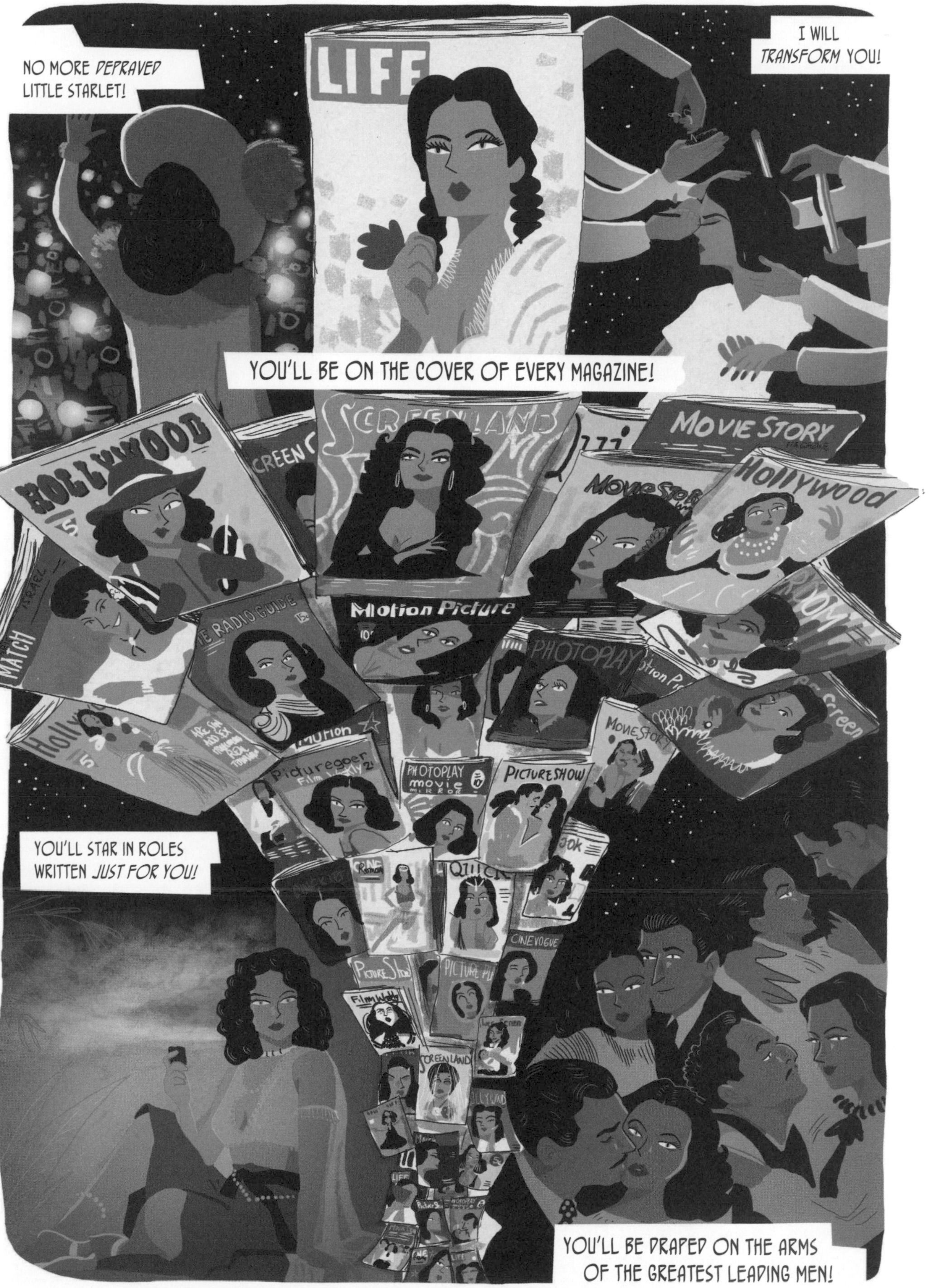
NO MORE *DEPRAVED* LITTLE STARLET!
LIFE
I WILL *TRANSFORM* YOU!
YOU'LL BE ON THE COVER OF EVERY MAGAZINE!
HOLLYWOOD
MOVIE STORY
Hollywood
Motion Picture
PHOTOPLAY
PHOTOPLAY movie MIRROR
PICTURESHOW
YOU'LL STAR IN ROLES WRITTEN *JUST FOR YOU!*
QUICK
CINEVOGUE
SCREENLAND
YOU'LL BE DRAPED ON THE ARMS OF THE GREATEST LEADING MEN!

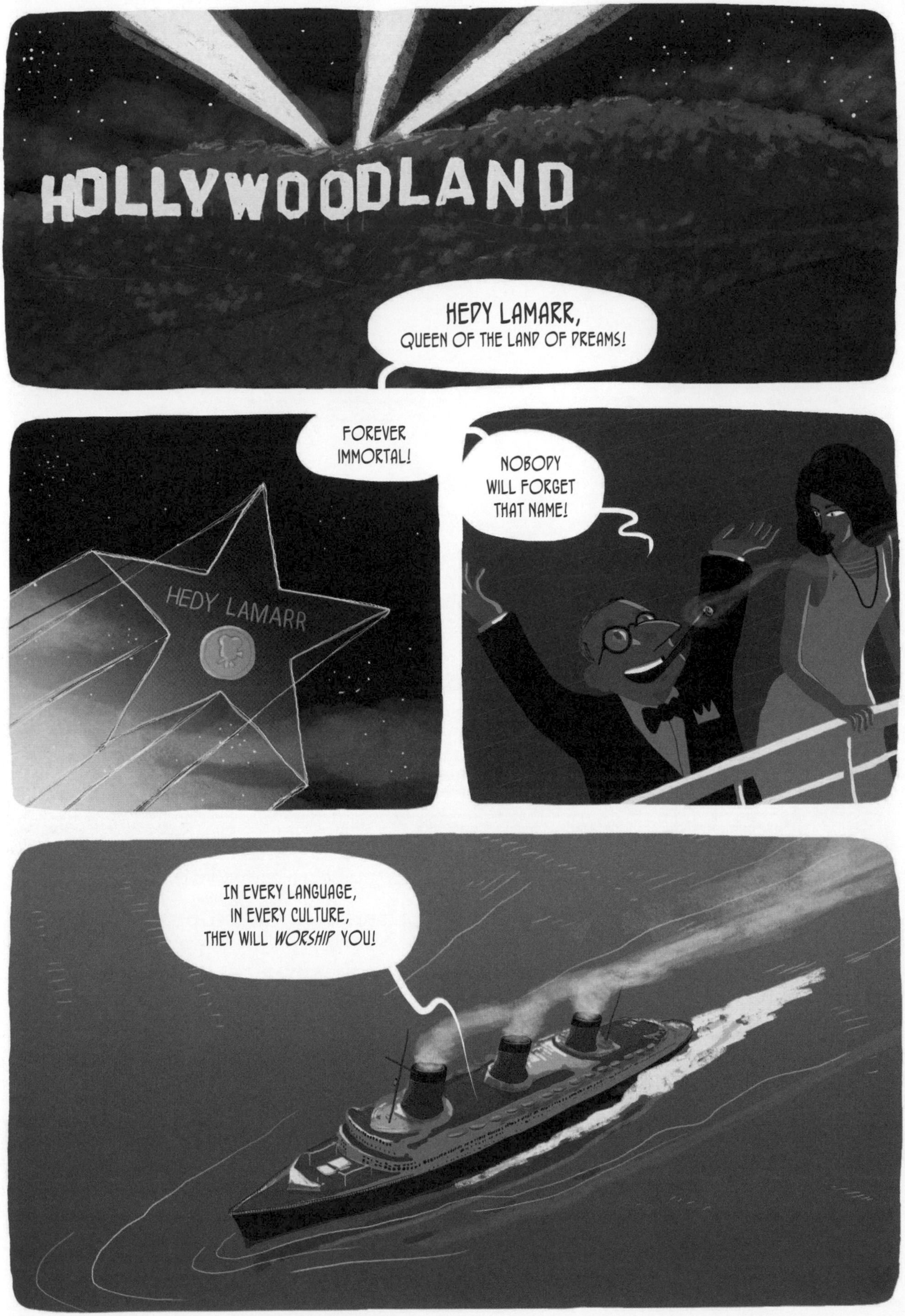
HOLLYWOODLAND
HEDY LAMARR, QUEEN OF THE LAND OF DREAMS!
FOREVER IMMORTAL!
HEDY LAMARR
NOBODY WILL FORGET THAT NAME!
IN EVERY LANGUAGE, IN EVERY CULTURE, THEY WILL *WORSHIP* YOU!

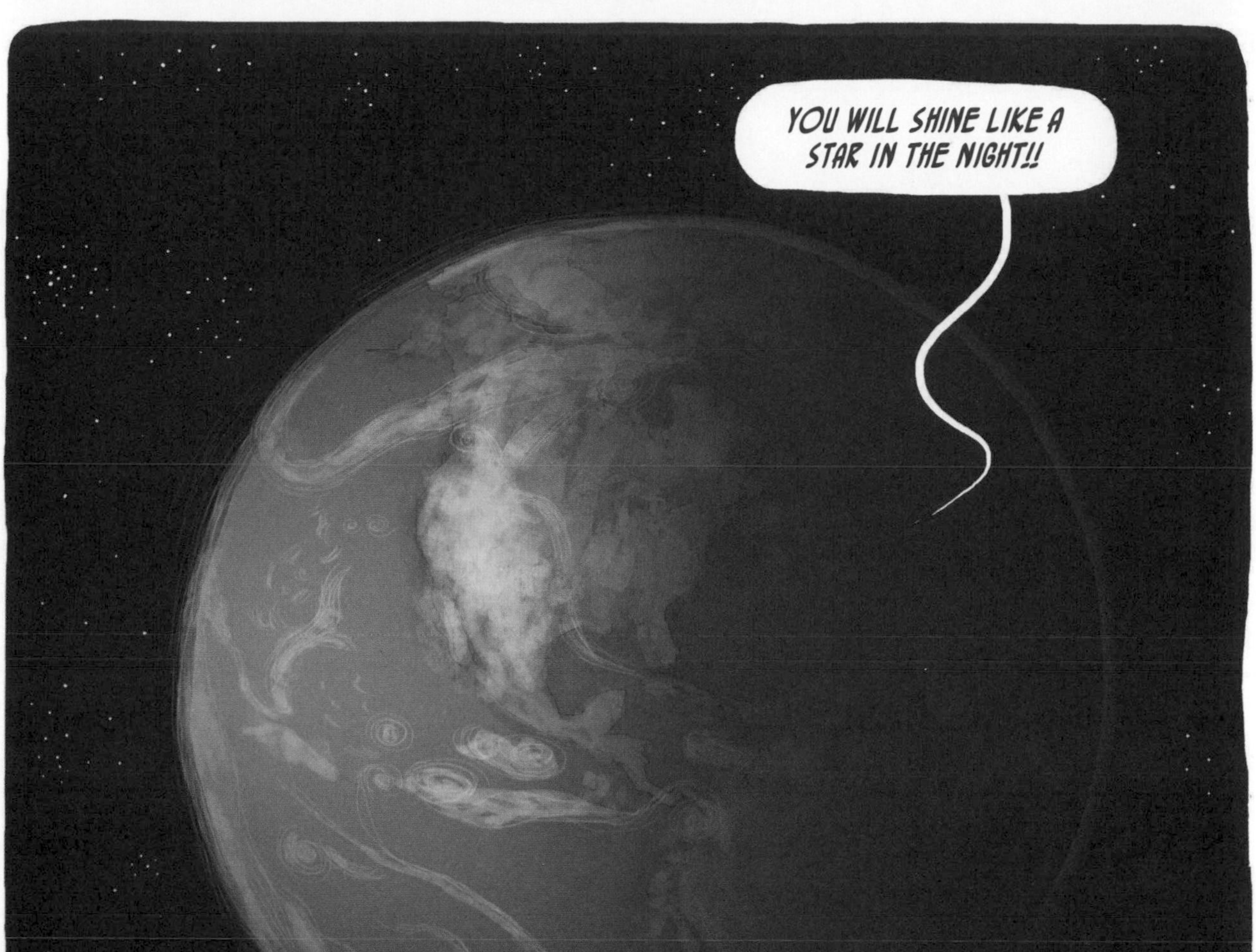
YOU WILL SHINE LIKE A STAR IN THE NIGHT!!

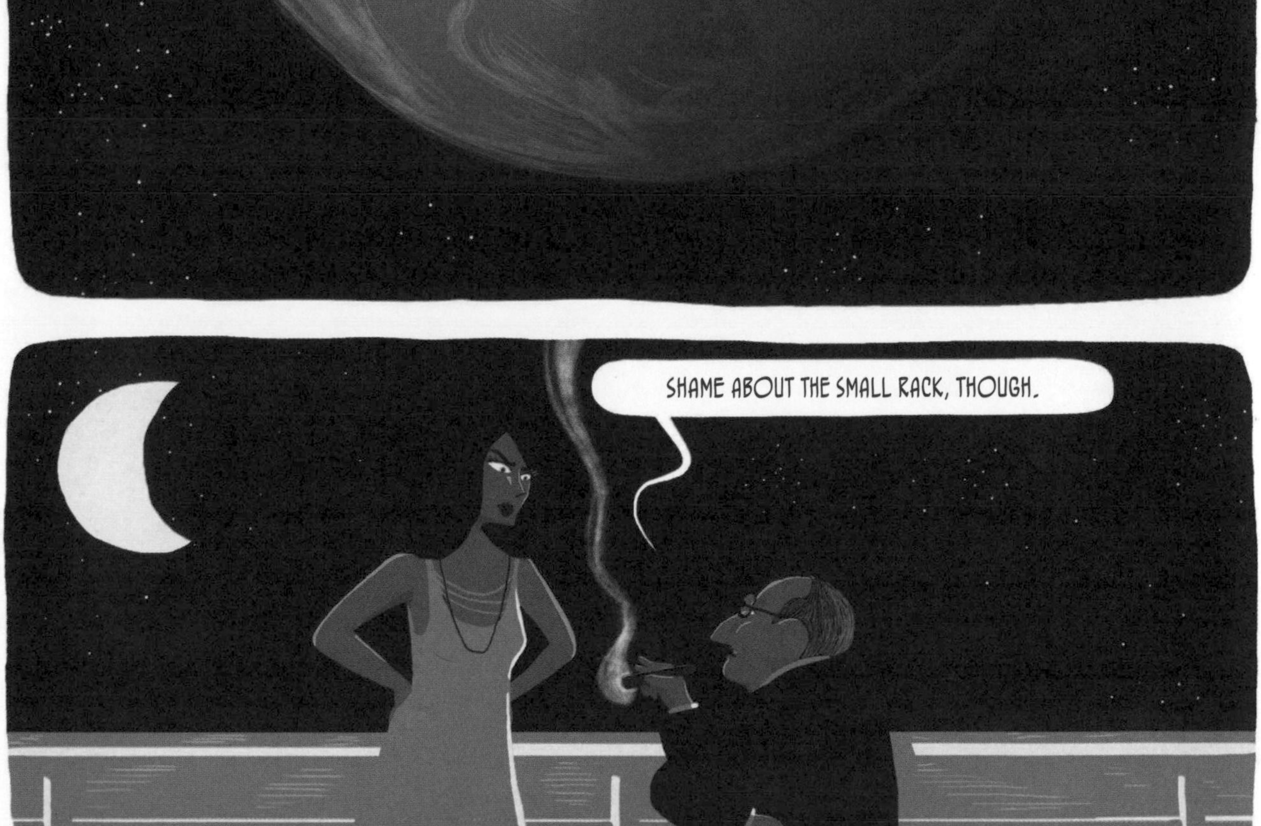
SHAME ABOUT THE SMALL RACK, THOUGH.

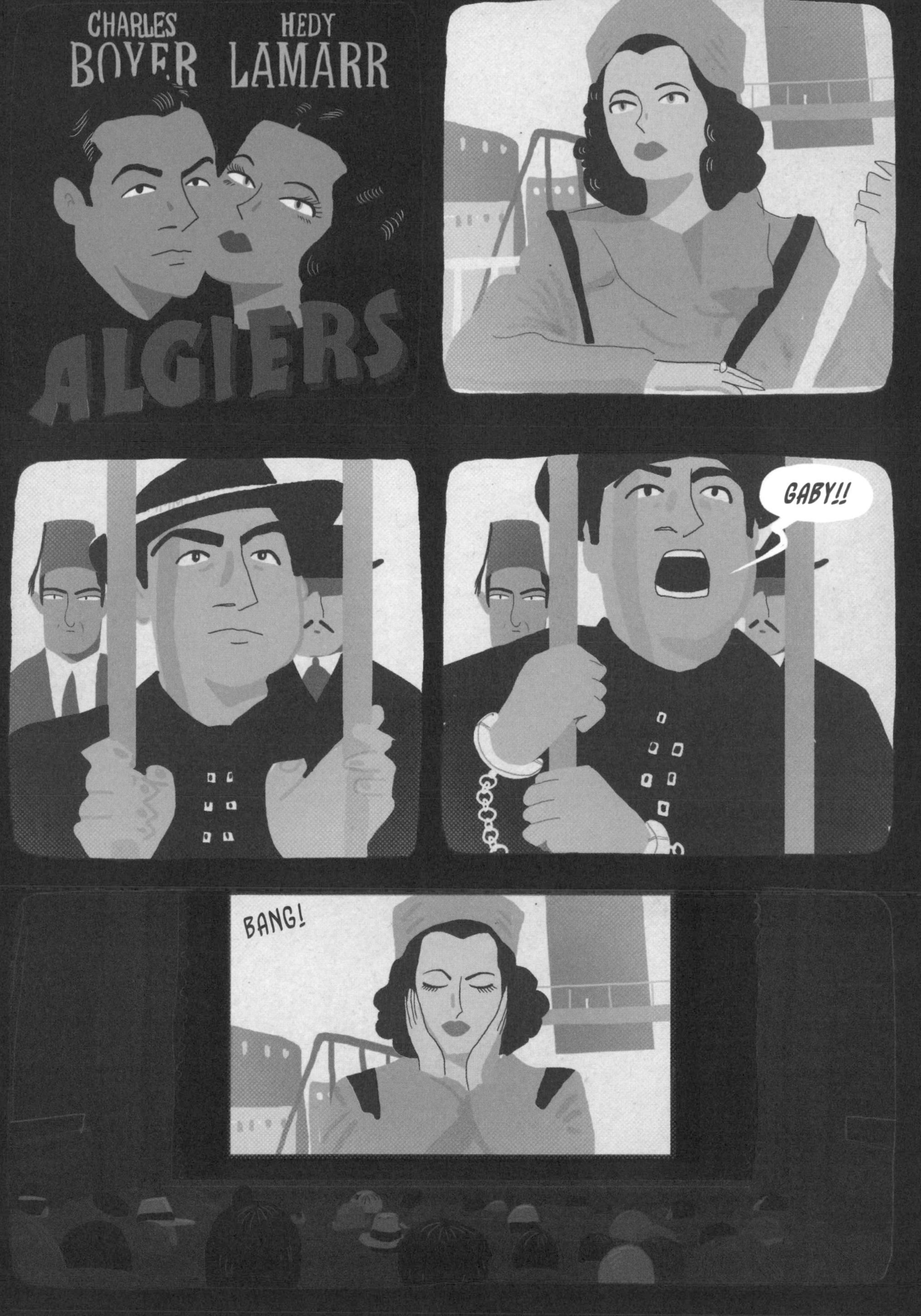
CHARLES
BOYER
HEDY
LAMARR
ALGIERS
GABY!!
BANG!

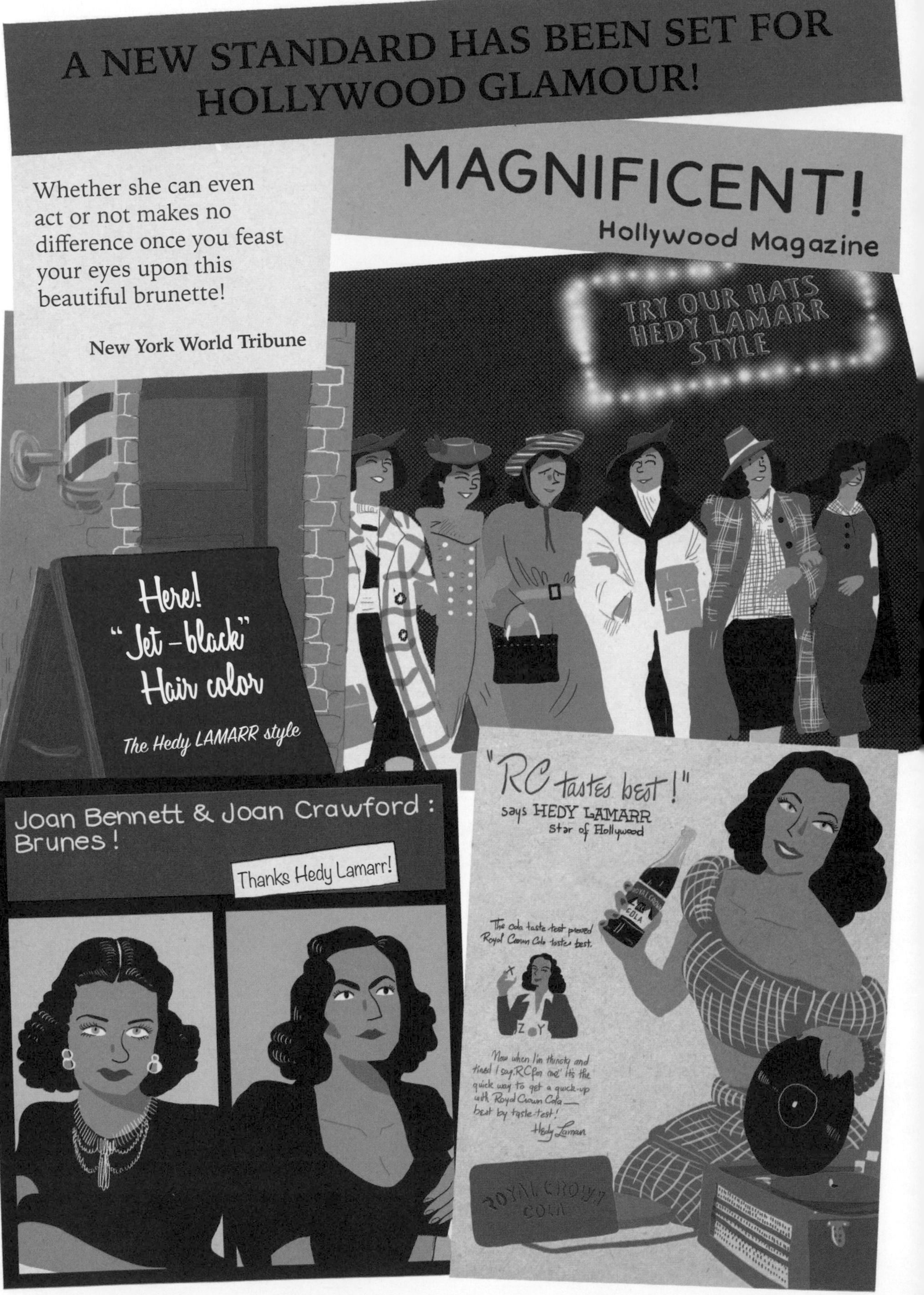
A NEW STANDARD HAS BEEN SET FOR HOLLYWOOD GLAMOUR!
Whether she can even act or not makes no difference once you feast your eyes upon this beautiful brunette!
New York World Tribune
MAGNIFICENT!
Hollywood Magazine
TRY OUR HATS HEDY LAMARR STYLE
Here! "Jet-black" Hair color
The Hedy LAMARR style
Joan Bennett & Joan Crawford : Brunes !
Thanks Hedy Lamarr!
"RC tastes best!"
says HEDY LAMARR
Star of Hollywood
The cola taste test proved Royal Crown Cola tastes best.
Now when I'm thirsty and tired I say, RC for me.' It's the quick way to get a quick-up with Royal Crown Cola— best by taste-test!
Hedy Lamarr

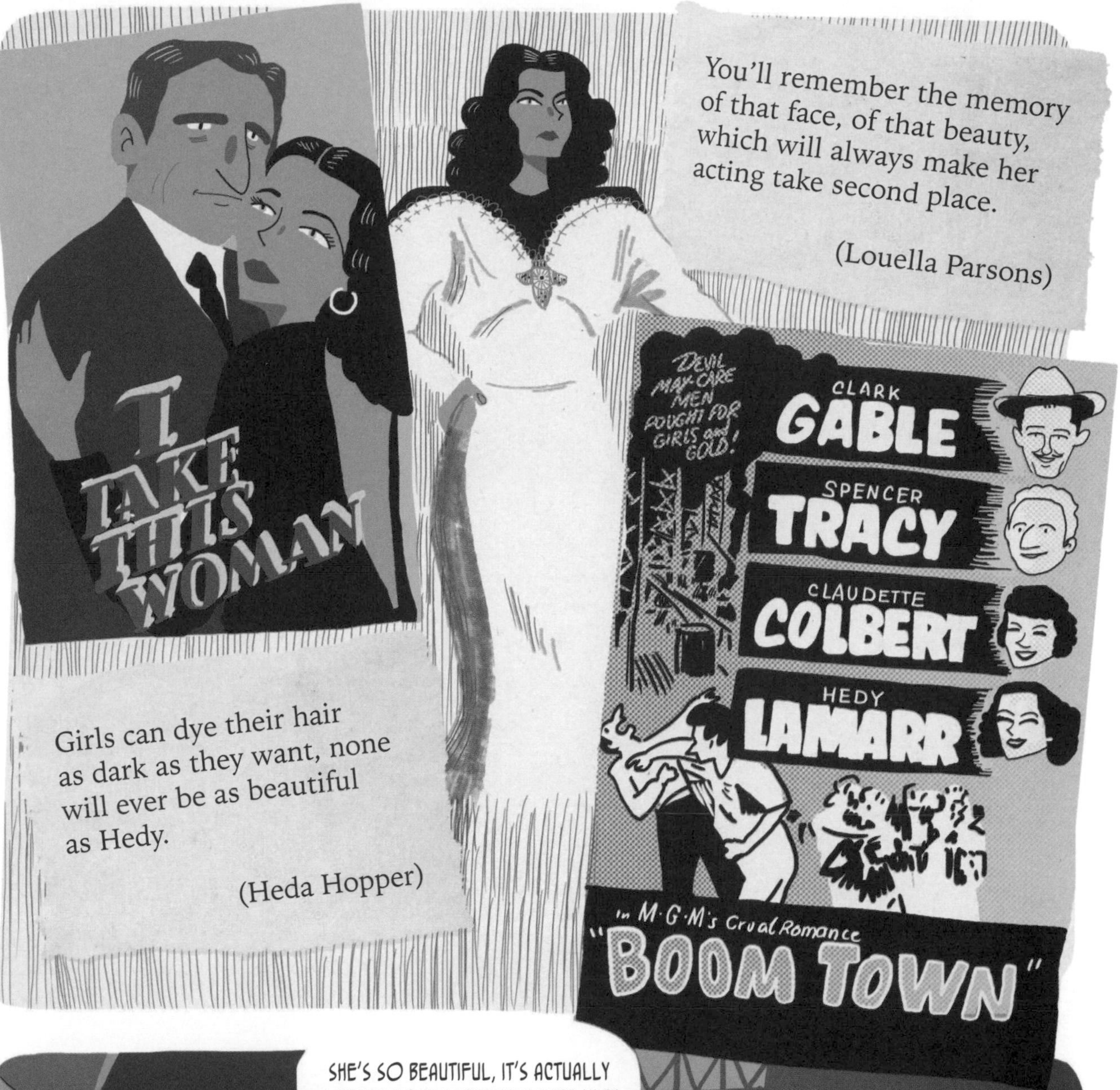
I TAKE THIS WOMAN
You'll remember the memory of that face, of that beauty, which will always make her acting take second place.
(Louella Parsons)
DEVIL MAY-CARE MEN FOUGHT FOR GIRLS and GOLD!
CLARK GABLE
SPENCER TRACY
CLAUDETTE COLBERT
HEDY LAMARR
in M·G·M's Crual Romance
"BOOM TOWN"
Girls can dye their hair as dark as they want, none will ever be as beautiful as Hedy.
(Heda Hopper)

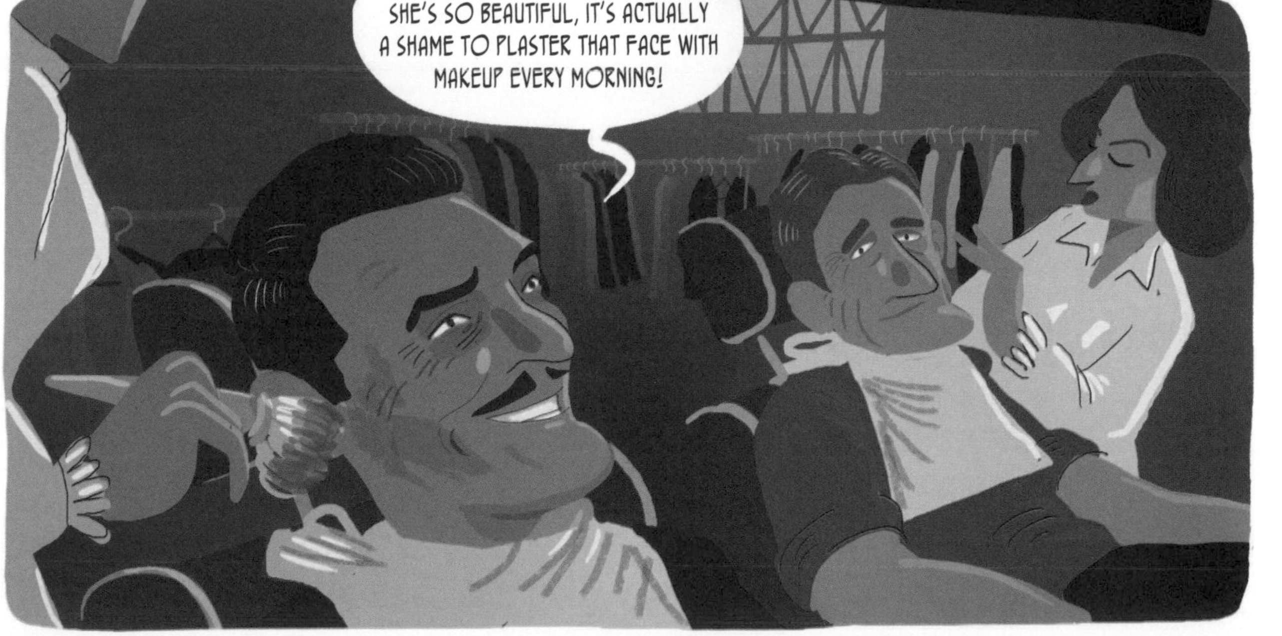
SHE'S SO BEAUTIFUL, IT'S ACTUALLY A SHAME TO PLASTER THAT FACE WITH MAKEUP EVERY MORNING!

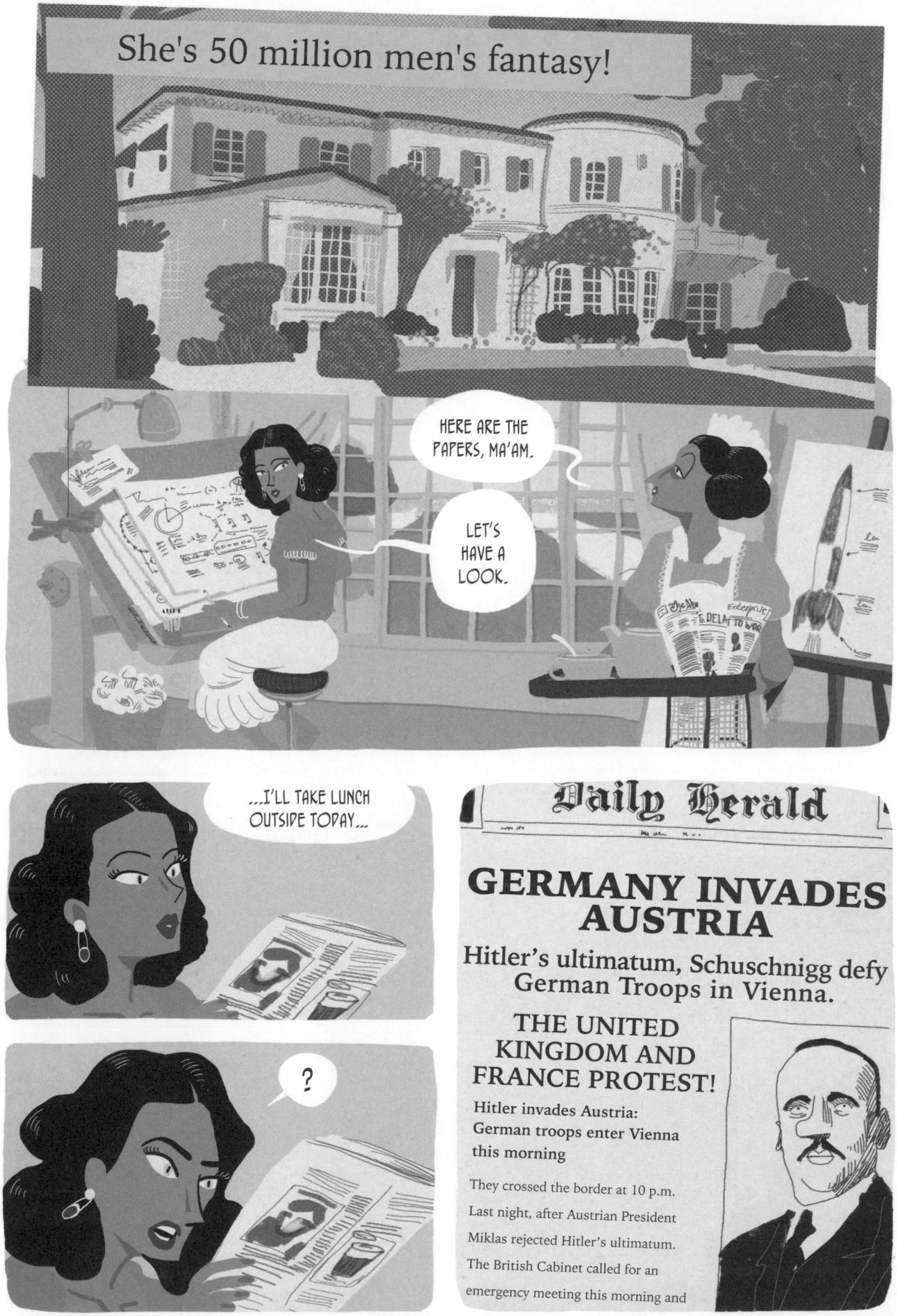
She's 50 million men's fantasy!
HERE ARE THE PAPERS, MA'AM.
LET'S HAVE A LOOK.
...I'LL TAKE LUNCH OUTSIDE TODAY...
?
Daily Herald
GERMANY INVADES AUSTRIA
Hitler's ultimatum, Schuschnigg defy German Troops in Vienna.
THE UNITED KINGDOM AND FRANCE PROTEST!
Hitler invades Austria: German troops enter Vienna this morning
They crossed the border at 10 p.m. Last night, after Austrian President Miklas rejected Hitler's ultimatum. The British Cabinet called for an emergency meeting this morning and

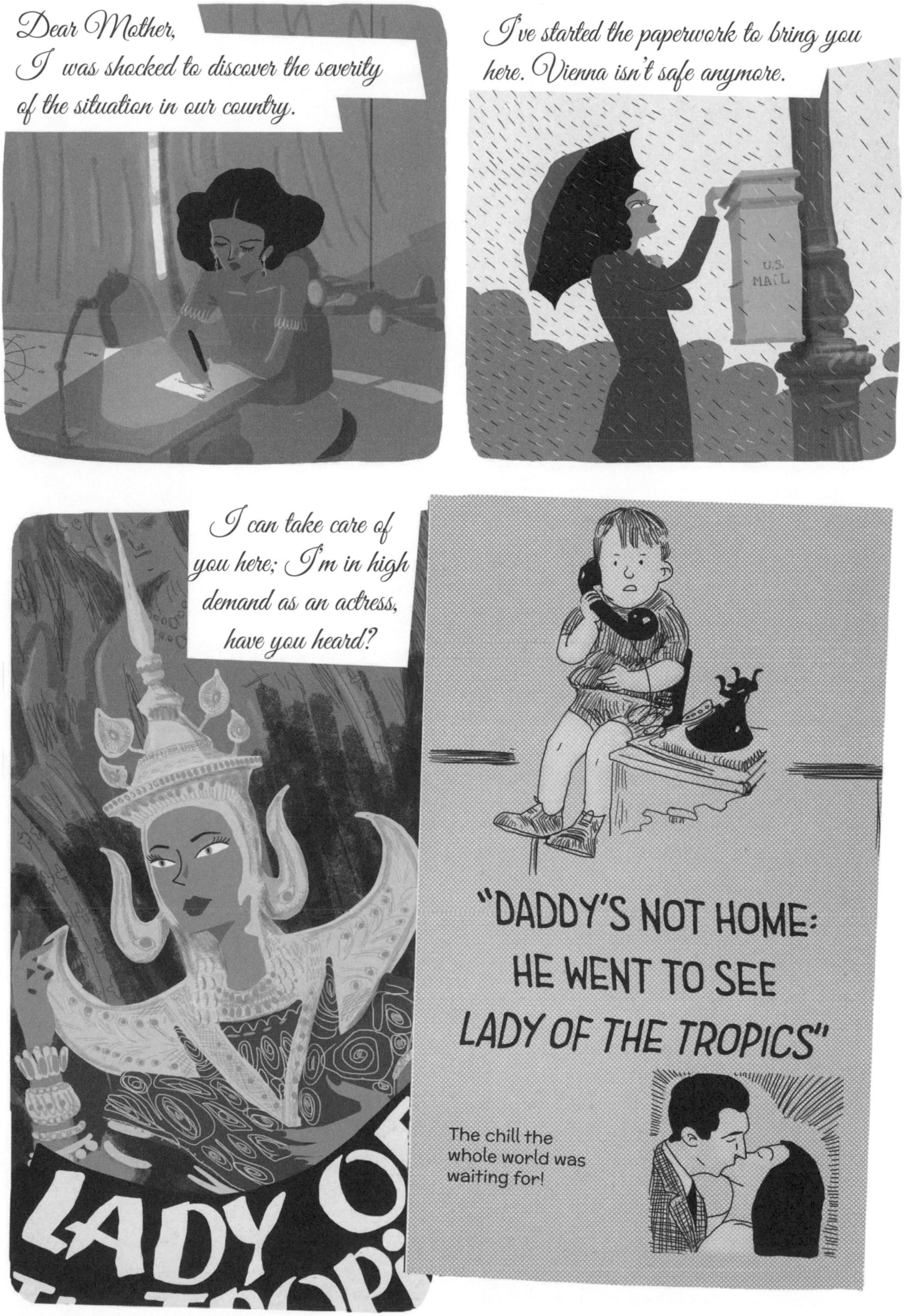
Dear Mother,
I was shocked to discover the severity of the situation in our country.
I've started the paperwork to bring you here. Vienna isn't safe anymore.
U.S. MAIL
I can take care of you here; I'm in high demand as an actress, have you heard?
LADY
"DADDY'S NOT HOME:
HE WENT TO SEE
LADY OF THE TROPICS"
The chill the whole world was waiting for!

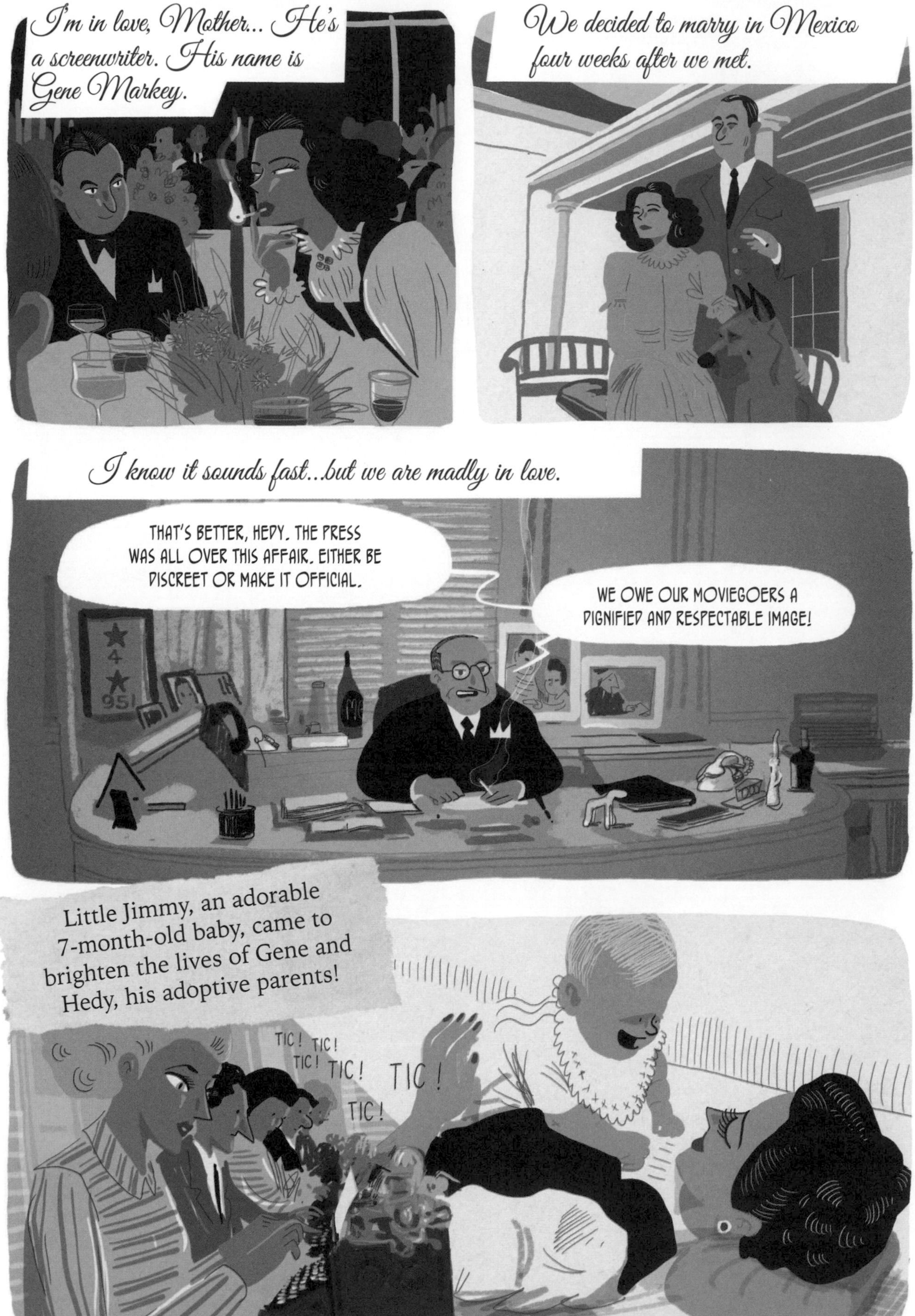
I'm in love, Mother... He's a screenwriter. His name is Gene Markey.
We decided to marry in Mexico four weeks after we met.
I know it sounds fast...but we are madly in love.
THAT'S BETTER, HEDY. THE PRESS WAS ALL OVER THIS AFFAIR. EITHER BE DISCREET OR MAKE IT OFFICIAL.
WE OWE OUR MOVIEGOERS A DIGNIFIED AND RESPECTABLE IMAGE!
Little Jimmy, an adorable 7-month-old baby, came to brighten the lives of Gene and Hedy, his adoptive parents!
TIC! TIC! TIC! TIC! TIC! TIC!

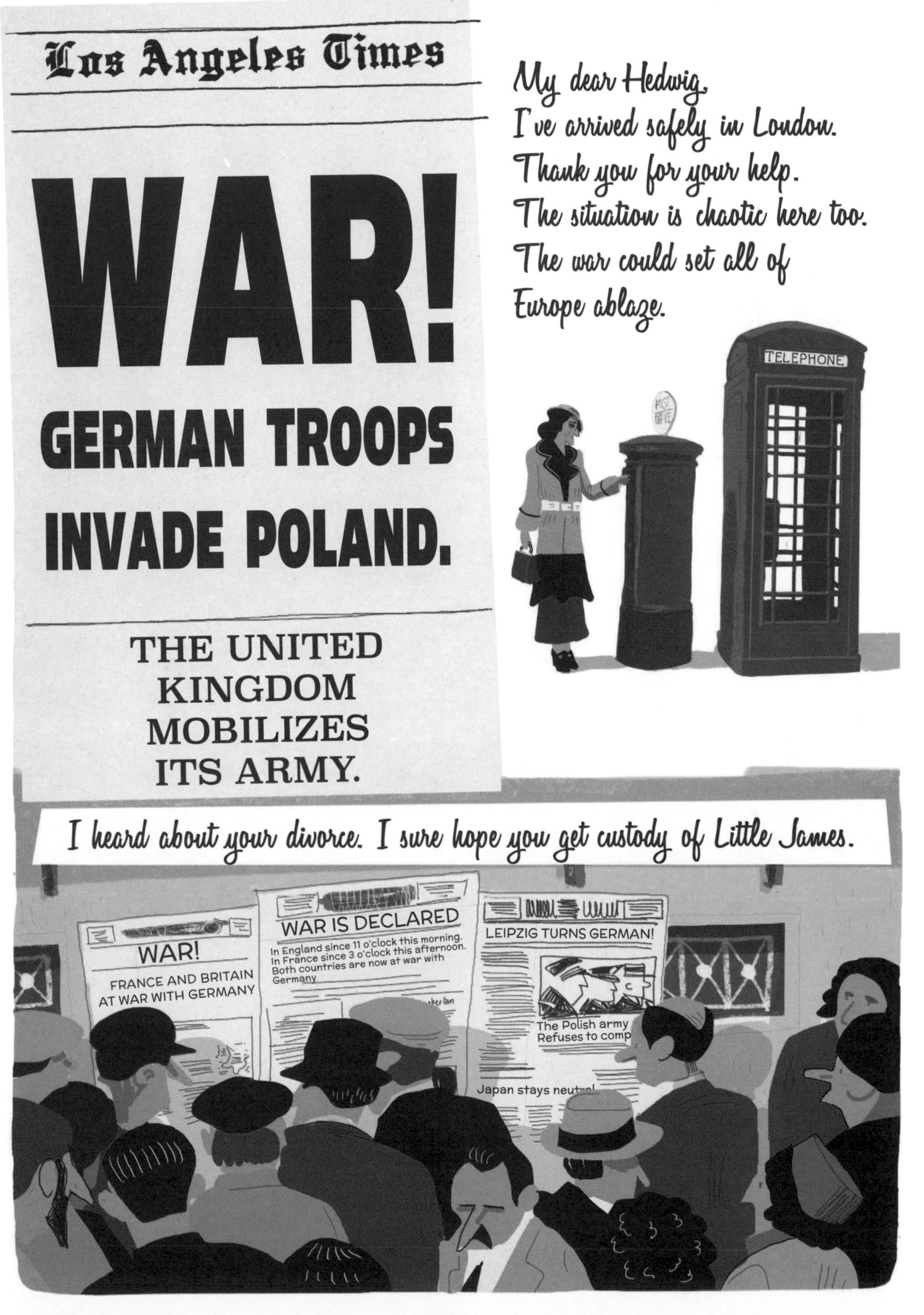

Los Angeles Times
WAR!
GERMAN TROOPS INVADE POLAND.
THE UNITED KINGDOM MOBILIZES ITS ARMY.
My dear Hedwig,
I've arrived safely in London.
Thank you for your help.
The situation is chaotic here too.
The war could set all of
Europe ablaze.
TELEPHONE
I heard about your divorce. I sure hope you get custody of Little James.
WAR!
FRANCE AND BRITAIN AT WAR WITH GERMANY
WAR IS DECLARED
In England since 11 o'clock this morning.
In France since 3 o'clock this afternoon.
Both countries are now at war with Germany
LEIPZIG TURNS GERMAN!
The Polish army
Refuses to comp
Japan stays neutr

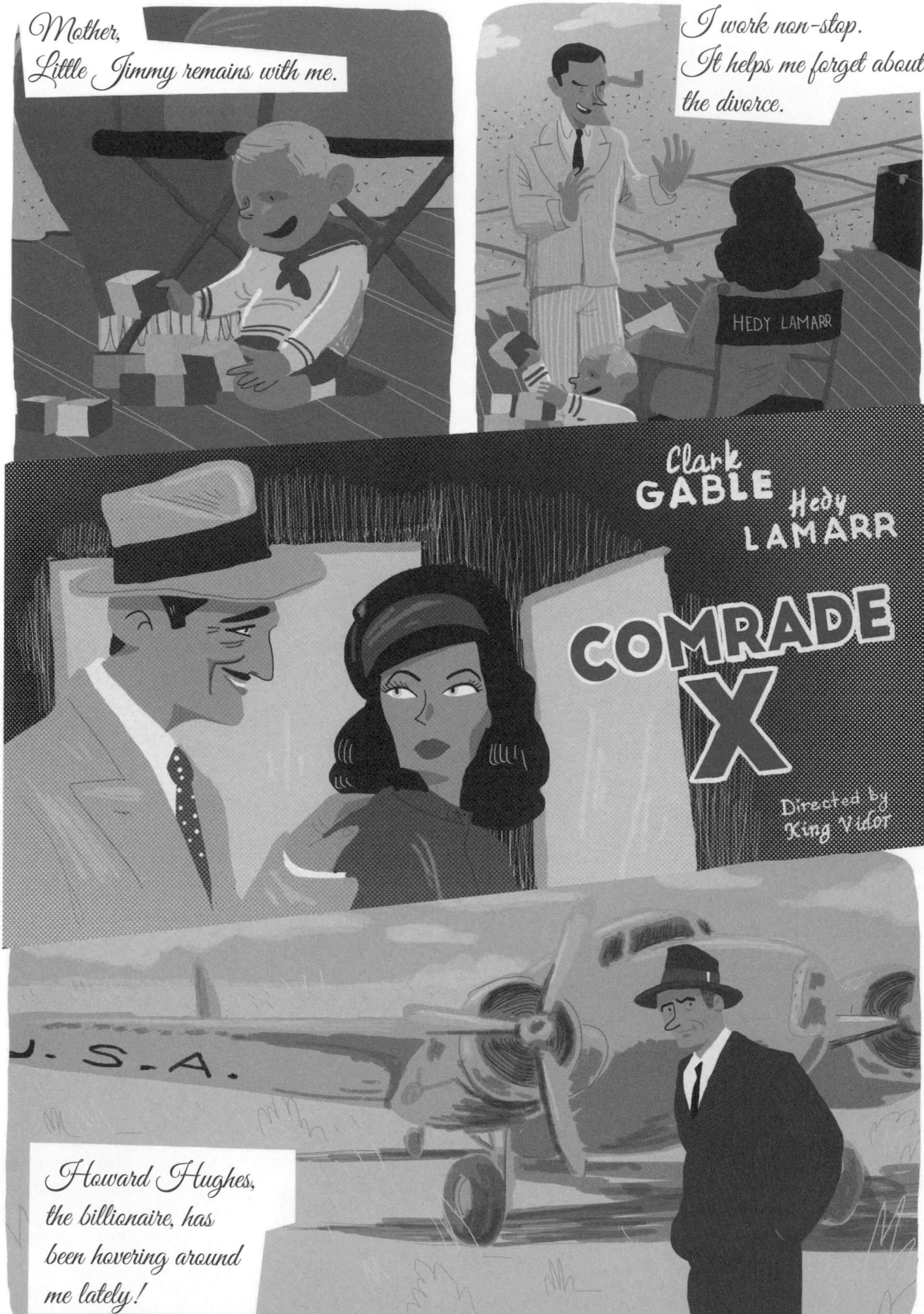
Mother,
Little Jimmy remains with me.
I work non-stop.
It helps me forget about
the divorce.
HEDY LAMARR
Clark
GABLE
Hedy
LAMARR
COMRADE
X
Directed by
King Vidor
U.S.A.
Howard Hughes,
the billionaire, has
been hovering around
me lately!

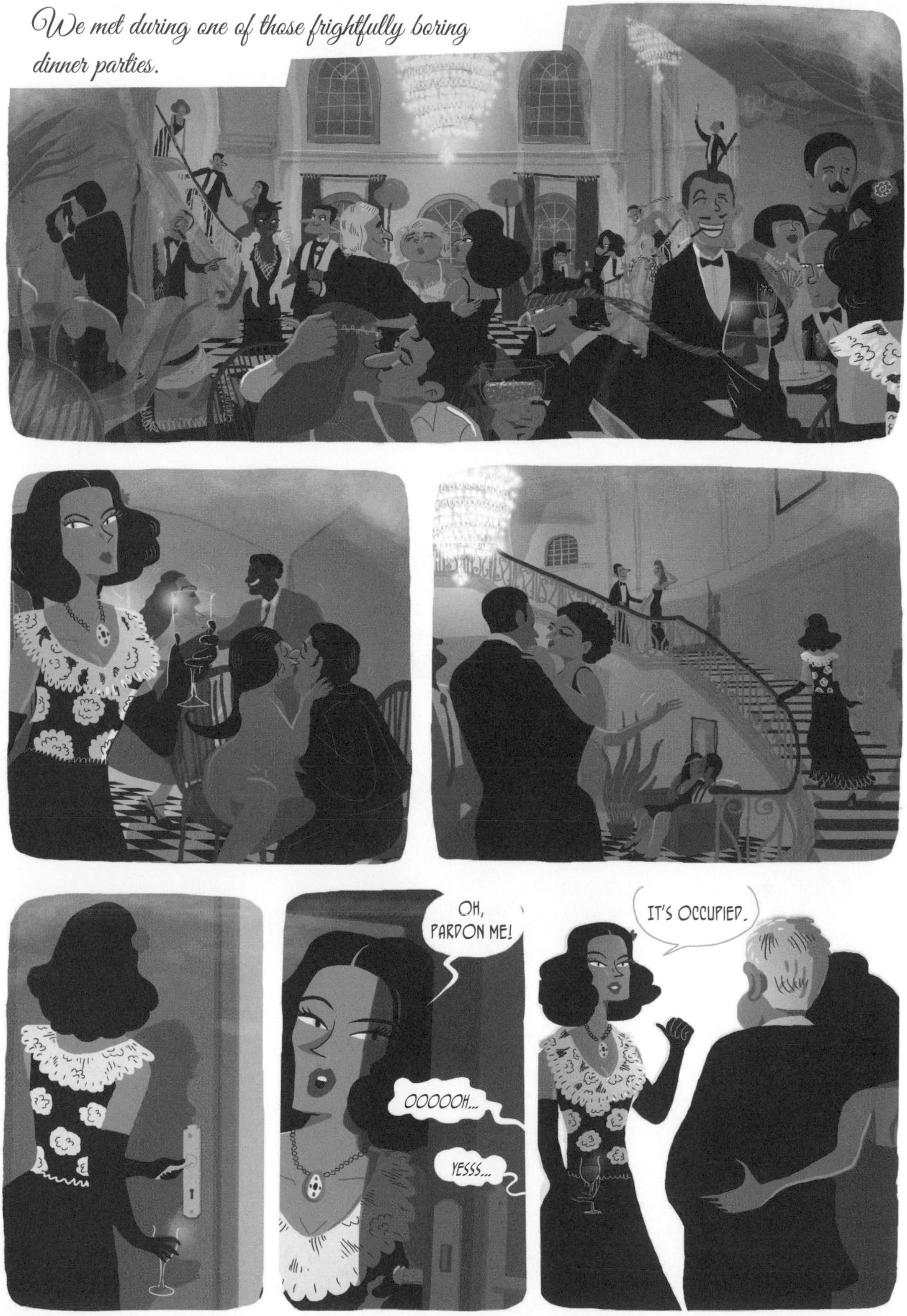
We met during one of those frightfully boring dinner parties.
OH, PARDON ME!
OOOOOH...
YESSS...
IT'S OCCUPIED.

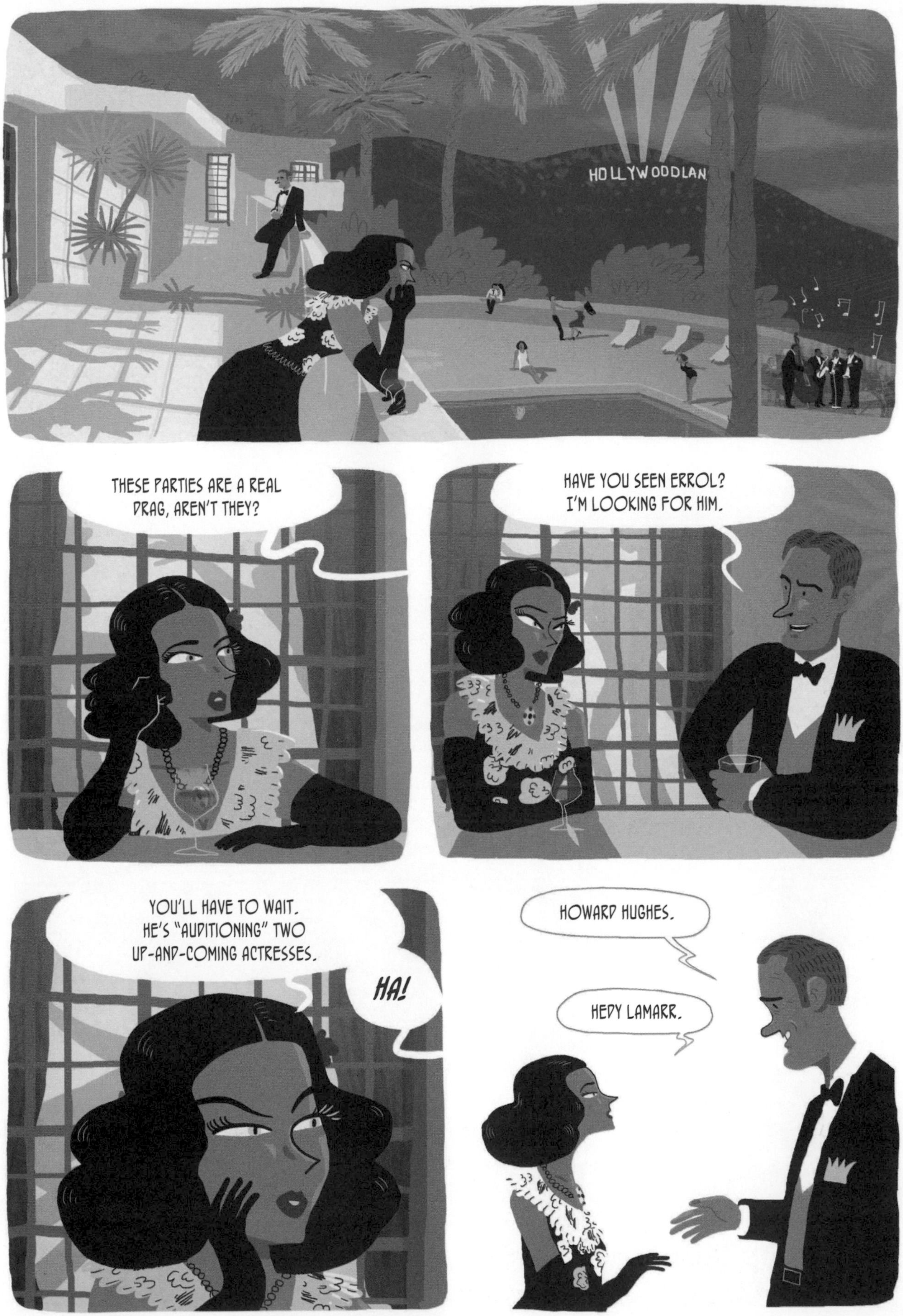
HOLLYWOODLAN
THESE PARTIES ARE A REAL DRAG, AREN'T THEY?
HAVE YOU SEEN ERROL? I'M LOOKING FOR HIM.
YOU'LL HAVE TO WAIT. HE'S "AUDITIONING" TWO UP-AND-COMING ACTRESSES.
HA!
HOWARD HUGHES.
HEDY LAMARR.

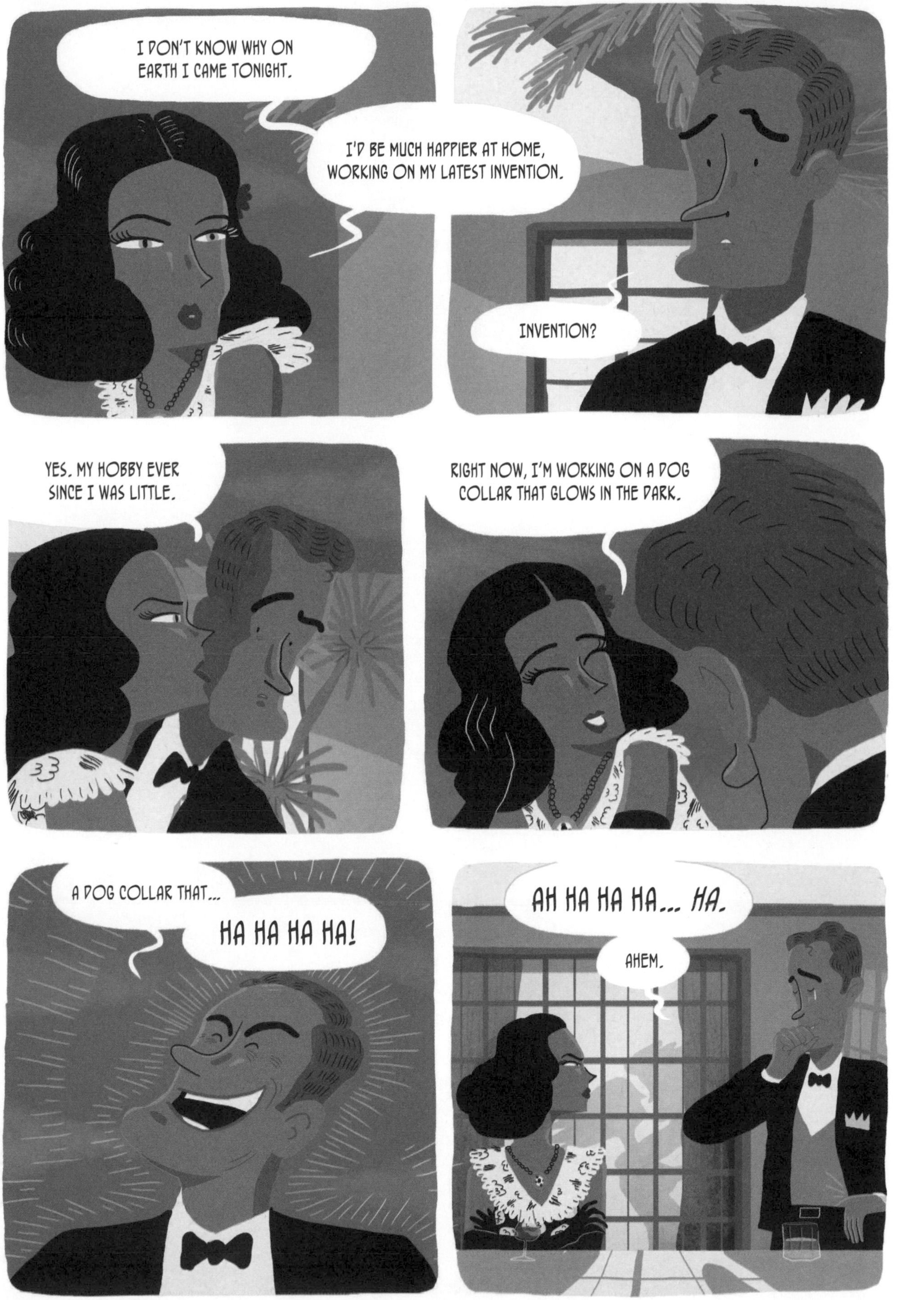
I DON'T KNOW WHY ON EARTH I CAME TONIGHT.
I'D BE MUCH HAPPIER AT HOME, WORKING ON MY LATEST INVENTION.
INVENTION?
YES. MY HOBBY EVER SINCE I WAS LITTLE.
RIGHT NOW, I'M WORKING ON A DOG COLLAR THAT GLOWS IN THE DARK.
A DOG COLLAR THAT...
HA HA HA HA!
AH HA HA HA... HA.
AHEM.

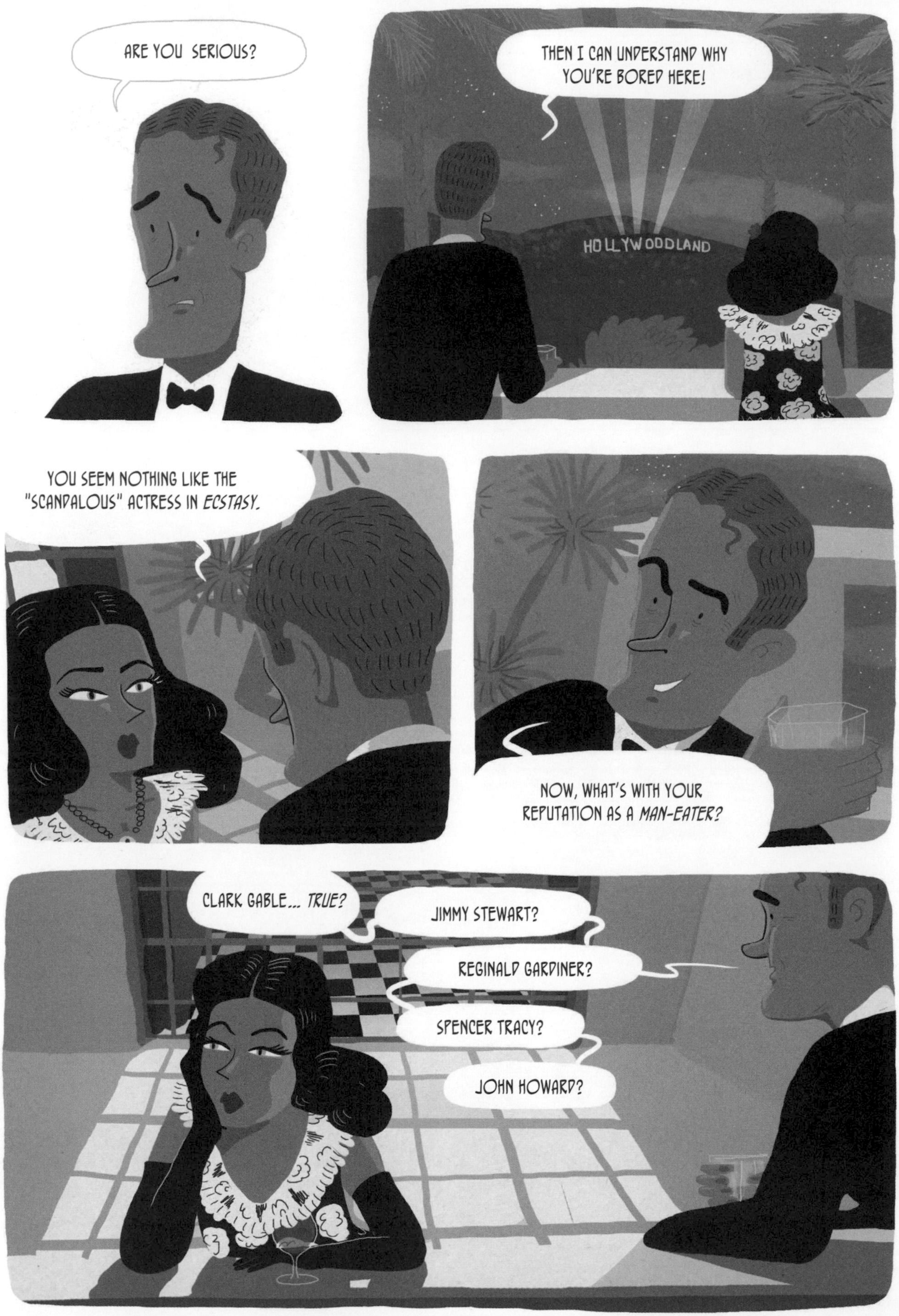
ARE YOU SERIOUS?
THEN I CAN UNDERSTAND WHY YOU'RE BORED HERE!
HOLLYWOODLAND
YOU SEEM NOTHING LIKE THE "SCANDALOUS" ACTRESS IN *ECSTASY.*
NOW, WHAT'S WITH YOUR REPUTATION AS A *MAN-EATER?*
CLARK GABLE... *TRUE?*
JIMMY STEWART?
REGINALD GARDINER?
SPENCER TRACY?
JOHN HOWARD?

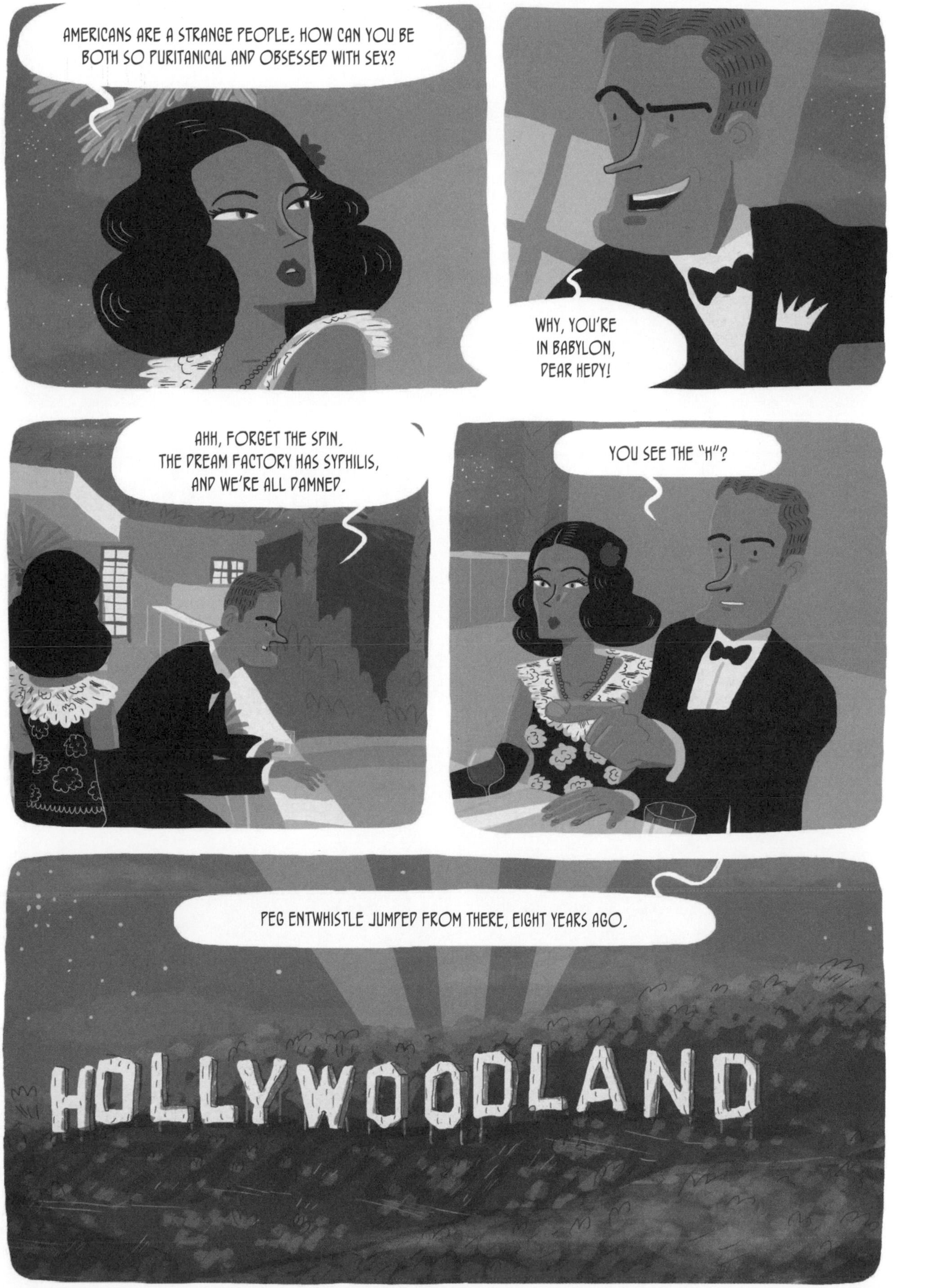
AMERICANS ARE A STRANGE PEOPLE: HOW CAN YOU BE BOTH SO PURITANICAL AND OBSESSED WITH SEX?
WHY, YOU'RE IN BABYLON, DEAR HEDY!
AHH, FORGET THE SPIN. THE DREAM FACTORY HAS SYPHILIS, AND WE'RE ALL DAMNED.
YOU SEE THE "H"?
PEG ENTWHISTLE JUMPED FROM THERE, EIGHT YEARS AGO.
HOLLYWOODLAND

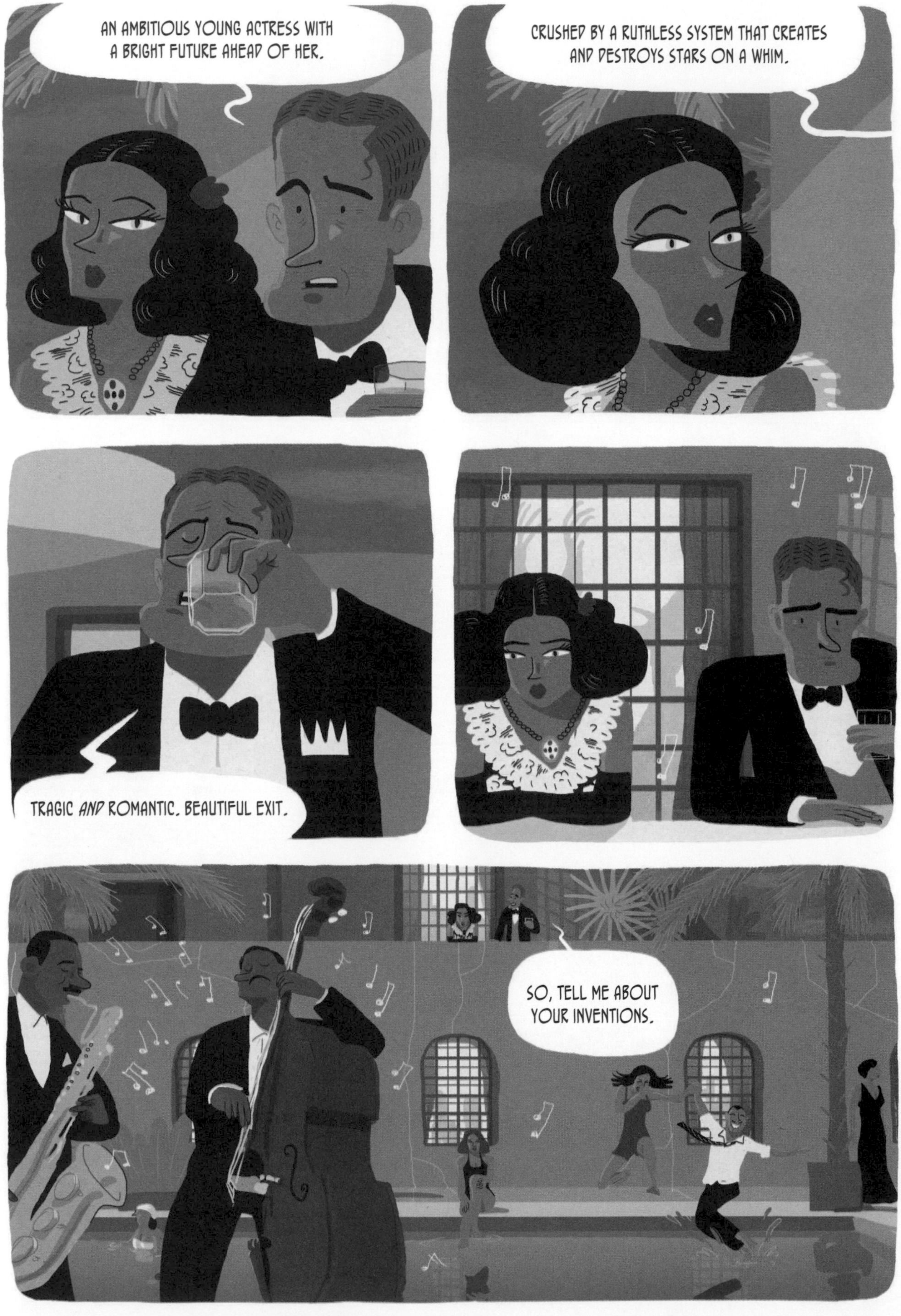
AN AMBITIOUS YOUNG ACTRESS WITH A BRIGHT FUTURE AHEAD OF HER.
CRUSHED BY A RUTHLESS SYSTEM THAT CREATES AND DESTROYS STARS ON A WHIM.
TRAGIC *AND* ROMANTIC. BEAUTIFUL EXIT.
SO, TELL ME ABOUT YOUR INVENTIONS.

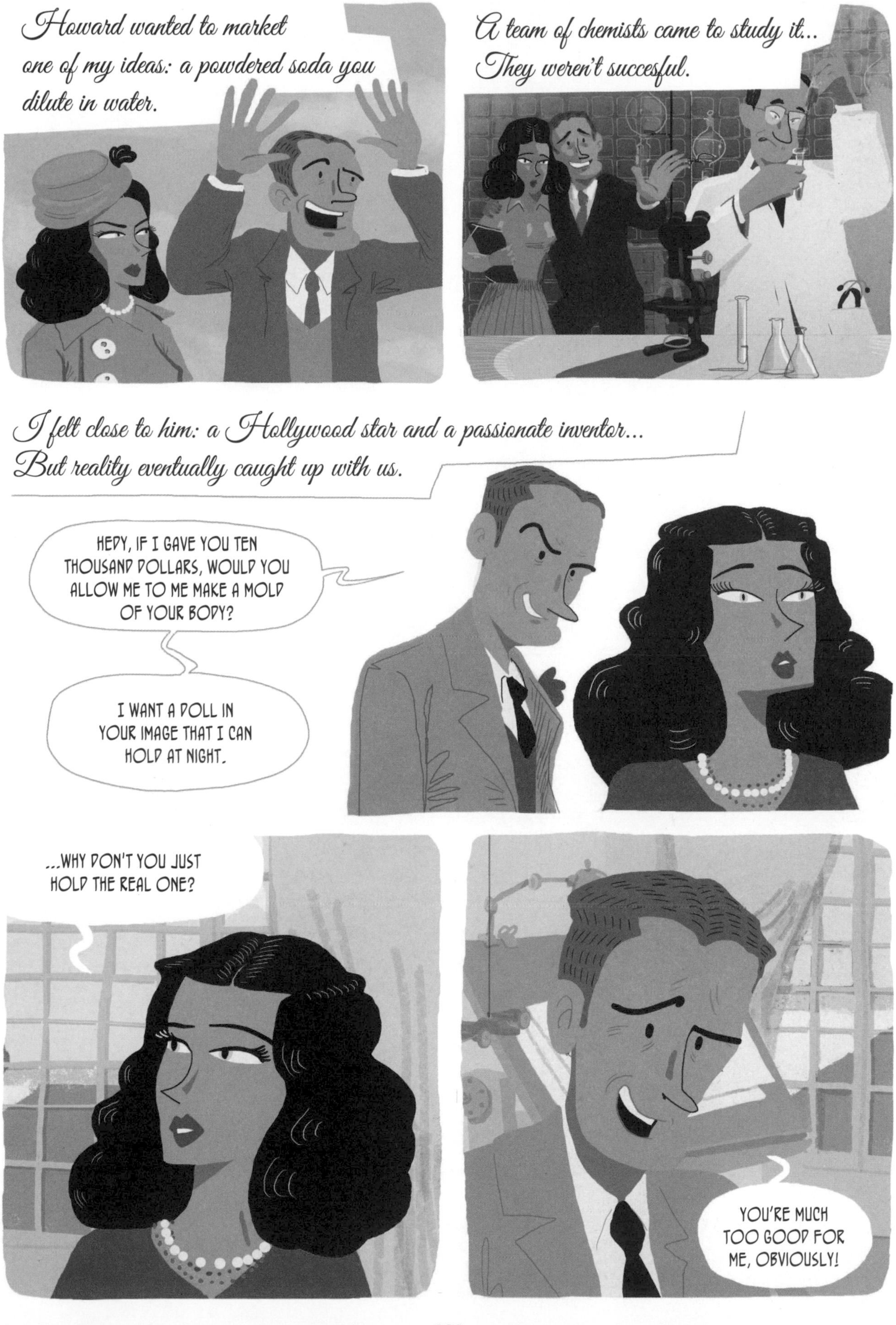
Howard wanted to market one of my ideas: a powdered soda you dilute in water.
A team of chemists came to study it... They weren't succesful.
I felt close to him: a Hollywood star and a passionate inventor... But reality eventually caught up with us.
HEDY, IF I GAVE YOU TEN THOUSAND DOLLARS, WOULD YOU ALLOW ME TO ME MAKE A MOLD OF YOUR BODY?
I WANT A DOLL IN YOUR IMAGE THAT I CAN HOLD AT NIGHT.
...WHY DON'T YOU JUST HOLD THE REAL ONE?
YOU'RE MUCH TOO GOOD FOR ME, OBVIOUSLY!

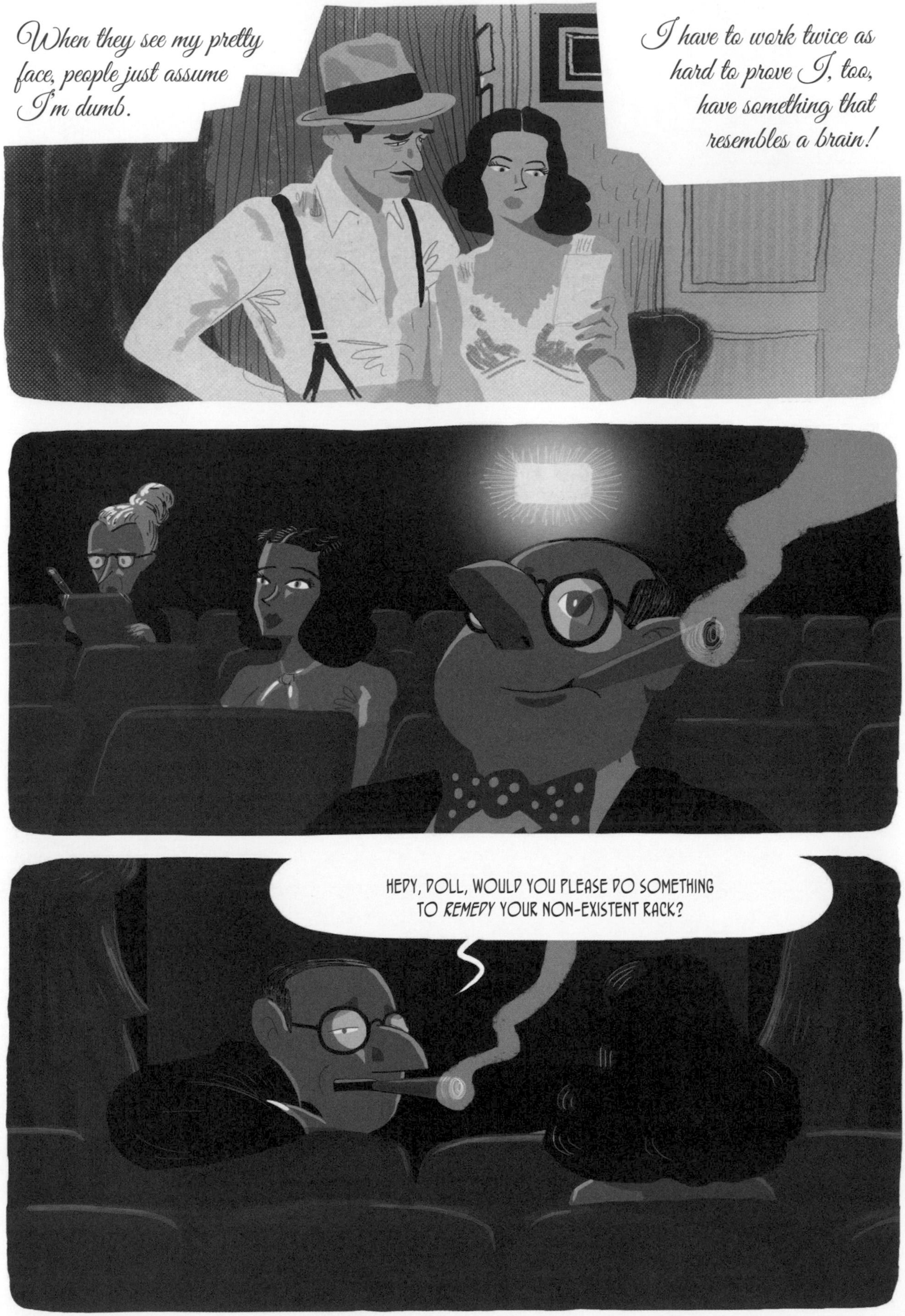
When they see my pretty face, people just assume I'm dumb.
I have to work twice as hard to prove I, too, have something that resembles a brain!
HEDY, DOLL, WOULD YOU PLEASE DO SOMETHING TO *REMEDY* YOUR NON-EXISTENT RACK?

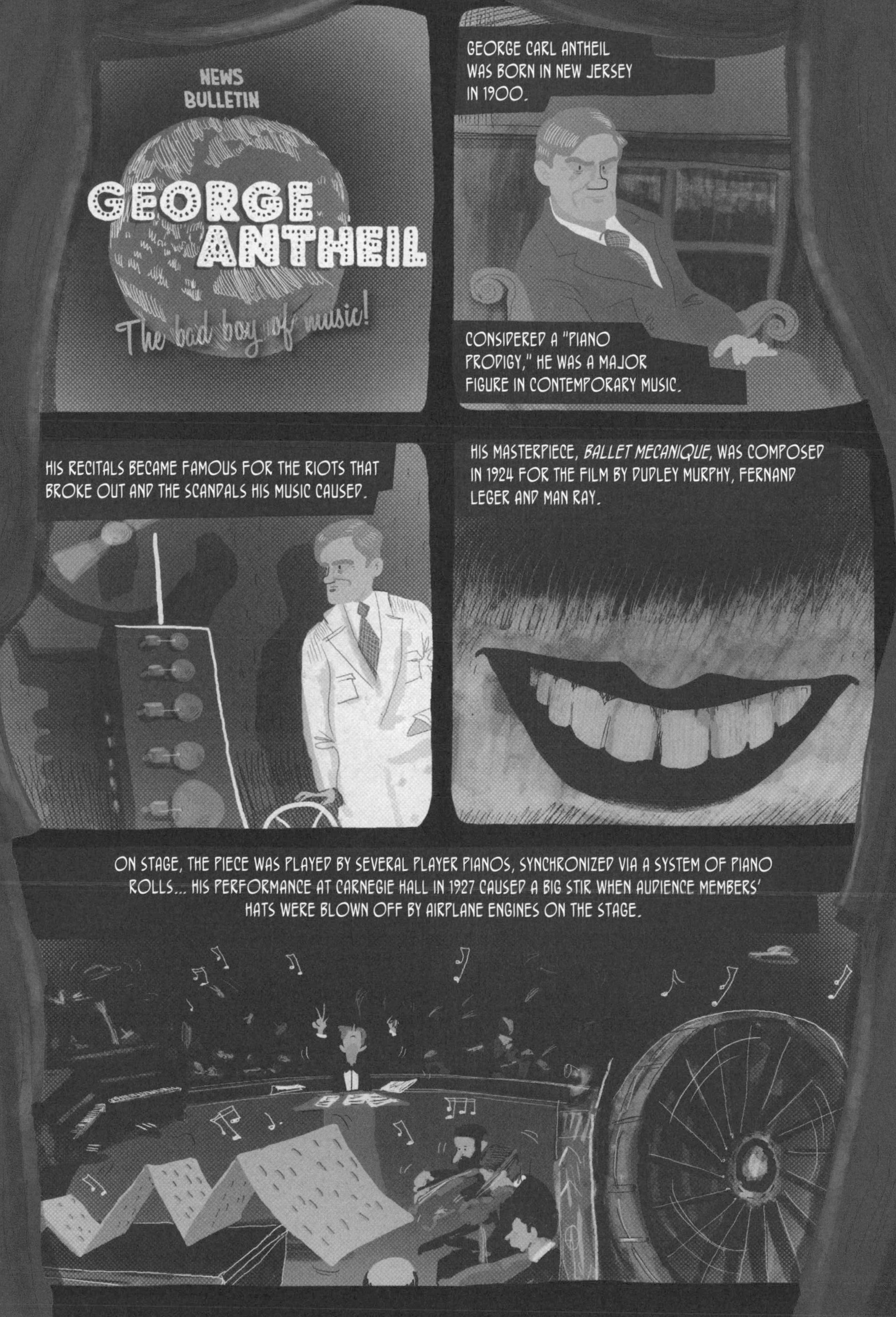

GEORGE ANTHEIL

The bad boy of music!

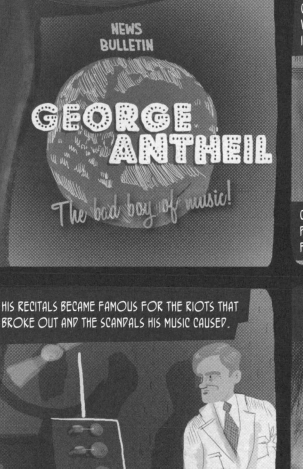

GEORGE CARL ANTHEIL WAS BORN IN NEW JERSEY IN 1900.

CONSIDERED A "PIANO PRODIGY," HE WAS A MAJOR FIGURE IN CONTEMPORARY MUSIC.

HIS RECITALS BECAME FAMOUS FOR THE RIOTS THAT BROKE OUT AND THE SCANDALS HIS MUSIC CAUSED.

HIS MASTERPIECE, *BALLET MECANIQUE*, WAS COMPOSED IN 1924 FOR THE FILM BY DUDLEY MURPHY, FERNAND LEGER AND MAN RAY.

ON STAGE, THE PIECE WAS PLAYED BY SEVERAL PLAYER PIANOS, SYNCHRONIZED VIA A SYSTEM OF PIANO ROLLS... HIS PERFORMANCE AT CARNEGIE HALL IN 1927 CAUSED A BIG STIR WHEN AUDIENCE MEMBERS' HATS WERE BLOWN OFF BY AIRPLANE ENGINES ON THE STAGE.

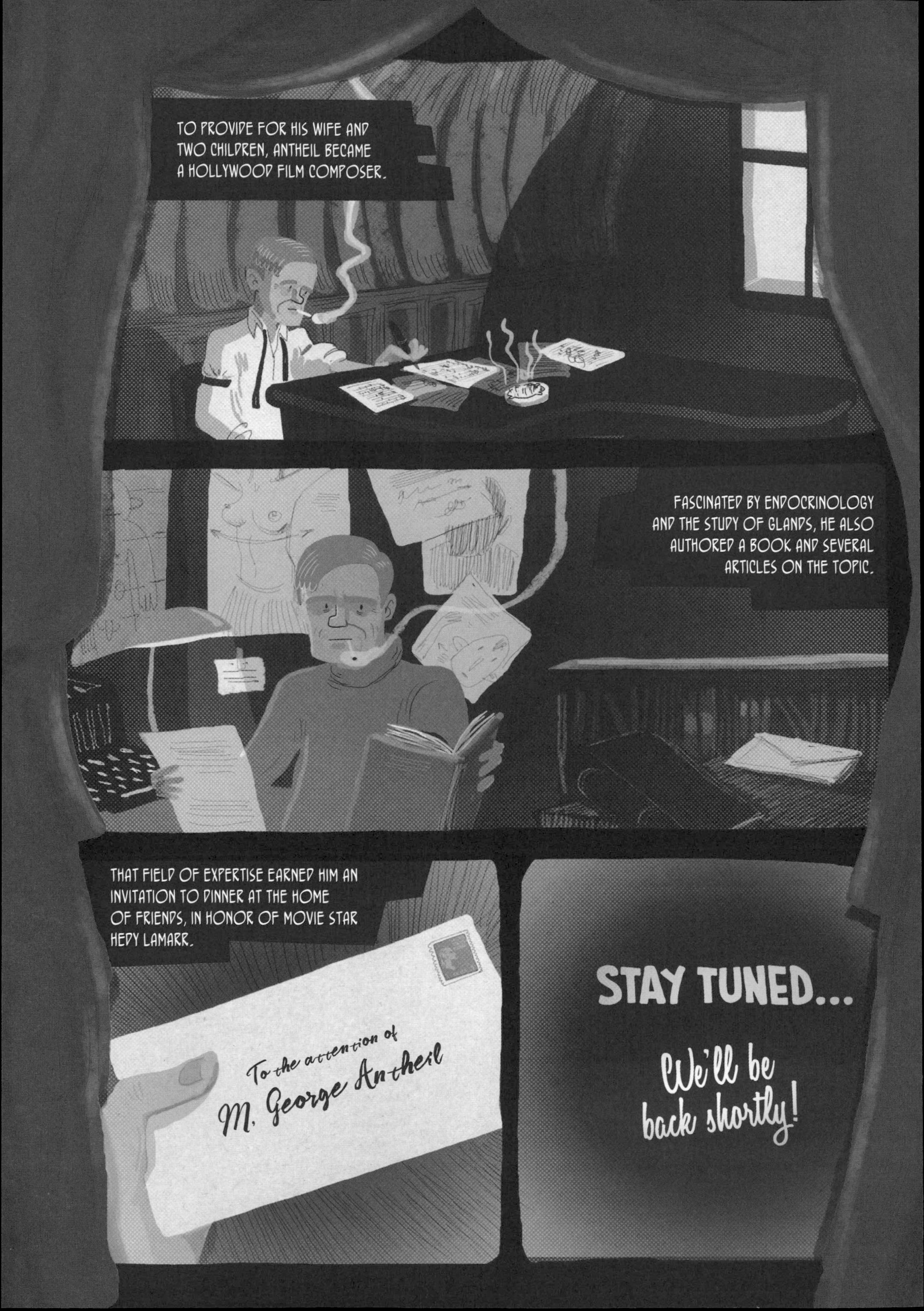
TO PROVIDE FOR HIS WIFE AND TWO CHILDREN, ANTHEIL BECAME A HOLLYWOOD FILM COMPOSER.
FASCINATED BY ENDOCRINOLOGY AND THE STUDY OF GLANDS, HE ALSO AUTHORED A BOOK AND SEVERAL ARTICLES ON THE TOPIC.
THAT FIELD OF EXPERTISE EARNED HIM AN INVITATION TO DINNER AT THE HOME OF FRIENDS, IN HONOR OF MOVIE STAR HEDY LAMARR.
To the attention of
M. George Antheil
STAY TUNED...
We'll be back shortly!

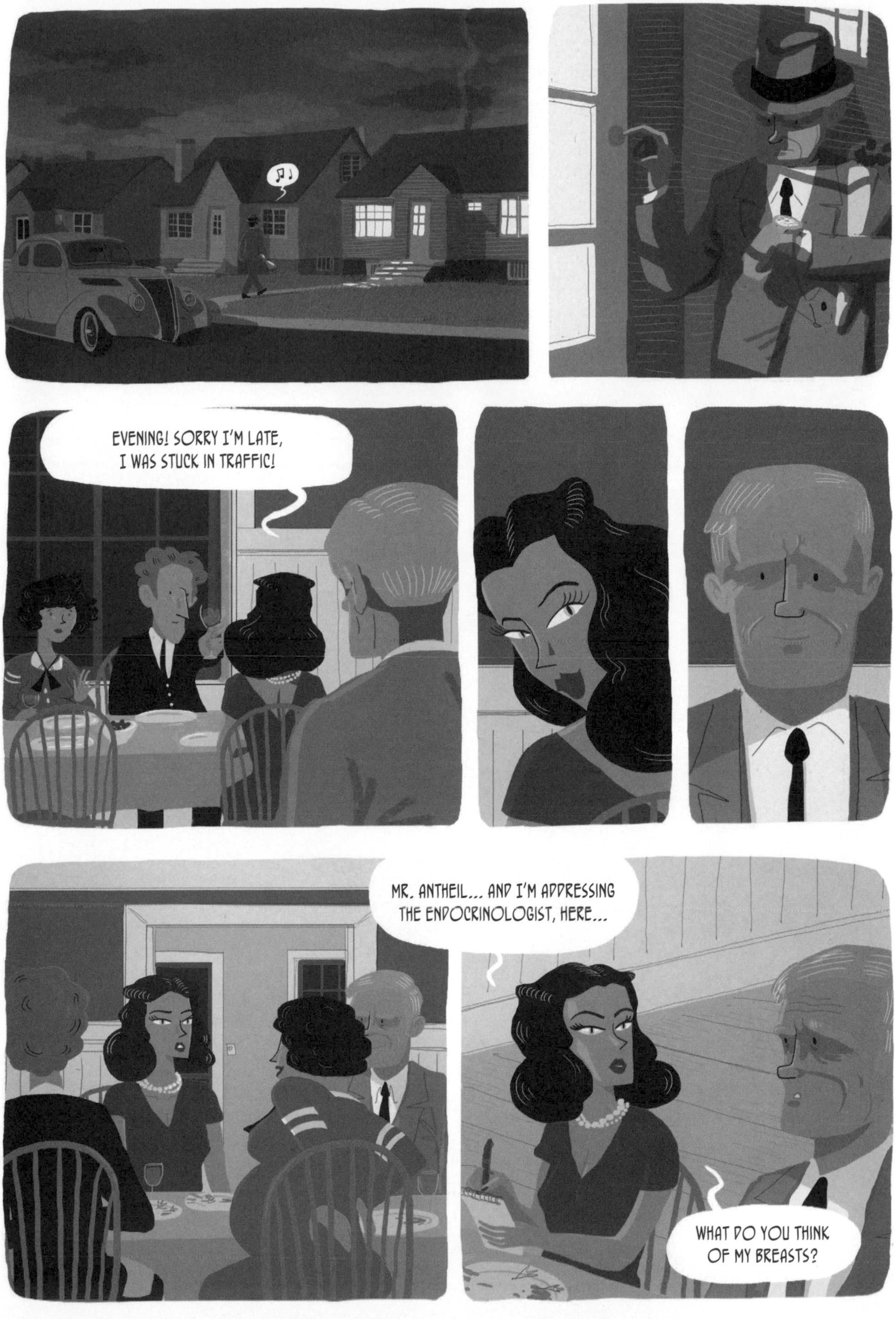
EVENING! SORRY I'M LATE, I WAS STUCK IN TRAFFIC!
MR. ANTHEIL... AND I'M ADDRESSING THE ENDOCRINOLOGIST, HERE...
WHAT DO YOU THINK OF MY BREASTS?

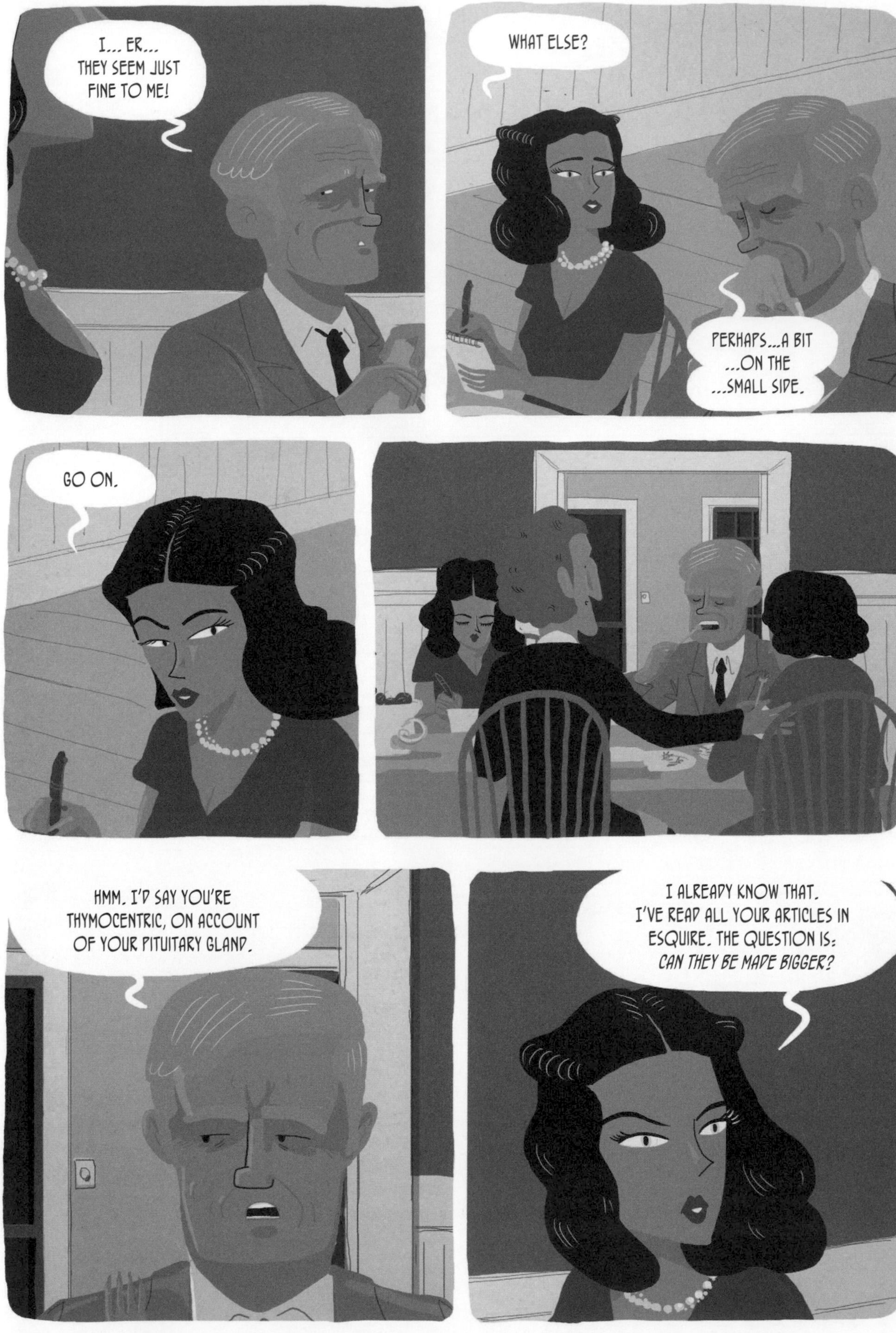
I... ER... THEY SEEM JUST FINE TO ME!
WHAT ELSE?
PERHAPS...A BIT ...ON THE ...SMALL SIDE.
GO ON.
HMM. I'D SAY YOU'RE THYMOCENTRIC, ON ACCOUNT OF YOUR PITUITARY GLAND.
I ALREADY KNOW THAT. I'VE READ ALL YOUR ARTICLES IN ESQUIRE. THE QUESTION IS: *CAN THEY BE MADE BIGGER?*

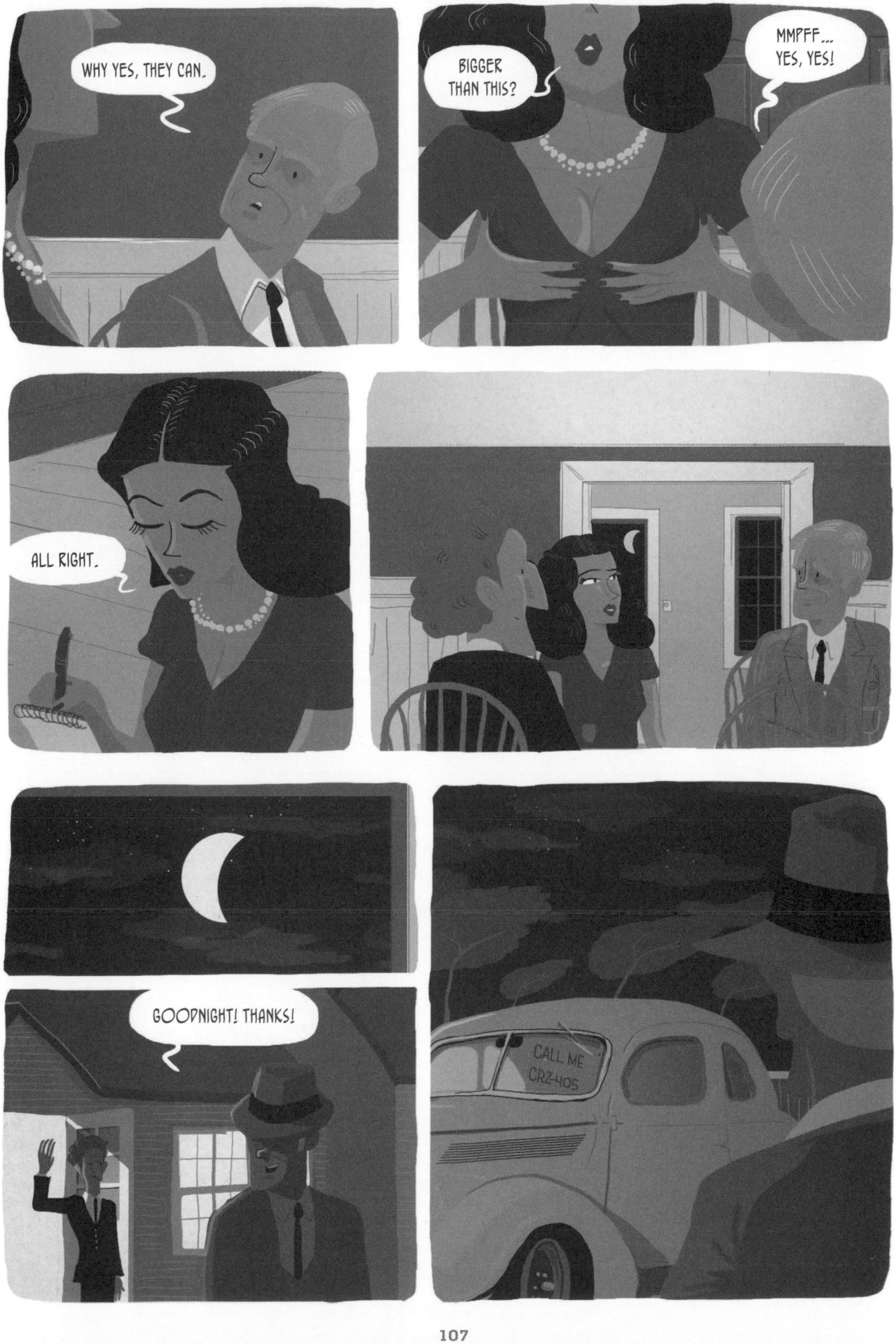
WHY YES, THEY CAN.
BIGGER THAN THIS?
MMPFF... YES, YES!
ALL RIGHT.
GOODNIGHT! THANKS!
CALL ME CRZ-405

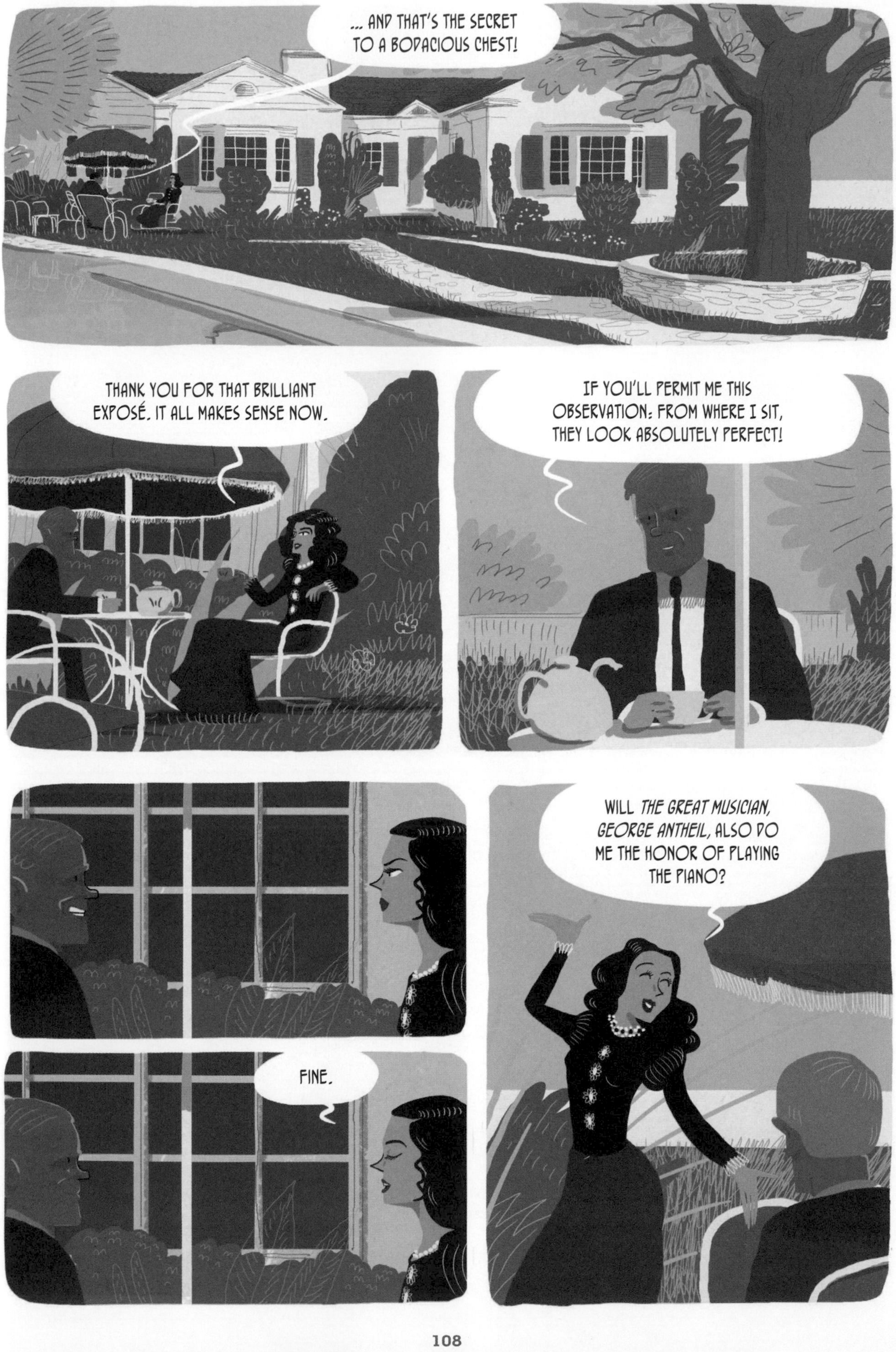
... AND THAT'S THE SECRET TO A BODACIOUS CHEST!
THANK YOU FOR THAT BRILLIANT EXPOSÉ. IT ALL MAKES SENSE NOW.
IF YOU'LL PERMIT ME THIS OBSERVATION: FROM WHERE I SIT, THEY LOOK ABSOLUTELY PERFECT!
WILL *THE GREAT MUSICIAN, GEORGE ANTHEIL,* ALSO DO ME THE HONOR OF PLAYING THE PIANO?
FINE.

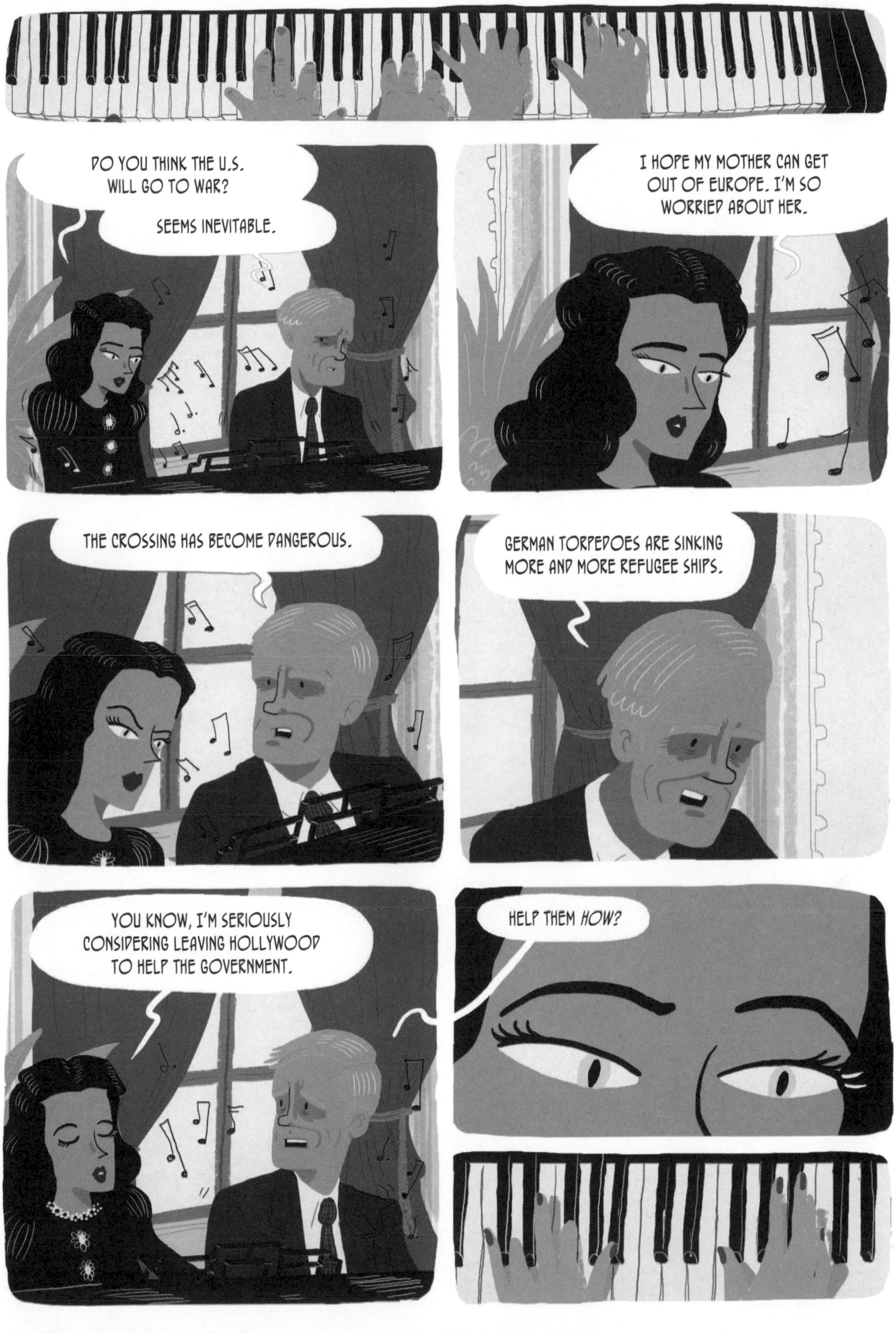

DO YOU THINK THE U.S. WILL GO TO WAR?
SEEMS INEVITABLE.
I HOPE MY MOTHER CAN GET OUT OF EUROPE. I'M SO WORRIED ABOUT HER.
THE CROSSING HAS BECOME DANGEROUS.
GERMAN TORPEDOES ARE SINKING MORE AND MORE REFUGEE SHIPS.
YOU KNOW, I'M SERIOUSLY CONSIDERING LEAVING HOLLYWOOD TO HELP THE GOVERNMENT.
HELP THEM *HOW?*

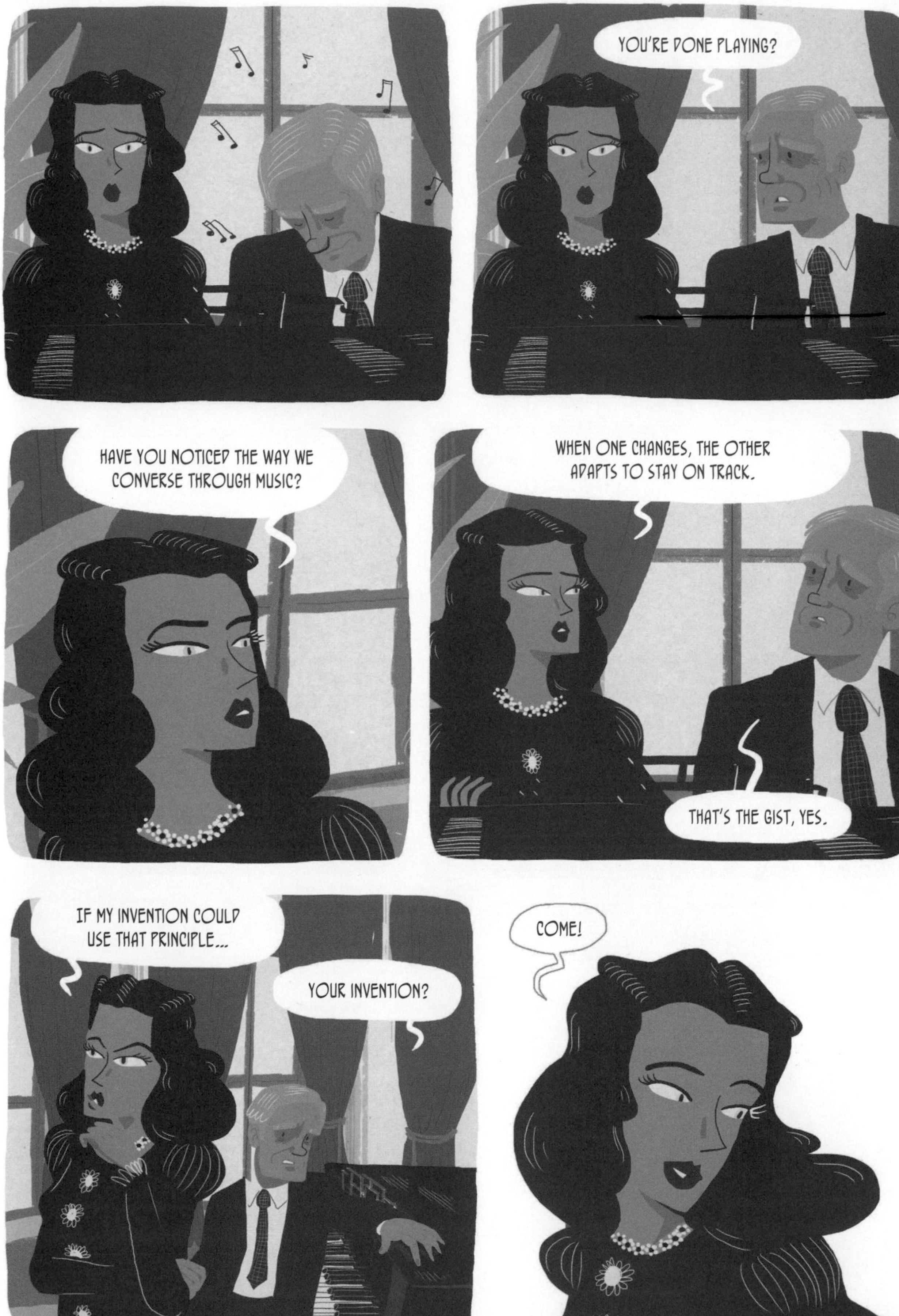
YOU'RE DONE PLAYING?
HAVE YOU NOTICED THE WAY WE CONVERSE THROUGH MUSIC?
WHEN ONE CHANGES, THE OTHER ADAPTS TO STAY ON TRACK.
THAT'S THE GIST, YES.
IF MY INVENTION COULD USE THAT PRINCIPLE...
YOUR INVENTION?
COME!

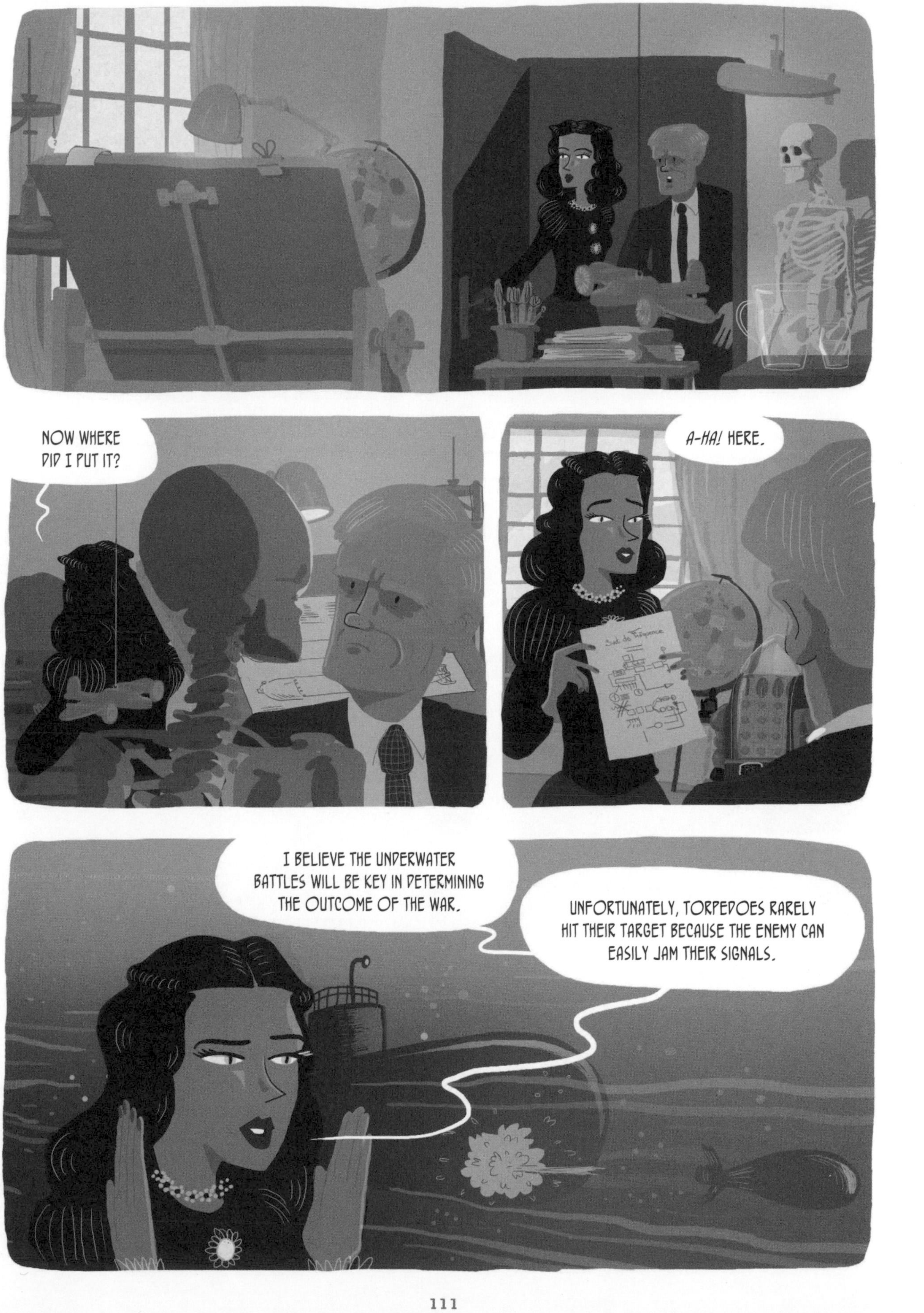
NOW WHERE DID I PUT IT?
A-HA! HERE.
I BELIEVE THE UNDERWATER BATTLES WILL BE KEY IN DETERMINING THE OUTCOME OF THE WAR.
UNFORTUNATELY, TORPEDOES RARELY HIT THEIR TARGET BECAUSE THE ENEMY CAN EASILY JAM THEIR SIGNALS.

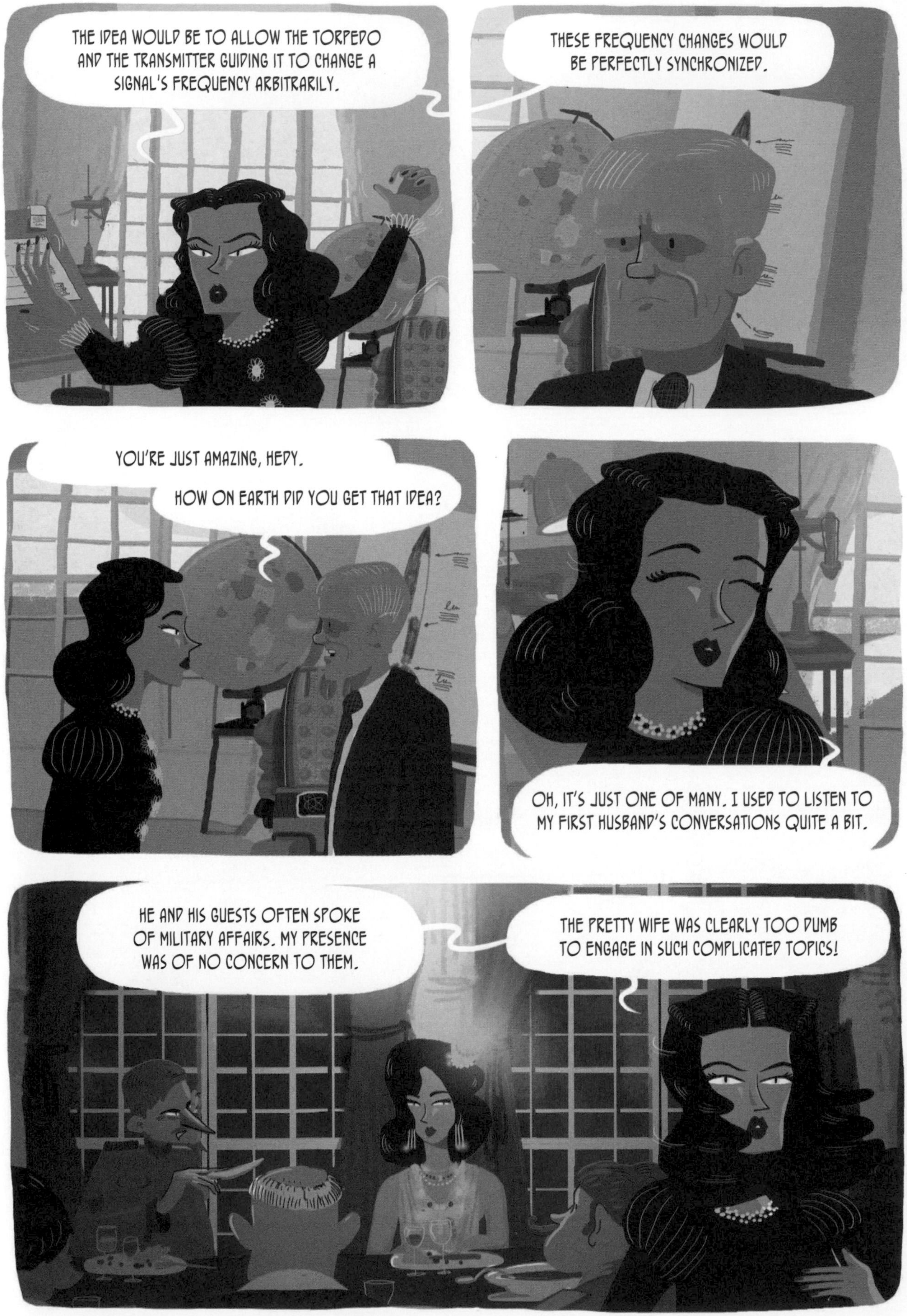
THE IDEA WOULD BE TO ALLOW THE TORPEDO AND THE TRANSMITTER GUIDING IT TO CHANGE A SIGNAL'S FREQUENCY ARBITRARILY.
THESE FREQUENCY CHANGES WOULD BE PERFECTLY SYNCHRONIZED.
YOU'RE JUST AMAZING, HEDY.
HOW ON EARTH DID YOU GET THAT IDEA?
OH, IT'S JUST ONE OF MANY. I USED TO LISTEN TO MY FIRST HUSBAND'S CONVERSATIONS QUITE A BIT.
HE AND HIS GUESTS OFTEN SPOKE OF MILITARY AFFAIRS. MY PRESENCE WAS OF NO CONCERN TO THEM.
THE PRETTY WIFE WAS CLEARLY TOO DUMB TO ENGAGE IN SUCH COMPLICATED TOPICS!

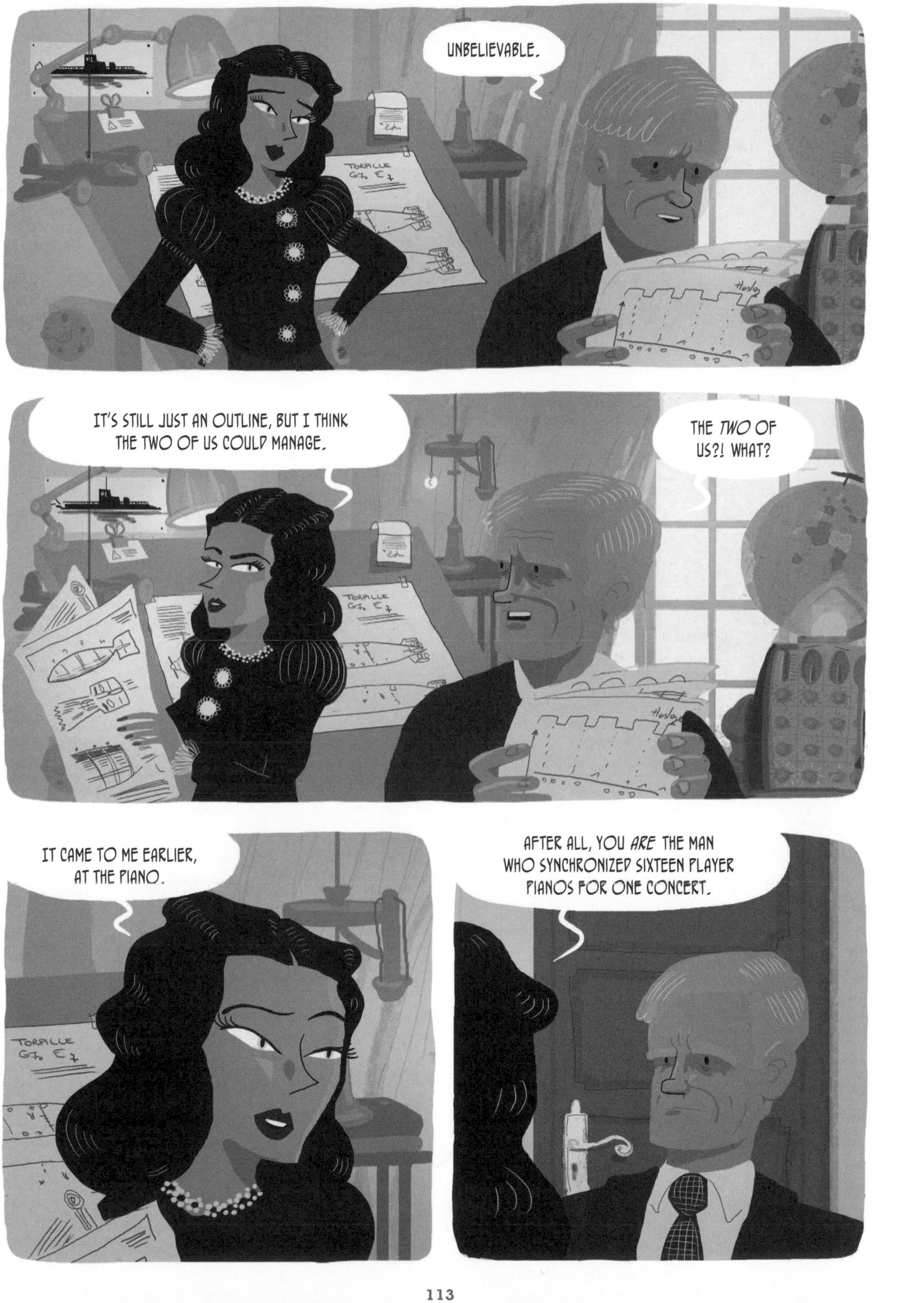
UNBELIEVABLE.
IT'S STILL JUST AN OUTLINE, BUT I THINK THE TWO OF US COULD MANAGE.
THE *TWO* OF US?! WHAT?
IT CAME TO ME EARLIER, AT THE PIANO.
AFTER ALL, YOU *ARE* THE MAN WHO SYNCHRONIZED SIXTEEN PLAYER PIANOS FOR ONE CONCERT.

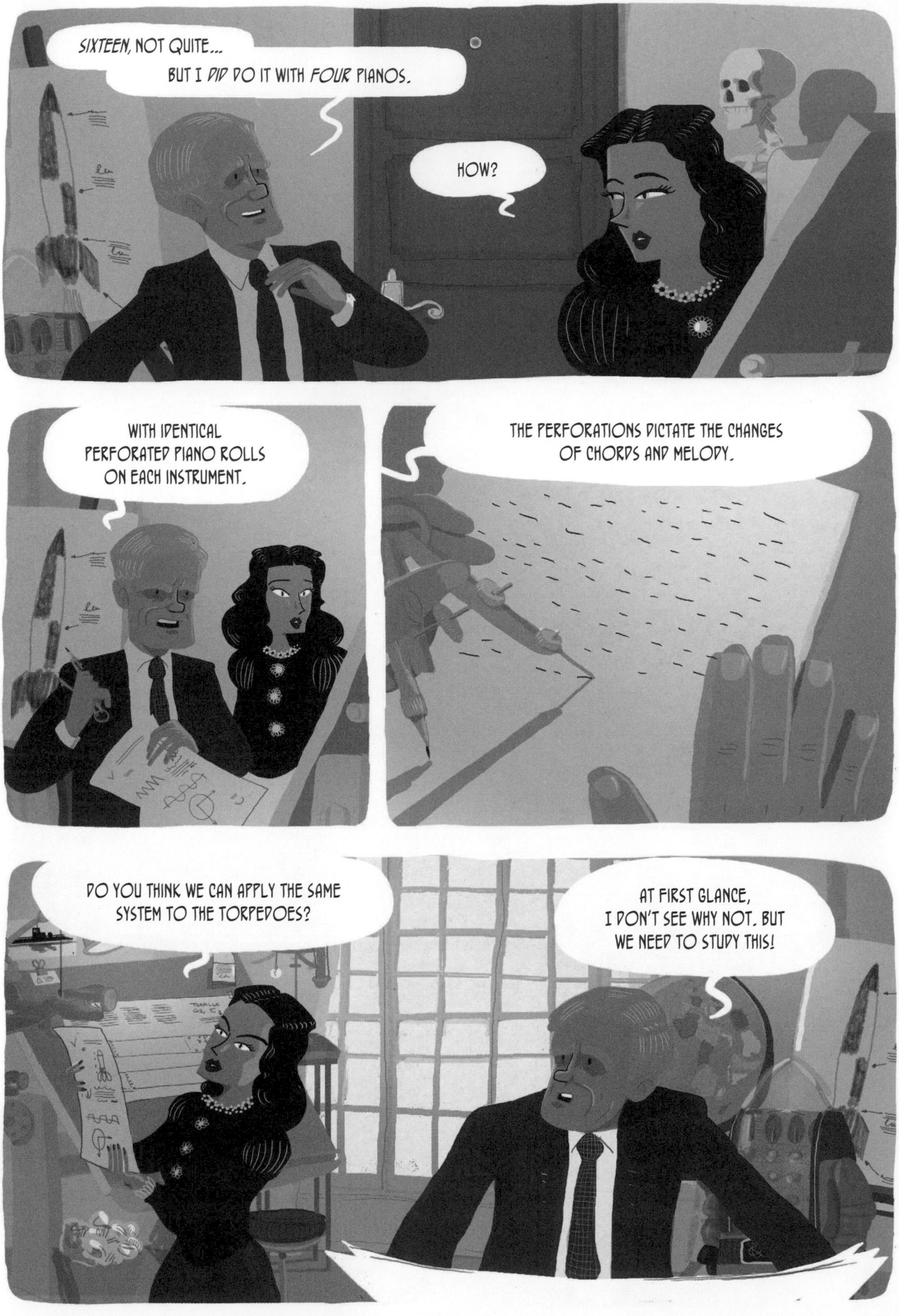
SIXTEEN, NOT QUITE... BUT I DID DO IT WITH FOUR PIANOS.
HOW?
WITH IDENTICAL PERFORATED PIANO ROLLS ON EACH INSTRUMENT.
THE PERFORATIONS DICTATE THE CHANGES OF CHORDS AND MELODY.
DO YOU THINK WE CAN APPLY THE SAME SYSTEM TO THE TORPEDOES?
AT FIRST GLANCE, I DON'T SEE WHY NOT. BUT WE NEED TO STUDY THIS!

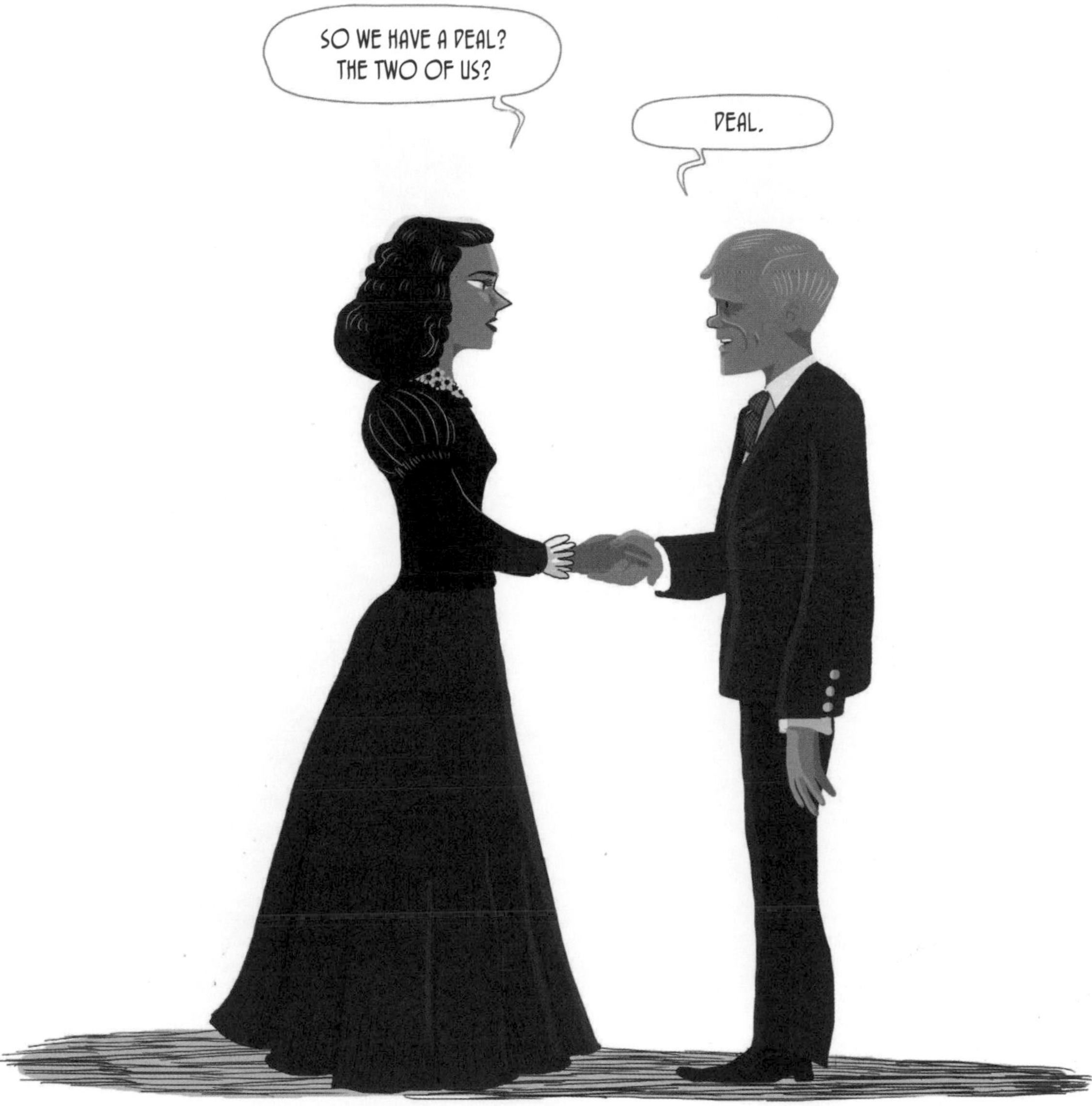
SO WE HAVE A DEAL?
THE TWO OF US?
DEAL.

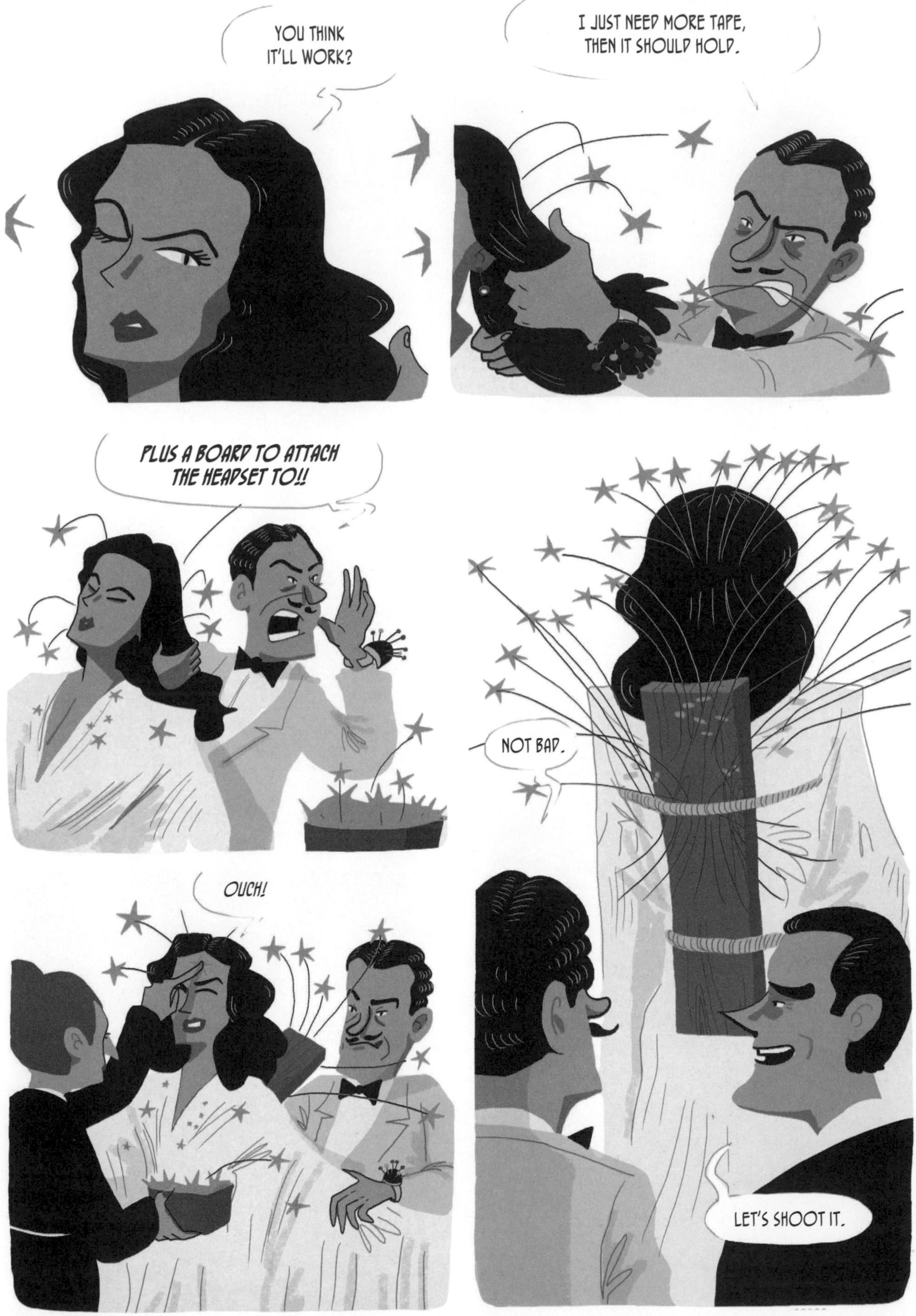
YOU THINK IT'LL WORK?
I JUST NEED MORE TAPE, THEN IT SHOULD HOLD.
PLUS A BOARD TO ATTACH THE HEADSET TO!!
OUCH!
NOT BAD.
LET'S SHOOT IT.

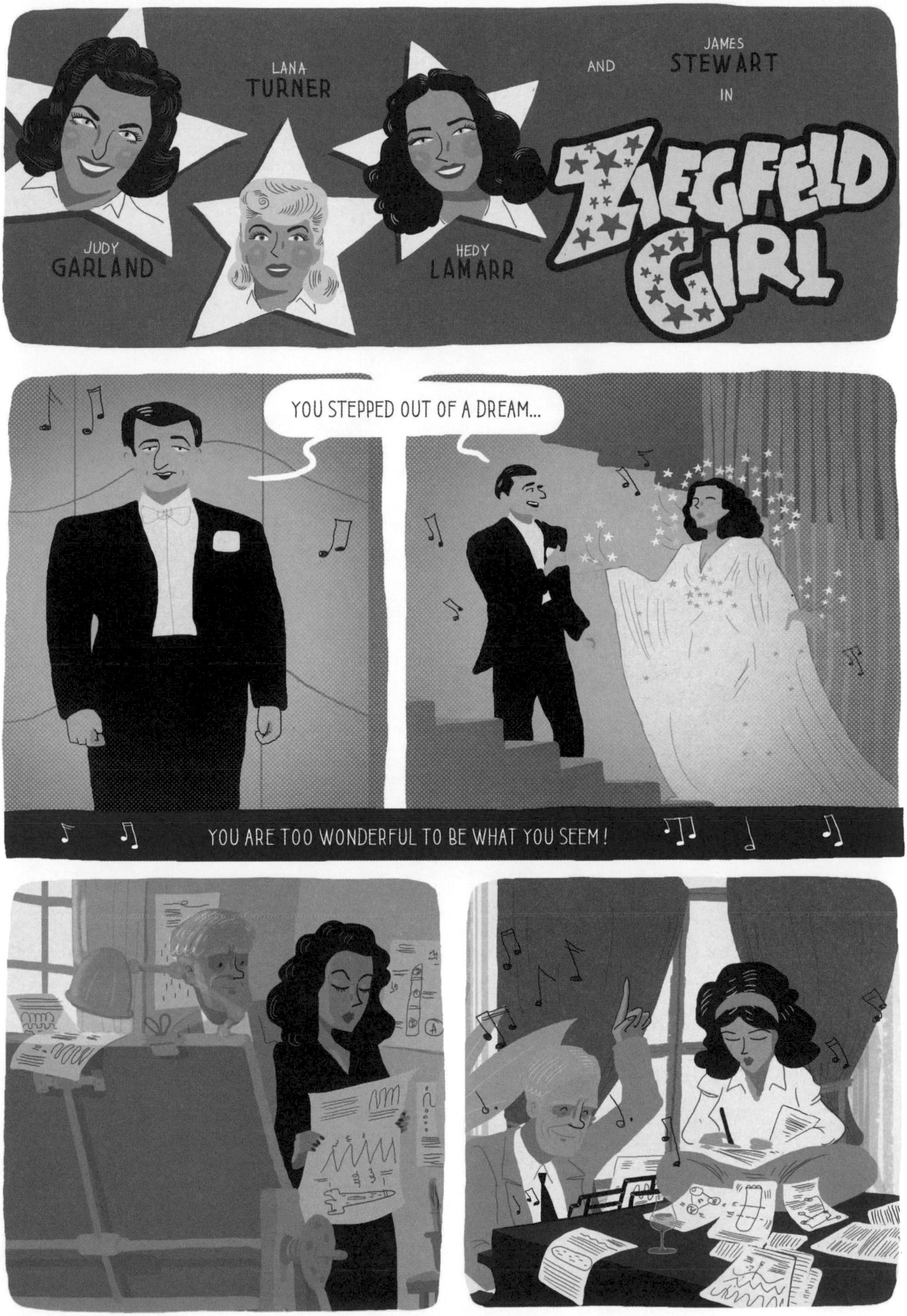
JUDY
GARLAND
LANA
TURNER
HEDY
LAMARR
AND
JAMES
STEWART
IN
ZIEGFELD
GIRL
YOU STEPPED OUT OF A DREAM...
YOU ARE TOO WONDERFUL TO BE WHAT YOU SEEM!

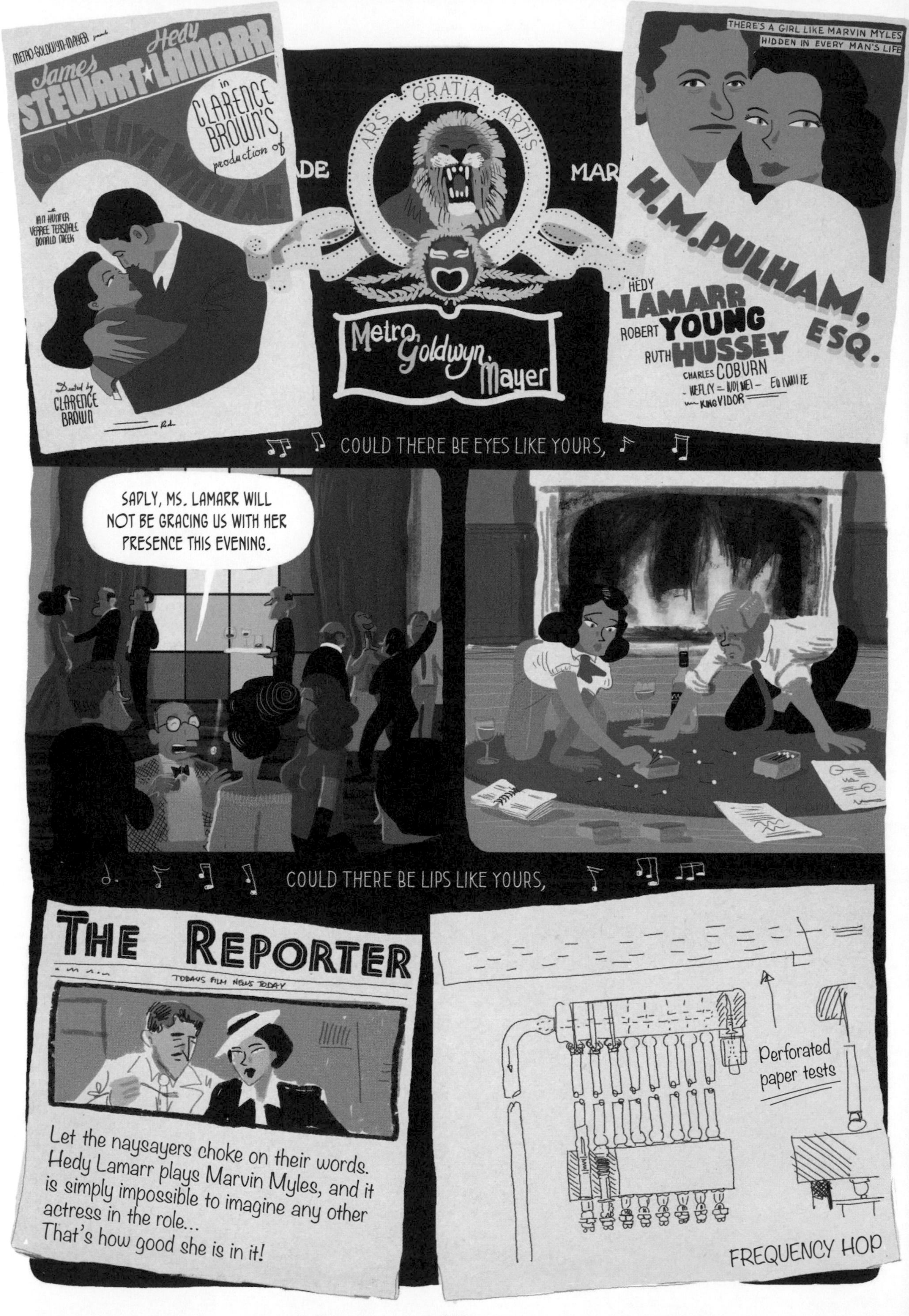
METRO-GOLDWYN-MAYER presents
James STEWART ★ Hedy LAMARR
in CLARENCE BROWN'S production of
COME LIVE WITH ME
IAN HUNTER
VERREE TEASDALE
DONALD MEEK
Directed by CLARENCE BROWN
ARS GRATIA ARTIS
Metro Goldwyn Mayer
THERE'S A GIRL LIKE MARVIN MYLES
HIDDEN IN EVERY MAN'S LIFE
H.M. PULHAM, ESQ.
HEDY LAMARR
ROBERT YOUNG
RUTH HUSSEY
CHARLES COBURN
KING VIDOR
COULD THERE BE EYES LIKE YOURS,
SADLY, MS. LAMARR WILL NOT BE GRACING US WITH HER PRESENCE THIS EVENING.
COULD THERE BE LIPS LIKE YOURS,
THE REPORTER
TODAY'S FILM NEWS TODAY
Let the naysayers choke on their words. Hedy Lamarr plays Marvin Myles, and it is simply impossible to imagine any other actress in the role...
That's how good she is in it!
Perforated paper tests
FREQUENCY HOP

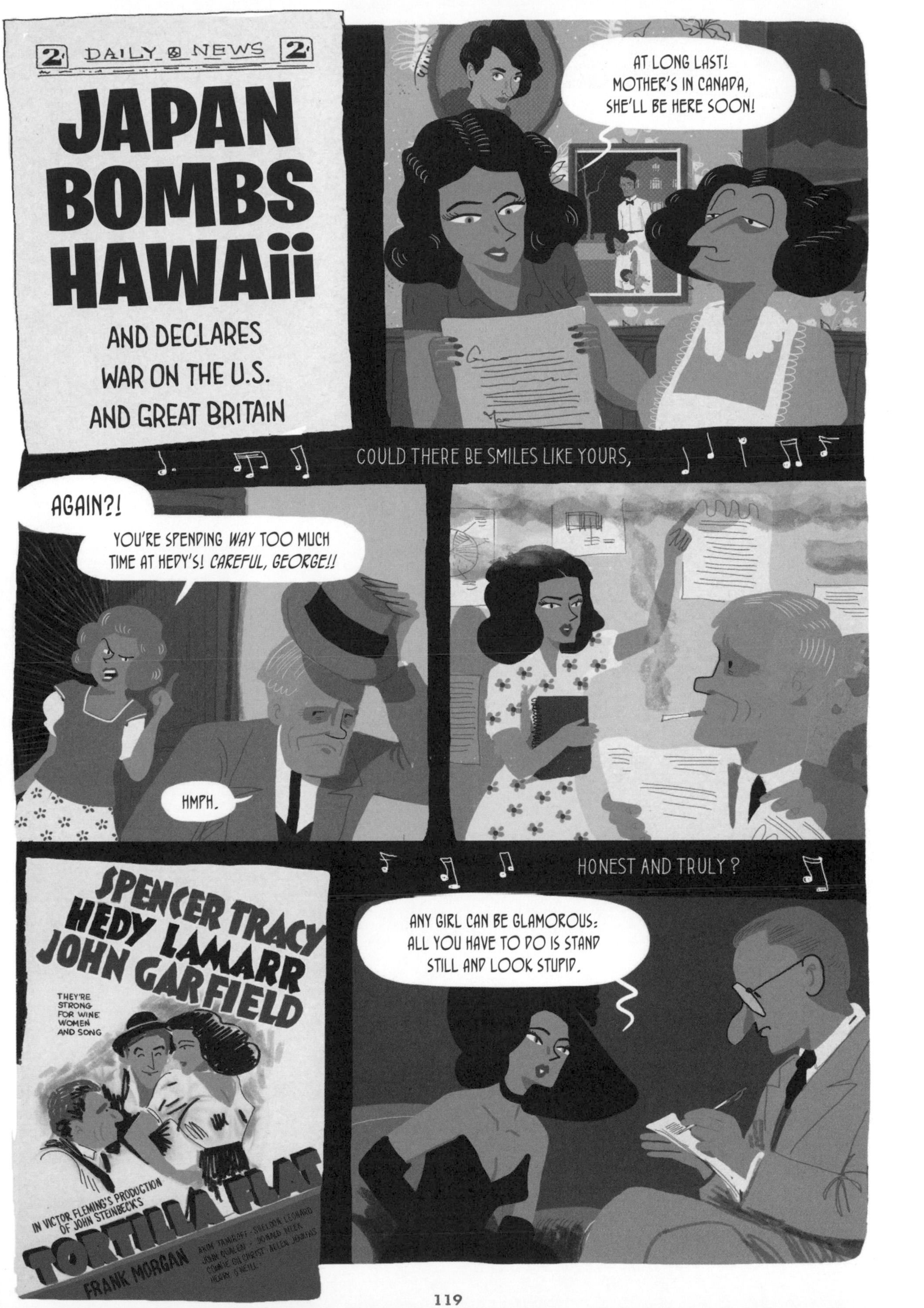

2 DAILY NEWS 2
JAPAN BOMBS HAWAii
AND DECLARES WAR ON THE U.S. AND GREAT BRITAIN
AT LONG LAST! MOTHER'S IN CANADA, SHE'LL BE HERE SOON!
COULD THERE BE SMILES LIKE YOURS,
AGAIN?!
YOU'RE SPENDING WAY TOO MUCH TIME AT HEDY'S! CAREFUL, GEORGE!!
HMPH.
HONEST AND TRULY?
SPENCER TRACY HEDY LAMARR JOHN GARFIELD
THEY'RE STRONG FOR WINE WOMEN AND SONG
IN VICTOR FLEMING'S PRODUCTION OF JOHN STEINBECK'S
TORTILLA FLAT
FRANK MORGAN
ANY GIRL CAN BE GLAMOROUS: ALL YOU HAVE TO DO IS STAND STILL AND LOOK STUPID.

Fig. 1.
OSC. 100~
OSC. 500~
VARIABLE FREQUENCY CARRIER OSCILLATOR
MODULATOR
AMPLIFIER
Fig. 2.
SELECTOR
AMPLIFIER
DETECTOR
100~ FILTER
RECTIFIER
500~ FILTER
RECTIFIER
Fig. 3.
TRANSMITTING STATION
TORPEDO
Fig. 4.
Fig. 6.
Fig. 5.
Inventors
Hedy Kiesler Markey
George Antheil
By Lyon & Lyon
Attorneys

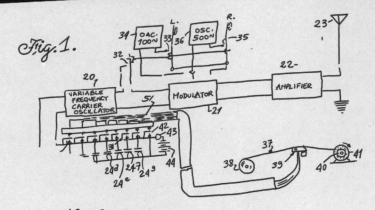

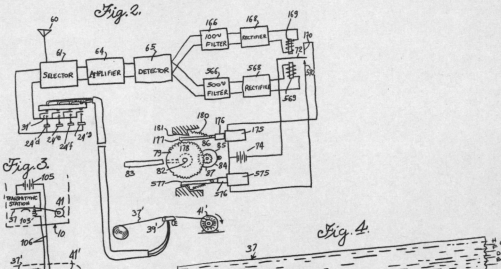

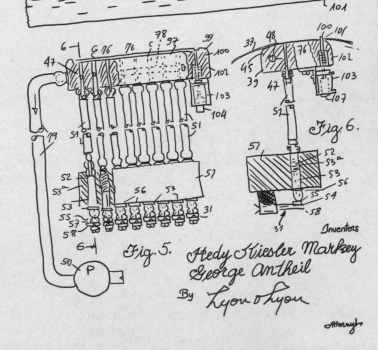

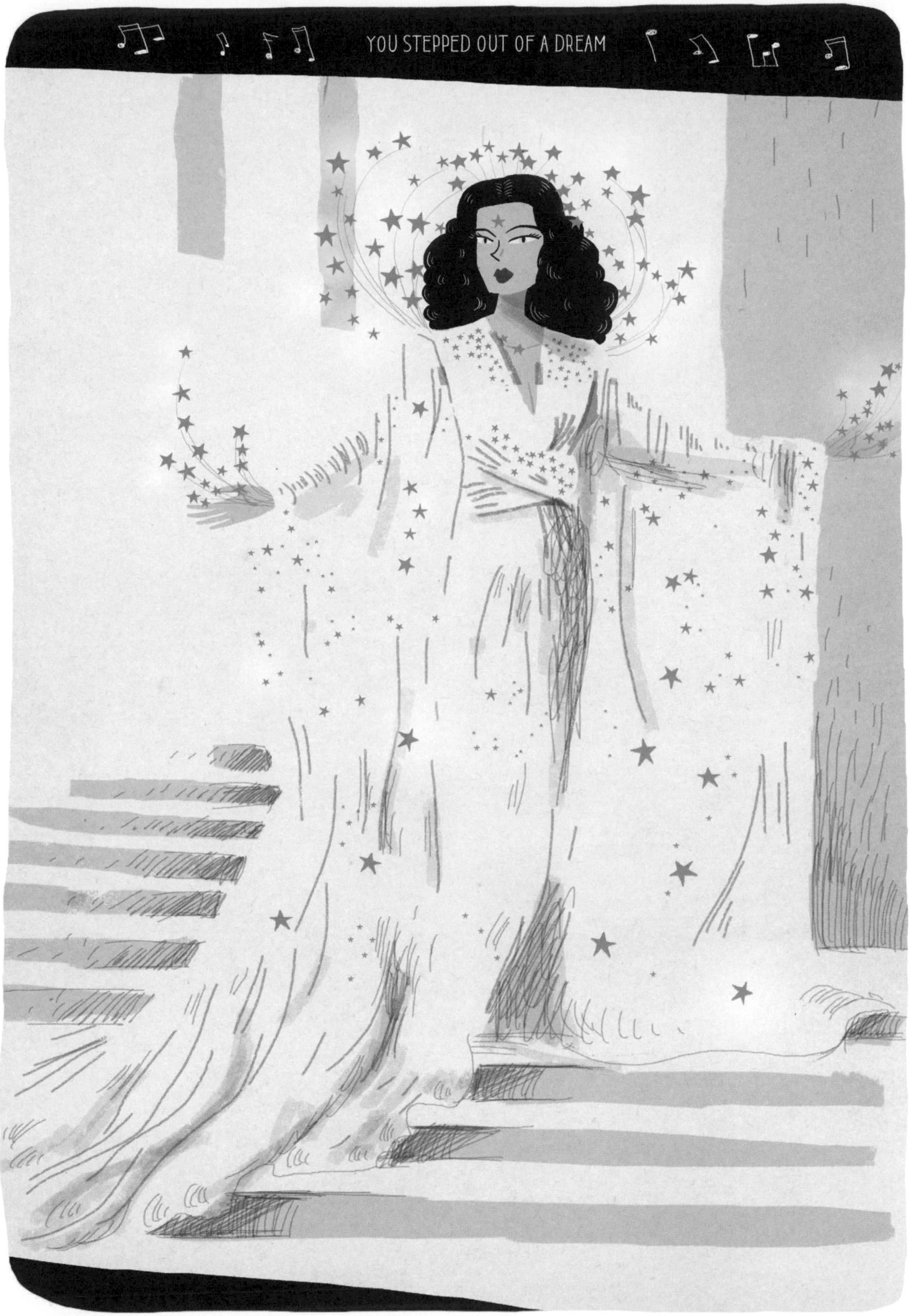
YOU STEPPED OUT OF A DREAM

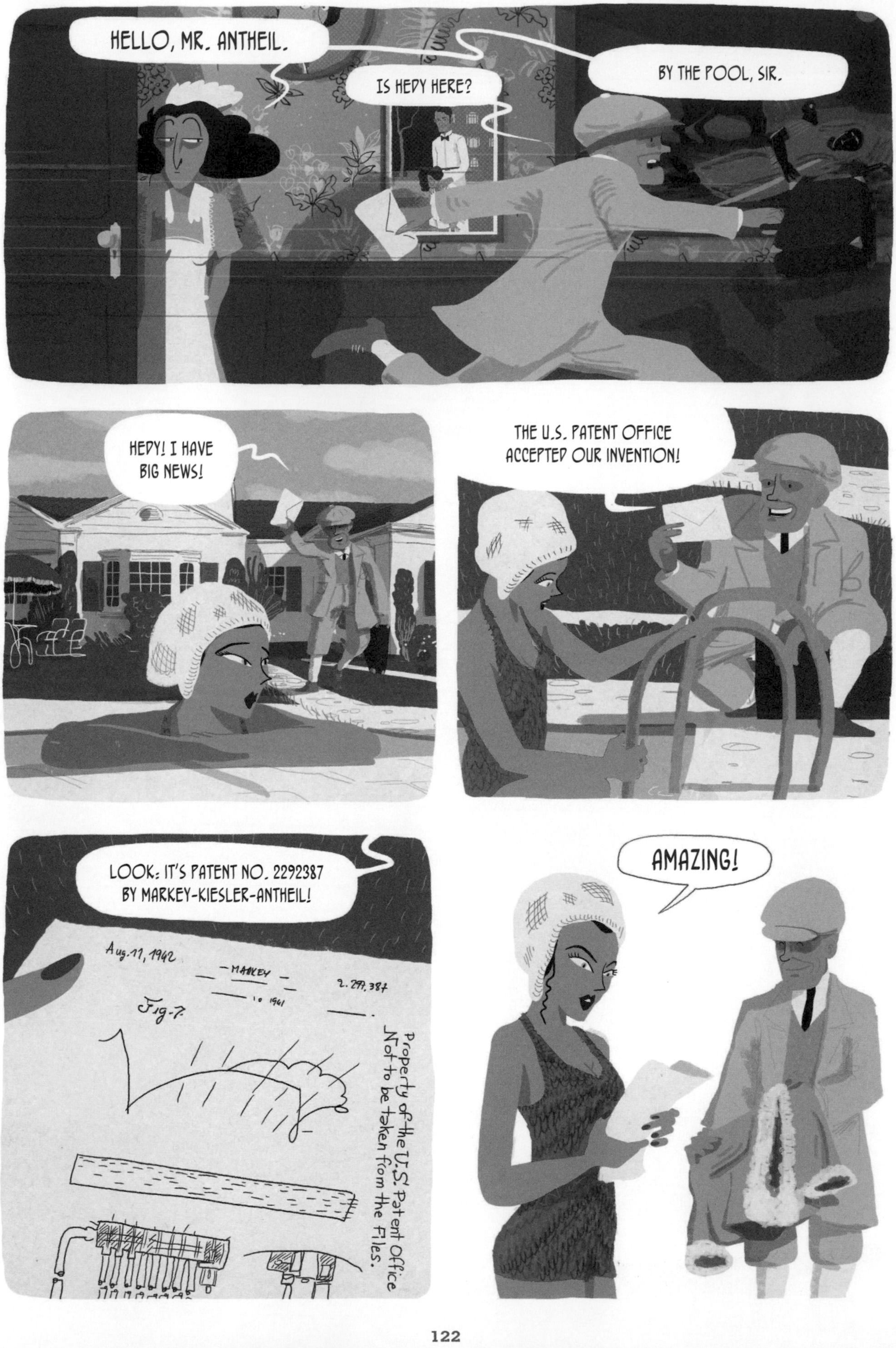
HELLO, MR. ANTHEIL.
IS HEDY HERE?
BY THE POOL, SIR.
HEDY! I HAVE BIG NEWS!
THE U.S. PATENT OFFICE ACCEPTED OUR INVENTION!
LOOK: IT'S PATENT NO. 2292387 BY MARKEY-KIESLER-ANTHEIL!
Aug. 11, 1942
MARKEY
2.297.387
1941
Fig. 7
Property of the U.S. Patent Office
Not to be taken from the files.
AMAZING!

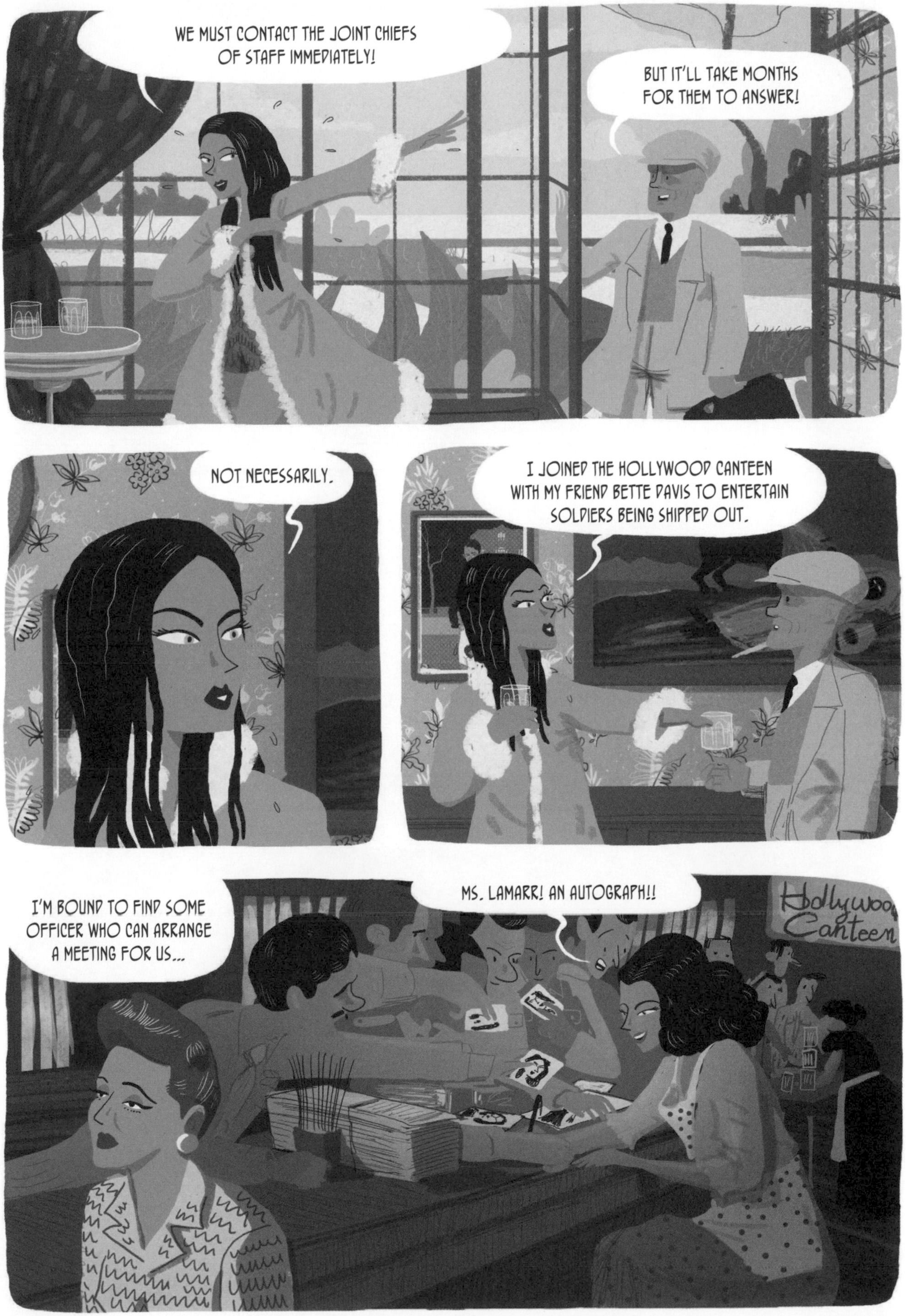
WE MUST CONTACT THE JOINT CHIEFS OF STAFF IMMEDIATELY!
BUT IT'LL TAKE MONTHS FOR THEM TO ANSWER!
NOT NECESSARILY.
I JOINED THE HOLLYWOOD CANTEEN WITH MY FRIEND BETTE DAVIS TO ENTERTAIN SOLDIERS BEING SHIPPED OUT.
I'M BOUND TO FIND SOME OFFICER WHO CAN ARRANGE A MEETING FOR US...
MS. LAMARR! AN AUTOGRAPH!!
Hollywood Canteen

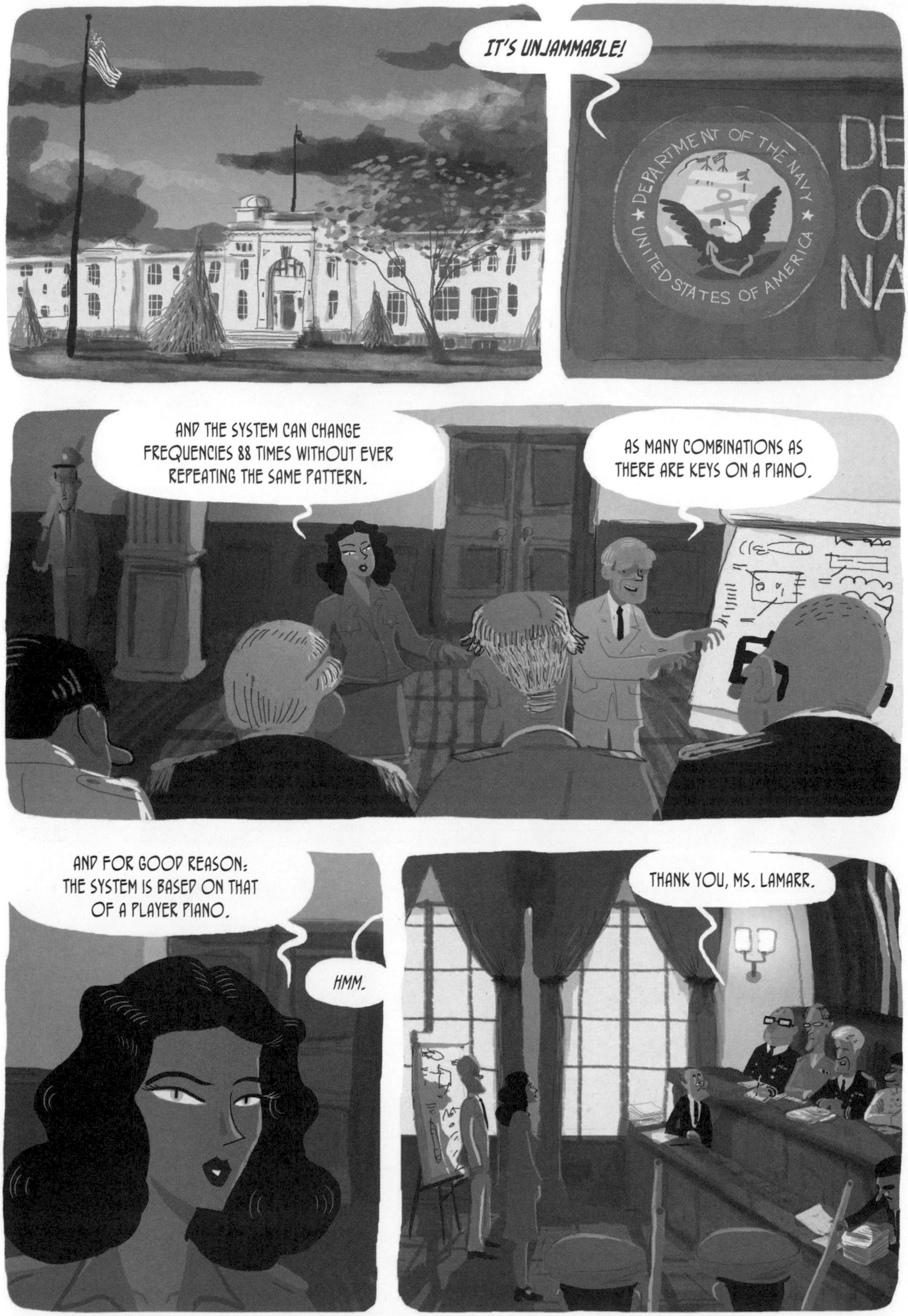

IT'S UNJAMMABLE!
DEPARTMENT OF THE NAVY
UNITED STATES OF AMERICA
AND THE SYSTEM CAN CHANGE FREQUENCIES 88 TIMES WITHOUT EVER REPEATING THE SAME PATTERN.
AS MANY COMBINATIONS AS THERE ARE KEYS ON A PIANO.
AND FOR GOOD REASON: THE SYSTEM IS BASED ON THAT OF A PLAYER PIANO.
HMM.
THANK YOU, MS. LAMARR.

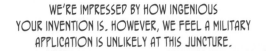

WE'RE IMPRESSED BY HOW INGENIOUS YOUR INVENTION IS. HOWEVER, WE FEEL A MILITARY APPLICATION IS UNLIKELY AT THIS JUNCTURE.

WHAT'S MISSING IS THE PRECISION OF A *REAL* SCIENTIST. BESIDES, THE SYSTEM IS TOO CUMBERSOME.

HOW THE HECK DO YOU INTEND TO FIT *A PLAYER PIANO* IN *A TORPEDO,* YOUNG LADY?

THAT'S NOT IT! *THEY DON'T GET IT AT ALL!* THE--

IT'S A UNANIMOUS "NO."

125

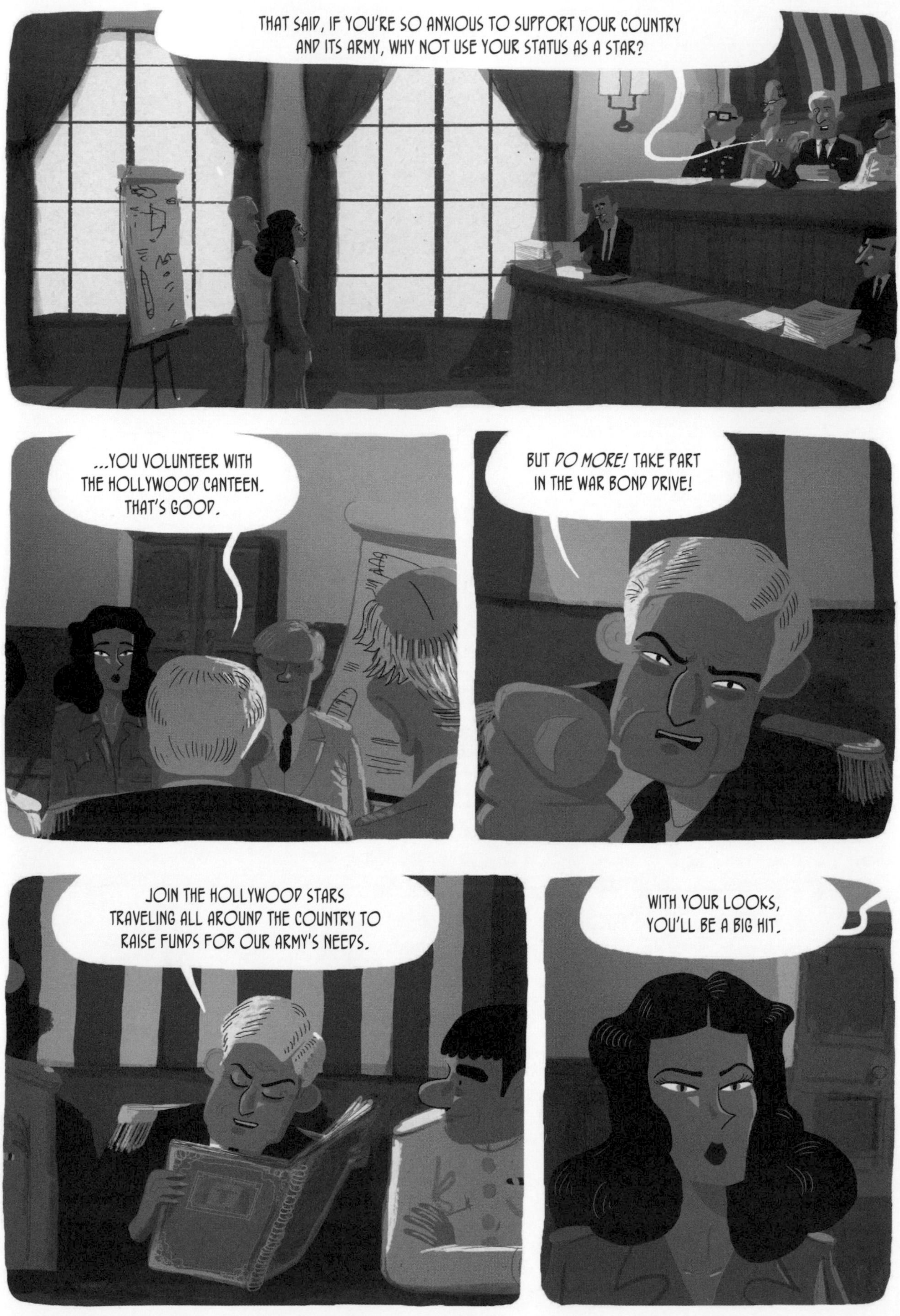
THAT SAID, IF YOU'RE SO ANXIOUS TO SUPPORT YOUR COUNTRY AND ITS ARMY, WHY NOT USE YOUR STATUS AS A STAR?
...YOU VOLUNTEER WITH THE HOLLYWOOD CANTEEN. THAT'S GOOD.
BUT *DO MORE!* TAKE PART IN THE WAR BOND DRIVE!
JOIN THE HOLLYWOOD STARS TRAVELING ALL AROUND THE COUNTRY TO RAISE FUNDS FOR OUR ARMY'S NEEDS.
WITH YOUR LOOKS, YOU'LL BE A BIG HIT.

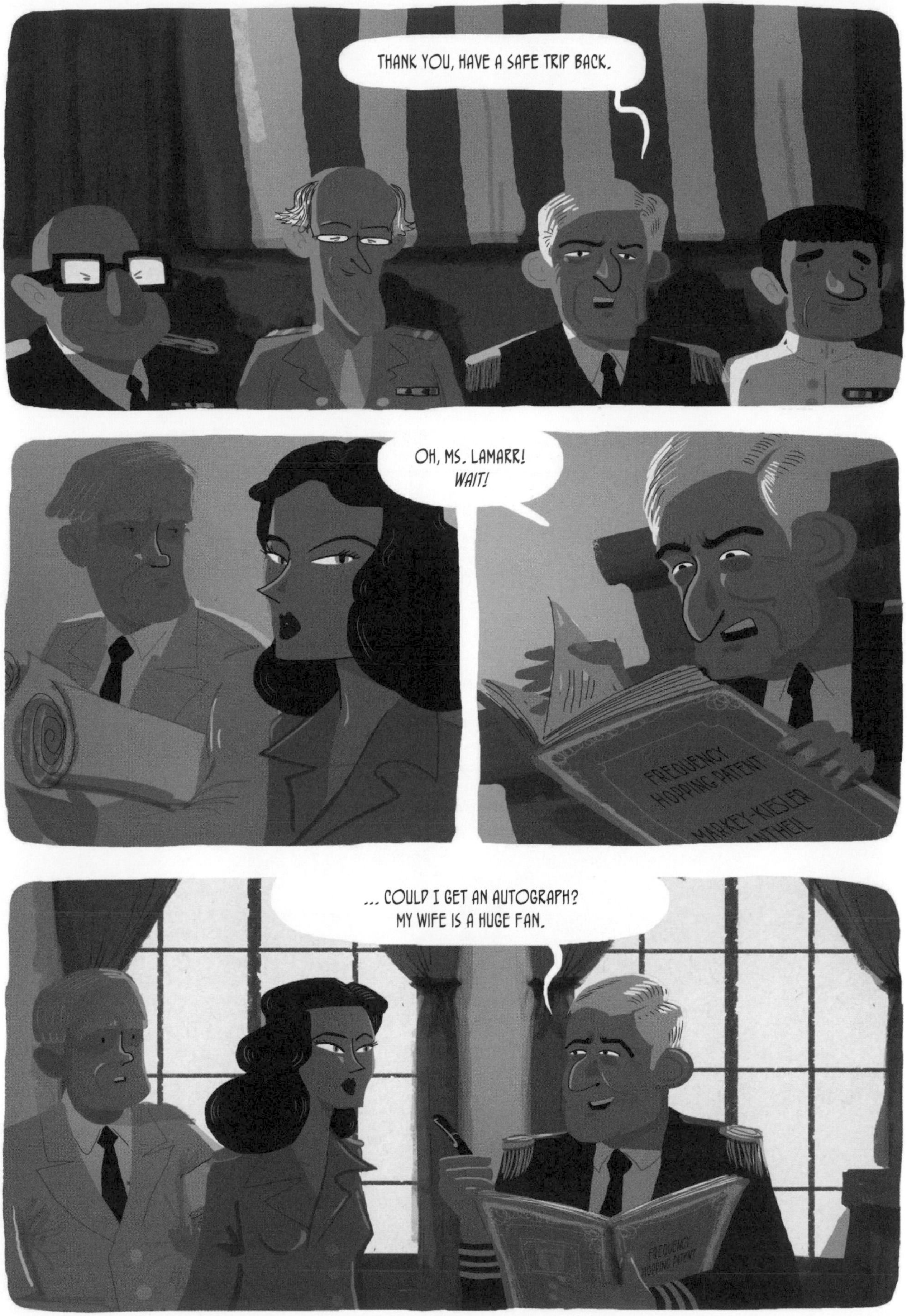
THANK YOU, HAVE A SAFE TRIP BACK.
OH, MS. LAMARR! *WAIT!*
FREQUENCY HOPPING PATENT
MARKEY-KIESLER ANTHEIL
... COULD I GET AN AUTOGRAPH? MY WIFE IS A HUGE FAN.
FREQUENCY HOPPING PATENT

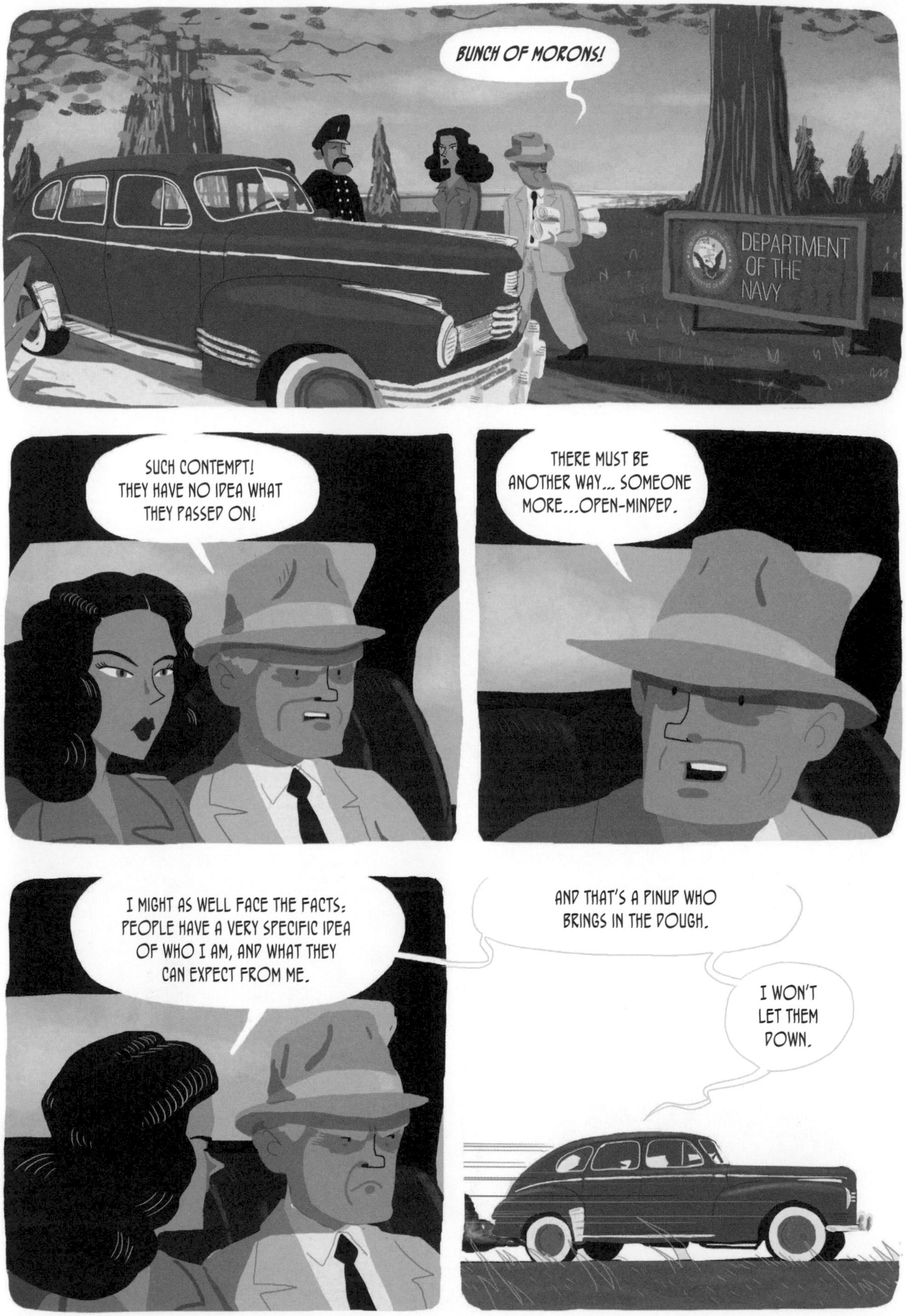
BUNCH OF MORONS!
DEPARTMENT OF THE NAVY
SUCH CONTEMPT! THEY HAVE NO IDEA WHAT THEY PASSED ON!
THERE MUST BE ANOTHER WAY... SOMEONE MORE...OPEN-MINDED.
I MIGHT AS WELL FACE THE FACTS: PEOPLE HAVE A VERY SPECIFIC IDEA OF WHO I AM, AND WHAT THEY CAN EXPECT FROM ME.
AND THAT'S A PINUP WHO BRINGS IN THE DOUGH.
I WON'T LET THEM DOWN.

A NEW RECORD!

HEDY LAMARR SELLS CLOSE TO 25 MILLION DOLLARS IN WAR BONDS!

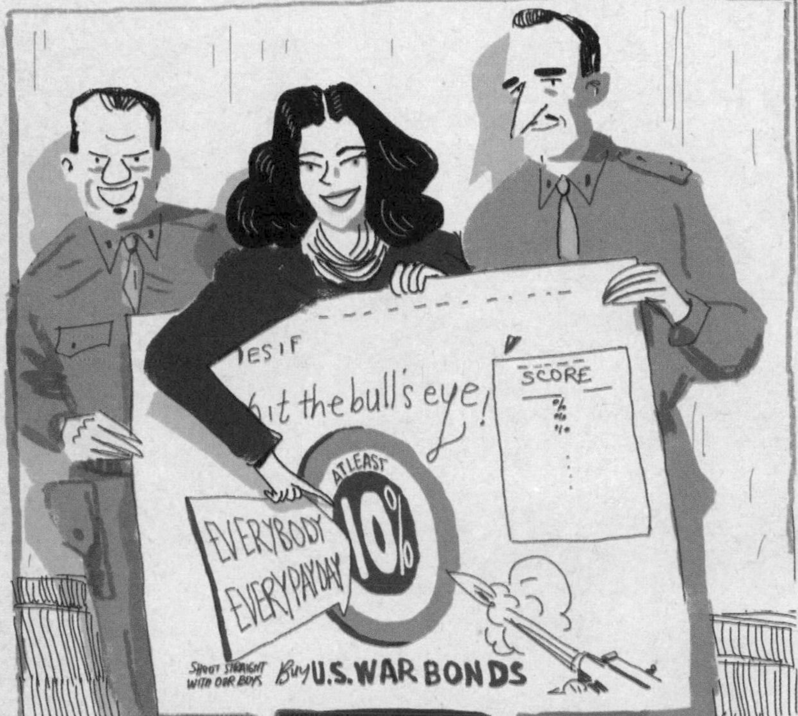

SCORE
AT LEAST
10%
EVERYBODY
EVERYPAYDAY
SHOOT STRAIGHT WITH OUR BOYS
Buy U.S. WAR BONDS

The War Bond Tour brought together today's biggest stars, including Bing Crosby, Bob Hope, Gene Tierney, James Cagney, Charles Laughton, and the comedy duo Abbott and Costello. But this campaign's real uproar was caused by Hedy Lamarr! In every city, a crowd of 20,000 people gathered, forcing local police to bring in reinforcements. Women fainted, the flashes of hundreds of cameras crackled. Everyone wanted a photo of the star. Whenever Mrs. Lamarr was driven around in an Army jeep, people on buses rose from their seats, drivers honked and countless teenagers tried to catch up with the convoy on bicycles!

"I'm here to help us win... But I have a feeling you're here to see what Hedy Lamarr looks like in real life. But we should all be here for the same reason. Knowing what Hedy Lamarr really looks like seems less important to me than knowing what Hirohito and Hitler are planning. Every time you reach for your pocket, you're letting those villains know the Yankees are coming! Help end the war soon! Don't ask what the people around you are going to do... Help fund the war effort!"

Those words by movie star, Hedy Lamarr, made a big impression on a crowd of Philadelphia residents who had come to see what the event was all about. (cont' on page 4)

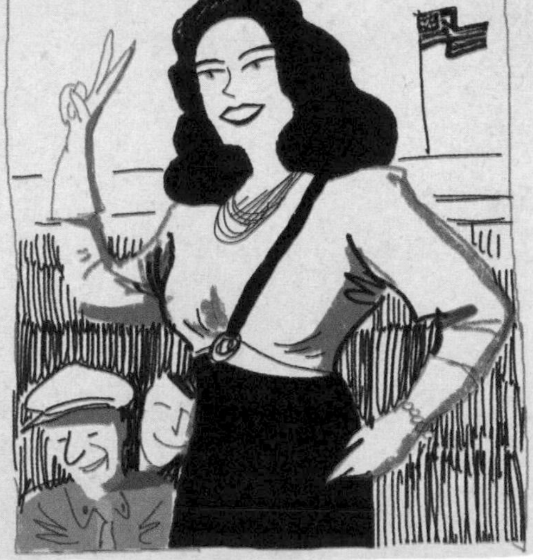

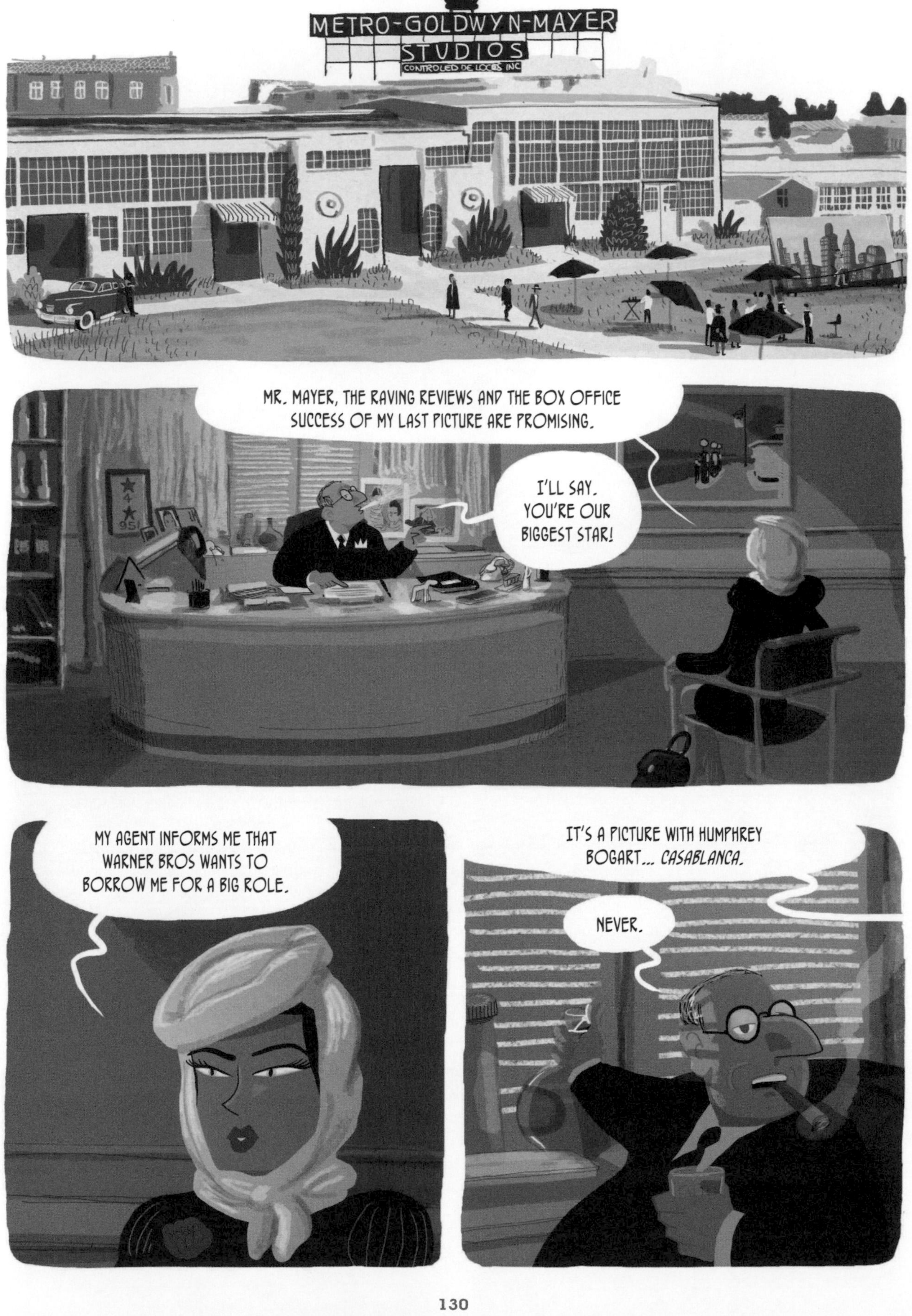
METRO-GOLDWYN-MAYER
STUDIOS
MR. MAYER, THE RAVING REVIEWS AND THE BOX OFFICE SUCCESS OF MY LAST PICTURE ARE PROMISING.
I'LL SAY. YOU'RE OUR BIGGEST STAR!
MY AGENT INFORMS ME THAT WARNER BROS WANTS TO BORROW ME FOR A BIG ROLE.
IT'S A PICTURE WITH HUMPHREY BOGART... *CASABLANCA.*
NEVER.

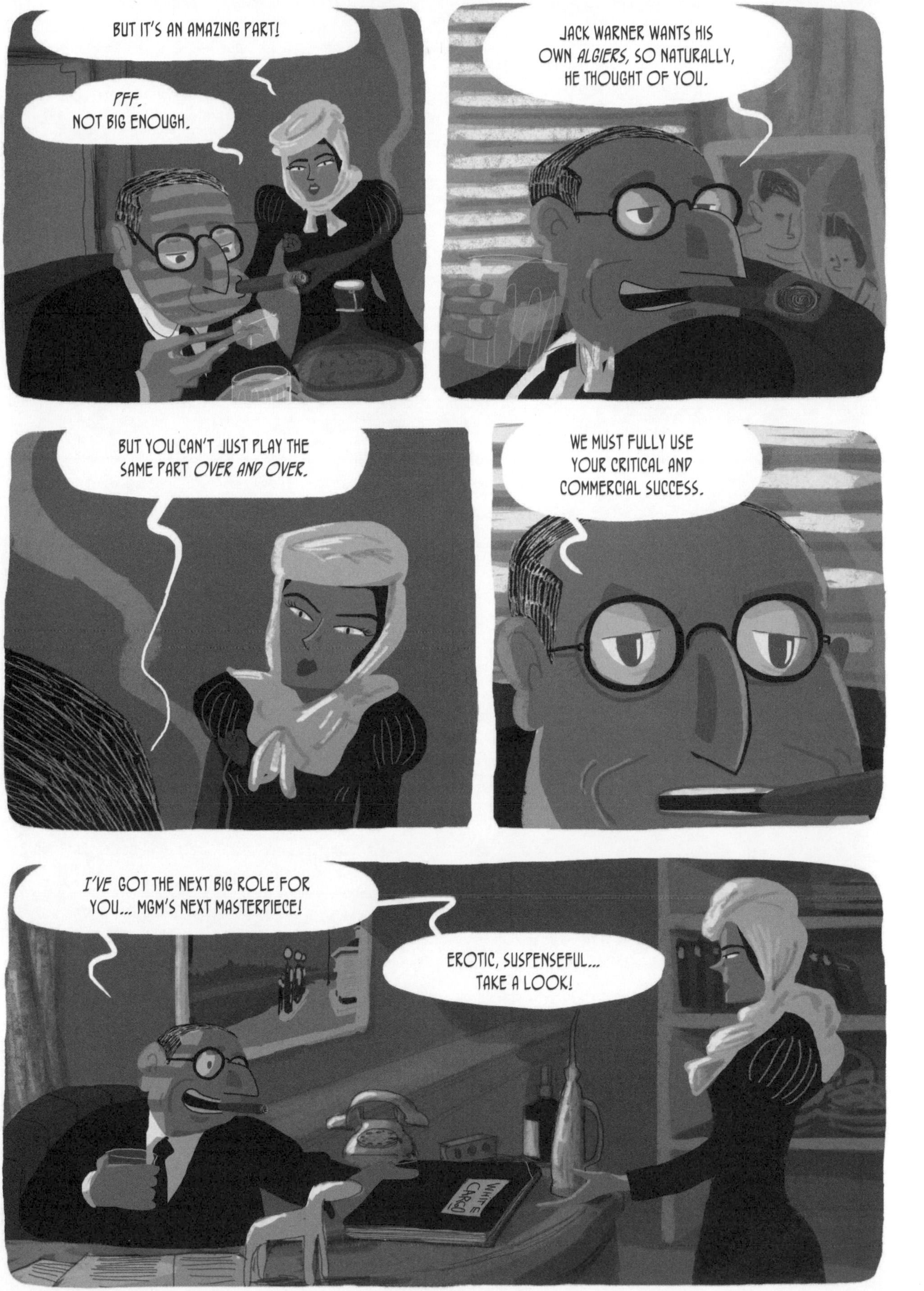
BUT IT'S AN AMAZING PART!
PFF. NOT BIG ENOUGH.
JACK WARNER WANTS HIS OWN *ALGIERS*, SO NATURALLY, HE THOUGHT OF YOU.
BUT YOU CAN'T JUST PLAY THE SAME PART *OVER AND OVER*.
WE MUST FULLY USE YOUR CRITICAL AND COMMERCIAL SUCCESS.
I'VE GOT THE NEXT BIG ROLE FOR YOU... MGM'S NEXT MASTERPIECE!
EROTIC, SUSPENSEFUL... TAKE A LOOK!
WHITE CARGO

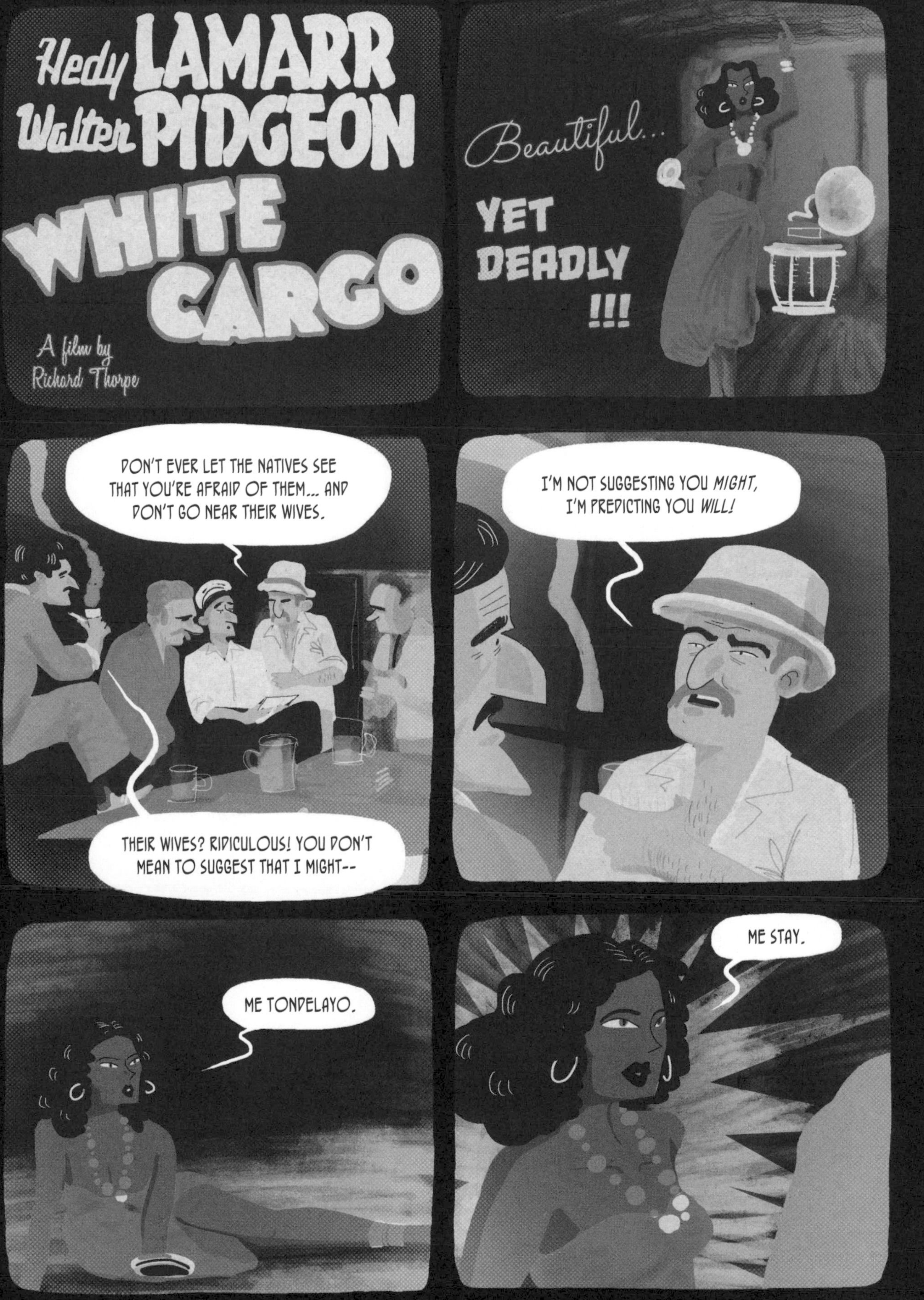

Hedy LAMARR
Walter PIDGEON
WHITE CARGO
A film by Richard Thorpe
Beautiful...
YET DEADLY !!!
DON'T EVER LET THE NATIVES SEE THAT YOU'RE AFRAID OF THEM... AND DON'T GO NEAR THEIR WIVES.
THEIR WIVES? RIDICULOUS! YOU DON'T MEAN TO SUGGEST THAT I MIGHT--
I'M NOT SUGGESTING YOU *MIGHT*, I'M PREDICTING YOU *WILL!*
ME TONDELAYO.
ME STAY.

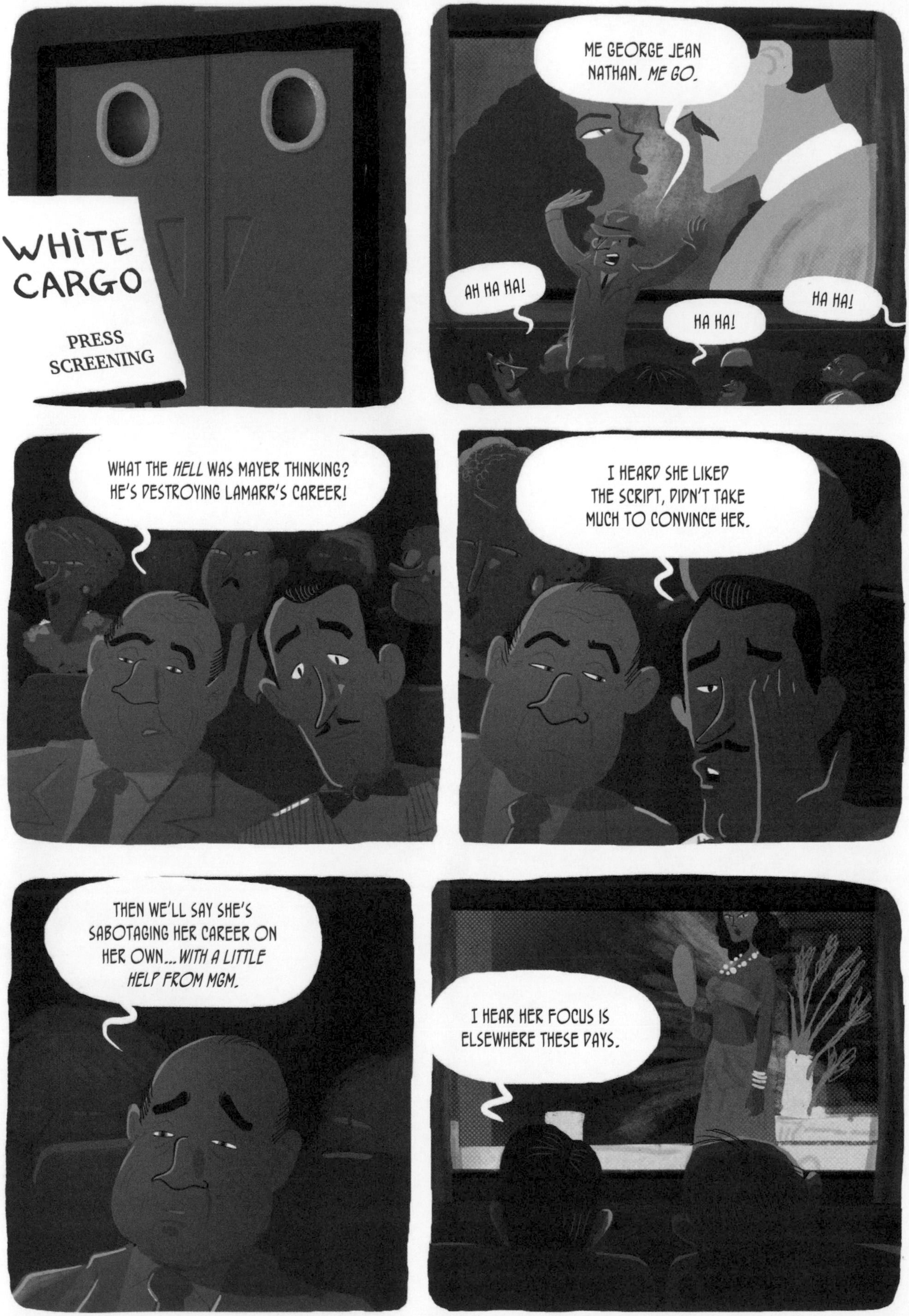
WHITE CARGO
PRESS SCREENING
ME GEORGE JEAN NATHAN. *ME GO.*
AH HA HA!
HA HA!
HA HA!
WHAT THE *HELL* WAS MAYER THINKING? HE'S DESTROYING LAMARR'S CAREER!
I HEARD SHE LIKED THE SCRIPT, DIDN'T TAKE MUCH TO CONVINCE HER.
THEN WE'LL SAY SHE'S SABOTAGING HER CAREER ON HER OWN... *WITH A LITTLE HELP FROM MGM.*
I HEAR HER FOCUS IS ELSEWHERE THESE DAYS.

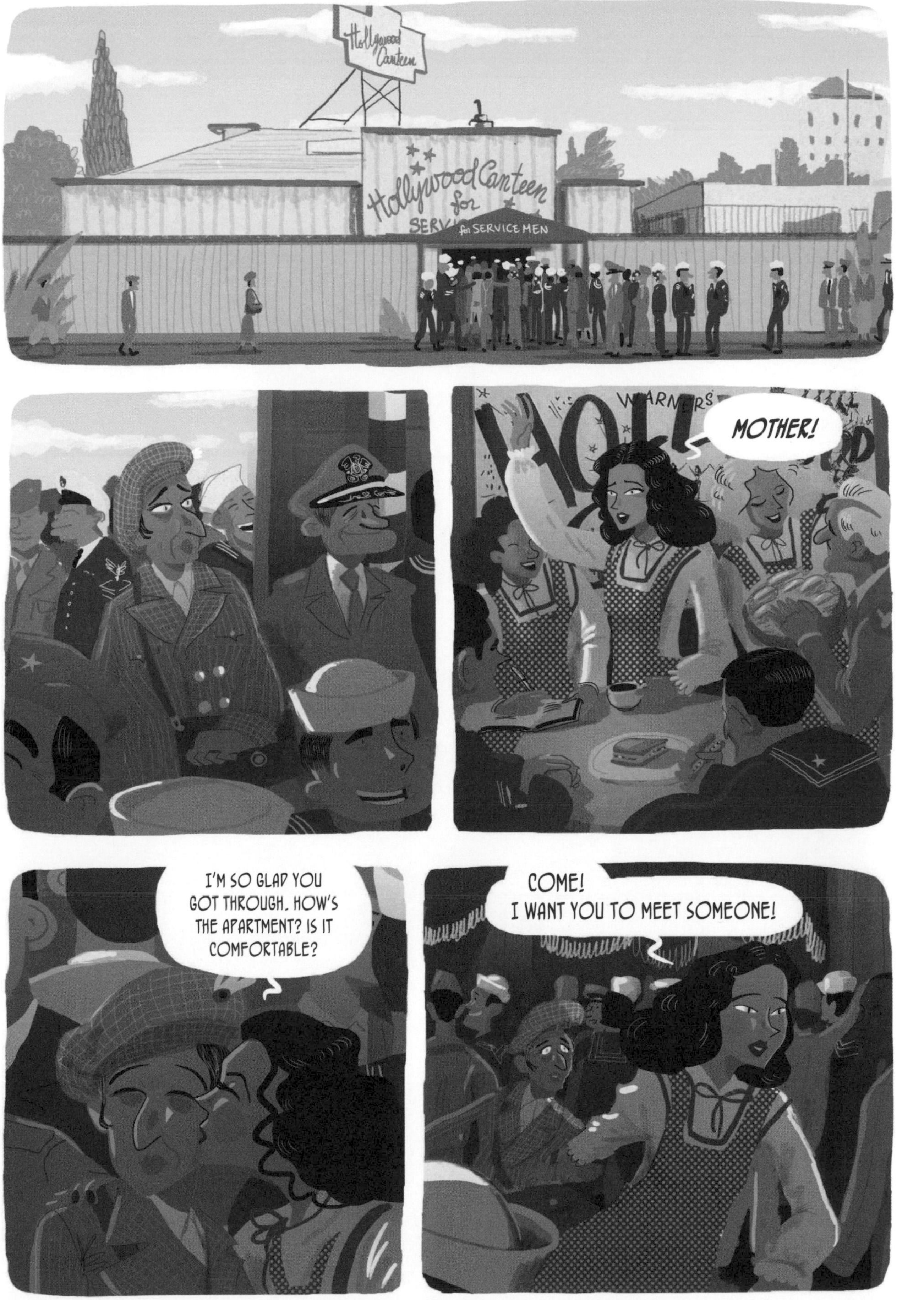
Hollywood Canteen
Hollywood Canteen for
for SERVICE MEN
WARNERS
MOTHER!
I'M SO GLAD YOU GOT THROUGH. HOW'S THE APARTMENT? IS IT COMFORTABLE?
COME! I WANT YOU TO MEET SOMEONE!

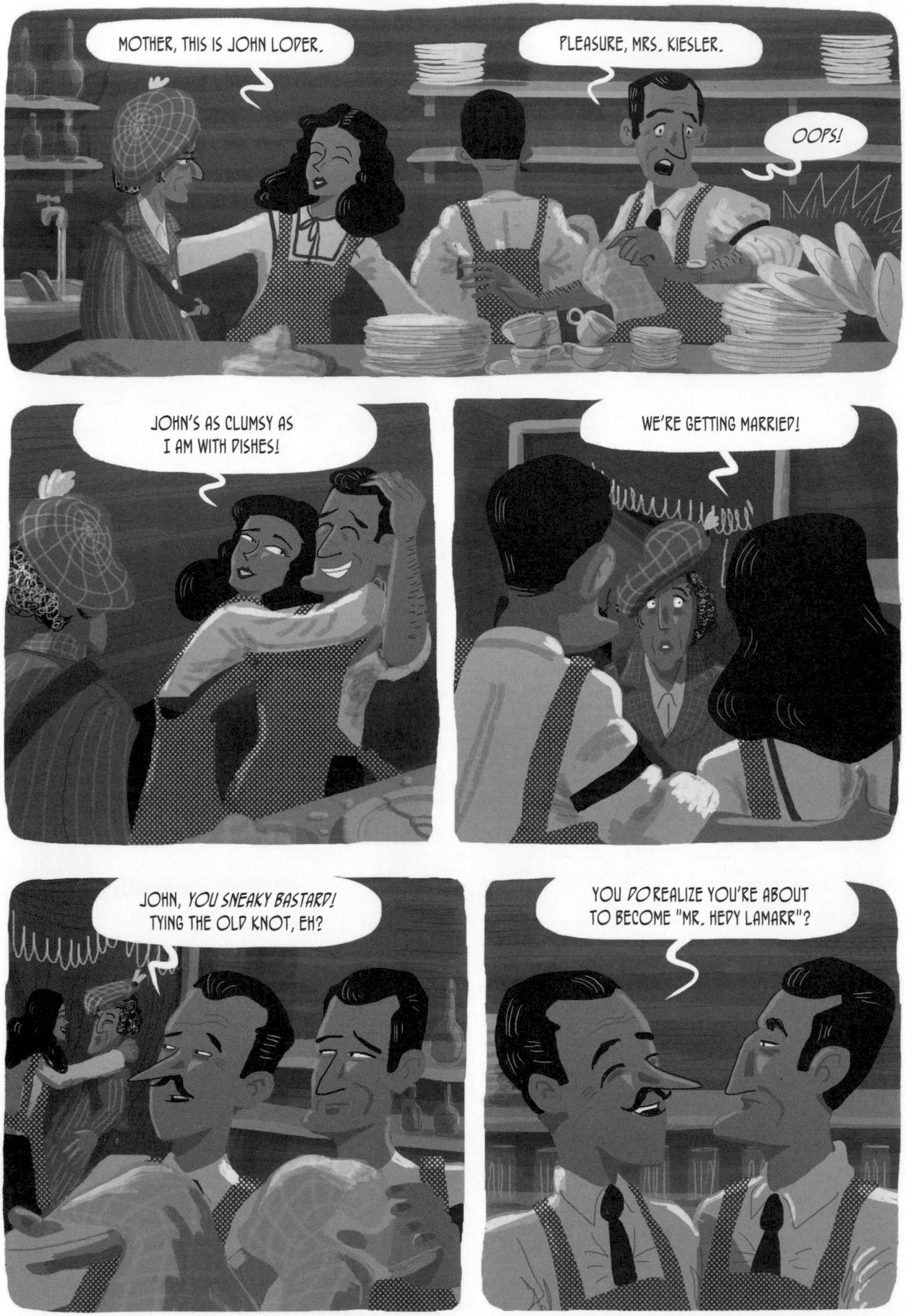
MOTHER, THIS IS JOHN LODER.
PLEASURE, MRS. KIESLER.
OOPS!
JOHN'S AS CLUMSY AS I AM WITH DISHES!
WE'RE GETTING MARRIED!
JOHN, *YOU SNEAKY BASTARD!* TYING THE OLD KNOT, EH?
YOU *DO* REALIZE YOU'RE ABOUT TO BECOME "MR. HEDY LAMARR"?

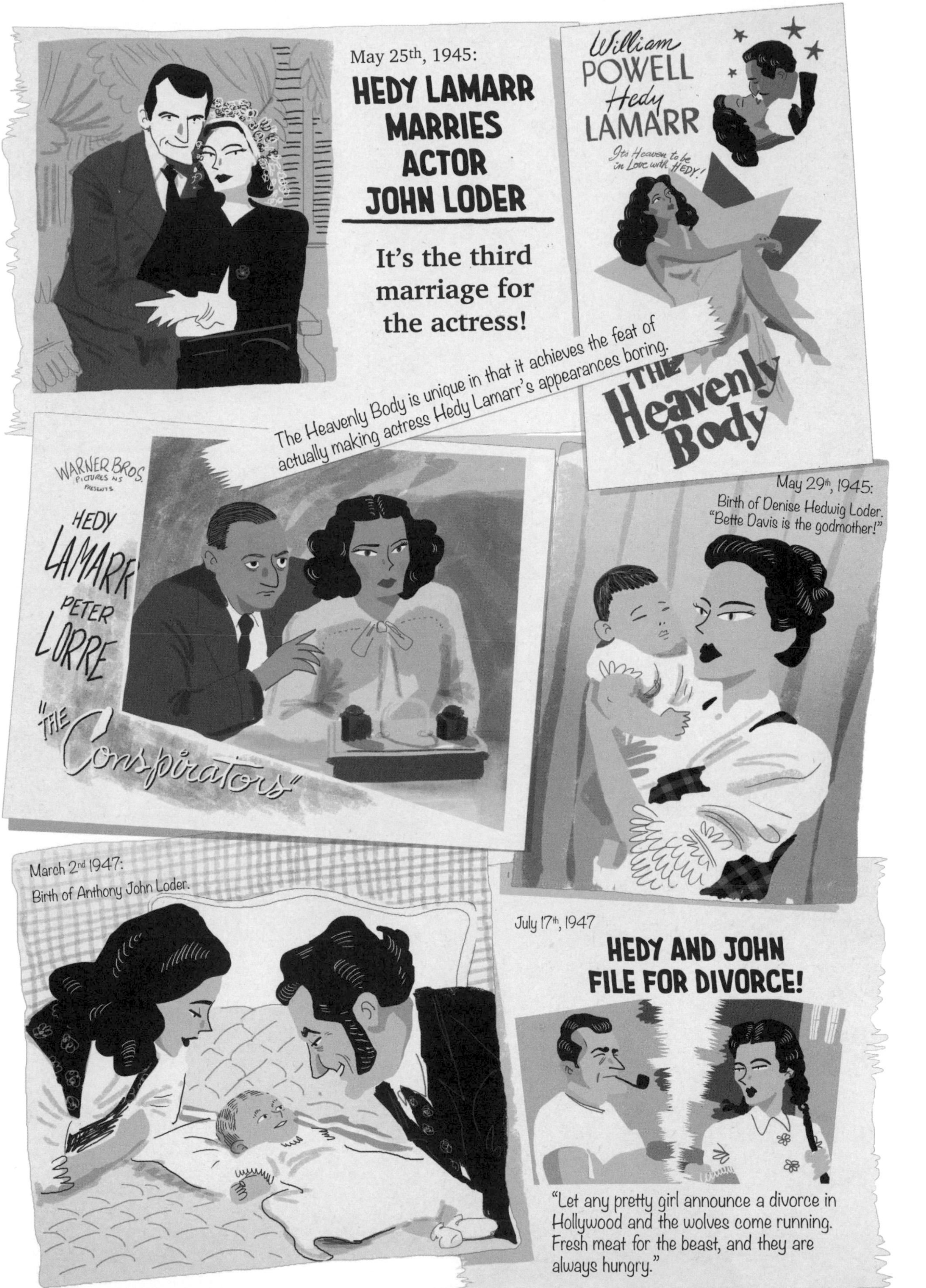
May 25th, 1945:
HEDY LAMARR MARRIES ACTOR JOHN LODER
It's the third marriage for the actress!
William POWELL Hedy LAMARR
It's Heaven to be in Love with HEDY!
THE Heavenly Body
The Heavenly Body is unique in that it achieves the feat of actually making actress Hedy Lamarr's appearances boring.
WARNER BROS.
HEDY LAMARR PETER LORRE
"THE Conspirators"
May 29th, 1945:
Birth of Denise Hedwig Loder.
"Bette Davis is the godmother!"
March 2nd 1947:
Birth of Anthony John Loder.
July 17th, 1947
HEDY AND JOHN FILE FOR DIVORCE!
"Let any pretty girl announce a divorce in Hollywood and the wolves come running. Fresh meat for the beast, and they are always hungry."

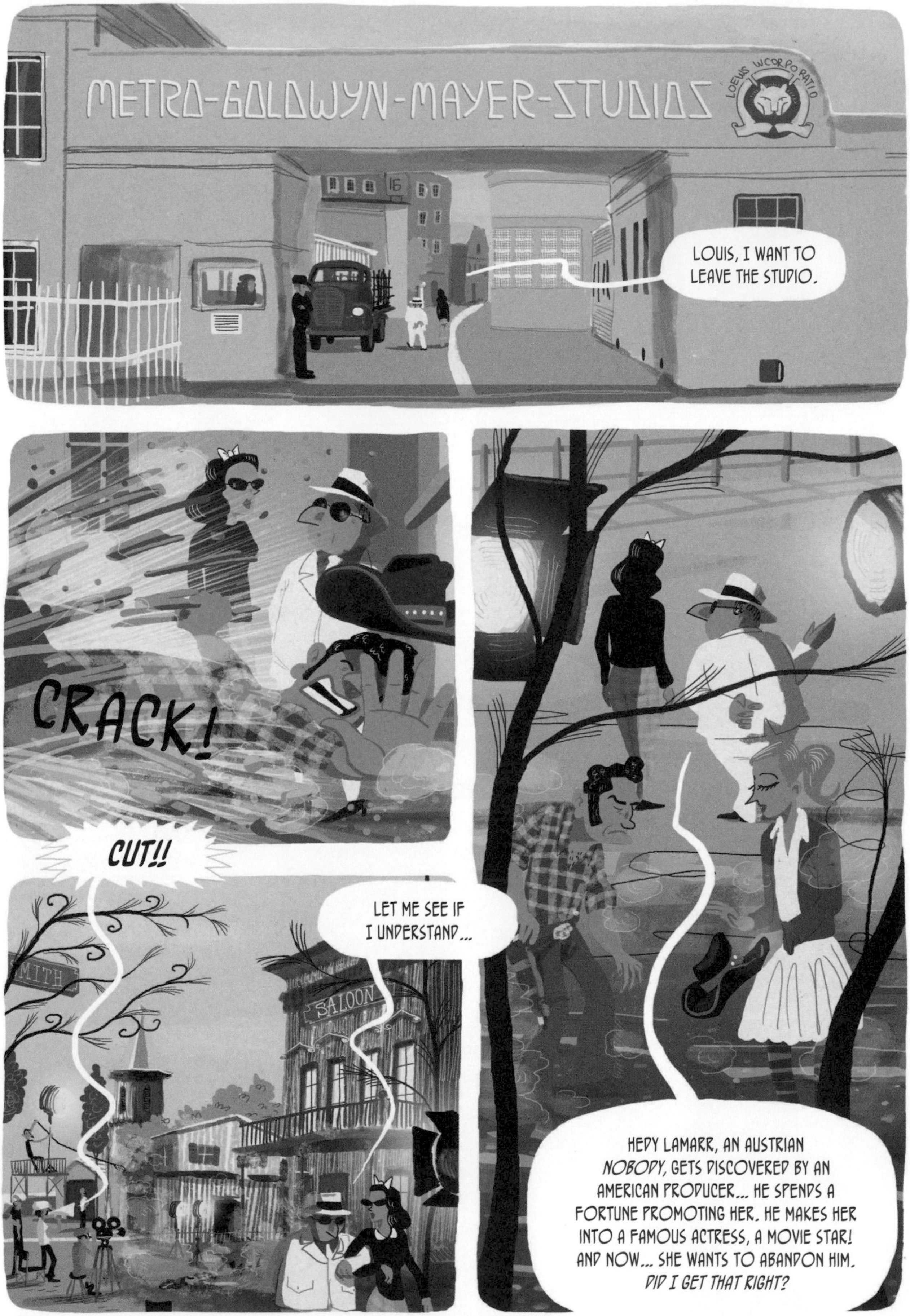
METRO-GOLDWYN-MAYER-STUDIOS
LOUIS, I WANT TO LEAVE THE STUDIO.
CRACK!
CUT!!
SALOON
LET ME SEE IF I UNDERSTAND...
HEDY LAMARR, AN AUSTRIAN *NOBODY*, GETS DISCOVERED BY AN AMERICAN PRODUCER... HE SPENDS A FORTUNE PROMOTING HER. HE MAKES HER INTO A FAMOUS ACTRESS, A MOVIE STAR! AND NOW... SHE WANTS TO ABANDON HIM. *DID I GET THAT RIGHT?*

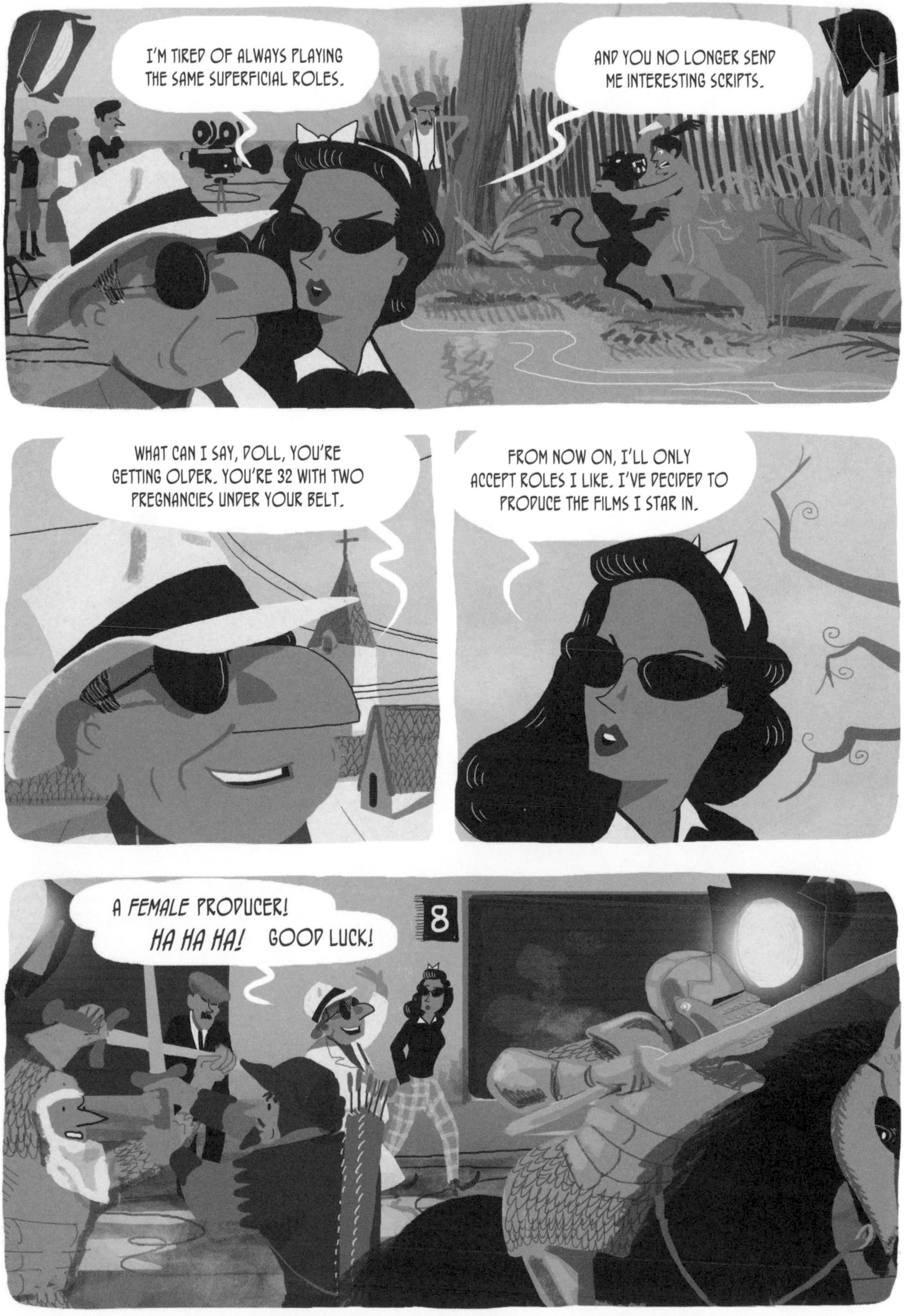
I'M TIRED OF ALWAYS PLAYING THE SAME SUPERFICIAL ROLES.
AND YOU NO LONGER SEND ME INTERESTING SCRIPTS.
WHAT CAN I SAY, DOLL, YOU'RE GETTING OLDER. YOU'RE 32 WITH TWO PREGNANCIES UNDER YOUR BELT.
FROM NOW ON, I'LL ONLY ACCEPT ROLES I LIKE. I'VE DECIDED TO PRODUCE THE FILMS I STAR IN.
A *FEMALE* PRODUCER! *HA HA HA!* GOOD LUCK!
8

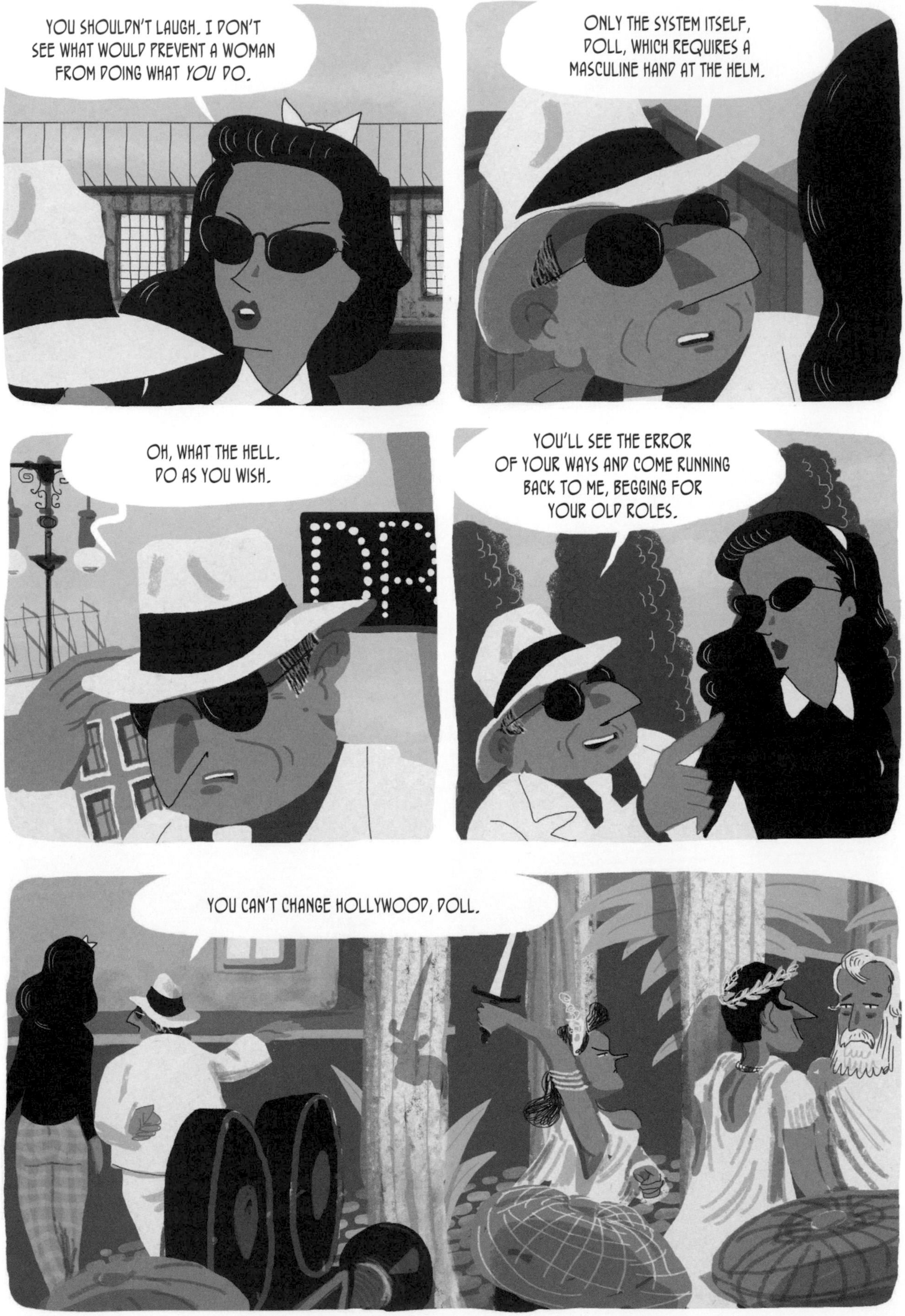
YOU SHOULDN'T LAUGH. I DON'T SEE WHAT WOULD PREVENT A WOMAN FROM DOING WHAT *YOU* DO.
ONLY THE SYSTEM ITSELF, DOLL, WHICH REQUIRES A MASCULINE HAND AT THE HELM.
OH, WHAT THE HELL. DO AS YOU WISH.
YOU'LL SEE THE ERROR OF YOUR WAYS AND COME RUNNING BACK TO ME, BEGGING FOR YOUR OLD ROLES.
YOU CAN'T CHANGE HOLLYWOOD, DOLL.

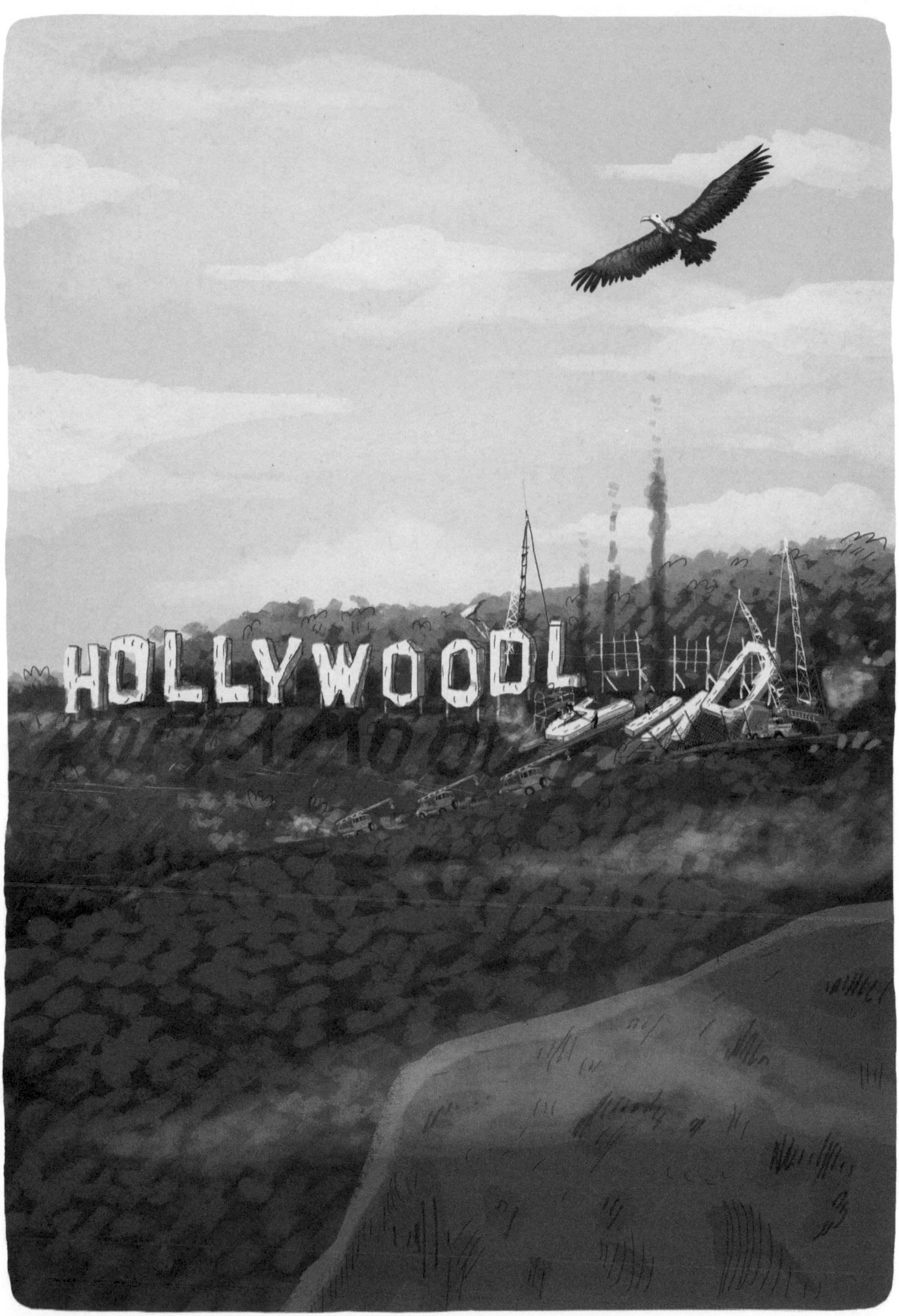
HOLLYWOODL

October 1957

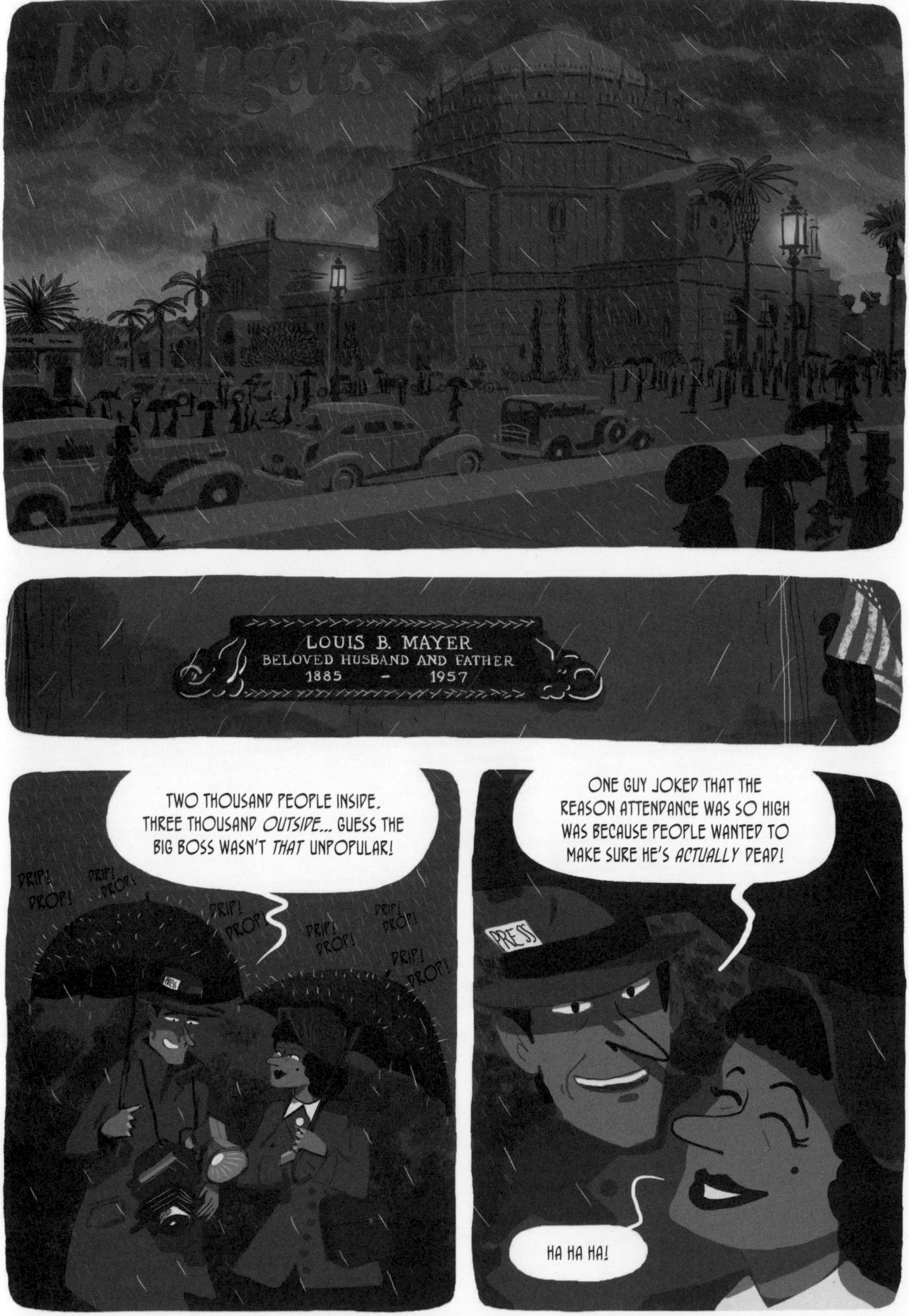
Los Angeles
LOUIS B. MAYER
BELOVED HUSBAND AND FATHER
1885 - 1957
TWO THOUSAND PEOPLE INSIDE. THREE THOUSAND *OUTSIDE*... GUESS THE BIG BOSS WASN'T *THAT* UNPOPULAR!
DRIP! DROP!
DRIP! DROP!
DRIP! DROP!
DRIP! DROP!
DRIP! DROP!
DRIP! DROP!
PRESS
ONE GUY JOKED THAT THE REASON ATTENDANCE WAS SO HIGH WAS BECAUSE PEOPLE WANTED TO MAKE SURE HE'S *ACTUALLY* DEAD!
PRESS
HA HA HA!

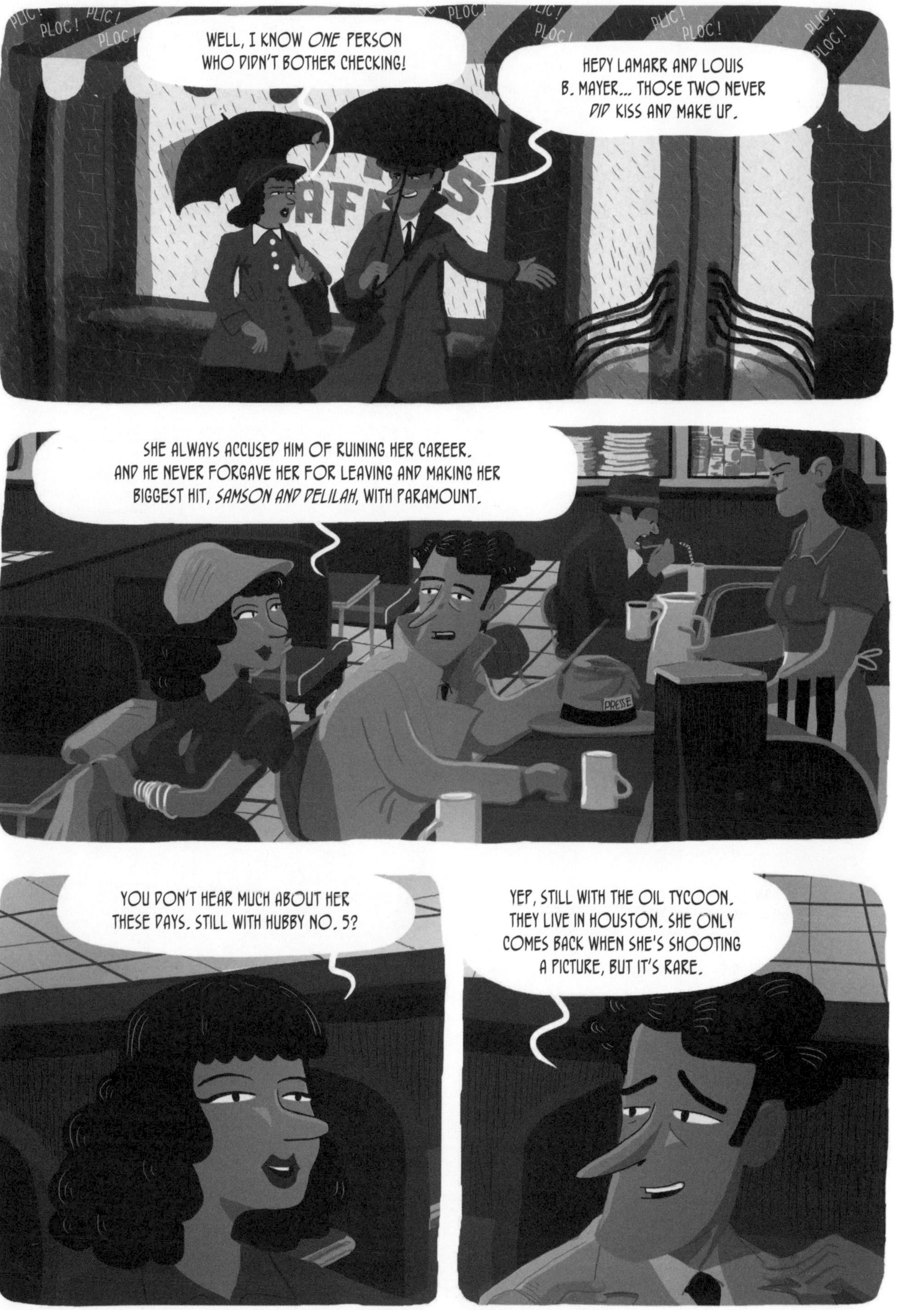
PLIC! PLOC! PLIC! PLOC!
WELL, I KNOW *ONE* PERSON WHO DIDN'T BOTHER CHECKING!
PLIC! PLOC! PLIC! PLOC! PLIC! PLOC!
HEDY LAMARR AND LOUIS B. MAYER... THOSE TWO NEVER *DID* KISS AND MAKE UP.
SHE ALWAYS ACCUSED HIM OF RUINING HER CAREER. AND HE NEVER FORGAVE HER FOR LEAVING AND MAKING HER BIGGEST HIT, *SAMSON AND DELILAH*, WITH PARAMOUNT.
PRESSE
YOU DON'T HEAR MUCH ABOUT HER THESE DAYS. STILL WITH HUBBY NO. 5?
YEP, STILL WITH THE OIL TYCOON. THEY LIVE IN HOUSTON. SHE ONLY COMES BACK WHEN SHE'S SHOOTING A PICTURE, BUT IT'S RARE.

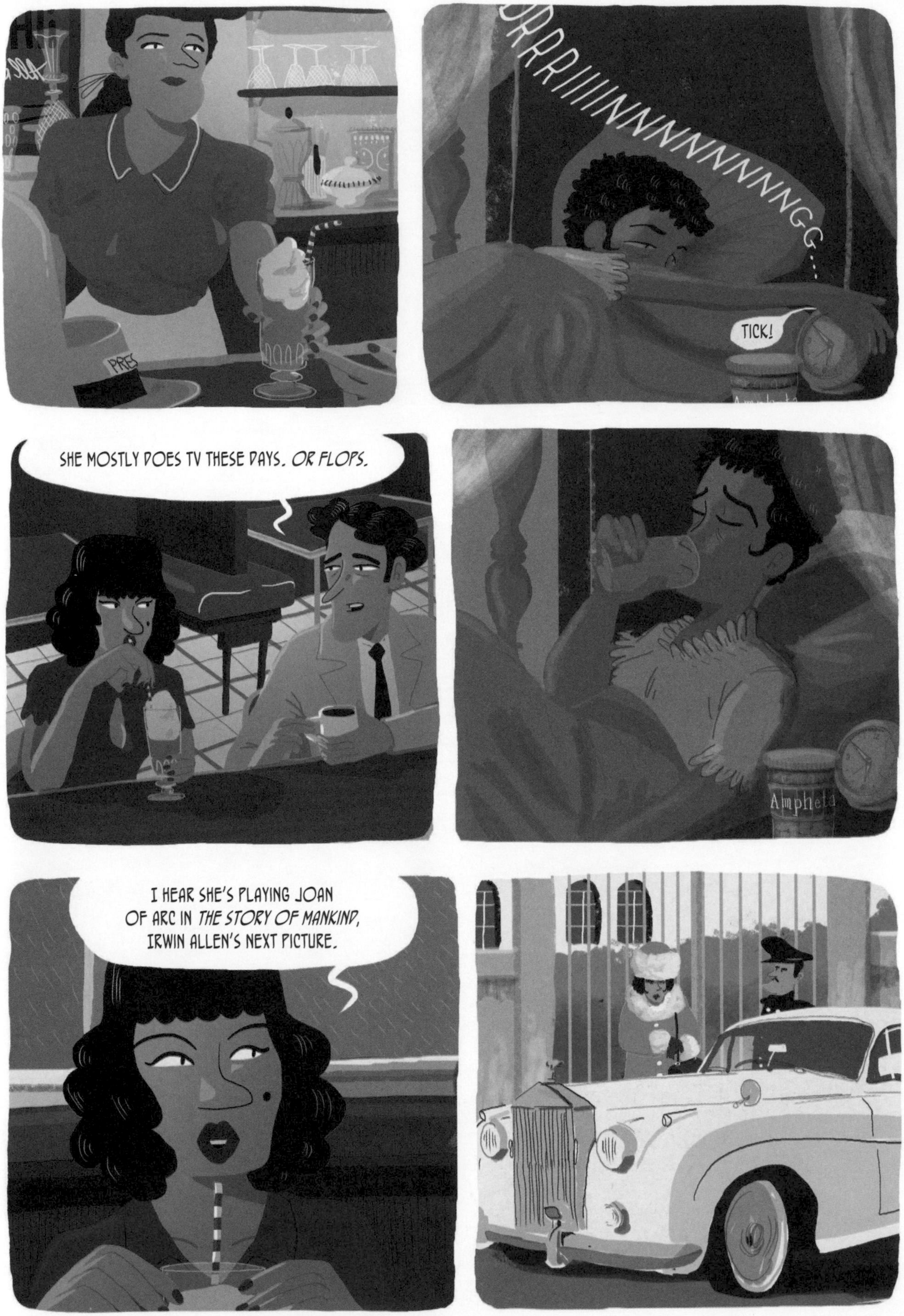
PRES
RRRIIIIINNNNNNNNNNGG...
TICK!
SHE MOSTLY DOES TV THESE DAYS. *OR FLOPS.*
Ampheta
I HEAR SHE'S PLAYING JOAN OF ARC IN *THE STORY OF MANKIND,* IRWIN ALLEN'S NEXT PICTURE.

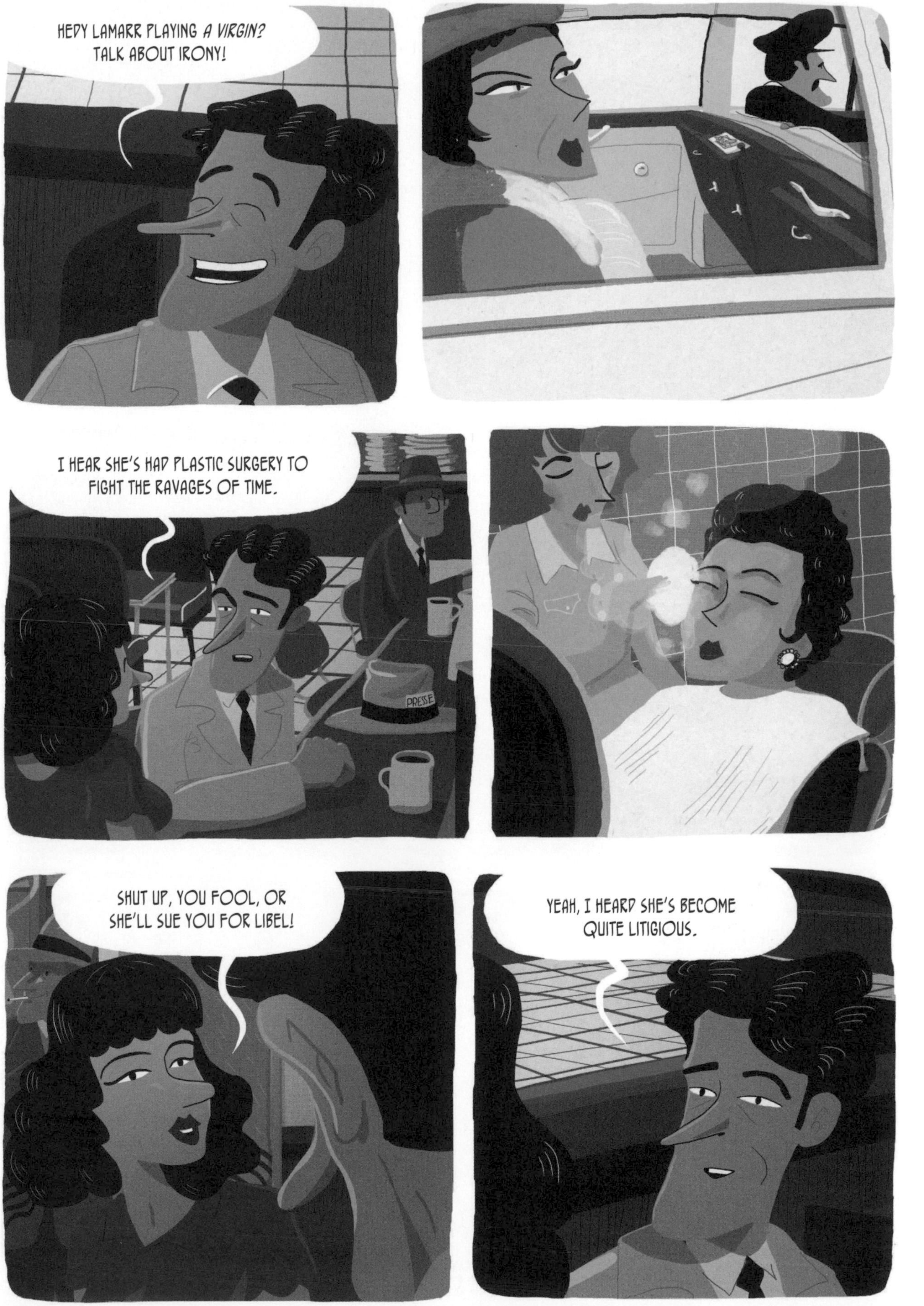
HEDY LAMARR PLAYING *A VIRGIN?* TALK ABOUT IRONY!
I HEAR SHE'S HAD PLASTIC SURGERY TO FIGHT THE RAVAGES OF TIME.
PRESSE
SHUT UP, YOU FOOL, OR SHE'LL SUE YOU FOR LIBEL!
YEAH, I HEARD SHE'S BECOME QUITE LITIGIOUS.

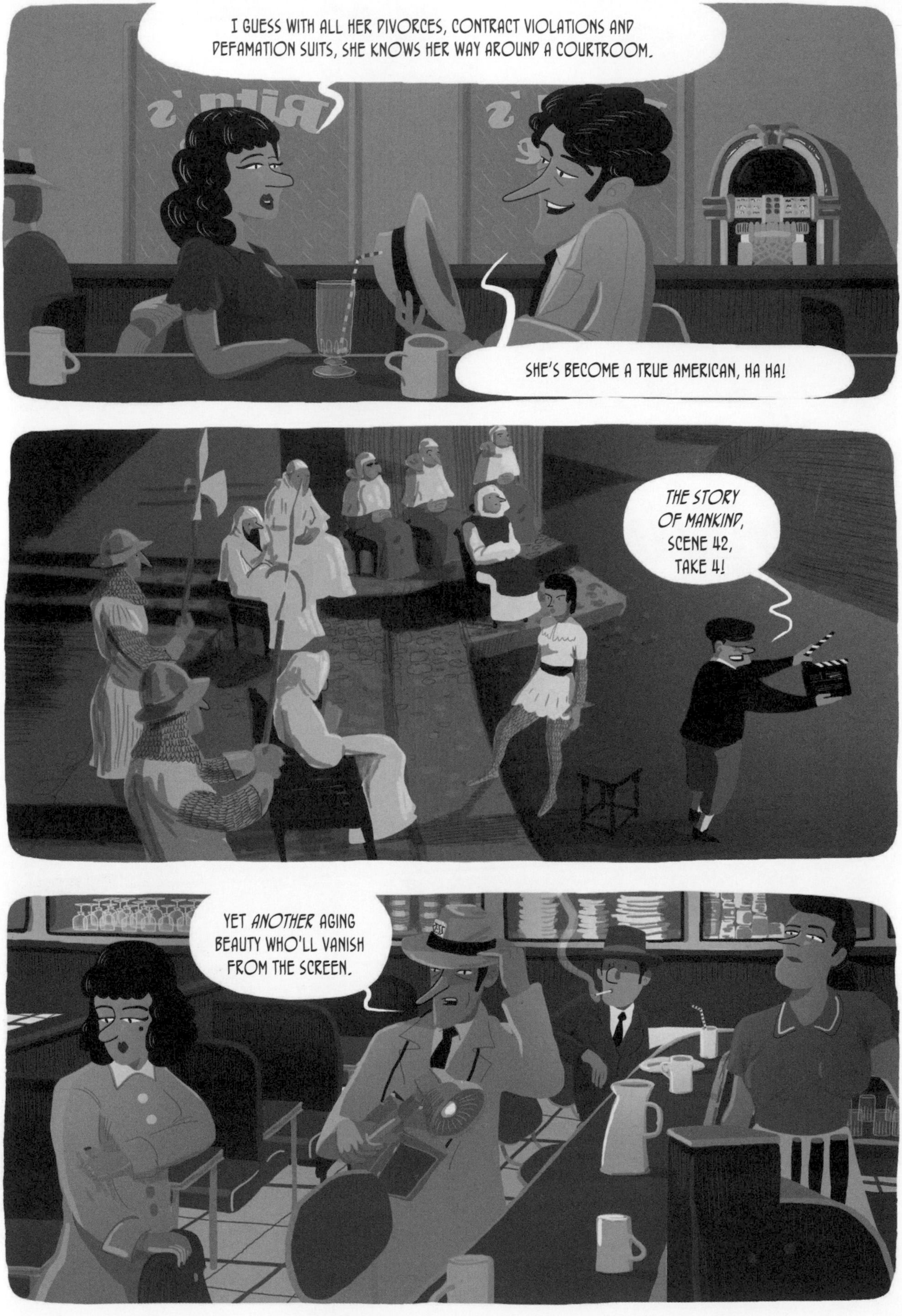
I GUESS WITH ALL HER DIVORCES, CONTRACT VIOLATIONS AND DEFAMATION SUITS, SHE KNOWS HER WAY AROUND A COURTROOM.
SHE'S BECOME A TRUE AMERICAN, HA HA!
THE STORY OF MANKIND, SCENE 42, TAKE 4!
YET *ANOTHER* AGING BEAUTY WHO'LL VANISH FROM THE SCREEN.

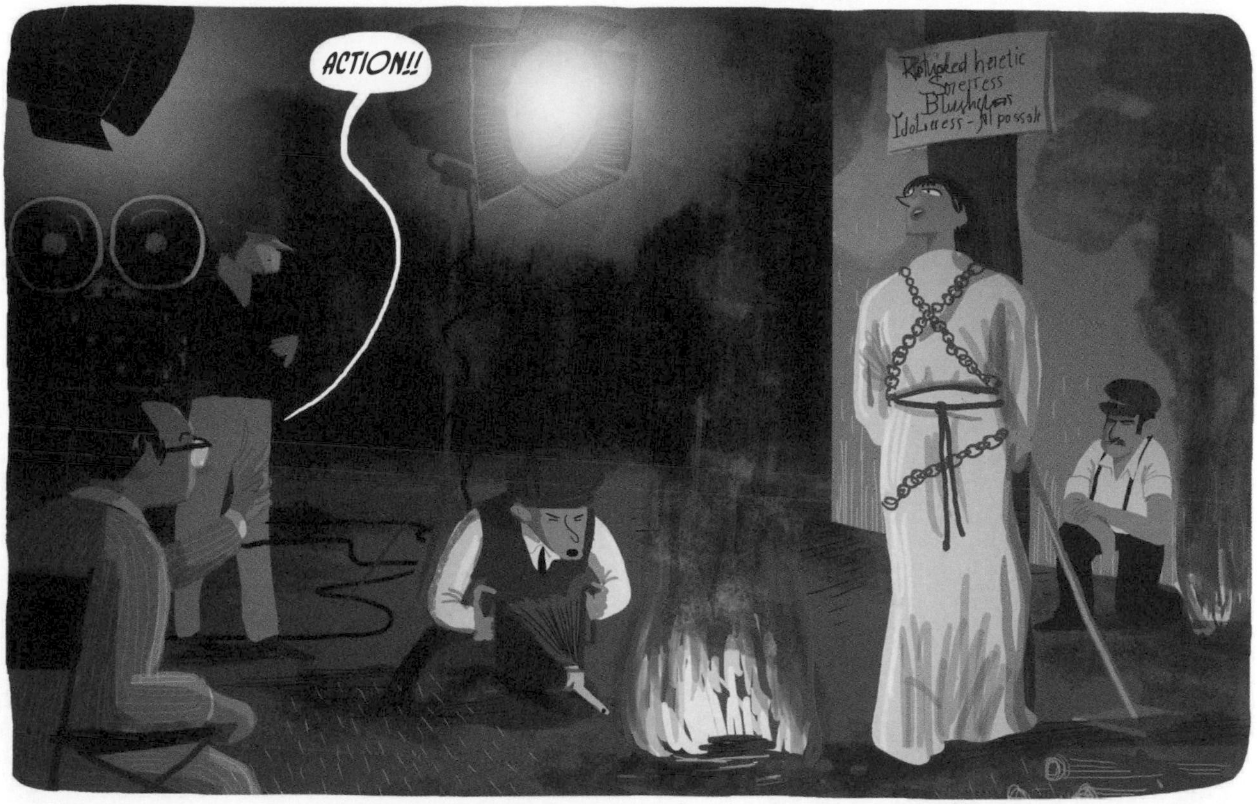
ACTION!!

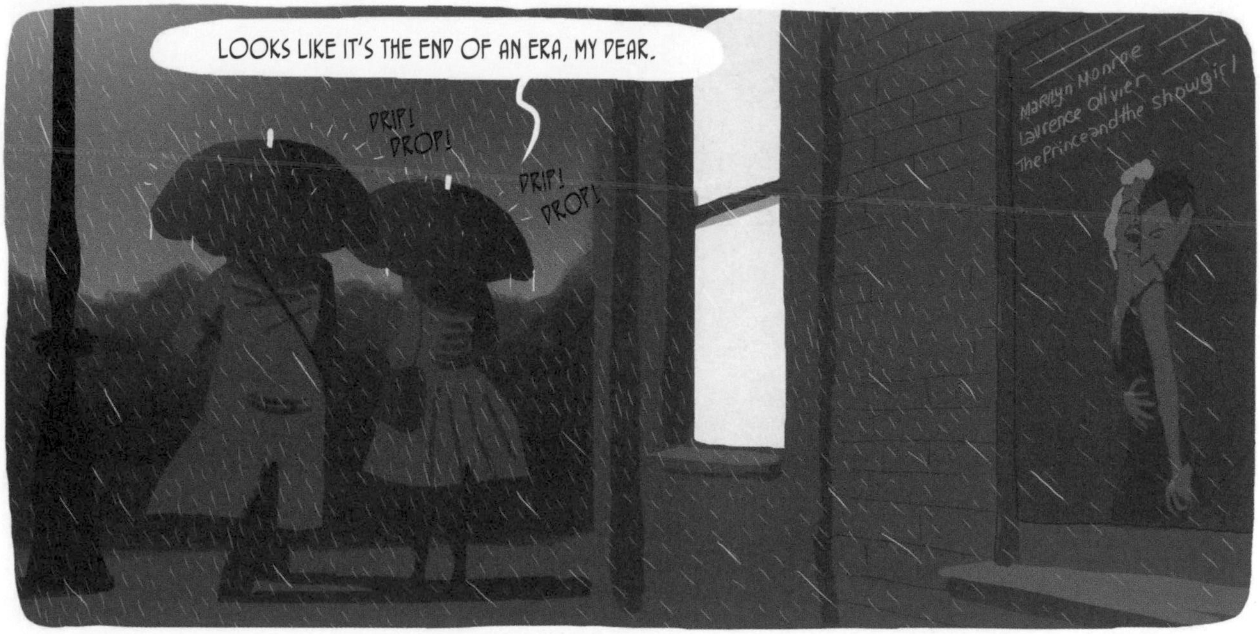
LOOKS LIKE IT'S THE END OF AN ERA, MY DEAR.
DRIP! DROP!
DRIP! DROP!
Marilyn Monroe
Laurence Olivier
The Prince and the Showgirl

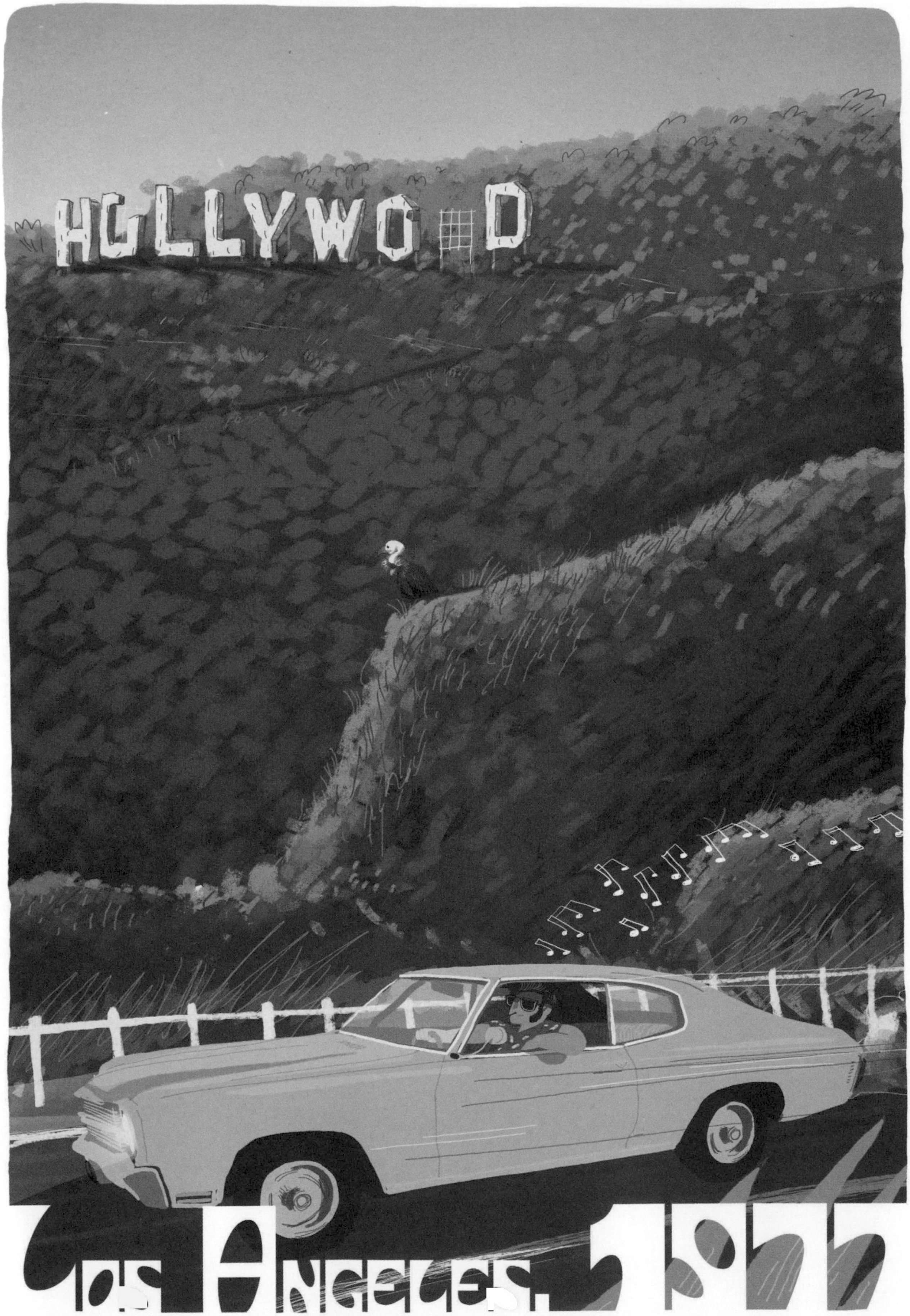
Los Angeles,

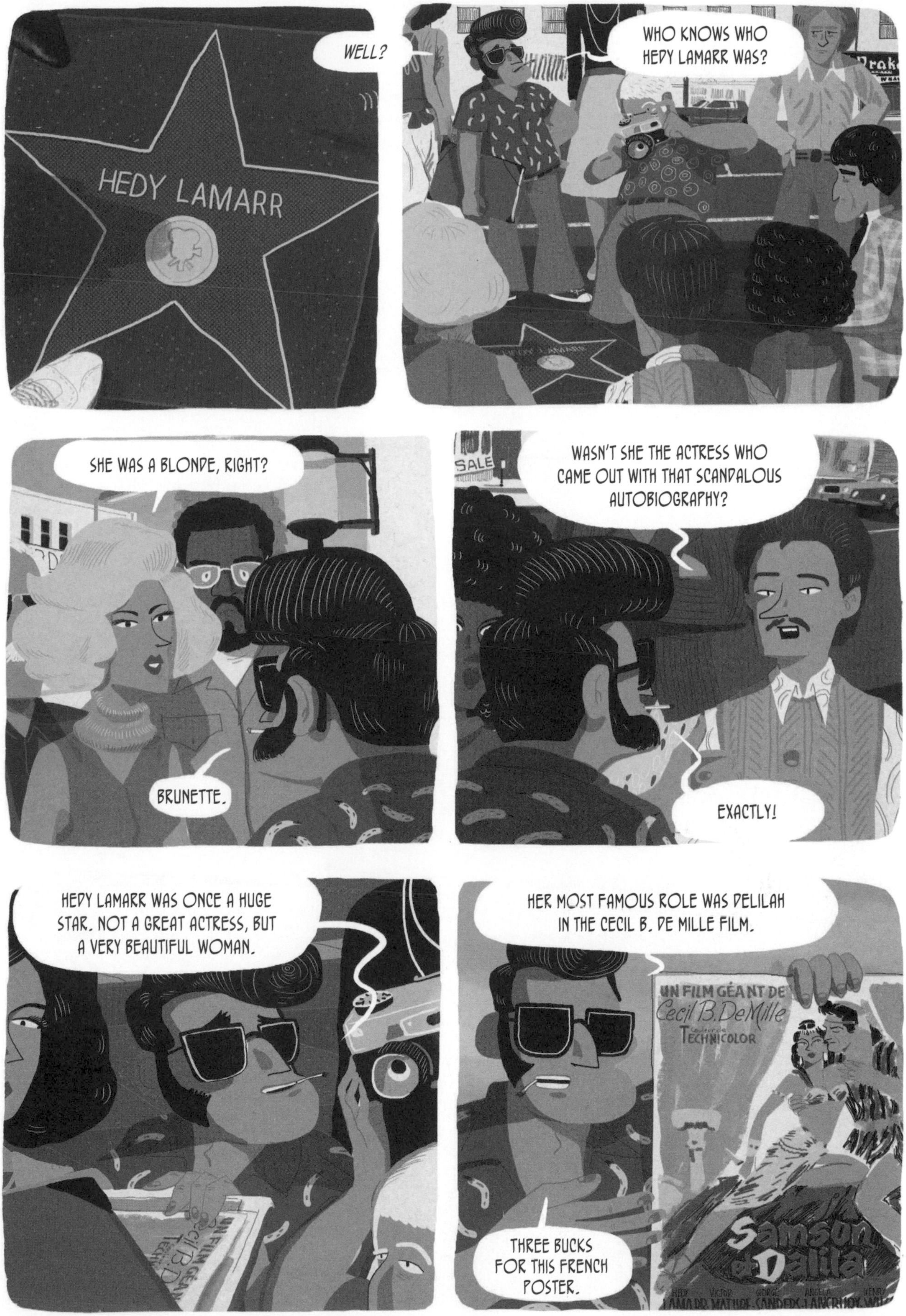
HEDY LAMARR
WELL?
WHO KNOWS WHO HEDY LAMARR WAS?
SHE WAS A BLONDE, RIGHT?
BRUNETTE.
WASN'T SHE THE ACTRESS WHO CAME OUT WITH THAT SCANDALOUS AUTOBIOGRAPHY?
EXACTLY!
HEDY LAMARR WAS ONCE A HUGE STAR. NOT A GREAT ACTRESS, BUT A VERY BEAUTIFUL WOMAN.
HER MOST FAMOUS ROLE WAS DELILAH IN THE CECIL B. DE MILLE FILM.
UN FILM GÉANT DE
Cecil B. DeMille
TECHNICOLOR
Samson et Dalila
THREE BUCKS FOR THIS FRENCH POSTER.

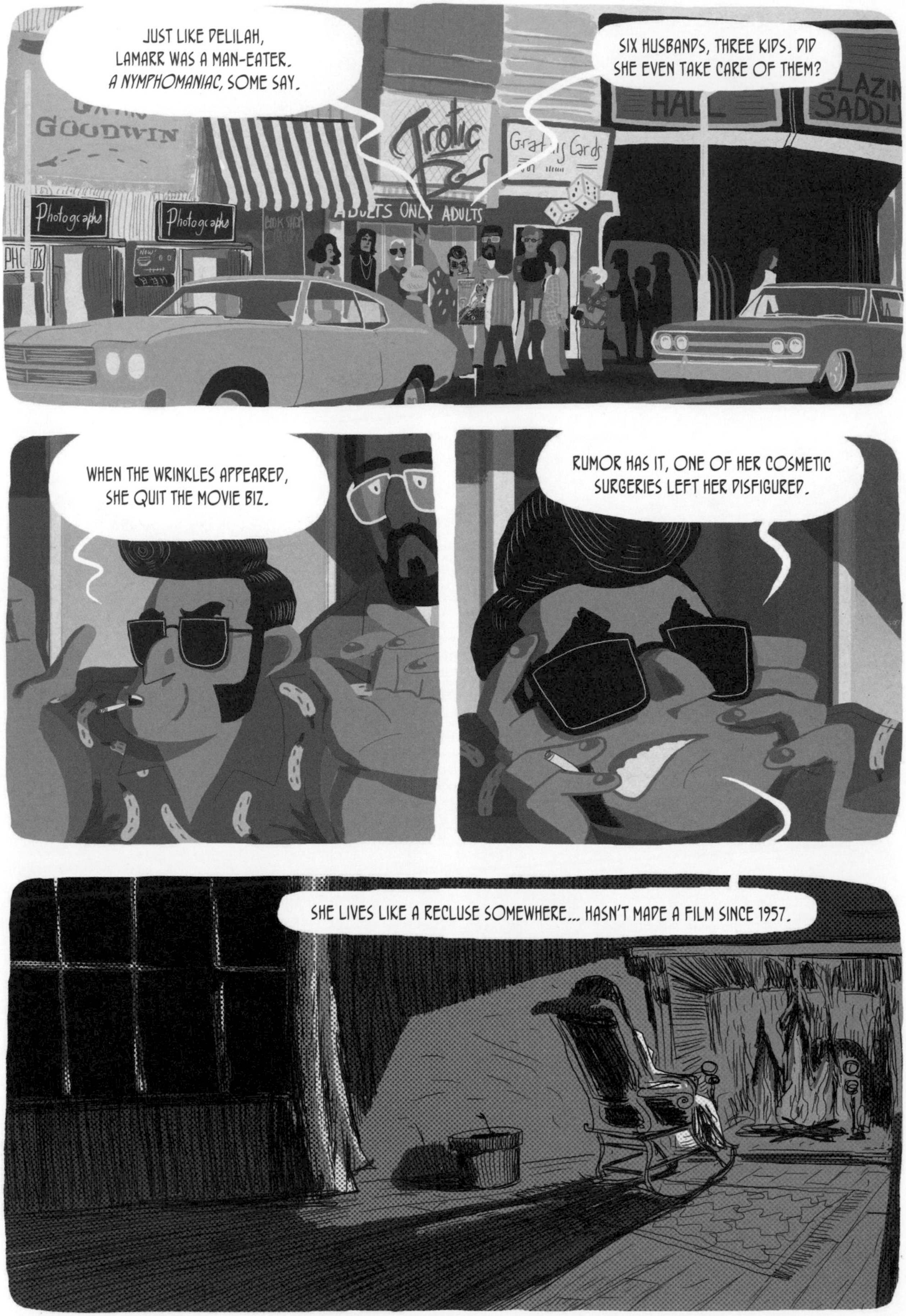
JUST LIKE DELILAH, LAMARR WAS A MAN-EATER. A NYMPHOMANIAC, SOME SAY.
SIX HUSBANDS, THREE KIDS. DID SHE EVEN TAKE CARE OF THEM?
GOODWIN
ADULTS ONLY ADULTS
WHEN THE WRINKLES APPEARED, SHE QUIT THE MOVIE BIZ.
RUMOR HAS IT, ONE OF HER COSMETIC SURGERIES LEFT HER DISFIGURED.
SHE LIVES LIKE A RECLUSE SOMEWHERE... HASN'T MADE A FILM SINCE 1957.

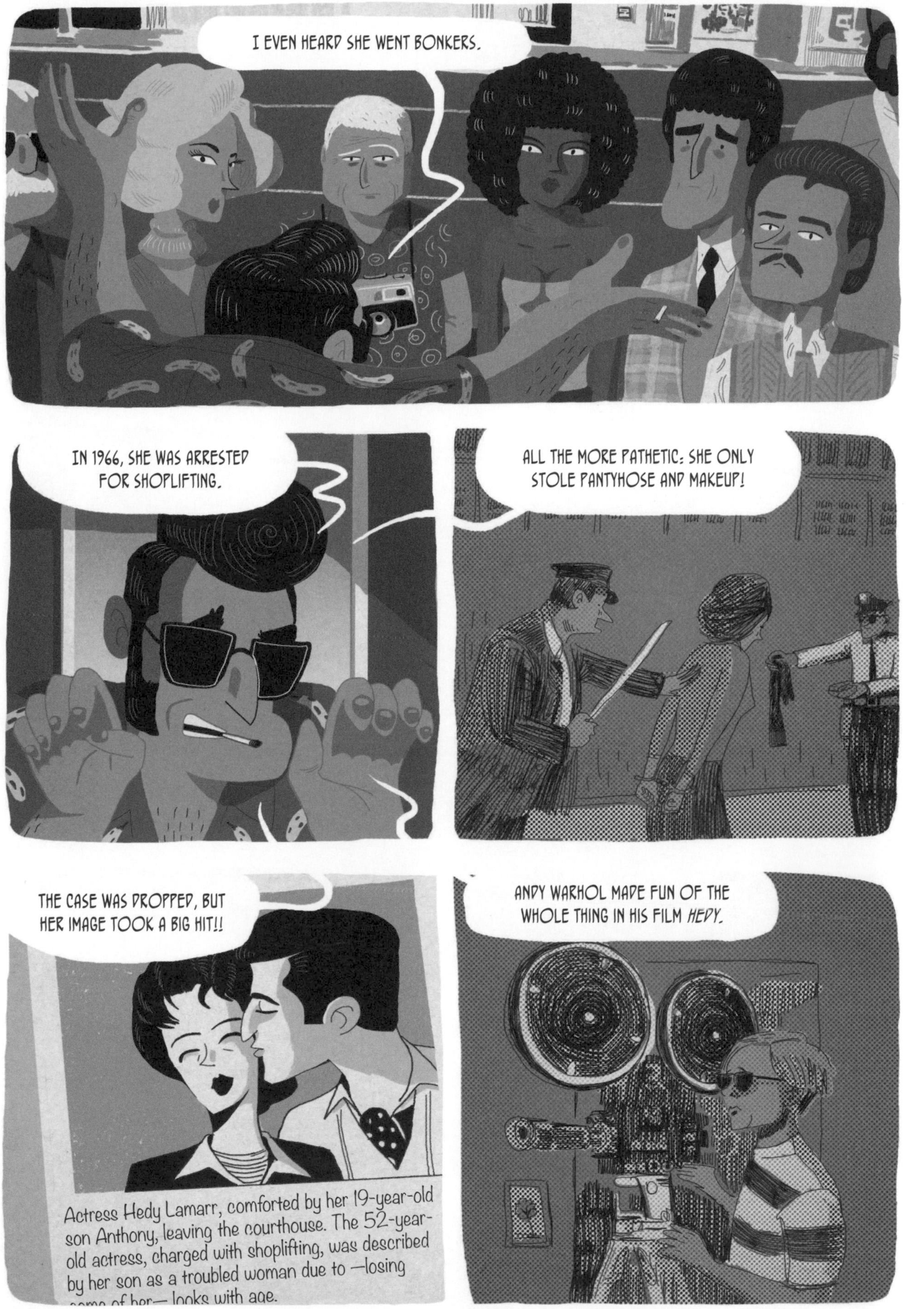
I EVEN HEARD SHE WENT BONKERS.
IN 1966, SHE WAS ARRESTED FOR SHOPLIFTING.
ALL THE MORE PATHETIC: SHE ONLY STOLE PANTYHOSE AND MAKEUP!
THE CASE WAS DROPPED, BUT HER IMAGE TOOK A BIG HIT!!
Actress Hedy Lamarr, comforted by her 19-year-old son Anthony, leaving the courthouse. The 52-year-old actress, charged with shoplifting, was described by her son as a troubled woman due to —losing some of her— looks with age.
ANDY WARHOL MADE FUN OF THE WHOLE THING IN HIS FILM *HEDY*.

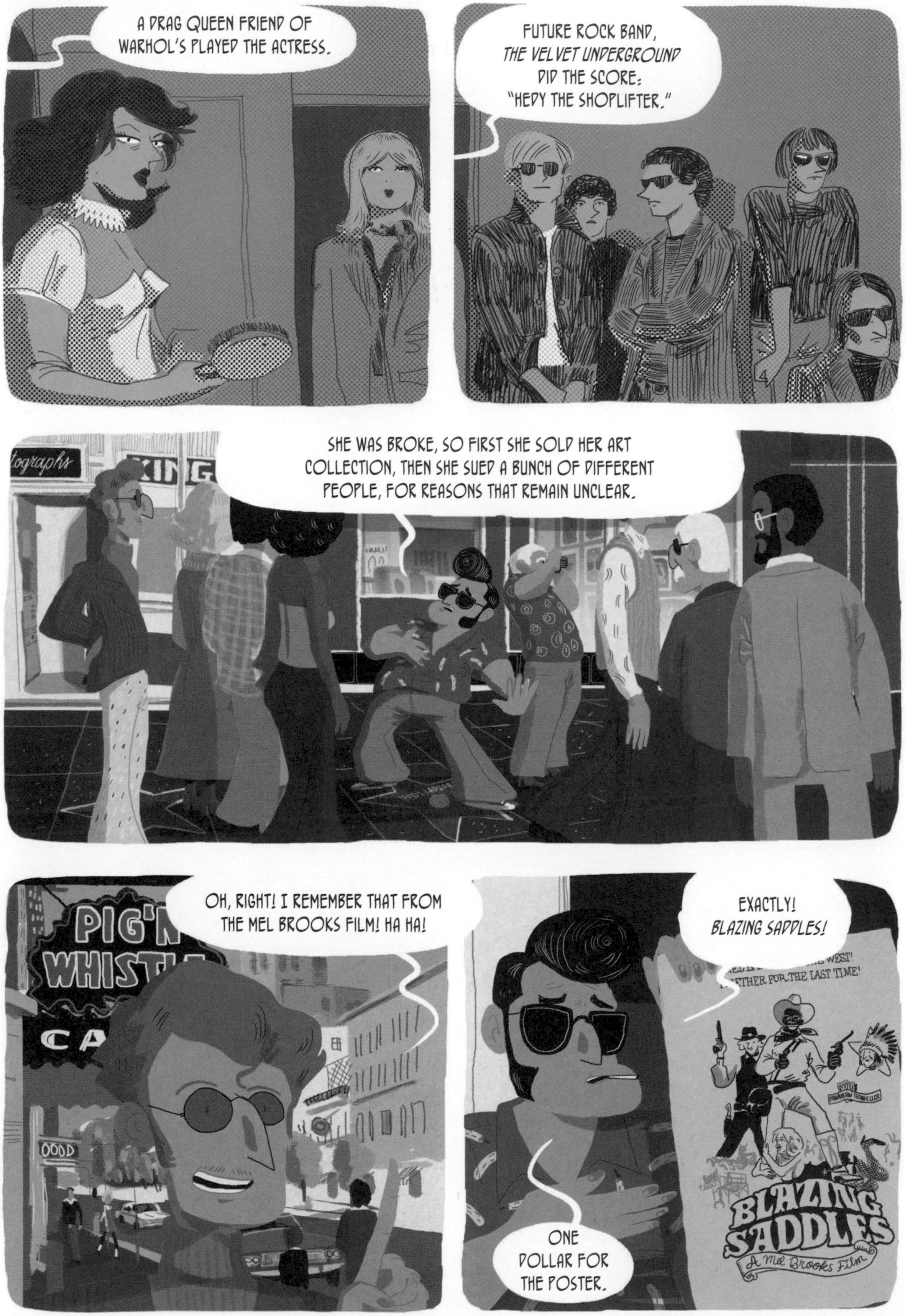
A DRAG QUEEN FRIEND OF WARHOL'S PLAYED THE ACTRESS.
FUTURE ROCK BAND, *THE VELVET UNDERGROUND* DID THE SCORE: "HEDY THE SHOPLIFTER."
SHE WAS BROKE, SO FIRST SHE SOLD HER ART COLLECTION, THEN SHE SUED A BUNCH OF DIFFERENT PEOPLE, FOR REASONS THAT REMAIN UNCLEAR.
OH, RIGHT! I REMEMBER THAT FROM THE MEL BROOKS FILM! HA HA!
PIG'N WHISTL
EXACTLY! *BLAZING SADDLES!*
ONE DOLLAR FOR THE POSTER.
BLAZING SADDLES
A Mel Brooks Film

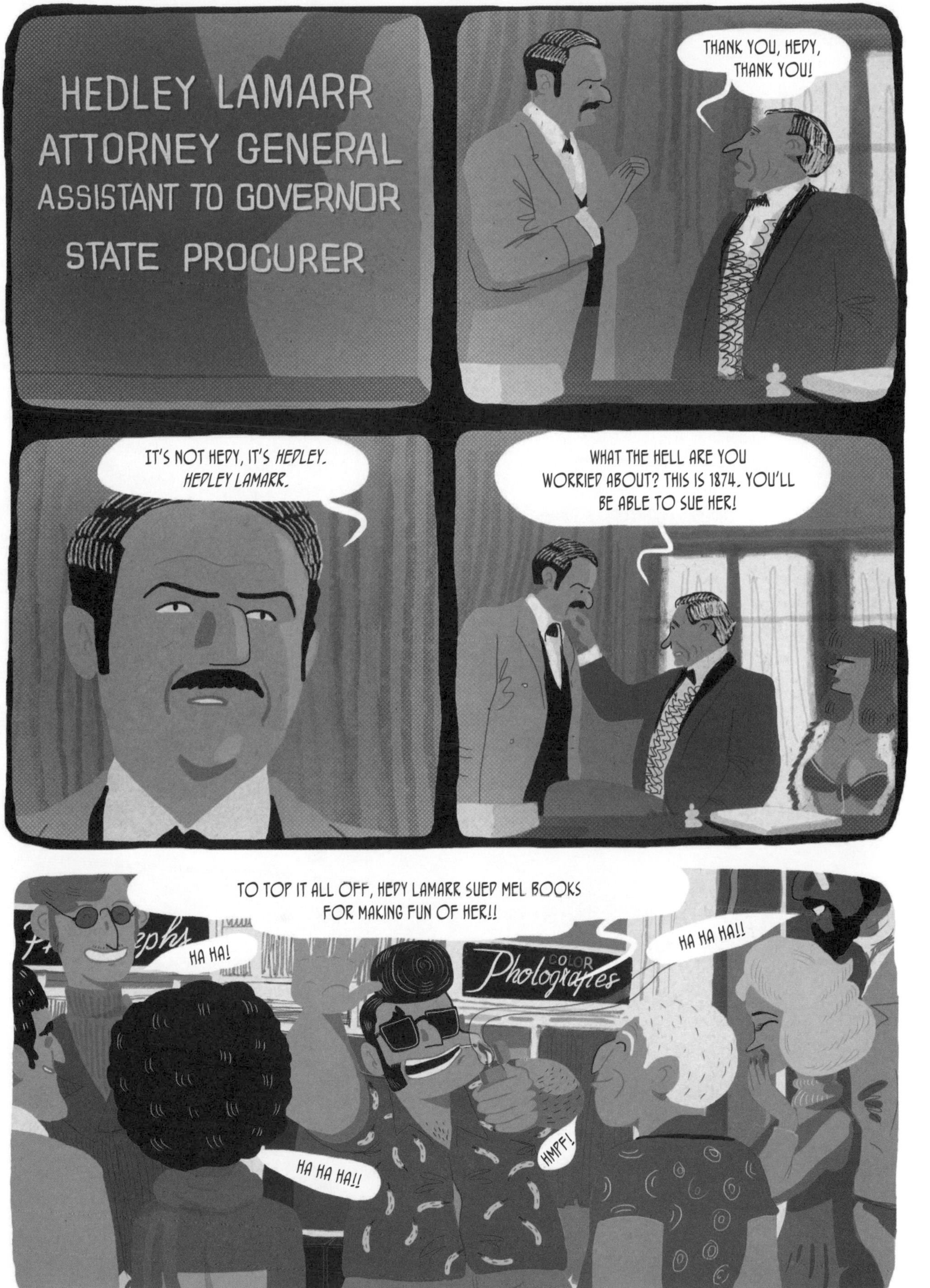
HEDLEY LAMARR
ATTORNEY GENERAL
ASSISTANT TO GOVERNOR
STATE PROCURER
THANK YOU, HEDY, THANK YOU!
IT'S NOT HEDY, IT'S HEDLEY. HEDLEY LAMARR.
WHAT THE HELL ARE YOU WORRIED ABOUT? THIS IS 1874. YOU'LL BE ABLE TO SUE HER!
TO TOP IT ALL OFF, HEDY LAMARR SUED MEL BOOKS FOR MAKING FUN OF HER!!
HA HA!
COLOR Photographes
HA HA HA!!
HA HA HA!!
HMPF!

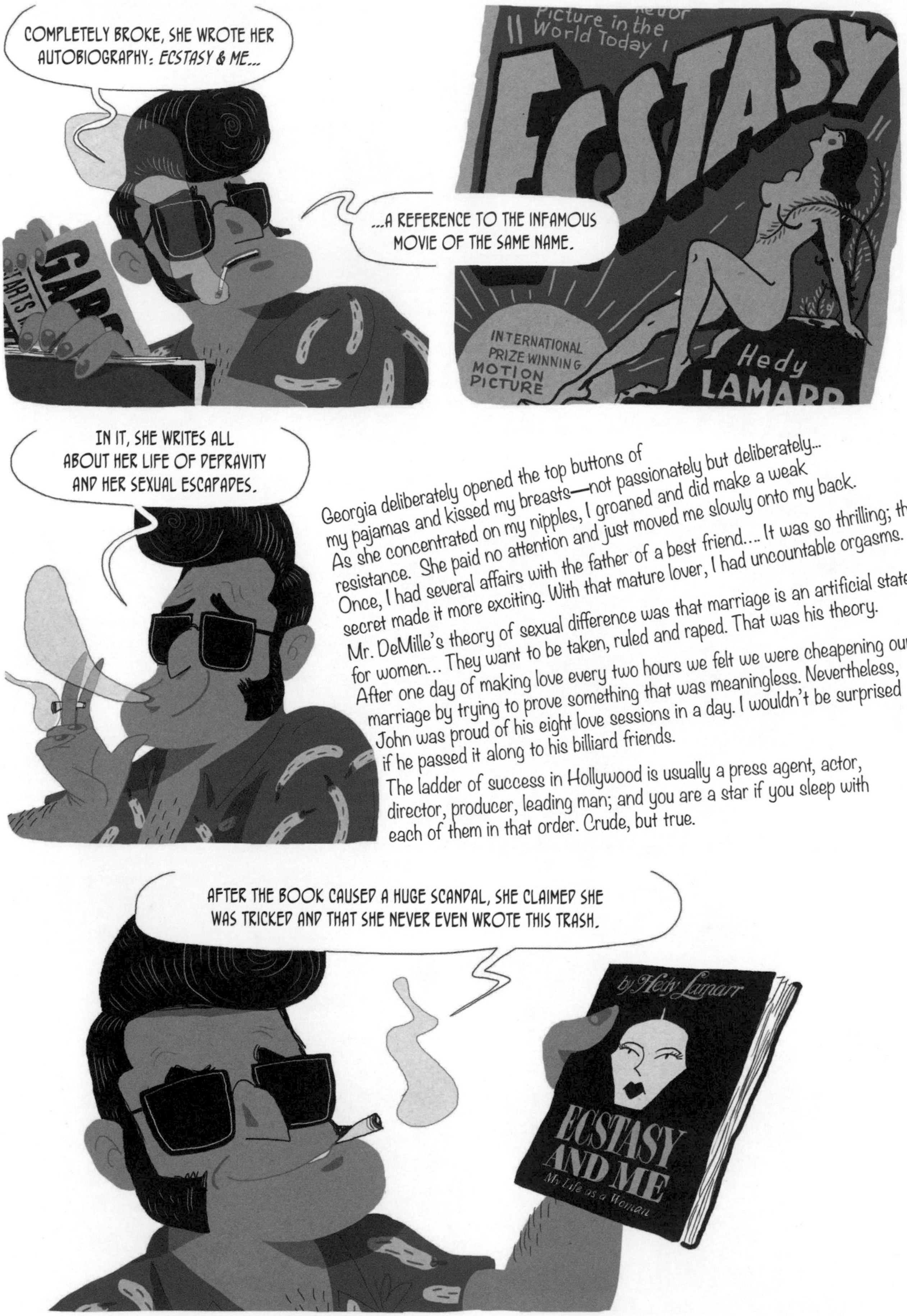
COMPLETELY BROKE, SHE WROTE HER AUTOBIOGRAPHY: *ECSTASY & ME*...
...A REFERENCE TO THE INFAMOUS MOVIE OF THE SAME NAME.
Picture in the World Today !
ECSTASY
INTERNATIONAL PRIZE WINNING MOTION PICTURE
Hedy LAMARR
IN IT, SHE WRITES ALL ABOUT HER LIFE OF DEPRAVITY AND HER SEXUAL ESCAPADES.
Georgia deliberately opened the top buttons of my pajamas and kissed my breasts—not passionately but deliberately... As she concentrated on my nipples, I groaned and did make a weak resistance. She paid no attention and just moved me slowly onto my back.
Once, I had several affairs with the father of a best friend.... It was so thrilling; the secret made it more exciting. With that mature lover, I had uncountable orgasms.
Mr. DeMille's theory of sexual difference was that marriage is an artificial state for women... They want to be taken, ruled and raped. That was his theory.
After one day of making love every two hours we felt we were cheapening our marriage by trying to prove something that was meaningless. Nevertheless, John was proud of his eight love sessions in a day. I wouldn't be surprised if he passed it along to his billiard friends.
The ladder of success in Hollywood is usually a press agent, actor, director, producer, leading man; and you are a star if you sleep with each of them in that order. Crude, but true.
AFTER THE BOOK CAUSED A HUGE SCANDAL, SHE CLAIMED SHE WAS TRICKED AND THAT SHE NEVER EVEN WROTE THIS TRASH.
by Hedy Lamarr
ECSTASY AND ME
My Life as a Woman

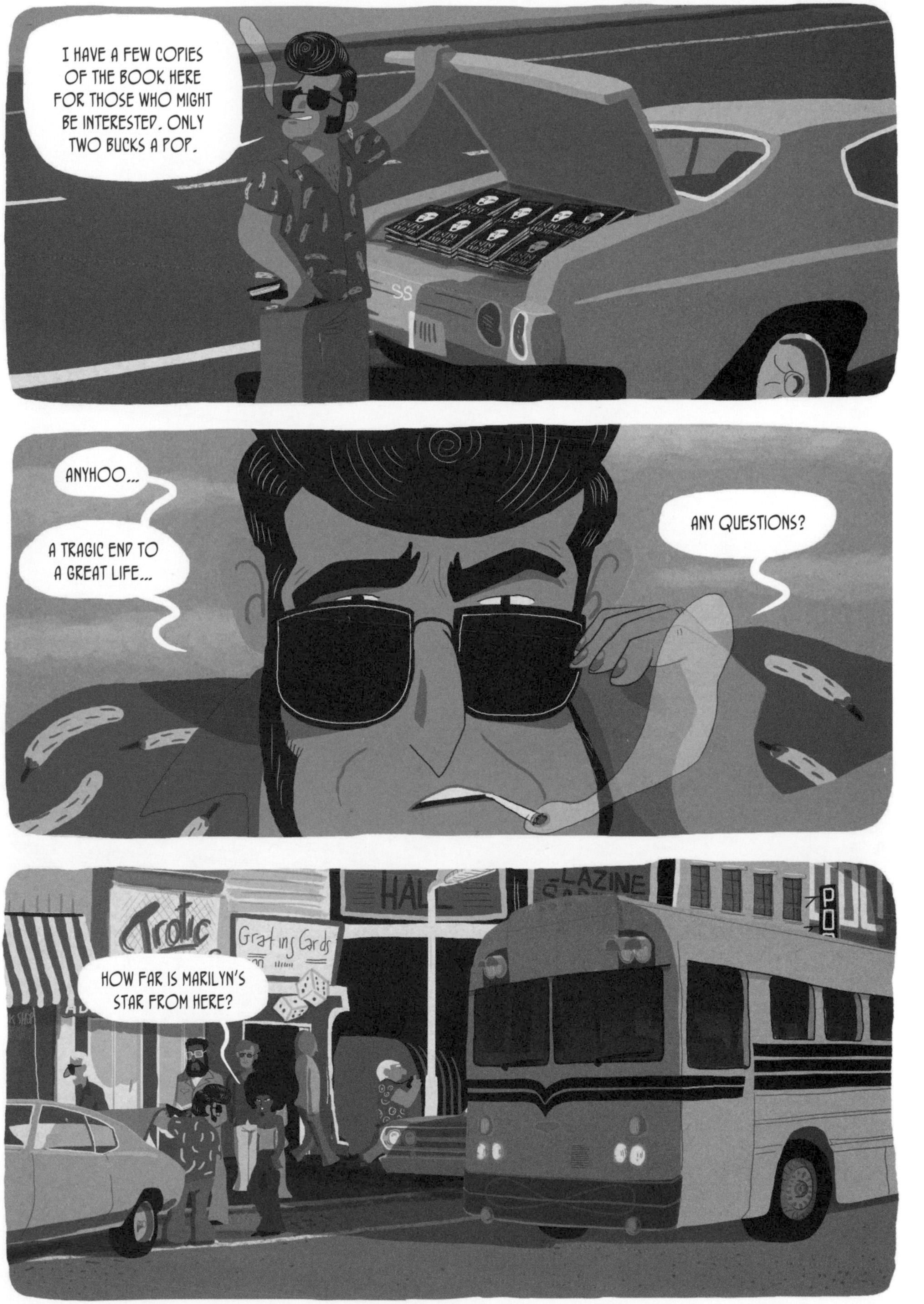

I HAVE A FEW COPIES OF THE BOOK HERE FOR THOSE WHO MIGHT BE INTERESTED. ONLY TWO BUCKS A POP.
SS
ANYHOO...
A TRAGIC END TO A GREAT LIFE...
ANY QUESTIONS?
HALL
LAZINE
Trotic
Grating Cards
HOW FAR IS MARILYN'S STAR FROM HERE?

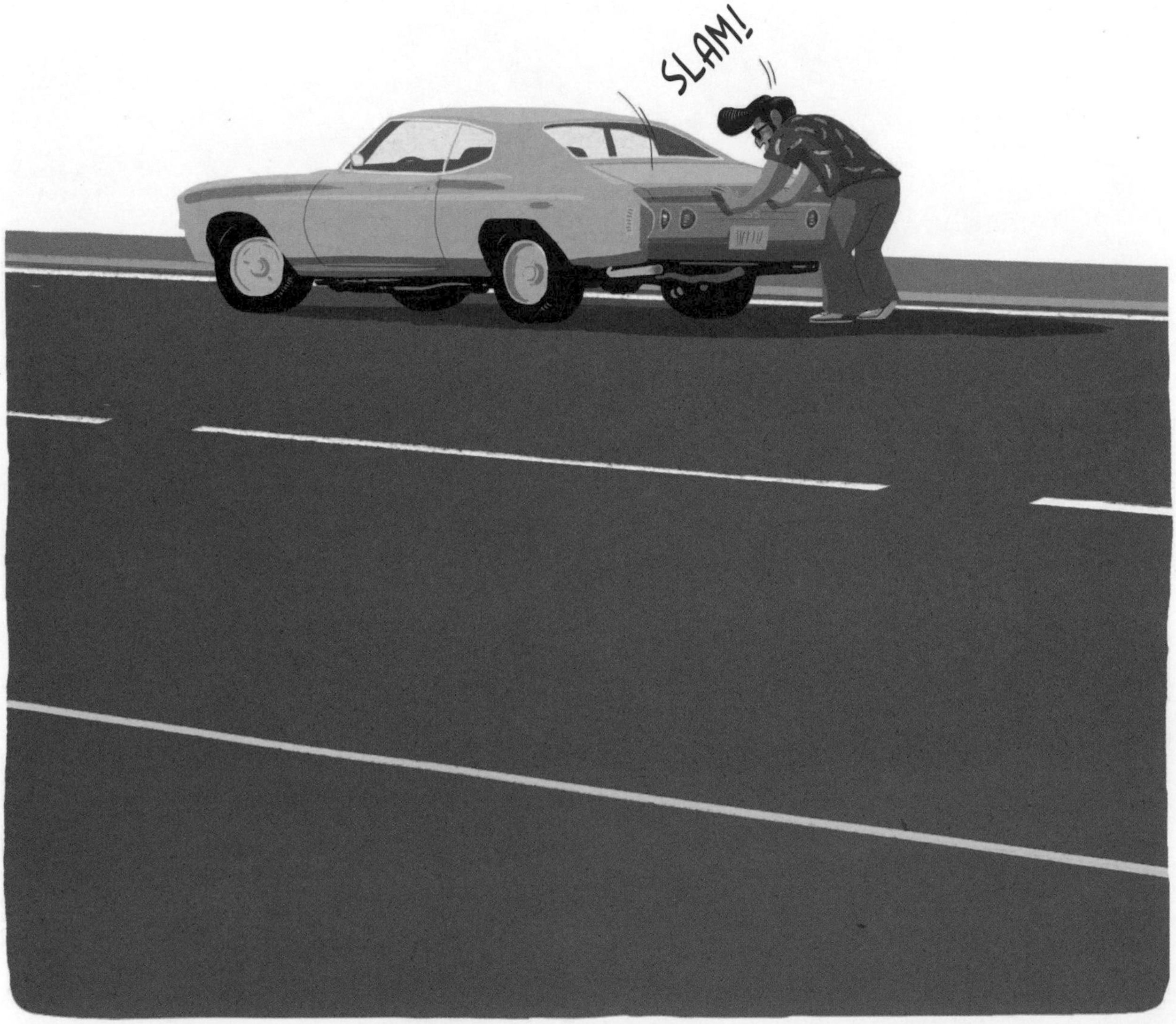
SLAM!

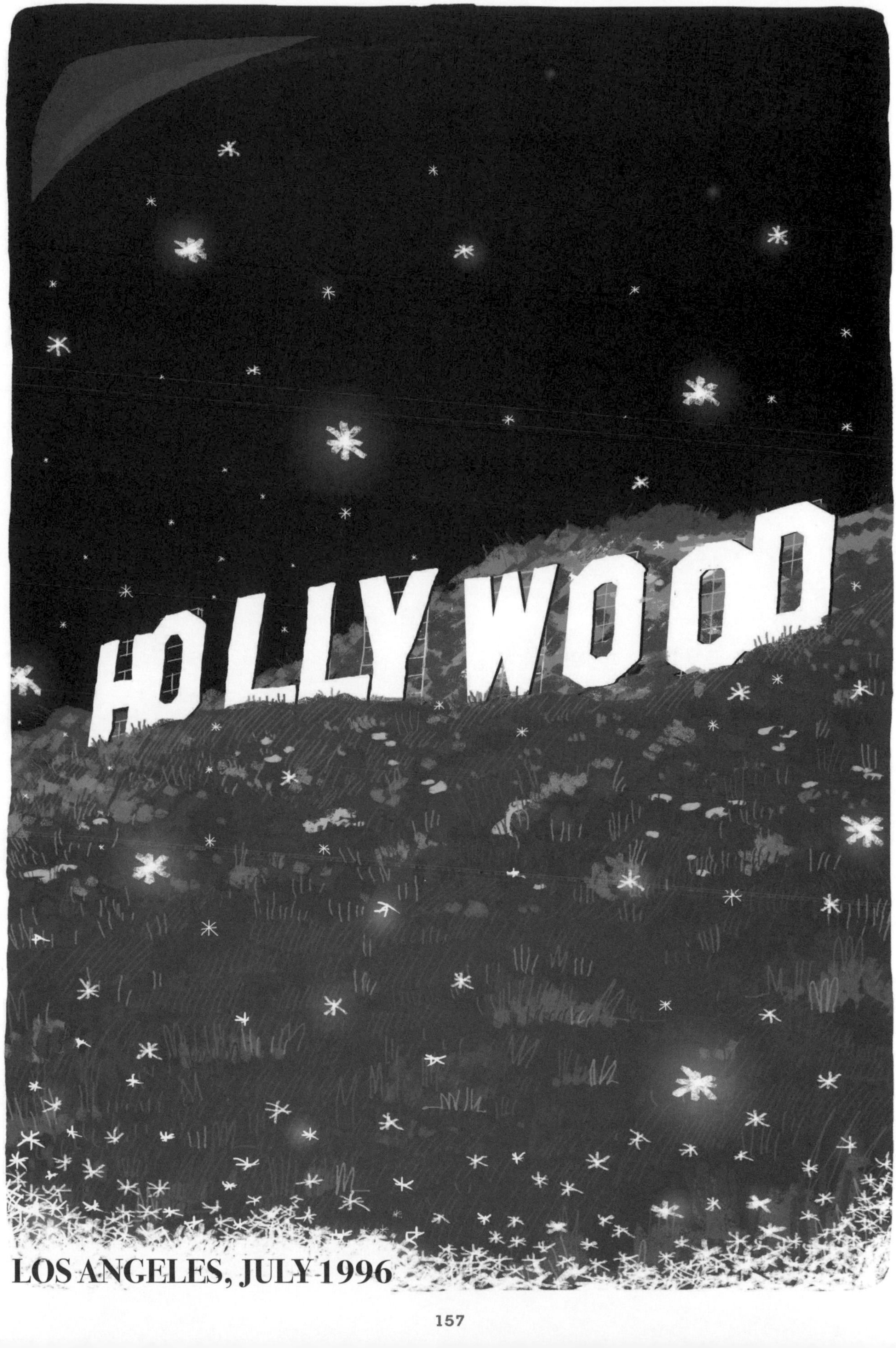
HOLLYWOOD

LOS ANGELES, JULY 1996

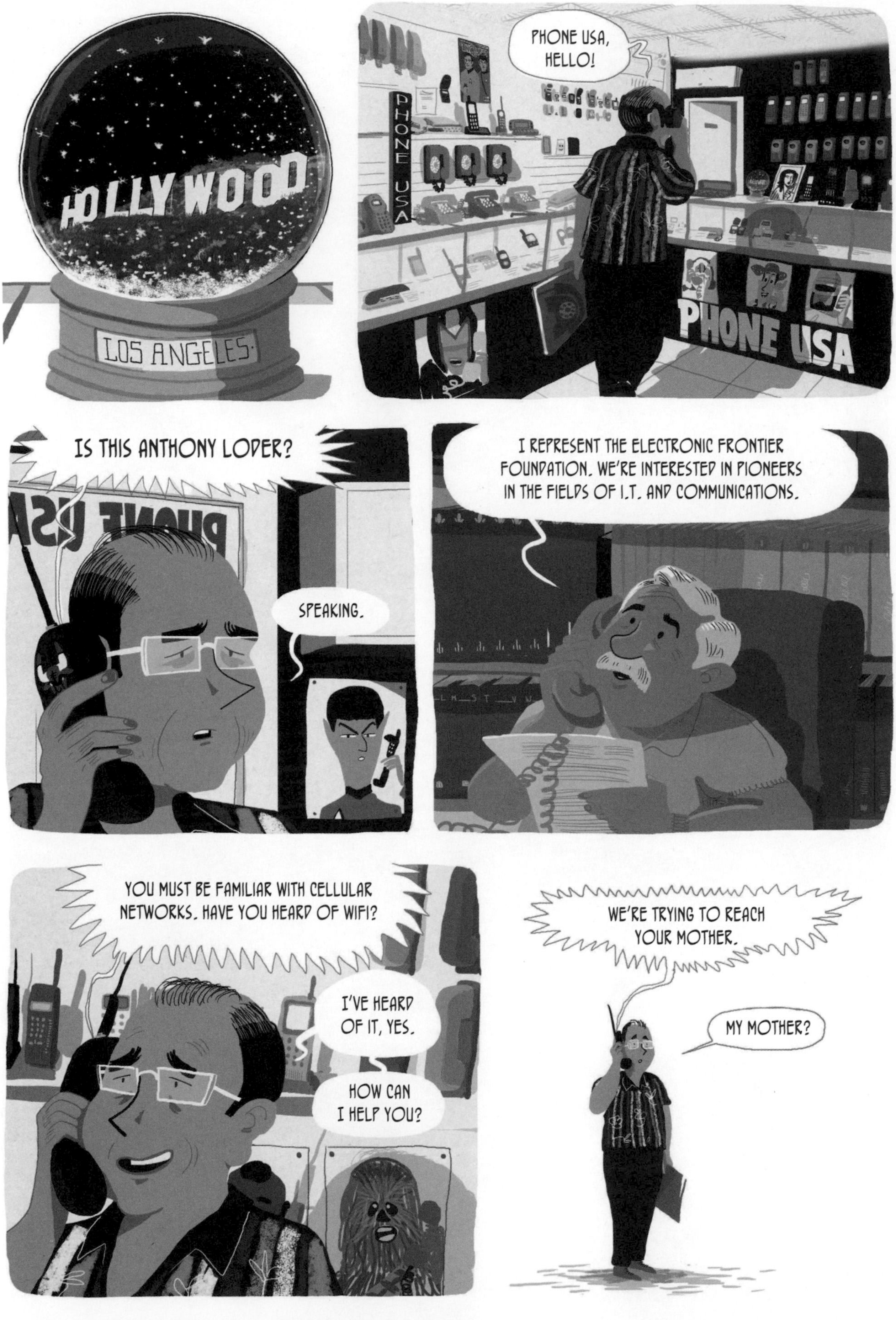
HOLLYWOOD
LOS ANGELES
PHONE USA, HELLO!
PHONE USA
PHONE USA
IS THIS ANTHONY LODER?
SPEAKING.
I REPRESENT THE ELECTRONIC FRONTIER FOUNDATION. WE'RE INTERESTED IN PIONEERS IN THE FIELDS OF I.T. AND COMMUNICATIONS.
YOU MUST BE FAMILIAR WITH CELLULAR NETWORKS. HAVE YOU HEARD OF WIFI?
I'VE HEARD OF IT, YES.
HOW CAN I HELP YOU?
WE'RE TRYING TO REACH YOUR MOTHER.
MY MOTHER?

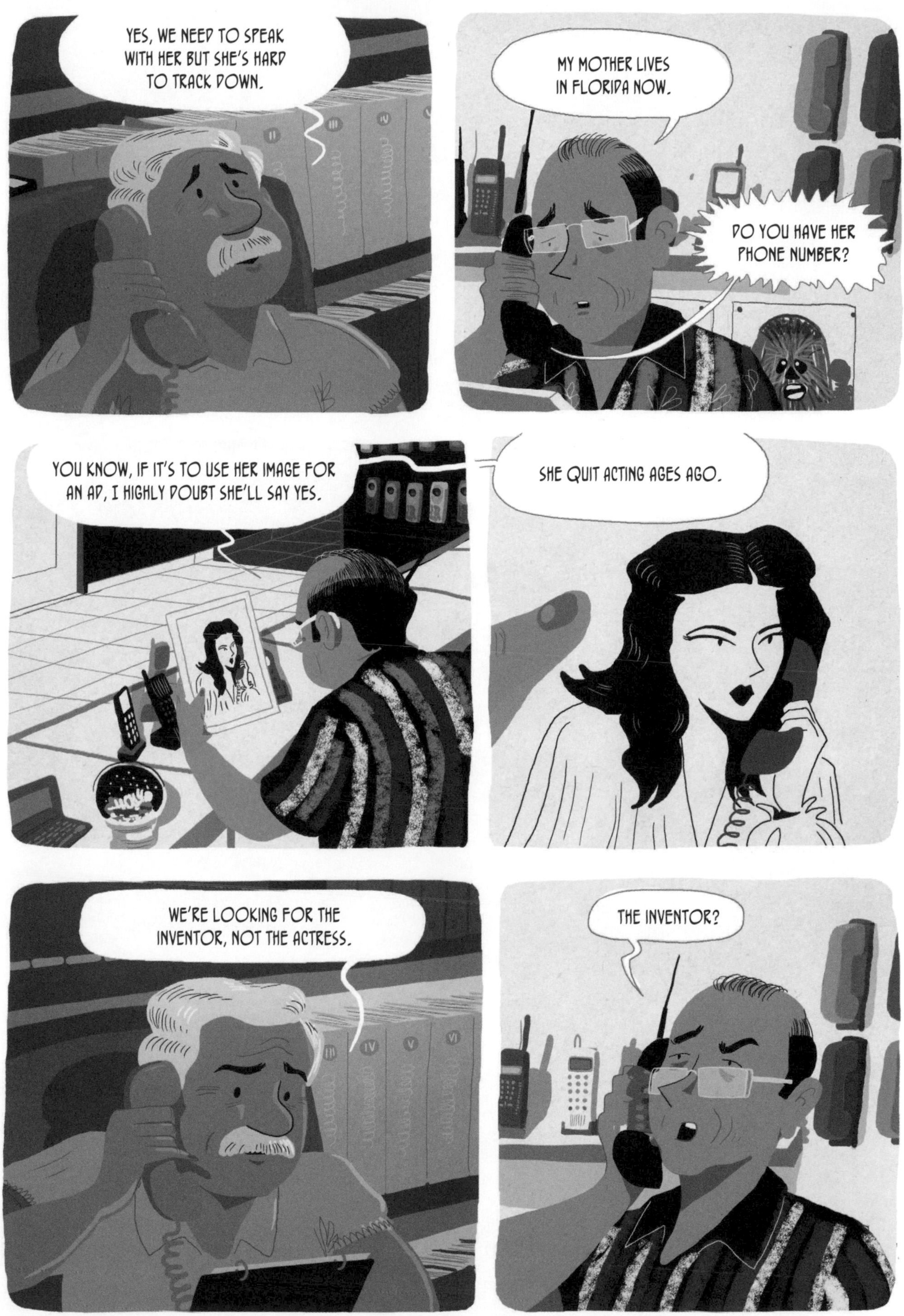
YES, WE NEED TO SPEAK WITH HER BUT SHE'S HARD TO TRACK DOWN.
MY MOTHER LIVES IN FLORIDA NOW.
DO YOU HAVE HER PHONE NUMBER?
YOU KNOW, IF IT'S TO USE HER IMAGE FOR AN AD, I HIGHLY DOUBT SHE'LL SAY YES.
SHE QUIT ACTING AGES AGO.
WE'RE LOOKING FOR THE INVENTOR, NOT THE ACTRESS.
THE INVENTOR?

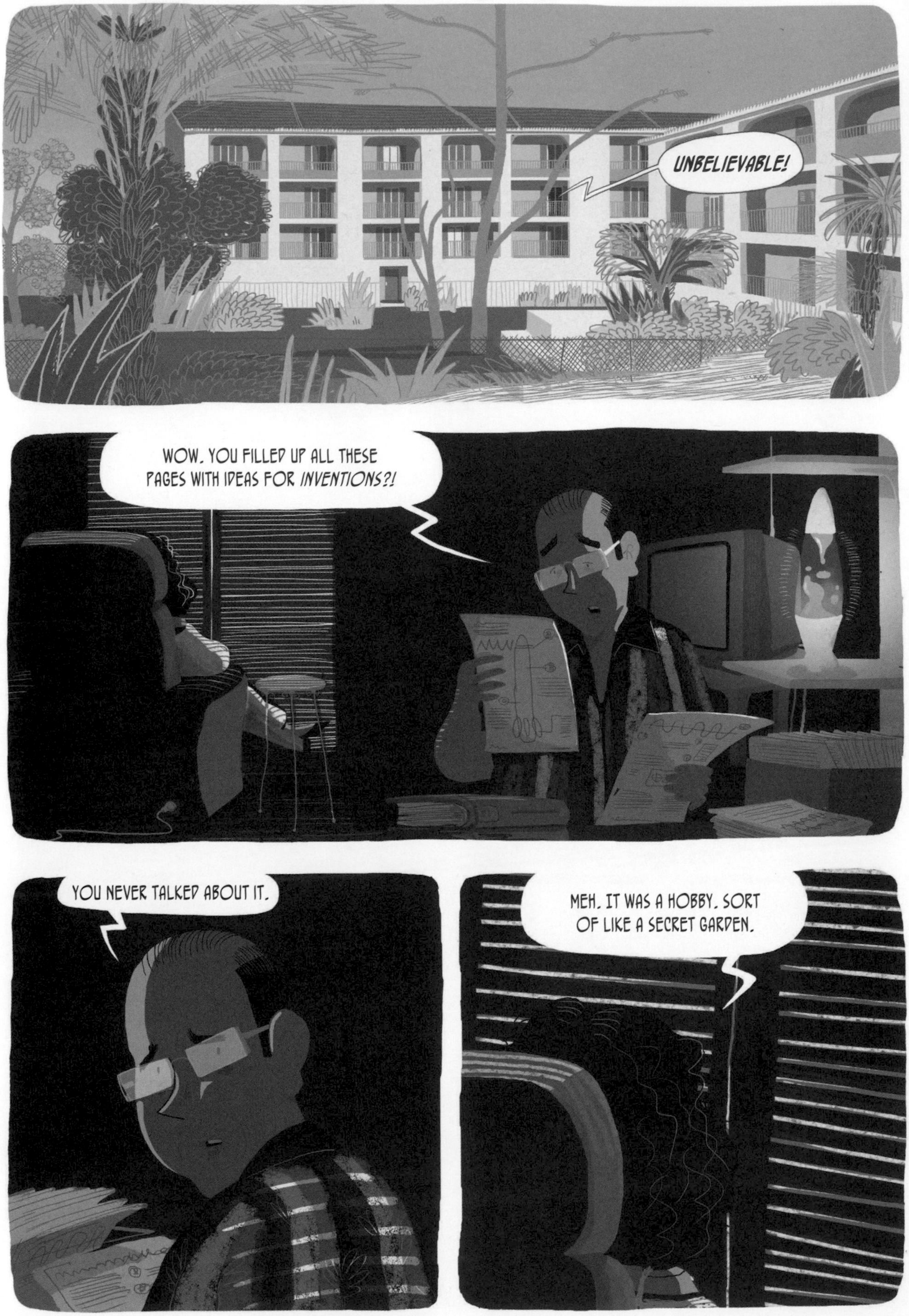
UNBELIEVABLE!
WOW. YOU FILLED UP ALL THESE PAGES WITH IDEAS FOR *INVENTIONS?!*
YOU NEVER TALKED ABOUT IT.
MEH. IT WAS A HOBBY. SORT OF LIKE A SECRET GARDEN.

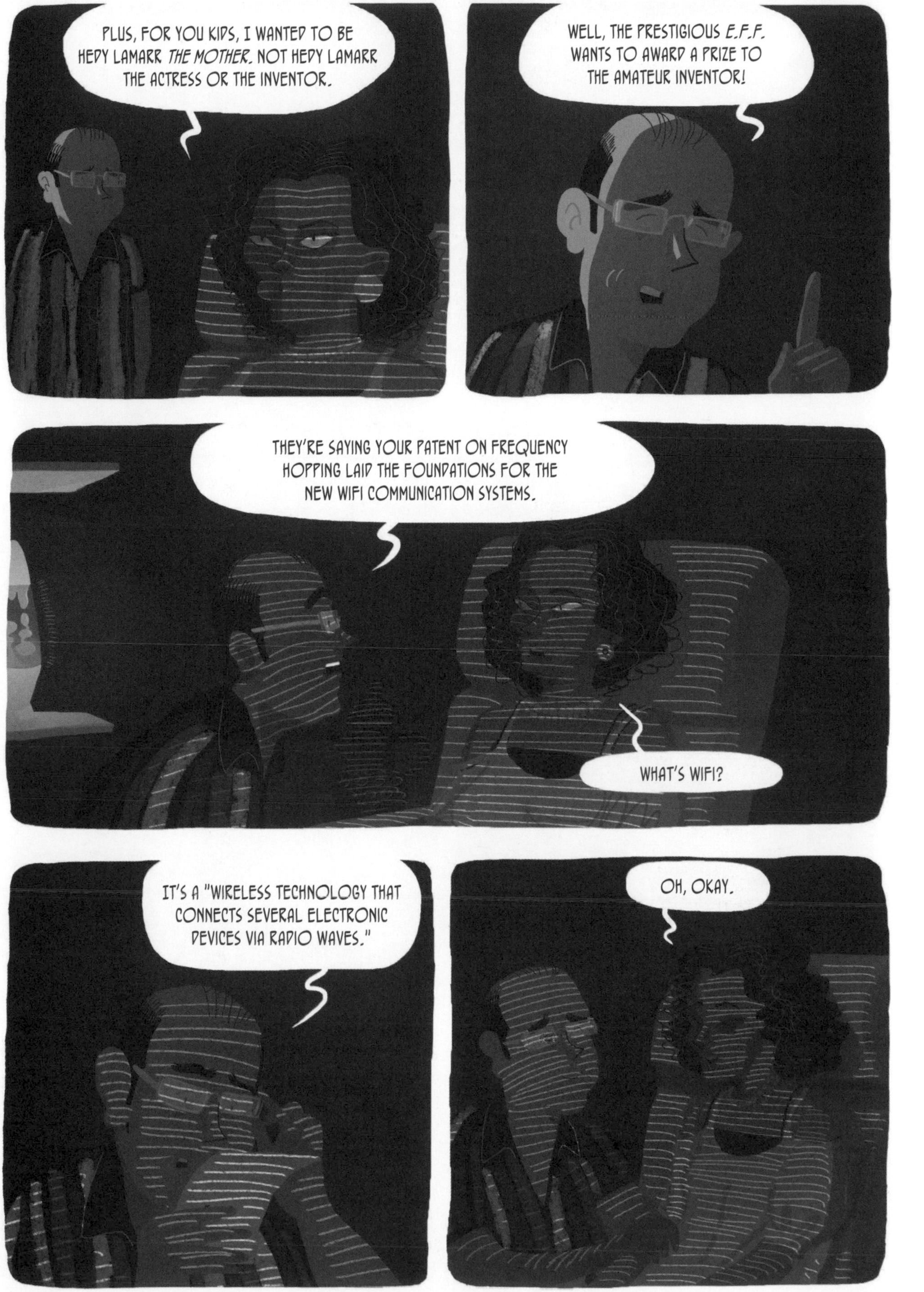
PLUS, FOR YOU KIDS, I WANTED TO BE HEDY LAMARR *THE MOTHER.* NOT HEDY LAMARR THE ACTRESS OR THE INVENTOR.
WELL, THE PRESTIGIOUS *E.F.F.* WANTS TO AWARD A PRIZE TO THE AMATEUR INVENTOR!
THEY'RE SAYING YOUR PATENT ON FREQUENCY HOPPING LAID THE FOUNDATIONS FOR THE NEW WIFI COMMUNICATION SYSTEMS.
WHAT'S WIFI?
IT'S A "WIRELESS TECHNOLOGY THAT CONNECTS SEVERAL ELECTRONIC DEVICES VIA RADIO WAVES."
OH, OKAY.

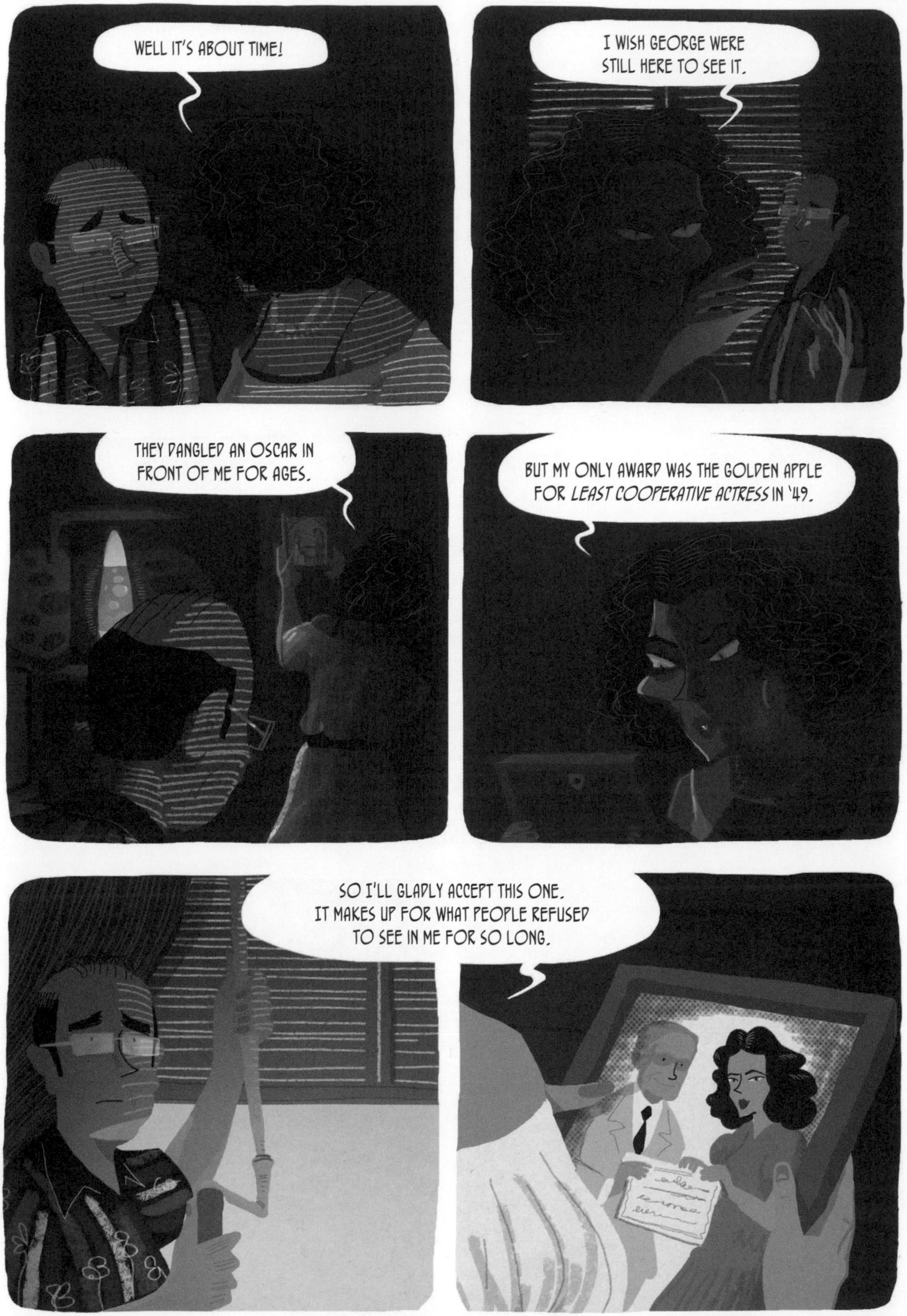
WELL IT'S ABOUT TIME!
I WISH GEORGE WERE STILL HERE TO SEE IT.
THEY DANGLED AN OSCAR IN FRONT OF ME FOR AGES.
BUT MY ONLY AWARD WAS THE GOLDEN APPLE FOR *LEAST COOPERATIVE ACTRESS* IN '49.
SO I'LL GLADLY ACCEPT THIS ONE. IT MAKES UP FOR WHAT PEOPLE REFUSED TO SEE IN ME FOR SO LONG.

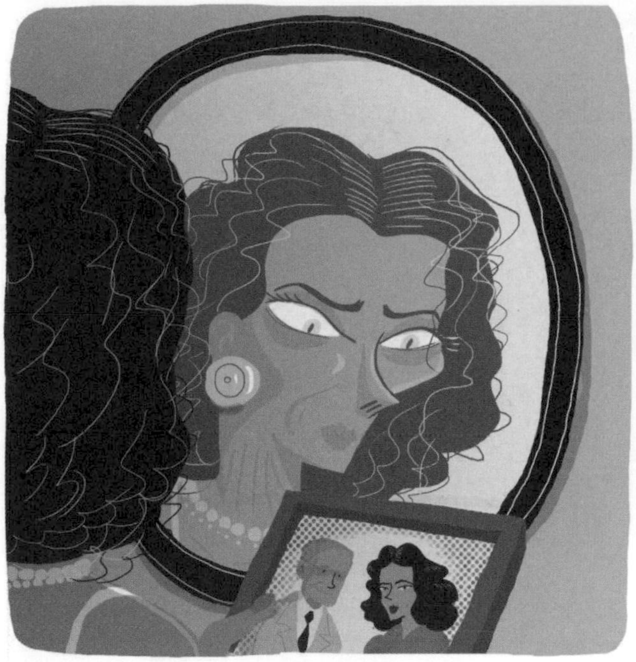

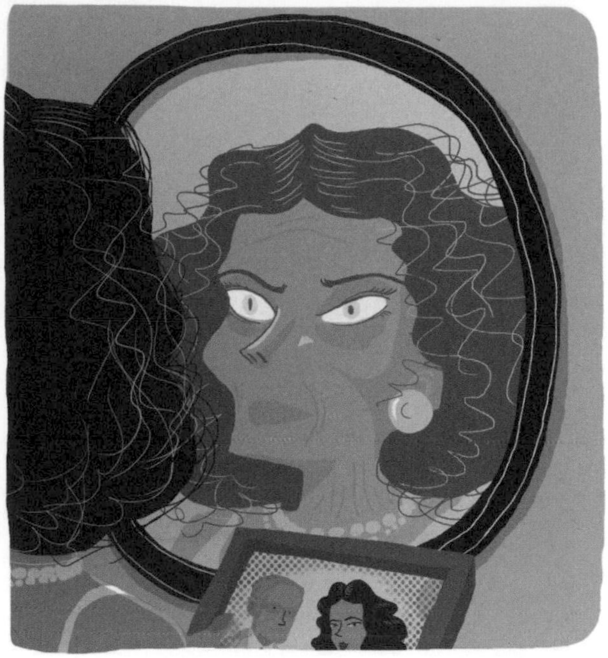

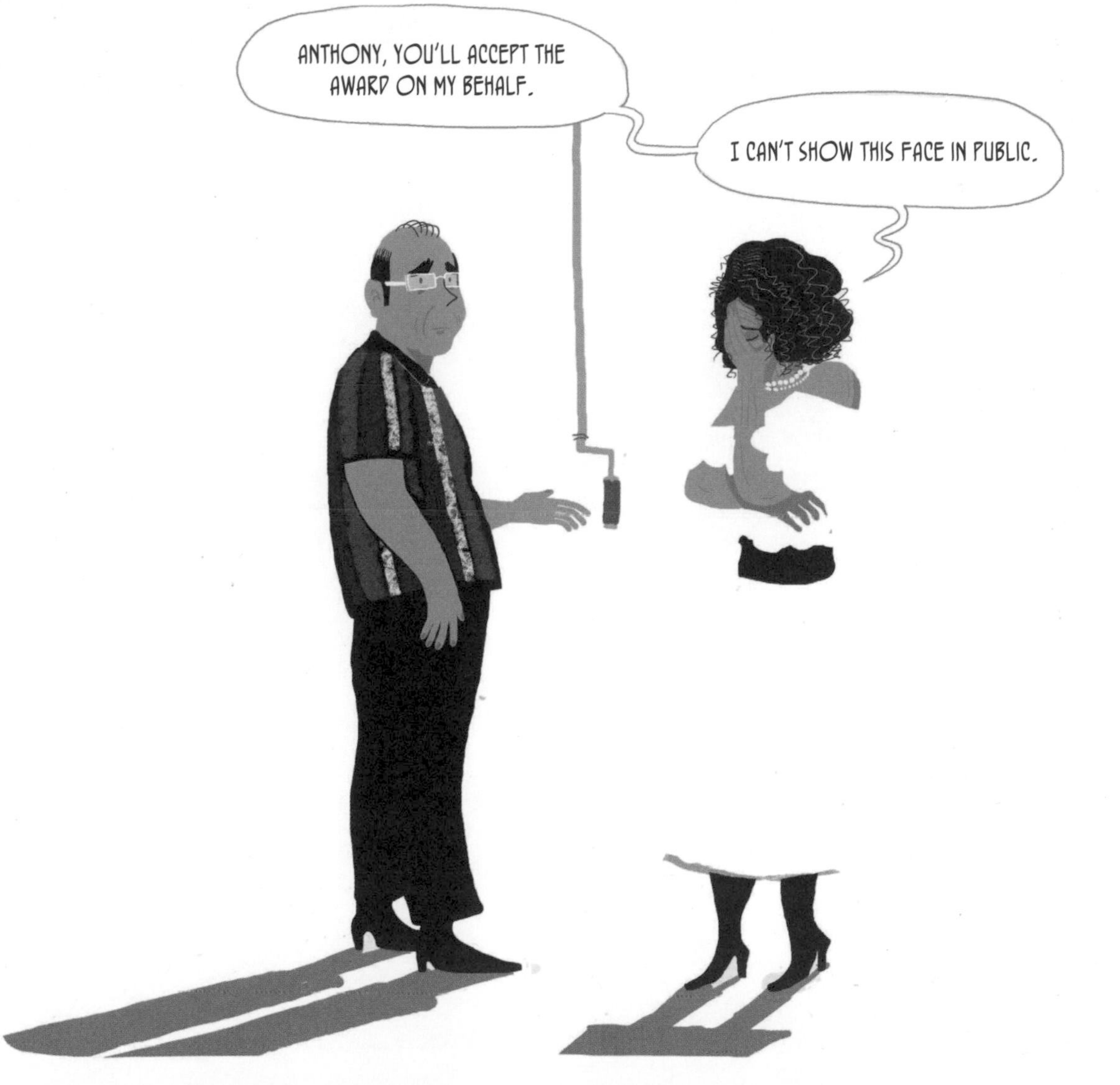
ANTHONY, YOU'LL ACCEPT THE AWARD ON MY BEHALF.
I CAN'T SHOW THIS FACE IN PUBLIC.

MARCH 12TH, 1997

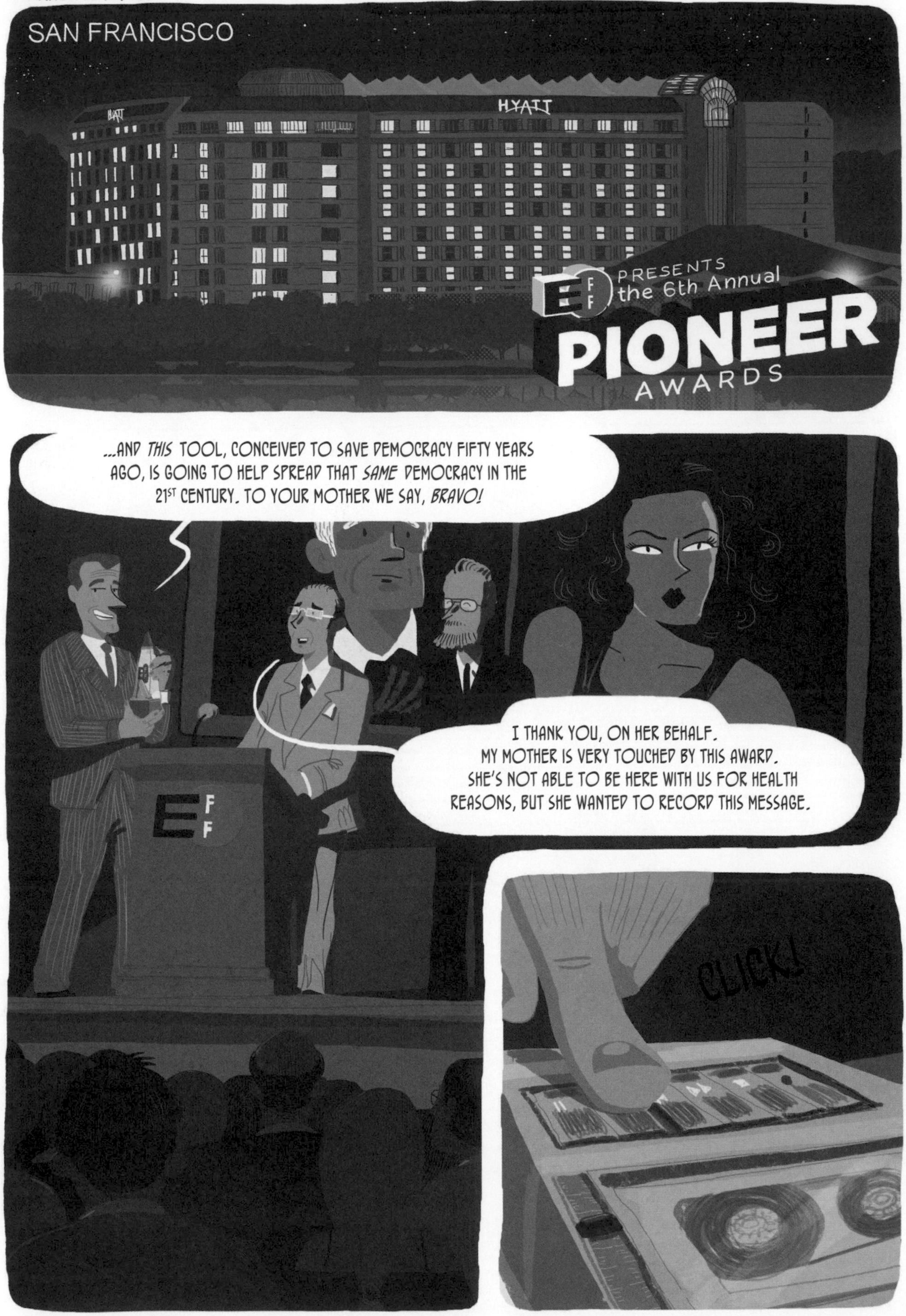
SAN FRANCISCO
HYATT
EFF PRESENTS the 6th Annual PIONEER AWARDS
...AND *THIS* TOOL, CONCEIVED TO SAVE DEMOCRACY FIFTY YEARS AGO, IS GOING TO HELP SPREAD THAT *SAME* DEMOCRACY IN THE 21ST CENTURY. TO YOUR MOTHER WE SAY, *BRAVO!*
EFF
I THANK YOU, ON HER BEHALF. MY MOTHER IS VERY TOUCHED BY THIS AWARD. SHE'S NOT ABLE TO BE HERE WITH US FOR HEALTH REASONS, BUT SHE WANTED TO RECORD THIS MESSAGE.
CLICK!

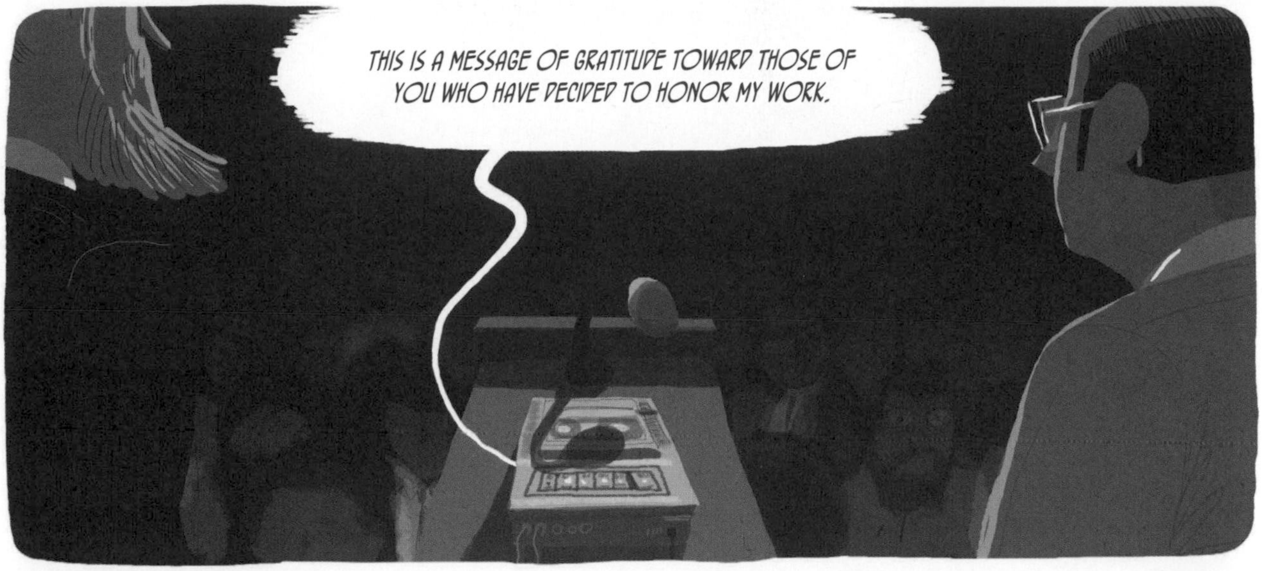
THIS IS A MESSAGE OF GRATITUDE TOWARD THOSE OF YOU WHO HAVE DECIDED TO HONOR MY WORK.

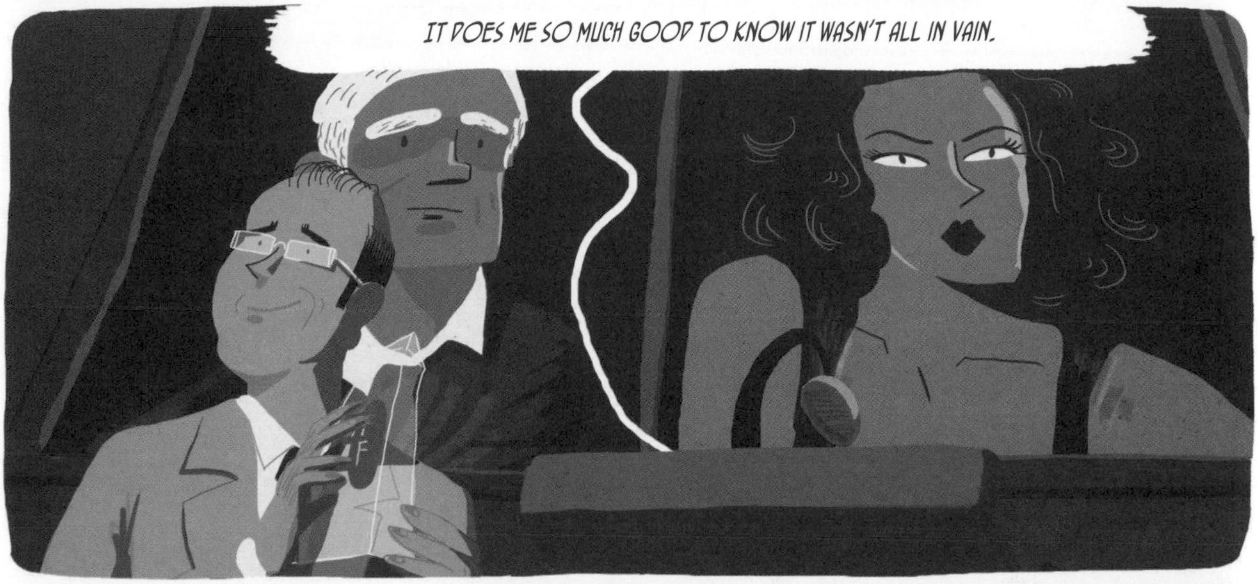
IT DOES ME SO MUCH GOOD TO KNOW IT WASN'T ALL IN VAIN.

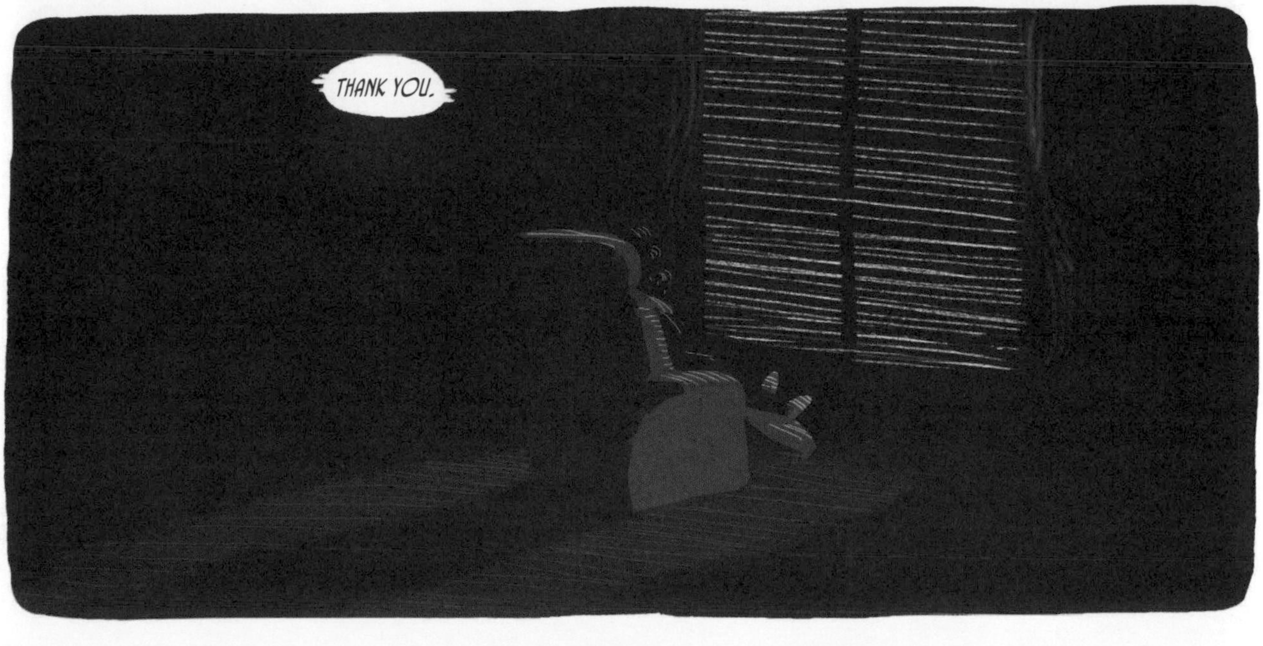
THANK YOU.

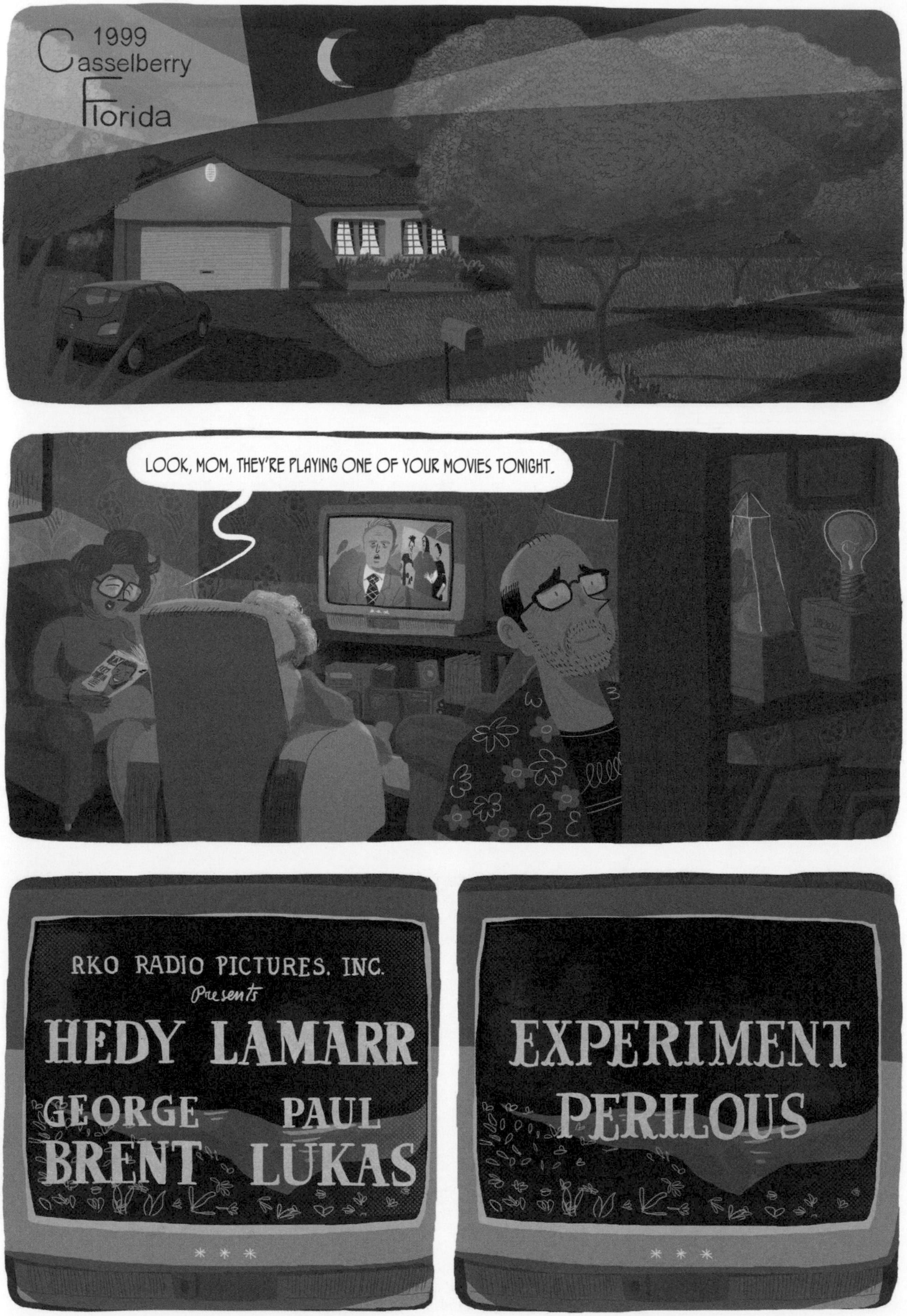
1999
Casselberry
Florida
LOOK, MOM, THEY'RE PLAYING ONE OF YOUR MOVIES TONIGHT.
RKO RADIO PICTURES. INC.
Presents
HEDY LAMARR
GEORGE BRENT
PAUL LUKAS
EXPERIMENT PERILOUS

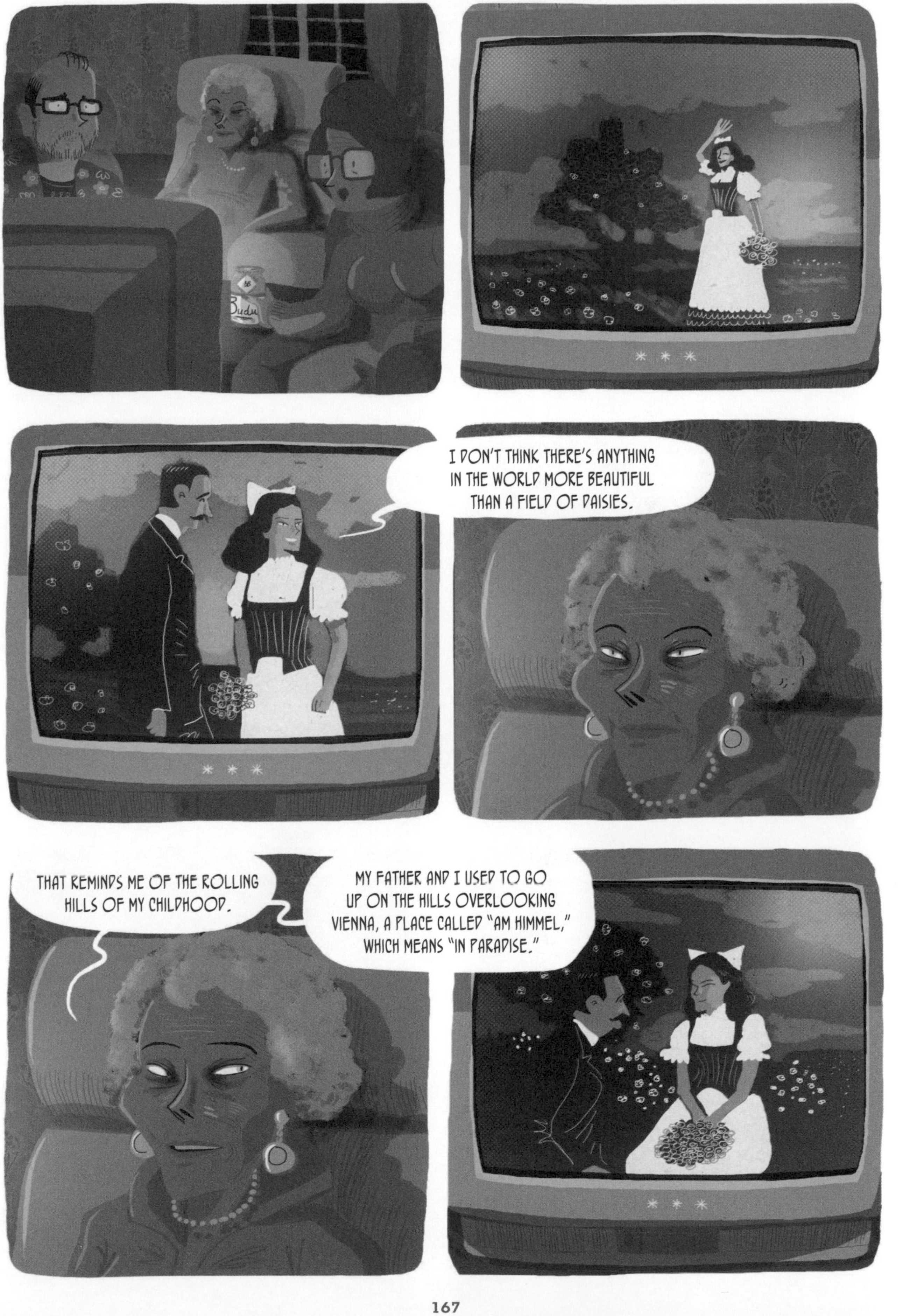
I DON'T THINK THERE'S ANYTHING IN THE WORLD MORE BEAUTIFUL THAN A FIELD OF DAISIES.
THAT REMINDS ME OF THE ROLLING HILLS OF MY CHILDHOOD.
MY FATHER AND I USED TO GO UP ON THE HILLS OVERLOOKING VIENNA, A PLACE CALLED "AM HIMMEL," WHICH MEANS "IN PARADISE."

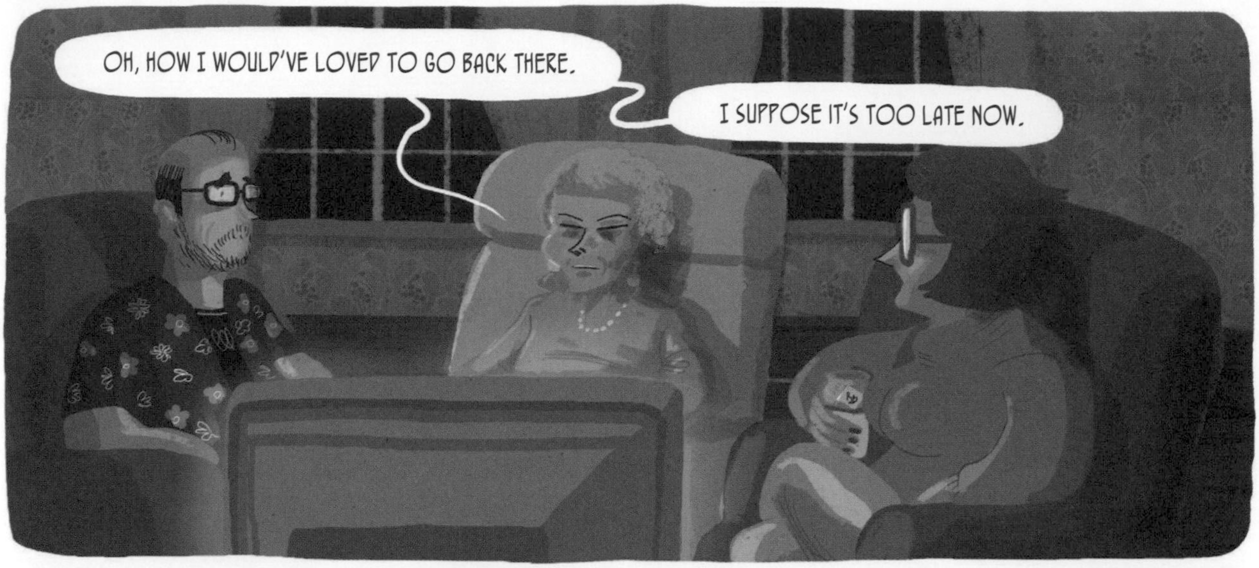
OH, HOW I WOULD'VE LOVED TO GO BACK THERE.
I SUPPOSE IT'S TOO LATE NOW.

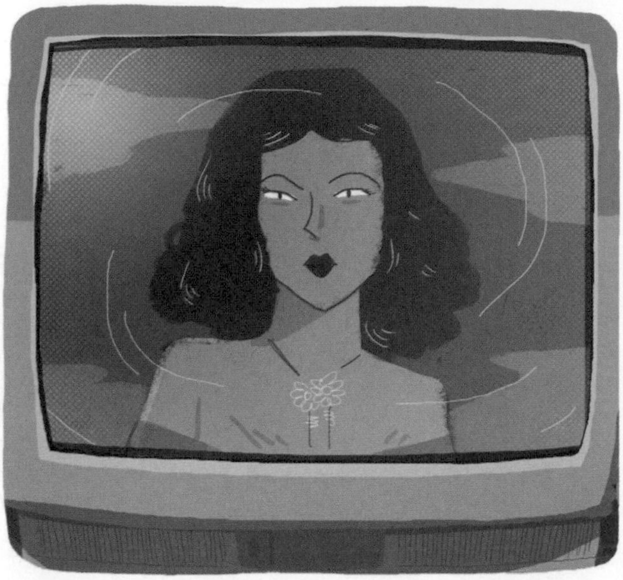

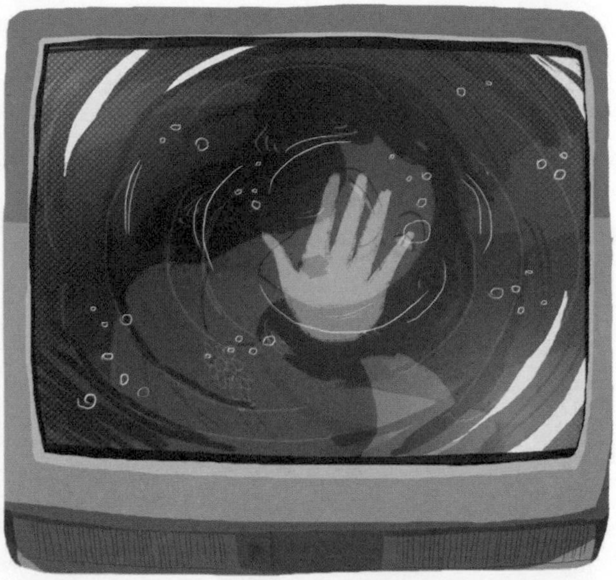

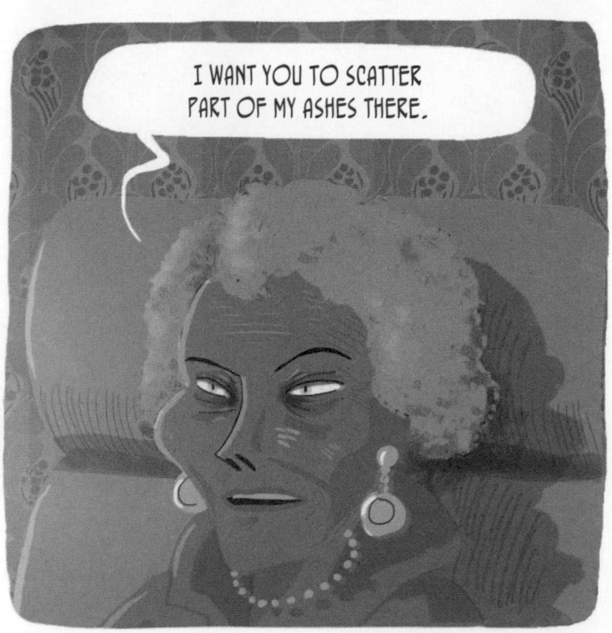
I WANT YOU TO SCATTER PART OF MY ASHES THERE.

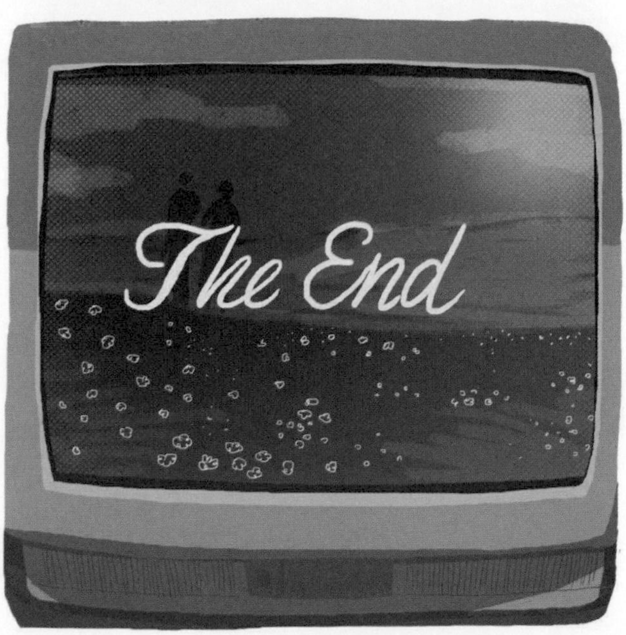
The End

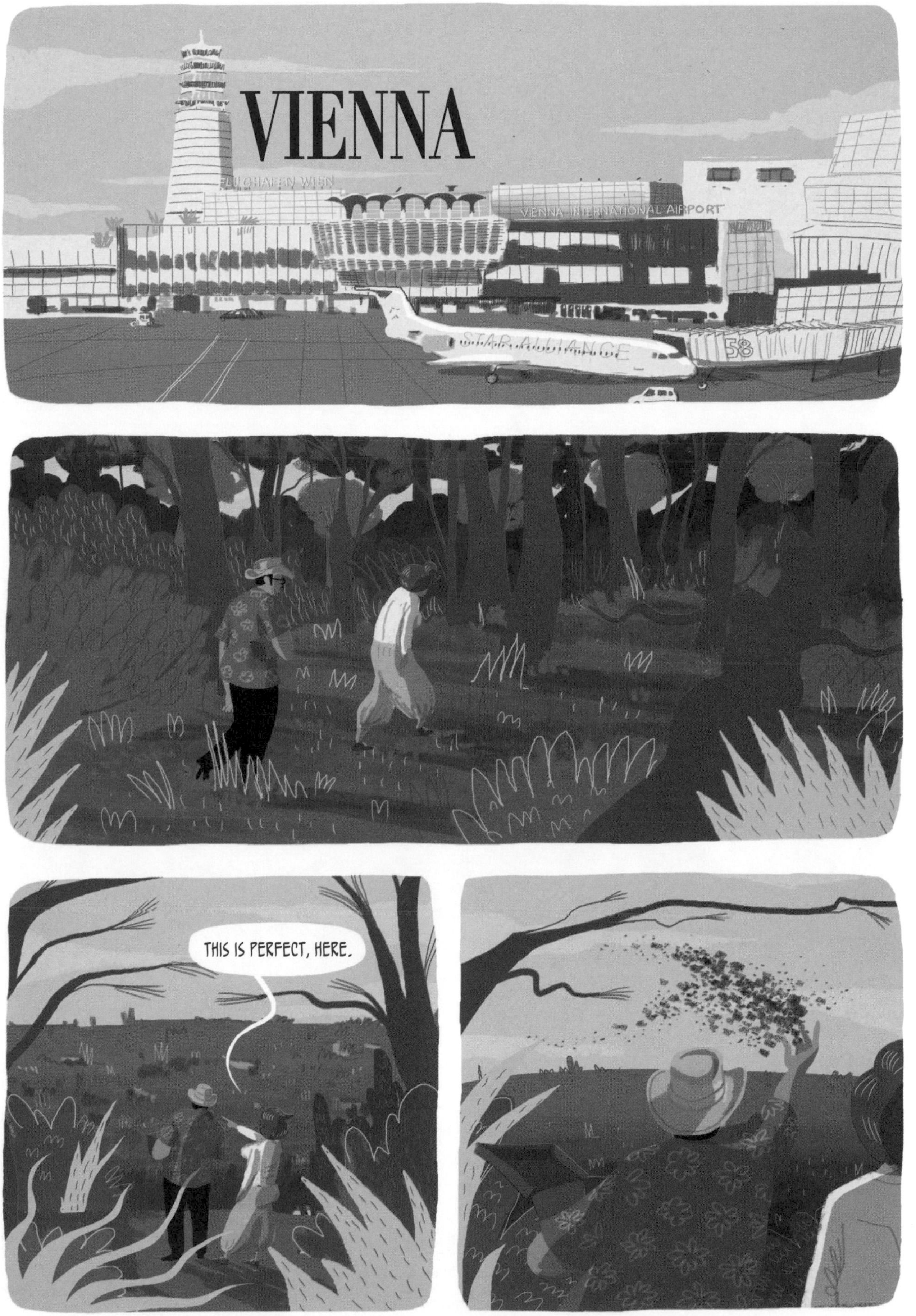
VIENNA
FLUGHAFEN WIEN
VIENNA INTERNATIONAL AIRPORT
STAR ALLIANCE
58
THIS IS PERFECT, HERE.

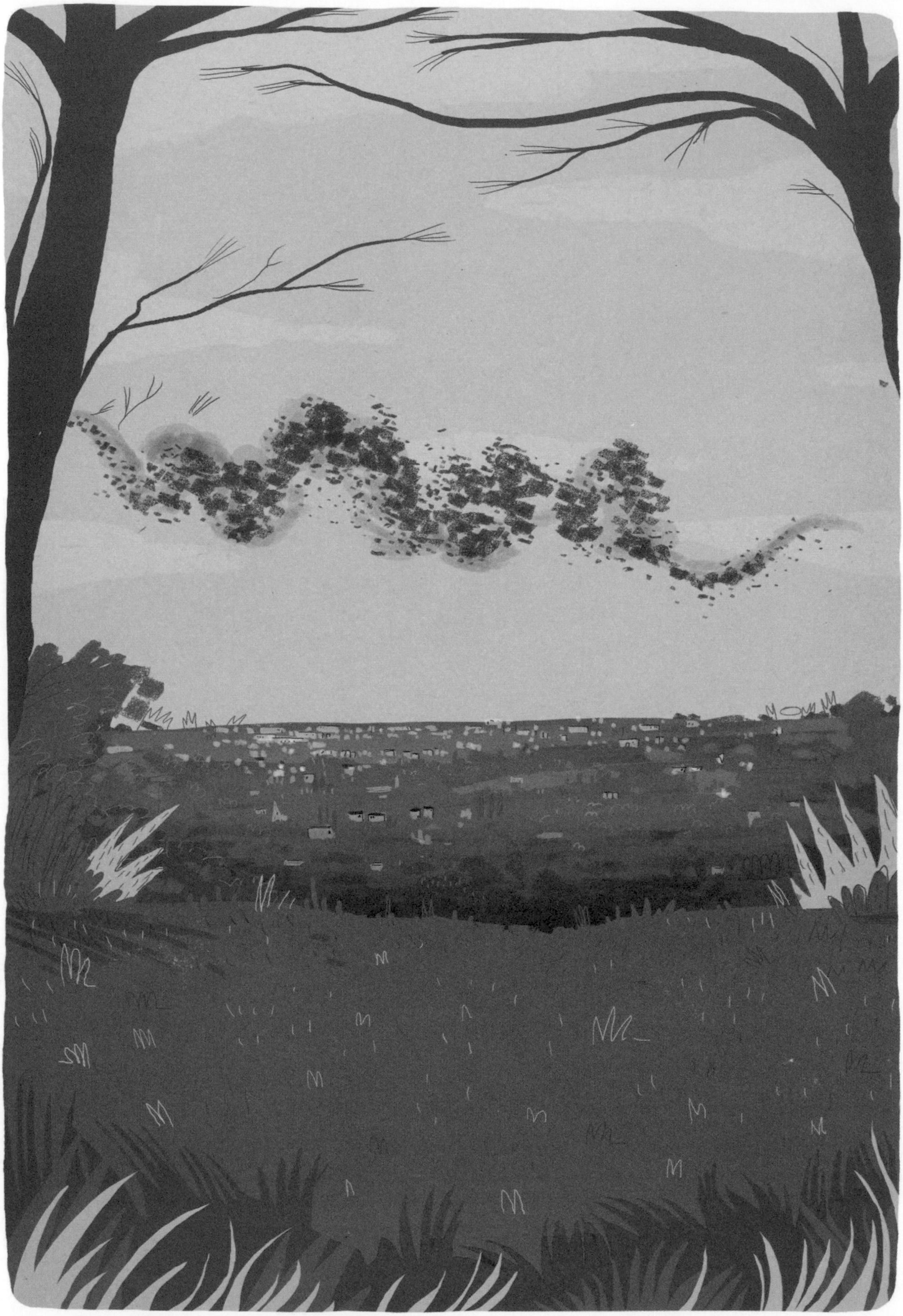

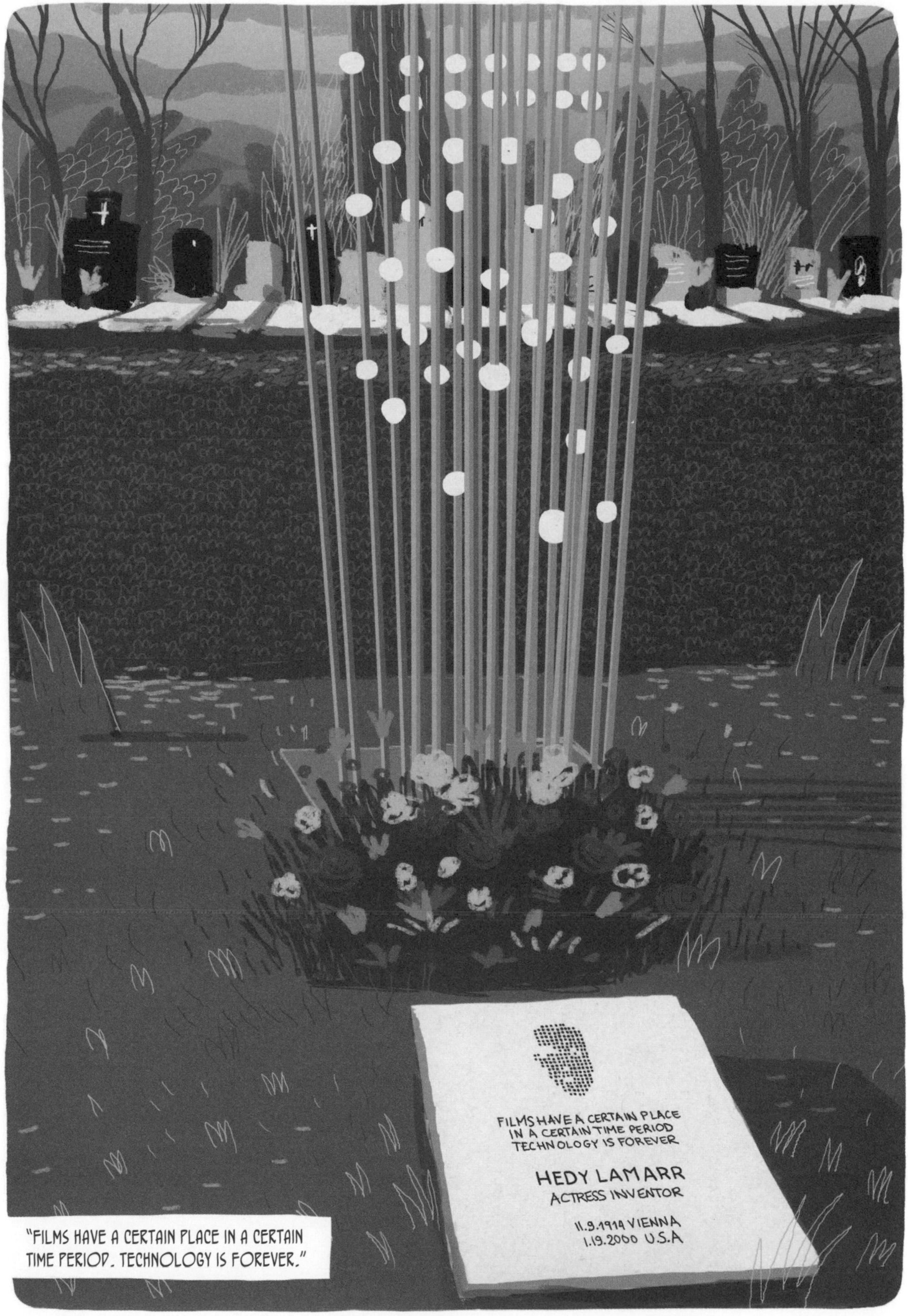
FILMS HAVE A CERTAIN PLACE
IN A CERTAIN TIME PERIOD
TECHNOLOGY IS FOREVER
HEDY LAMARR
ACTRESS INVENTOR
11.9.1914 VIENNA
1.19.2000 U.S.A
"FILMS HAVE A CERTAIN PLACE IN A CERTAIN TIME PERIOD. TECHNOLOGY IS FOREVER."

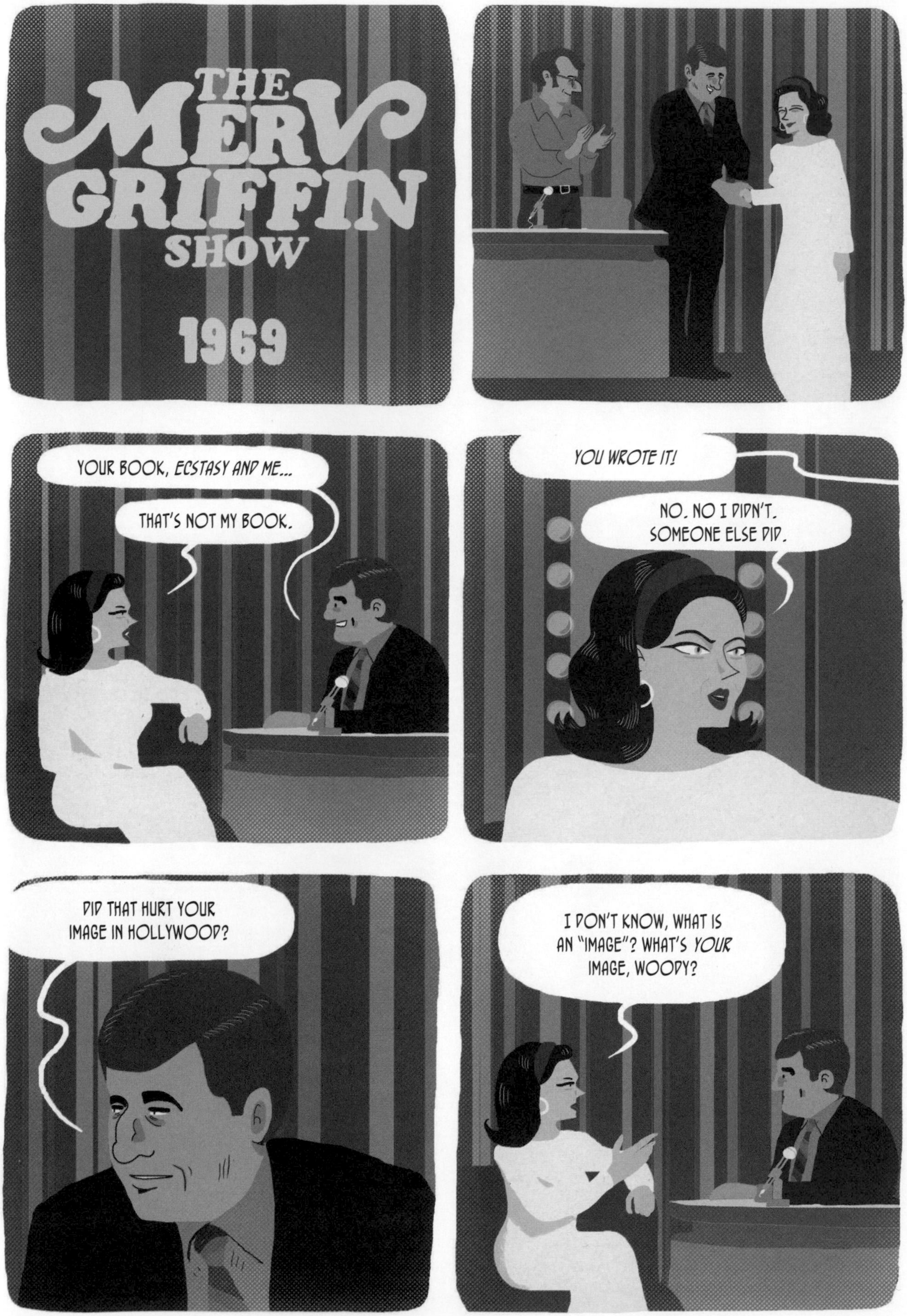
THE MERV GRIFFIN SHOW
1969
YOUR BOOK, *ECSTASY AND ME*...
THAT'S NOT MY BOOK.
YOU WROTE IT!
NO. NO I DIDN'T. SOMEONE ELSE DID.
DID THAT HURT YOUR IMAGE IN HOLLYWOOD?
I DON'T KNOW, WHAT IS AN "IMAGE"? WHAT'S *YOUR* IMAGE, WOODY?

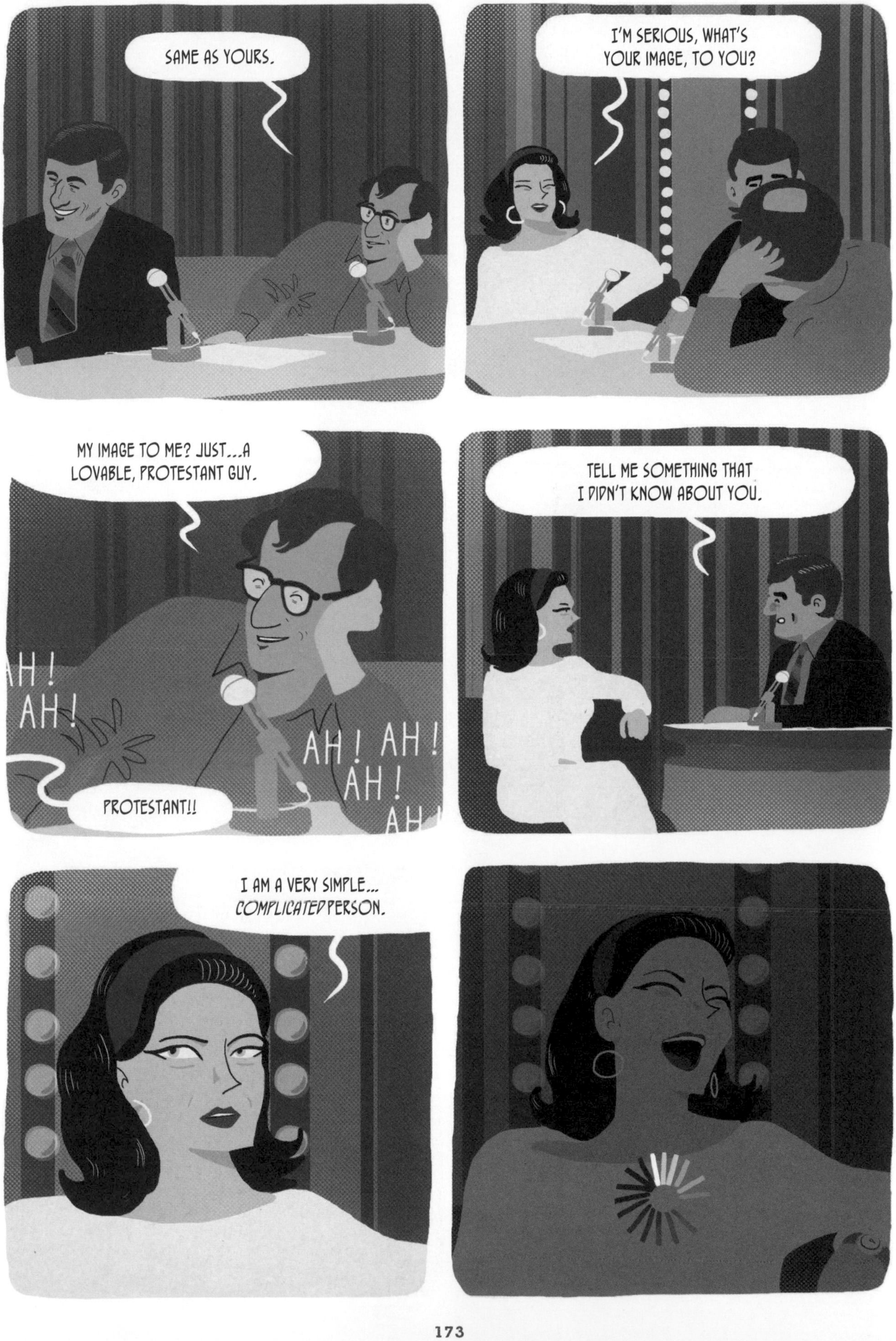
SAME AS YOURS.
I'M SERIOUS, WHAT'S YOUR IMAGE, TO YOU?
MY IMAGE TO ME? JUST...A LOVABLE, PROTESTANT GUY.
AH! AH!
AH! AH! AH! AH!
PROTESTANT!!
TELL ME SOMETHING THAT I DIDN'T KNOW ABOUT YOU.
I AM A VERY SIMPLE... *COMPLICATED* PERSON.

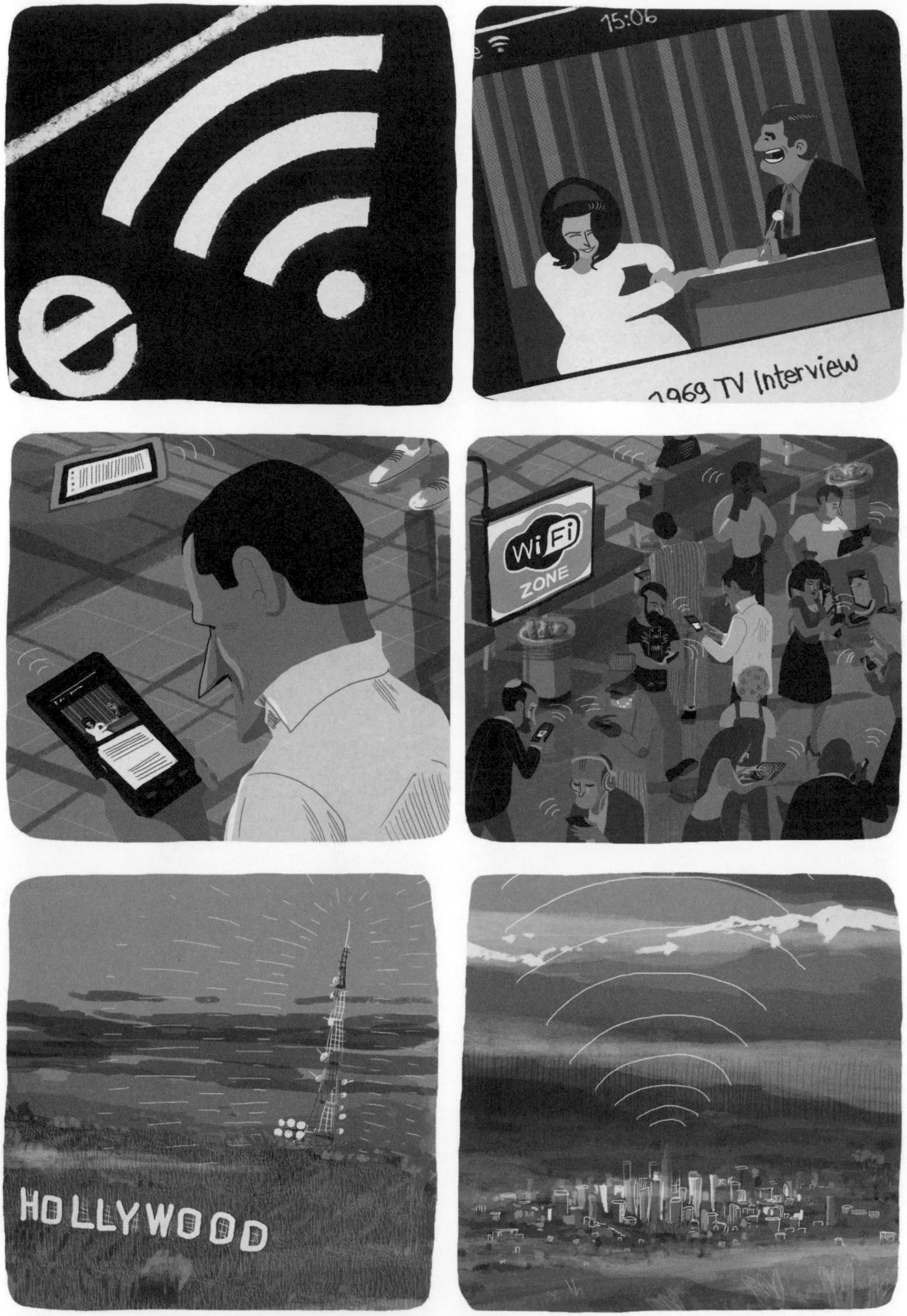
15:06
1969 TV Interview
WiFi
ZONE
HOLLYWOOD

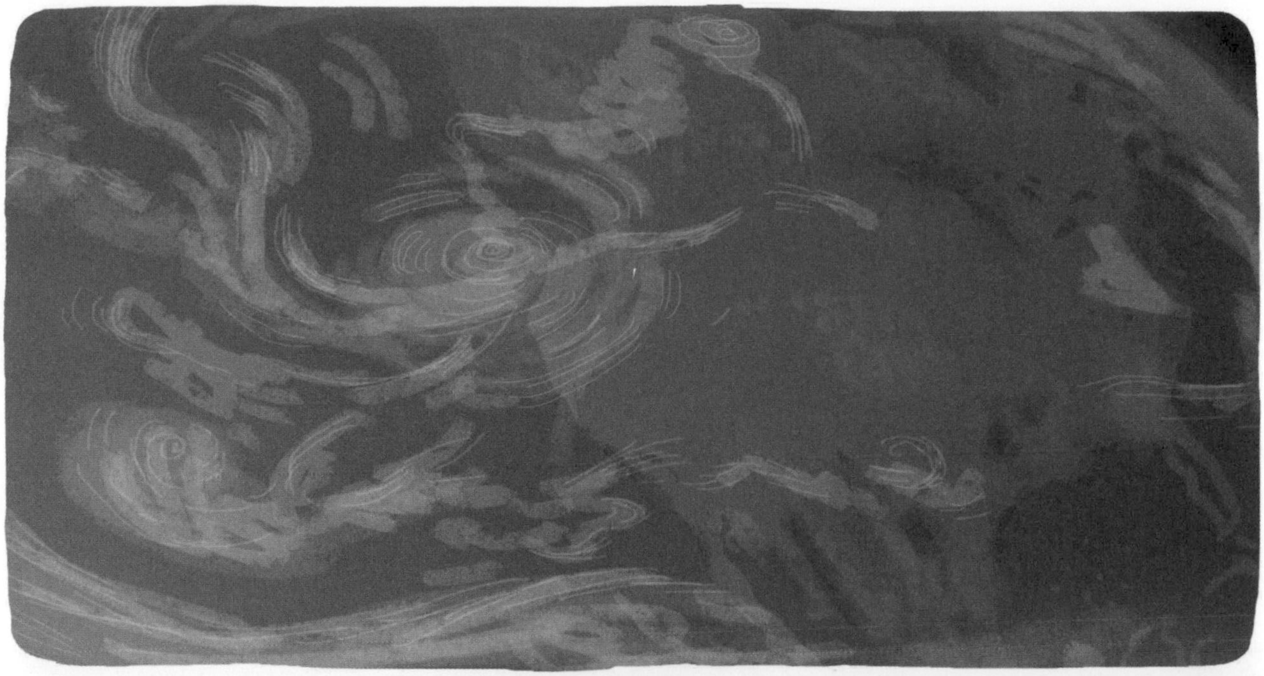

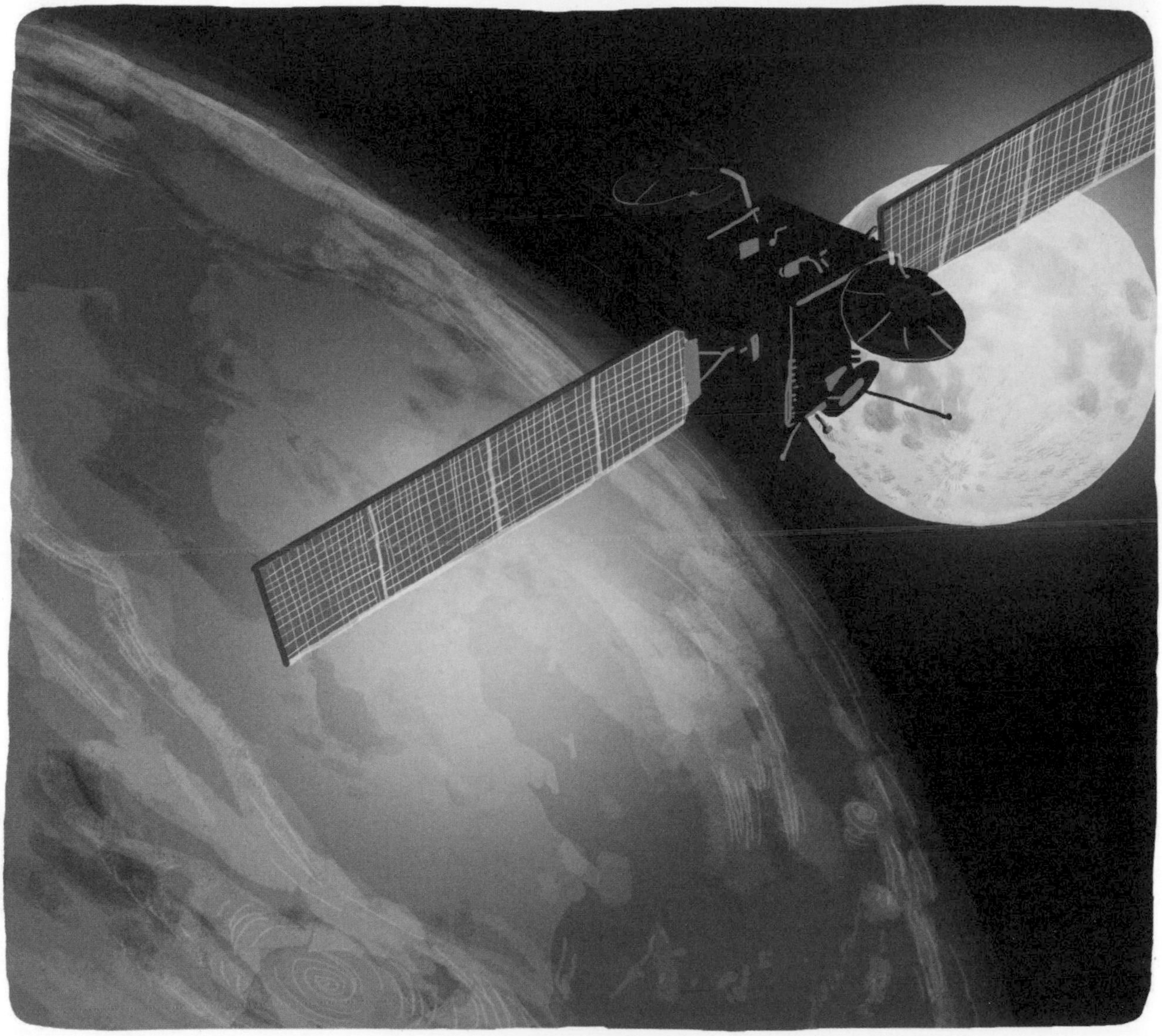

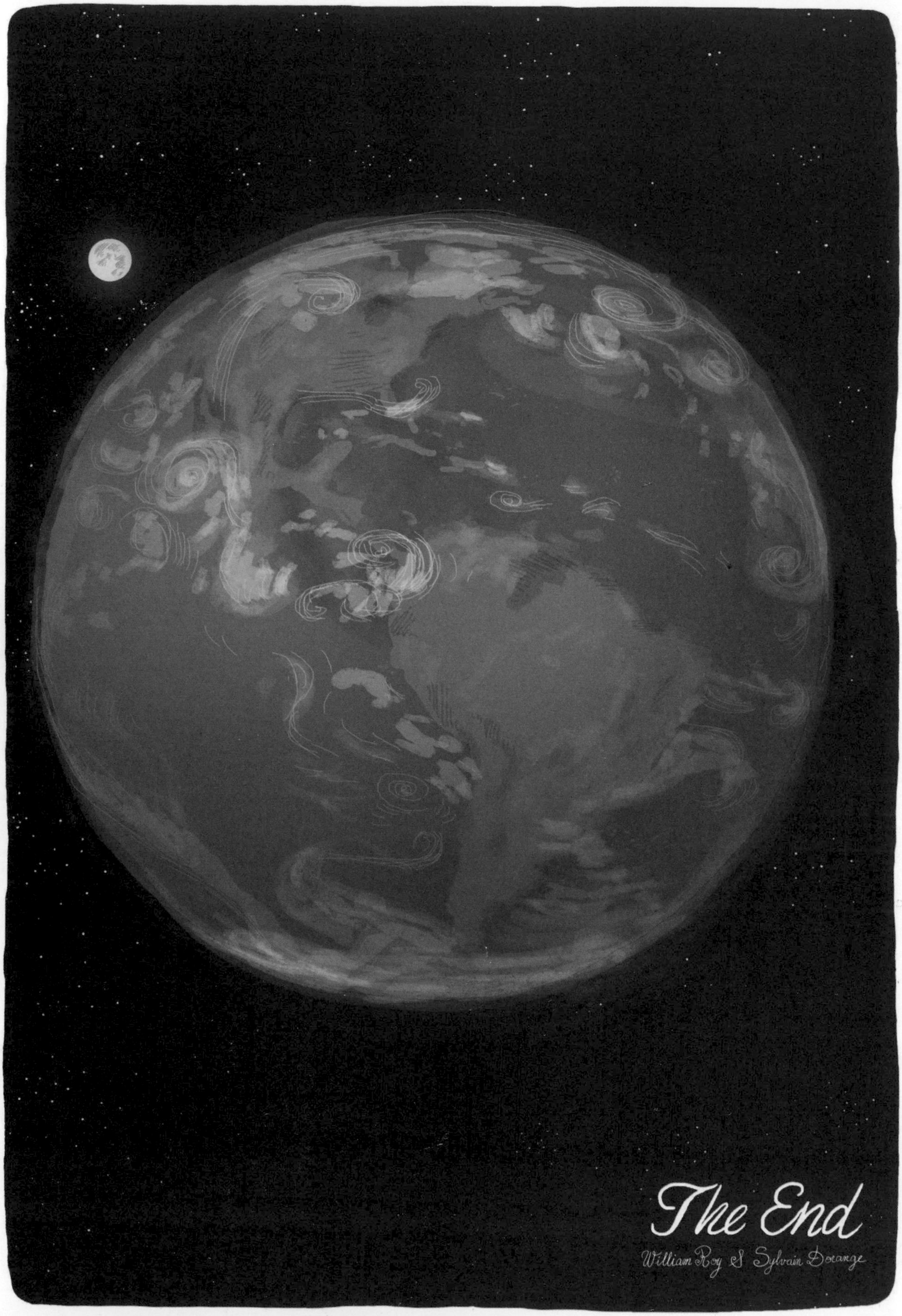
The End
William Roy & Sylvain Dorange